GENDER, KINSHIP AND PROPERTY RIGHTS

A girl dressed up for *Tiruvaadirai*

GENDER, KINSHIP AND PROPERTY RIGHTS

Nagarattar Womanhood in South India

YUKO NISHIMURA

DELHI
OXFORD UNIVERSITY PRESS
CALCUTTA   CHENNAI   MUMBAI
1998

Oxford University Press, Great Clarendon Street, Oxford OX2 6DP

Oxford New York
Athens Auckland Bangkok Calcutta
Cape Town Chennai Dar es Salaam Delhi
Florence Hong Kong Istanbul Karachi
Kuala Lumpur Madrid Melbourne Mexico City
Mumbai Nairobi Paris Singapore
Taipei Tokyo Toronto

and associates in

Berlin Ibadan

Typeset byRastrixi, New Delhi 110070
Printed at Pauls Press, Okhla, New Delhi 110020
and published by Manzar Khan, Oxford University Press
YMCA Library Building, Jai Singh Road, New Delhi 110001

Acknowledgements

This work is based on the fieldwork conducted for eleven months between January 1991 to November 1991 in southern India funded by the Central Research Fund (University of London). I was also helped by the ORS Award while I was writing up the thesis. The data is partially renewed and supplemented thanks to my post-doctoral visits during 1994 which were funded in part by the Tokyo Women's Foundation. I am grateful for these funds which enabled me to conduct my fieldwork. I am also indebted to Komazawa University's Special Research and Publication Fund which assisted me to complete this book in 1997. During my stay in London, two professors passed away in Japan. I would like to express thanks for the encouragement they gave me; Professor Keiichi Yanagawa of Tokyo University and Professor Tadahiko Hara of Tokyo University of Foreign Studies. They guided me while I was a postgraduate student of Religious Studies in the Graduate Division of Humanities at Tokyo University. In India, I am deeply indebted to Dr P.V. Krishnamoorty and his wife Raj, Nacchiammai and her husband Dr Manickawasagar as well as Sandya Narasimman and her family who looked after me while I was in Chettinadu in South India. I express my gratitude to all the Nagarattars I met there, especially to Uma Aacchi, Lakshmi Aacchi, Sita Aacchi, Devaki Aacchi, Meena Aacchi, and Sigappi Aacchi with whom I have developed long-lasting friendships. I dare not mention other names as their privacy must be protected. This work was written by me, but the Nagarattar women are my collaborators, as it is about their lives and marriages. (When necessary, I have used aliases in order to protect their privacy.)

I would also like to express my special thanks to Professor Pat Caplan, University of London who put me up in her house for a few days when I first came to London for an interview at LSE. Since I met her and her family, she has remained as one of my role models and I am grateful for being fortunate to have known her. Her constant moral support and encouragement in academic studies has boosted my sense of mission to complete this work.

Academically, I am deeply indebted to the Department of Social Anthropology at the LSE and those academics I met who stimulated me and helped me decide to pursue this path. During my study at LSE, Professor C.J. Fuller trained me with amazing patience. Without his in-depth criticism and academic discipline, I would not have been able to finish the dissertation. The training he has given me made me realize how difficult but important it is to be sincere in my academic work.

I also express my deepest gratitude to Professor Anthony Good whom I met for the first time as an external examiner of my Ph.D. dissertation. His academic sincerity impressed me, and he has been a patient commentator on my manuscripts. Without his help, I could not have completed this work.

In Tokyo, I was supported by my longtime friend, Malini Subramaniyam and her husband. Without their encouragement, I would have given up this path long ago.

Lastly, I thank Noboru, my husband. Without his understanding, support and sharing of my experiences, this work would never have been written, and in this sense, he is its co-author. He also helped me in drawing most of the illustrations which appear here.

London   *Yuko Nishimura*
March 1997

Contents

List of Tables

List of Figures

Note on Transliteration and Spelling of Non-English Words

The non-English vocabulary from Tamil and Sanskrit is transcribed by modifying the system of Tamil Lexicon and removing of their diacritical marks. Longer vowels are spelt as 'aa' and 'ee' in order to avoid unnecessary confusion (eg. *danam* and *daanam*). In some cases, I have also followed local oral pronunciation and modified the literal spellings. As for transliteration of other writers' works, I have tried to follow their transliteration, but have also stripped the diacritical marks. In most cases, I have followed the standard Anglo-Indian spelling accepted locally for the individual names and local places.

INDIA

JAMMU &
KASHMIR

HIMACHAL
PRADESH

PUNJAB

HARYANA

DELHI

ARUNACHAL
PRADESH

MEGHALAYA

SIKKIM

RAJASTHAN

UTTAR
PRADESH

ASSAM

NAGA-
LAND

MANIPUR

BIHAR

W.
BENGAL

TRIPURA

MIZORAM

GUJARAT

MADHYA PRADESH

MAHARASHTRA

ORISSA

ANDHRA
PRADESH

GOA

KARNATAKA

ANDAMAN

&

NICOBAR IS.

LAKSHADWEEP

KERALA

TAMIL
NADU

Chapter 1

Introduction

1.1 The Beginning

MY initial encounter with the Nagarattars took place in 1985, as I was on the brink of completing my first stint of long-term fieldwork. I had been staying in the village of Mahamai Puram, near Tirumayam in the Pudukottai District of Tamil Nadu. Dozens of the local castes congregate annually in this particular village to worship in the temple dedicated to the mother goddess, Mariyamman. The Nagarattars, along with other local castes such as the Pallars, Parayas, Mukkulatturs, Dasaris, and Pandarams, traditionally have one *mandahappadi* day during the twelve days of the festival. When it is a particular caste or group's *mandahappadi* day, that group is responsible for all expenses incurred, including the *puja* (rituals) and the entertainment. In return, the group has the honour of being the first to receive the blessing from the deity.

On the festival's third day the *mandahappadi* fell to the Nagarattars of the village Kadiyabatti, near Mahamai Puram. Kadiyabatti, one of the Chettinadu villages, had an abundance of magnificent Nagarattar houses, which were beautifully decorated with exotic carvings and statues. These houses seemed palatial: I had become accustomed to mud houses and thatched huts without tap water or toilets. The Nagarattars differed greatly from the other castes who lived in the area. Their grand houses were indicative of a different lifestyle and their attitude towards their *mandahappadi* day illustrated their aloof disposition. The third *mandahappadi* day had fallen to the Nagarattars, but they did not attend. They appointed instead, a non-Nagarattar caretaker to receive the honour on their behalf. It became apparent that the Nagarattars' payment for their *mandahappadi* day had been automatically drawn from the common bank account designated for charity.

Upon arriving in Kadiyabatti via Tirumayam, I was astonished at the sight of this settlement. Architecturally these beautiful and unusual houses combined Western and Hindu styles — the tops of the mansions were decorated with Western angels and figures reminiscent of the Virgin Mary, intermingled with Hindu deities, and the windows were decorated with stained glass. However, my astonishment turned to puzzlement when it appeared that these beautiful houses stood in a ghost town. There were very few pedestrians and many of the mansions seemed deserted. It was explained to me that Kadiyabatti was at its most prosperous and successful in the 1920s when the village teemed with construction workers building these Nagarattar houses with the teak wood transported from Burma. However, when the Burmese Government severed all links with the Nagarattars, their prosperity collapsed. I was told that nowadays, most of the Nagarattars who had ancestral homes in Kadiyabatti lived in cities such as Madras and

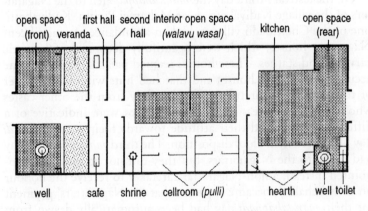

Fig. 1.1. House plan

Madurai and that they seldom returned to the village other than on ceremonial occasions.

While I was staying in Mahamai Puram, I was invited to lunch by an old Nagarattar woman who lived in one of the grandest mansions in Kadiyabatti. I imagine that she became curious when she discovered that a Japanese woman was researching the Mariyamman festival while living in a hamlet of low castes. In any case, she sent her servant to invite me to her house. This was an unusual event in Tamil Nadu where the women were rarely so bold or independent as to invite a stranger to their house, even if the stranger was a foreigner and female — and so her curiosity was matched by my own.

When I told them about the invitation, my neighbours, Dasaris and Pandarams, said that as I was visiting a Nagarattar house, the food would be of a very high standard. It was with this thought in mind that I went to meet an *aacchi* (a married Nagarattar woman) for the first time.

The house was a fabulous church-like mansion, protected by high walls and several thick, heavy teak doors. The *aacchi* gave me a guided tour of the whole house pointing out the rows of cupboards where she stored vessels, bed linen, silver goods, etc., which were to be used in the event of a wedding. In the spacious attic there was a wardrobe which stretched from floor to ceiling simply to store mattresses and pillows. The vast difference between the lifestyle of this woman and that of the people in the village in which I was staying, where there was no tap water nor even a toilet, was striking. No one in the village owned a refrigerator, there was no gas for cooking, and of course, no one had a car. The huge gap shocked me and left me baffled as to how castes in such diverse circumstances could share the joy of the same village festival.

This *aacchi* was surrounded by servants including a male cook, a maid, and 'agents', or domiciliary managers who dealt with most of the domestic affairs. Having male servants at home is quite unusual by South Indian standards, since sexual segregation is quite strict, and women are not supposed to talk to males unless they are close kin. The *aacchi* seemed to have been living there alone, receiving her relatives, her husband (who lived in Bombay) and her children and grandchildren, as occasional visitors. They all lived in cities such as Bombay, Madras, and even as far away as the USA, and came back occasionally to see her.

This lifestyle was anomalous amongst the Indians. Most of the village women that I encountered would have regarded being away from their family for even one day as exceptional. The old *aacchi* said that she even went to visit one of her daughters in Los Angeles, but added that life in the USA was not attractive. 'There, you have to do everything yourself. You have to cook, prepare tea, and do the dishes. What a labour! I need servants. The life there was not at all comfortable.'

The huge, high-ceilinged entrance hall of the house was decorated with magnificent stained glass, fine Italian chandeliers, Burmese teak and rosewood furniture, foreign porcelain collections, and big sofas covered with white sheets to protect them while they were not being used. Passing through these Westernized rooms, I was guided to the women's quarter, where they had a *walavu waasal*, an open space, in which they were drying chillies in a basket. Here, an old female servant in a worn and threadbare cotton *saree* was eating cold rice from a plantain (banana) leaf beside a water-tap. This sight is quite common in most Hindu houses, yet the contrast between the imposing, spacious, westernized rooms and the daily routine life of drying chillies and eating cold rice which was taking place in the *walavu waasal* left a deep impression on me. The juxtaposition, in one house, of two such contradictory lifestyles was baffling.

On the walls of the corridor surrounding the *walavu waasal* hung the photographs of nineteenth-century ancestors and foreign visitors. Again I noted with interest that some of the men were in Western dress while the Nagarattar women wore blouses with puffed sleeves underneath their *sarees*. In a smaller dining room, I had a delicious vegetarian lunch with the *aacchi*, who had been quite friendly from the beginning. She was well over sixty and spoke some English, although she said she had attended school for only six years. She gave instructions to her servants in Tamil; her manner was brisk and her instructions were indicative of a well-organized mind. Good organization is central to the Nagarattar caste character, as they are very financially conscious and this has been the basis of their wealth and prosperity. This view was shared by lower and upper-class Nagarattars alike. As soon as we had finished our meal, the *aacchi* asked each of her servants how many *chapattis* they would want for their next meal, and, adding it to the number she wanted, she ordered the cook to make the precise amount. She had no difficulty in thinking ahead: though she had just finished eating, she was perfectly capable of planning the next meal.

Later, I ascertained that what I had noticed in her was typical of the Nagarattar character: they are parsimonious and excellent organizers. It was generally said that the Nagarattars are rich because they know how to save money, eking an existence out of very little. It was also said that the first test a mother-in-law would give her daughter-in-law would be to observe the quantity of salt the daughter-in-law put on her banana leaf — she should be careful not to use too much. Nagarattar women are also meticulous in checking the conduct of their servants: the first test is to leave out a small amount of money while a newly hired servant is cleaning the house. If she does not touch the money, or if she informs the *aacchi* of its whereabouts, the servant passes the test. I was told that this testing continues for several months.

The Nagarattars are friendly to non-Nagarattars and always honour guests with good food. That which was served to me was of a quality that showed the high standard of their food culture. Although I often ate with non-Nagarattar castes, the standard of food used to vary, while the Nagarattars, whether rich or not, usually served good food. Even if they were financially stricken, and ate cold rice and chutney every day in order to save money, they would be too proud to show it, and therefore, would pour kerosene over the banana leaf before throwing it away outside, to mask that they could not afford to pour *ghee* (purified butter) over the rice. The measure of wealth in a Nagarattar family was regarded as the indication of family status, and a decline in that wealth would affect both their alliances and business opportunities. Later, I became familiar with the marked contrast in the big Nagarattar houses — there was an appearance of opulence but in reality there was often much poverty.

The Nagarattar woman I met for the first time was very careful with money and would not waste food, but she was also very proud. She, like other rich Nagarattars, would make large religious and charitable donations. I had heard from the Mariyamman temple trustee that her father built a hospital to treat local people free of charge, and she still maintained the hospital from the fund left by her father. During the Mariyamman festival which I researched, the local leaders of the festival visited her and asked for a donation to repair the wall of the temple. She gave them Rs 5000 instantly from her own pocket.[1] I was impressed by the independence that was shown by her in making such a quick decision without consulting her husband. In South India, women cannot usually give away large sums of money without first consulting their husbands. In fact, it is quite rare for non-Nagarattar women to be so financially independent, even if they are rich. However the villagers also suggested that the Nagarattars' donations to the temple are made not simply from altruistic motives but also out of the desire to impress others.

Since the invitation to lunch was extended by a woman to a complete stranger, I considered that there might be some cultural tradition amongst her caste that allowed such freedom to women. My curiosity was increased by the fact that adjacent to the mansion in which she lived, was another which belonged to her husband and his *pangaalis* or patrilineally connected male relatives (see Chapter 3). Several *pangaalis* lived with their nuclear families *(pullis)* within the house and each family had its own hearth which appeared to be an indication of their economic independence from the joint family housed under the same roof.

While I was dining with the *aacchi*, she answered my questions and talked about her caste, explaining that there were nine clan Shiva temple divisions which functioned just like Brahmanic *gootras* as marriage regulators. However, she said that they worshipped *kula deivams* (lineage gods) more ardently than Shiva, although these deities were mostly minor local deities and non-vegetarian gods such as Karuppan, Madurai Veeran, Mariyamman, Selliyamman, and Kaliyamman. She talked about her father's *kula deivam*, a goddess called Adai Kattaan, who was a widow and the ancestress who started the line. By the time I left the Nagarattar woman's house, I was determined to study her caste, especially the *aacchis*, as my next research topic.

1.2 The Discovering of *Acchihood*

In late January 1991, I went back to Tamil Nadu, and started fieldwork in the Chettinadu area. I stayed in Karaikkudi, a town situated in the north of Madurai, in the heartland of Chettinadu, until October 1991 and after nine months, I moved to Madras

---

[1] At that time the salary of a college professor, or a bank branch manager, was around Rs 2,500 per month.

and stayed there for one and a half months to clarify some field data before I went back to London. My data was collected mostly in Karaikkudi and nearby Chettinadu villages such as Kottayur, Kadiyabatti, Pallattur, Kanadukattan, Kandanur, Nattasan Kottai, Pillaiyarpatti, Padarakkudi, Tulavur, etc., although I frequently travelled to Madras to meet the Nagarattars. In a way, this was unavoidable, since the *aacchis* themselves were used to shuttling between Chettinadu and the town or city where they lived. A lot of them had become used to travelling alone in order to attend various ceremonies and look after the ancestral house in Chettinadu. Among the non-Nagarattar women of South India, it is unusual to travel alone especially if one is unmarried. It would also be unusual for an elderly married woman to live alone. I realized that the old *aacchi* I had met on my previous visit was an excellent example of some of the differences I would find between Nagarattar women and South Indian women in general.

During my time with the Nagarattars I learned many things, but one of the things which impressed me most was their strength,

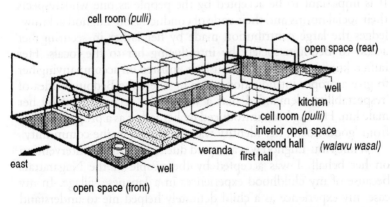

Fig. 1.2. Three dimensional view of the ancestral house

deriving from their sense of autonomy. After several months with them, I came to realize the distinct existence of what I might call 'aacchihood', i.e. the idealized goal which is to be achieved by a Nagarattar woman after marriage.

In fact, most senior aacchis who were respected in their own circles were not only economically autonomous but also capable of handling their resources cleverly. For example, aacchis greatly respected those widows who had brought up their children and married them off with money that they had skillfully saved. Such autonomy is especially important to elderly Nagarattar widows, as they seem to be far more autonomous than those of other castes.

As a researcher, I agree with what Rabinow (1977) calls 'inter-subjectivity', since the anthropological text is written through the interwoven subjectivity of the researcher and the informant, and this intersubejctivity should still be critically assessed by the re-searcher while she is collecting data as well as when producing her anthropological paper. Creating such common ground is in itself problematic. For example, Abu-Lughod, an American, who did fieldwork among the Bedouins maintains that data collection in-volves addressing certain theoretical difficulties (1986: 10). Person-ality, social location of the community, intimacy of the contact between the anthropologist and the host(s), are listed as factors which strongly influence a work, although she does not deny that a little bit of luck is also needed for good research. An anthropologist, as Abu-Lughod maintains, should also introduce herself properly and clarify her identity in the society in which she does the fieldwork. It is important to be accepted by the people as one who respects their social norms and their code of conduct. Abu-Lughod acknow-ledges the large contribution made by her father in securing her access to Bedouin society by introducing her to the locals. Her father, knowing the Bedouin custom, insisted on accompanying her to give a proper introduction, since he knew the Bedouins' idea of 'respectability' demanded that a woman be accompanied by her male kin. Having been introduced by her father as a proper Muslim from 'good stock', her identity was established in the community.

While Abu-Lughod was accepted due to her father's intervention on her behalf, I was accepted by the people of the Nagarattars because of my childhood experiences in a Japanese village. In my case, my experience as a child definitely helped me to understand and integrate with the lifestyle of the Nagarattars. In fact, I may have tried to recover the lost world of an old Japanese village in northern Japan where I was brought up surrounded by relatives and servants. After the initial surprise of seeing the grand Nagarattar houses and experiencing different climate, food and kinship relationships, I quickly felt comfortable with them. Soon I had no problem in associating with many *aacchis* who were as orthodox as my deceased grandmother but far more open-minded. I could understand the joys and sorrows of these *aacchis* because of my childhood experiences. In addition to the strong influence of my childhood memories, I also had the advantages of being an Asian woman. Because of this, the Indian people felt even closer to me, and the fact that I was a woman helped me to have a close relationship with the women. Yet the really privileged access to the woman's world only comes when a researcher is trusted. To me, the real process of in-depth interaction only started after my research had finished: after writing my Ph.D. thesis, I visited them every year. These visits opened my eyes to the lifestyle of the Nagarattar women as I saw the real change in the process of a young bride becoming a mother and her baby growing up and going to nursery school.

I also met Nagarattars in London and Singapore, as well as in Tokyo, who would carry news about fellow Nagarattars back home and sustain the ties with those who were in their village or in Madras. I was especially close to several *aacchis* and their families who are in Madras: most of my ideological framework for *aacchihood* is through the contact with these people. My previous fieldwork experiences helped me a great deal in interacting with these people yet their rich experiences of travelling and being exposed to many kinds of people also made our mutual understanding easier. Although senior *aacchis* in general have not experienced working outside the home, they have broader experiences of travelling. In fact, they travel almost every month and are interested in knowing different people.

During my research, I found men in general were more interested in prestige, social status, and the glory of Nagarattar activities and less interested in actual human interactions. They were also secretive about details of marriage expenses and property issues despite my assurances that I would not reveal this information to the tax officers!

Compared to the women, I found the men fairly uninteresting, although it is male Nagarattars who have written about the history and glorious achievements of their community. Thus, had I known only male informants, my knowledge would have been based mainly on written material and I would not have noticed the real complement between the male and female worlds which takes place in day-to-day interactions. Women, i.e. mothers, wives, and daughters, on the other hand, were extremely informative and could supplement the fragmentary and somewhat 'formal' information given by their men. I could better understand the men's information in a wider context. My research would not have progressed without the co-operation of many *aacchis,* both prominent and non-prominent. They introduced me to a large number of people through their networking.

Aacchis in general are open-minded and full of curiosity, fond of mixing with people. They have their own share of responsibility for household management, and make it a duty to attend ceremonies and manage their ancestral household in the village. As a result, they frequently travel alone, between cities and villages in Chettinadu. In this way *aacchis* share important family work with their husbands, although the kind of work they do is circumscribed by their gender. For example, although it is still men who engage in wage-work or business, it is women who check the household expenses. Women can also look after the farms and estates, giving workers instructions and checking the accounts. They arrange ceremonies, particularly the auspicious ones, and visit the houses of their relatives with news. Previously, women were not accustomed to wage-work since working for somebody was considered degrading. Men would work for wages as agents only if there was no choice, but women never would. Although this situation has changed significantly within the last ten to twenty years, women in the olden days had no experience of working outside. However, since *aacchis* traditionally appreciate hardworking women, wage-work has become more common than before among Nagarattar women: women with earning power are generally appreciated provided the job does not demean the family status.

The Nagarattars appreciate autonomy, if not individualism. They respect the autonomy of each household. Even between mother-in-law and daughter-in-law, there exists an unwritten code of etiquette concerning non-interference with each other's property or household affairs. A respectable Nagarattar housewife would feel ashamed to borrow even a single kitchen utensil from her mother-in-law while she in turn would not dare to take away a single cup from her daughter-in-law's possession. This respect for each other's territory is also supposed to exist, ideally speaking, between husband and wife. The wife does not interfere with her husband's business especially as it is often jointly organized with his own brothers and father. The husband, on the other hand, leaves management of domestic issues including the household accounts and the children's education to his wife, although he may insist that he should be kept informed of what is going on at home. Management of the household does not confine itself to nursing children, cooking, and cleaning. The Nagarattar household managed by women includes much wider areas: property, management of farms and land, as well as networking among kin and affines. Even if they only talk about family affairs when they meet each other, in Chettinadu men do not consider it as mere chit-chatting, since they understand that these very activities produce productive relationships: various levels of organizing and networking of Nagarattar kinship are the means of yielding wealth and fame. Through kinship networking, *aacchis* arrange marriages, get economic and political assistance, and acquire social identity and prestige.

Well-known senior *aacchis* from prosperous houses can arrange marriages for relatives and non-relatives. They can play an important part in finding appropriate partners and helping financially. As 'fixers' for the caste, they would be invited to most of the major weddings and funeral ceremonies. Having such *aacchis* present at a wedding and *saandi* (the sixtieth birthday celebration of a married man) shows that the family is well connected. Prominent *aacchis* can ask their male relatives to find a job for someone, or obtain a seat for someone else's child at a college or at school. They agree to give donations to charities, and assist at functions by taking home-cooked food. While their business-bound husbands may not be able to deal with such day-to-day problems, the *aacchis* are more accessible, especially through the women's network.

Aacchis are expected to manage the house in a budget-conscious way. They keep a check on the daily account however busy they may be. Even *aacchis* from the richest families know the price of vegetables, including the price rise during rainy seasons. *Aacchis*, whether rich or poor, manage their daily account by themselves. They know each nook and cranny of the house so that they can supervise the work of the servants. Although most non-Nagarattar housewives may not be particular about small change, one senior *aacchi* from a well-to-do family told me, 'If my servant did not return the five paisa change, I would certainly ask him why. It should be correct.'

Aacchis are also involved in extra-household activities. Although *aacchis* in the middle-income group may not deal with many marriage alliances or school admissions, they still try to be in touch with other *aacchis*. As in other relationships, friendship, affection, respect, prestige, or economic interests are the bonds of their social relationship. Through such networking of their mothers, wives, or even sisters, men of lower social status can also visit *aacchis* of higher status for help, especially because *aacchis* are more accessible at home than their husbands. Such interaction between sexes is quite unusual in India where most extra-household interactions take place between a same sex group unless they are relatives. Moreover, men visiting unrelated women to ask a favour is almost unheard of.

While I was in Karaikkudi, I hired a local research assistant, a Brahman girl, who could give me a different perspective on the Nagarattars. She also introduced me to Nagarattar women who belonged to a lower-middle class and middle class level. We frequently visited them in their houses to interview them. Being interviewed by a foreigner and a Brahman girl often had a liberating effect on the Nagarattar women, since they could express criticism about their caste. For example, I often heard unmarried Nagarattar girls criticizing their own caste as being 'money minded' and 'not artistic' (as compared to the Brahmans). It would have been difficult to hear such criticisms if I had had a Nagarattar assistant who might want to protect the name of her caste from such criticism. However, though I did not have a research assistant for the entire research period, she was able to come with me for about one-third of the time, and her role as my assistant and as a non-Nagarattar local informant was invaluable. In general, I noticed that the Brahman girls were proud of their own caste, claiming their intellectual and ritual superiority to the Nagarattars. However, even they are sometimes critical of the economic insecurity and the lower status in the conjugal relationship of married Brahman women. Thus my research assistant used to express her envy whenever she came across the Nagarattar tradition of protecting married women's property rights.

During my research, I regularly met and interviewed around

thirty to forty people. They were mostly Nagarattars, except for a few non-Nagarattars who provided me with crucial information. Meeting regularly, sharing meals, and gossiping was useful in making me feel part of their culture. However, I was not usually able to take notes at such times without it seeming inappropriate. Regular visits were also necessary for me, since my knowledge of Tamil was not good enough to pick up information in only one or two visits. Taking notes on rituals and ceremonies was essential, as well as studying genealogy, although I was never good at it. In these procedures, I was greatly helped by senior Nagarattar women who were able to talk to me in English and supplement the information from various sources.

I also used to exchange opinions with local people about the Nagarattars, comparing them with the Brahmans and non-Brahmans in the Chettinadu area. Most people I met were frank with me because I was not a Nagarattar but a foreigner, an alien, who could not possibly pass such information on to local people.

Although the Nagarattars are Shaivas who are entitled to be initiated by Shaiva Brahmans, their 'pollution rule' is much more relaxed than that of the Brahmans or Pillais. As a result, the Nagarattars are quite positive about the reproductive power of women: a woman's first menstruation after her wedding used to be celebrated quite openly by her married family in contrast to the Brahmanic ideology which maintains that the bride's first menstruation pollutes the groom's natal family. The conceptual difference about purity and pollution between the Nagarattars and the Brahmans was especially noticeable because I had hired a Brahman girl as my research assistant.

Although most Nagarattar kitchens are far cleaner and far better organized than the average Brahman kitchen, my young Brahman assistant, although in her early twenties, like other Brahmans, insisted on the ritual purity of Brahmans especially in the kitchen. For example, she declined to eat in a Nagarattar house where both vegetarian and non-vegetarian meals are cooked in the same kitchen: 'they would cook my meal in a pan which is used to cook their chicken! I cannot stand it.' Therefore, I had to give up meals in a Nagarattar house if my assistant was accompanying me. Although otherwise quite friendly, her grandmother would not let any non-Brahman (including me) into the kitchen while she was visiting her daughter's house.

Having hired a Brahman girl, I have had the advantage of knowing the acute cultural differences between the Brahmans and the Nagarattars. I also had additional 'benefits' by hiring a girl who belonged to such a conservative family as she helped me to understand the conservative aspects of village life. Although using a female assistant helped me a great deal in utilizing the 'women's network', a young unmarried girl, especially in a conservative village area, restricts the area and time of research. In an orthodox area like Chettinadu, a girl's conduct is closely scrutinized by her neighbours. I lived nearby and would accompany her home at night for fear of causing a scandal. Yet she insisted on my 'luck' of being a woman researcher, since she maintained she would never have worked with me if I were a man. No woman would be willing to talk to a male researcher unless compelled to by her parents or husband. Because of cultural constraints, she had to be home before supper, could not accompany me on trips, and was often unavailable because of domestic work assigned to her. In spite of such inconveniences, a woman assistant was still a bonus especially because these very experiences alerted me to the actual conditions and restrictions imposed on women in her culture.

I also admit that being a foreigner was an advantage since I could accompany men as an exceptional case. After initial introductions through wives and daughters, I could visit their husbands in the office. I could also go to the cremation ground with the men and the corpse, observing the process of cremation, which an Indian woman would not be allowed to do. I could sit in the men's quarter at weddings, eat with them, and give a speech at their meetings. In this respect, I was not exactly a 'woman', but something more like a foreigner who happens to be a female. In this way, I fully understood the advantageous position of being a foreigner. In a community where foreign guests are well received, a guest also has an obligation: he or she should be good company and worth talking to.

1.3 The Nagarattars: A History

The Nagarattars call themselves 'Chettiyars' (merchants). The name *chetti* is used to denote mercantile castes, as a more or less honorific title (Thurston and Rangachari 1909: ii. 91). According to Thurston

Fig. 1.3. Front entrance of a prominent Nagarattar house

(1909: v. 249), the word Nagarattar is derived from their word for 'fort', which is where their ancestors lived.

Somalay (1953) gives a similar explanation concerning this point: since many of the Nagarattar Chettiyars lived in big houses resembling forts, they came to be called 'Nattukottai Chettiyars'. 'Nattukottai' translated literally, means 'fort in the country'. According to Somalay, the term is derived from the word *'nagaram'*, a town. Since the term *nagaram* means town, those who came from the *nagaram* were known as the Nagarattars (Somalay 1953: 14–15).

Thurston names four of the best known Chettis: the Beri Chettis, the Nagarattu Chettis, the Kasukkar Chettis, and the Naattukottai Chettis (Thurston and Rangachari 1909: ii. 92). Venkatarama Ayyar, in the *Pudukottai Manual,* mentions the Nattukottai Chettis, and also a few other Chettis claiming that both Sundaram Chettis and the Nattukottai Chettis must have derived from the Ariyur Chettis (Ayyar 1938: 120–1), though, at the moment, no connection has been made between these three castes. With regard to wealth, the Nattukottai Chettis are the most prominent Chettiyars in South India, and have attracted the most attention.

The homeland of the Nattukottai Chettiyars is in the area called Chettinadu, or the land of Chettiyars, which is bound on the north by the Vellaru river, in the south by the Vaigai river, in the west by Piramalai and in the east by the Bay of Bengal (Somalay 1953: 12). They are distributed among seventy-eight villages, fifty-eight of which are located in the Ramanathapuram District (which is now split into Ramnad District and Pasumpon-Thevar Thirumagan District), the other tewnty are in the Pudukottai District.

According to legend, they started as jewellery merchants and had moved to Kanchipuram by the seventh to eighth century BC. Sometime during the seventh century, eight thousand families were compelled to commit suicide in protest, as the king had illegally imprisoned several (ten to twenty) of their women. Only 1502 boys were saved and they later married local Vellalar (the agricultural caste) girls, creating a new caste which is the foundation of the Nagarattars of today. In connection with the marriage to the Vellalar girls, the founders of the Nagarattars made several mutual agreements with the original three Vellalar castes from whom they had taken the girls. First, the Vellalar parents would give dowries for the girls so that they could maintain their maid servants after marriage. Second, the Vaisya (mercantile caste) men would not give their daughters to the Vellalars, and thus the marriage rituals performed by the girls' brothers and relatives would not be performed until after one or two generations. This means that the Vellalar girls' natal families would not remain as affines to the Vaisya families. As I explain in Chapter 4, the wedding ritual performed by the maternal uncle and other kin on the girl's side is a symbol of the reconfirmation of reciprocal exchange of women between the kin and the affine in the following generations. Refusal of this ritual leads to the cessation of the relationship. Thirdly, the girls were to be given separate *madams* (religious institutions) for gaining the initiation for becoming a Shaiva from their own *guru*. This *madam* still exists in Tulavur and gives initiation exclusively to women of the Nagarattar community. Traditionally, the *guru* is of Shaiva Vellalar caste, belonging to the lineage of the *guru* who was the first mentor for Nagarattar women.

Early in the eighth century, the Nagarattars migrated and settled in Pandya country following the request of the Pandya king. This area (where they still remain) is now called Chettinadu. As legend maintains, they were already Shaivas (worshippers of Shiva) well before the eighth century, having their own religious *madam* with their own *gurus*. At present, there are two *madams* which were installed for the purpose of initiating caste members; the one exclusively for men is located in Padarakkudi and the women's is located in Tulavur. Another *madam* which has a *guru* of the Nagarattar caste was established in Kovilur in the seventeenth century. The Nagarattars have numerous religious institutions in almost all the renowned pilgrimage spots in India, including Benares. Therefore, their prestigious status as the 'high and religious caste' seems to have been established through long-term capital investment in religious institutions. Both Price and Rudner point out that some powerful Nagarattars even purchased the title of the local *Zamindar* (chieftain) (Price 1979: 195–6; Rudner 1985: 114–16).

Indigenous historical records kept at Palani temple and collected by Rudner confirm the Nagarattar oral tradition that the caste was primarily involved in salt trade in a small area around their Chettinadu homeland in the seventeenth century (Rudner 1985: 48). In order to get prestige, the Nagarattars were continually investing in religious institutions. However, as Mahadevan (1978) and Dirks (1987) have shown, most of the assets of the Nagarattars were first established abroad. In Ceylon, Malaya, and Burma, they earned huge sums as agents for British firms, middlemen for local investment, as well as in their traditional role as moneylenders. And, as I mentioned earlier, they built grand houses (Dirks 1987: 370):

Armed with huge sums of money made overseas, the *cettiyar* men returned to their native villages where they had always maintained their home base, kept their women, celebrated their marriages, and in general continued their tightly knit social and religious life. There they built large and impressive houses, importing tons of Burmese teak and rare Ceylonese satin wood to support and decorate these new palatial structures. The *cettiyars* also tried to buy land, which became increasingly possible because of the new market in land created by the settlement of the latter half of the [19th] century. In particular, the *cettiyars* cornered the market on *brahmadeyas*, buying whole Brahman villages after the Inam Settlement of 1888. The *cettiyars* were particularly interested in buying these lands because they were among the most fertile, came in large packages, and had very low tax assessments through the provisions of the Inam

Settlement. The Brahmans sold these lands because their holdings had fragmented with each new generation, more and more of them having mortgaged their lands already for cash in what became an escalating move to the towns and cities, where they could obtain education, and then government employment as office workers and bureaucrats.

The *cettiyars* also invested their money in temples. Here they ran into major resistance. For the *cettiyars* invested in temples not only out of religious fervour, but to secure higher honours in important regional temples, if possible displacing or at least superseding the regnant *nattars.* Not that religious fervour was unimportant; the *cettiyars,* like other groups of Indian merchants, saw a direct relationship between their temple worship and business success. (ibid.: 371)

Concerning the influence of the Nagarattar capital on the Burmese economy, Siegleman (1962) claims that the vast fertile lands of Lower Burma were created by the funds provided by the moneylenders of the Nagarattars, thus making the Nagarattars' involvement in the local economy a positive one:

The first [cause] is the series of British attempts to fill the wastelands of Lower Burma with population; it was this population and the immigrants from Upper Burma that provided the clientele for Chetty's early economic administrations. The second is the expansion of cultivated area in Lower Burma; it was in this conversion of millions of acres from jungle to paddy fields that Chetty capital played such an indispensable role. (ibid.: 82)

However, Siegleman also contends that such a heavy investment together with the economic squeeze on the local farmers created much tension between the Nagarattars and the Burmese, which eventually forced the former to retreat from Burma in the late 1930s. Moreover, Mahadevan (1978) claims that the conflict between the Nagarattars and the local farmers was unavoidable, since the former exploited the latter, especially when the world economy was suffering from the Depression. Mahadevan quotes from the report of the Madras Banking Enquiry Commission of 1929 and concludes that the Chettiyars obtained 50 per cent of the crop of the agriculturist in return for the loan advanced. Mahadevan further stated, 'by acquiring paddy in this way and selling it, they could, given the upward trend in the prices of paddy, easily secure repayment of their loan and the interest' (ibid.: 351). Siegleman argues that the Burmese were the largest rice exporters in the world market during the 1920s and 1930s, and that this was made possible by the capital provided by the Nagarattars (1962: 97). However, Mahadevan points out that the Nagarattars also made huge profits by providing funds for the farmers, demanding high interest, and then repossessing or purchasing the land from the impoverished farmers. They then became landlords and exploitation became so acute that the local government had to intervene.

With the money acquired, the Nagarattars entered into business with other enterprises such as rice mills and rubber estates, while also continuing with their tradition of lending money to middle and small-scale farmers in Burma. The conflict between the landlord-cum-moneylender Nagarattars and the local Burmese increased as the anti-Indian sentiment grew. Mahadevan claims that by 1929–30, the Chettiyars owned as much as 570,000 acres of fertile land in the thirteen main districts of lower Burma, and this was 6 per cent of the total occupied land, which was 'no mean figure by any standard' (1978: 353). By the 1930s, the conflict between 'the Chettiyar and the Burmese cultivators had entered into its final, most acute stage' (Siegleman 1962: 298). In the Depression, the price of rice and land plummeted in the world market. And European banks, which began calling in the loans they had advanced to the big Nagarattars and the North Indian merchants (Marwari firms), intensified the crisis. In 1941 the Land Purchase Act was effected by the Burmese Government to purchase the lands held by the Nagarattars at a minimal cost, in order to redistribute the land to the impoverished Burmese farmers. The result of this was that the Nagarattars finally had to leave Burma, losing as they went, a huge amount of investment.

According to Ito, most of the Nagarattars' community assets (i.e. about three-fifths of their working funds invested abroad) were in Burma. Yet because of the Depression, the invasion of the Japanese army, and the subsequent independence of Burma, they lost it all. However, in spite of such a huge loss, the community as a whole survived and were re-established as the 'modern capitalists in their own country' (Ito 1966: 372). Ito locates the bankruptcy of the Nagarattars' traditional economic activities and the shift towards modern capitalistic activities at a point which coincided with the period of the 1930s and 1940s, when India's capitalism was gradually expanding. Nowadays, they are most closely connected with the cotton textile industry and one-fifth of the total spinning mills of the four states of southern India are owned by the Nagarattars. In addition, they control four banks of various sizes, and hold one quarter of the total bank deposits in southern India (ibid.). A few of them entered other industries such as the metal and engineering industry, the sugar industry, and the fertilizer and other chemical industries.

The chief business combines (business conglomerates) which have been extremely successful are the Rajah Sir Group (now divided into the Raja Sir Muttaiah, M.A. Chidambaram, and M. Ct. M groups), Tiagarajan group, and the AMM Group (TI Cycles). Ito, comparing the Nagarattar groups with other major North Indian business combines such as the Tatas and Birlas, the Mafatlals, the Walchands, and the Mahindras, claims that excepting the first two (i.e. the Tatas and Birlas), the combined figures of the above mentioned Nagarattar groups exceed the other big North Indian business combines both in scale and in assets.

1.4 Entrepreneurship and Kinship:
Individualism or Collectivism?

Ito claims that the motivation for profit-making among Indian entrepreneurs is 'not the individual as in western Europe, but the minimum unit of enterprises is the joint family' (Ito 1966: 368). He also claims that part of the strength of the Nagarattar entrepreneurship exists in the minimum nuclear unit *(pulli)* which consists of a husband, a wife, and their unmarried children. According to him, for each *pulli*, autonomous economic activities are encouraged, which helps each *pulli* take quick decisions, without consulting the head of the joint family. For example, Ito cites the TI group as consisting of a total of six nuclear families including those of two brothers, a son, and three nephews who are formally separated but in fact have jointly built up a group of companies called the AMM group.[2] In order to compete with the big business combines in North India such as Tata and Birla, Ito claims that competition as well as cooperation are encouraged. It is increasingly necessary for the Nagarattar business combines to unite, since:

---

[2] The AMM and the Raja Sir Annamalai groups are *pangaalis* (patrilineally related male members and their families). I shall discuss the details of their kinship relationship in Chapter 3.

Fig. 1.4. A Nagarattar family in the 1920s

Mobilization of funds for the enterprises in the group from sources both inside and outside the group by means of the group's own banks, investment companies, managing agents, etc. is an extremely profitable mechanism under the conditions of an economy in which investment requires immense funds in the light of present levels of technology and in which capital accumulation is lagging behind. (ibid.: 378)

Contrary to the encouragement of the economic autonomy of nuclear households, this does not lead the Nagarattars to start up enterprises individually that are then managed separately. According to Ito, the tendency is that the familial bonds, i.e. the joint family organizations, are strengthened. As an objective result, the allocation among the families of the management of the various enterprises included in the group is more or less fixed, and important decisions are made jointly under the leadership of their head, usually the eldest. In other words, Ito's argument claims that the combination of the economic autonomy of the nuclear household and the power of the joint household creates a potent force.

As seen above, Ito's concept of the *pulli's* economic activity does not imply the husband/wife unit as the business enterprise but rather the 'business' carried out by a man who is the head of the household, and also the joint business carried out by him and his unmarried sons. As the sons get married, they may split from their father's business to start separate businesses of their own, but Ito stresses that the sons who split from their father's business do not need to consult their fathers for their own business: thus there is a balance between the joint family enterprise (group business) which provides the pool of capital and that of the individual enterprise. His paper is mainly based on research done on the TI group, the AMM family business, which was started by four brothers. As I discuss in Chapter 3, Ito's argument regarding the *pulli* has a serious setback, as he neglects the importance of the interrelationship between kin and the affines which actually support the *pulli*: in other words, each *pulli* has two economic supports, i.e. the husband's and the wife's, and the economic autonomy of the *pulli* against the husband's *pangaali* is maintained by the support of the wife's side. The very example of the TI group which Ito quoted well exemplifies this, since there are more cases of cross-cousin marriage than non-relative marriages among them (see Chapter 3).

However, Rudner (1994: 112) refutes Ito's argument concerning the decision-making power of the *pulli* and maintains that there is no implication of the *pulli* being an independent economic unit. He claims that the *pulli* is not even the residential unit, since 'even most of their properties and business activities were held as part of the undivided estate of a *walavu*, the Nagarattar joint family unit to which the *pulli* belonged' (ibid.). Instead, Rudner stresses the collectivism of the Nagarattars based on their clans, lineages, panchayats, and the elite bankers, all of which succeeded in maintaining the cross-cutting segmentation and equality among the members (ibid.: 228).

As I discuss in the following chapters, Rudner's argument is seriously flawed as it ignores the autonomous aspect of the *pulli* and the fact of the Nagarattars' preference for cross-cousin marriage (I shall discuss this in Chapter 3). Although I agree with Rudner that the Nagarattars' principle of equality among themselves is based on symmetrical exchange, it is not that they 'reject any rule that would perpetuate ties of marriage alliance' (ibid.: 218), rather the opposite — Nagarattars have a strong preference for cross-cousin marriage and for its perpetuation down through the generations.

As for the economic autonomy given to the *pulli*, the following remarks of Nagarajan (1983) vividly describe how the economic independence of sons at an early stage is encouraged. Somalay (1984: 17–18) also describes the process of how they built the large ancestral homes *(walavu viidu)* with the money earned abroad. According to him, it was normally *pangaalis*, i.e. father, his brothers, and their sons etc. who would share the cost, and build the house and its extensions. The rest of the money sent by each earning member would usually be pooled as joint property, although the man would regain his share when he left the joint house to get married. Therefore, although the house was jointly made so that it would impress others as the business firm, and the capital of individuals was pooled, they nevertheless kept individual accounts within the house.

The joint ancestral house existed as a symbolic unity, and each member kept his share of the joint house, in the form of a small store room *(ul viidu)*, which would be handed down to his children. When the store room got too small, the next generation could also build a house for their own family so that they would be able to give one room of this house to each of their own children. In this way, the joint houses of the *pangaalis* were built side by side so that they would be able to utilize all the facilities of the houses of the *pangaalis*. Nagarajan, writing about the richest man of the Nagarattar community in the early twentieth century, i.e. Raja Sir Annamalai, writes as follows:

On his marriage Annamalai Chettiyar set up house on his own. It would be more correct to say, his parents set him up in a household of his own. That did not mean 'moving house'. A couple of rooms of the family house and a kitchen were set apart for him and he was supposed to run them. In point of fact, it was his parents who ran the establishment until he and his wife accustomed themselves to the routine and learned to follow it. Extremely frugal and socially well knit, the Chettiyars believed in early beginnings. Annamalai Chettiyar's elder brothers were already married and they had households of their own. The parents kept a watchful eye on them, guided their steps at every turn and groomed them to blossom into competent householders. The need to have a good look at both sides of the family rupee was ever present to their minds for, though their means were ample, the need for thrift was ever present. . . . The sons were also trained in the family business. They were unpaid apprentices, apprentices who were coached in account-keeping and letter-writing. They had no other ambitions. Accounts came in from the family businesses abroad every month, from Ceylon, Burma and Malaya and from the firms in India. (Nagarajan 1983: 17)

After marriage, Raja Sir Annamalai had four sons, and they shared the property alike (father and sons) and each one was entitled to a fifth share of the family properties which included every item of property from the business at home and abroad, houses, lands, gardens, etc. . . . Everything was divided. The partition is usually effected in a family council at which near relations and friends assist. Preferences are respected where there is no special objection and the partition is reduced to writing. (ibid.: 23)

In addition to the property share given to the sons as small entrepreneurs, there is also a share for the daughters, although this is much smaller in comparison (see Chapter 4). However, the final partition takes place when the father dies. Sometimes the final partition does not come at all, if the *pangaalis* decide to continue a jointly held company. If sons get married and receive their share from their fathers, they are expected not to ask for any further share until the death of their father. It is the wife's family who should help him thereafter.

According to Rudner (1994), the success of the Nagarattar business derives from three elements, i.e. the *pangaalis,* the agents, and the local caste group governed by the local caste leaders who take decisions for the regional caste members. The role of the *pangaalis* as the patrilinearly joined property group, according to Rudner, is to succeed in pooling credit and reserving and accumulating capital within the joint business. In the past, important decisions were made by the eldest male members of the *pangaali* group (i.e. head of the *walavu)* and each conjugal family headed by the male householder was expected to follow the decisions (ibid.: 112–14). He claims that while men were away overseas, women and children were supposed to be under the control of these elderly males who were the *pangaalis* of the husbands (ibid.: 112). Therefore, although Ito (1966: 370) argues that the Nagarattars 'nuclear families' (i.e. the *pulli)* had maintained economic independence, and the head of each nuclear family was allowed to make decisions on the business started on their own, Rudner claims that the decision-making power in most business transactions was in the hands of the eldest males of the *pangaalis,* and although the household budget for each individual conjugal unit was acknowledged, there was no reason to believe that the *pulli* had business activity of its own. Therefore, Rudner refutes Ito's point that the Nagarattars show the 'individualistic economic motivation which is comparable to western capitalistic entrepreneurship' (ibid.).

I disagree both with Ito and Rudner on these points; since both ignore the underlying mechanism of isogamy based on the Nagarattars' preference for bilateral cross-cousin marriage, which is the foundation of their kinship-oriented capital pooling system. Thus both of them fail to see the trans-generational aspect of the capital pooling system which maintains the circulation of funds among several families as well as the bi-linearity of the property transfer systems which I am going to discuss in this book (see Chapter 4).

Therefore, although Ito claims that the conjugal family used to have the power to take individual decisions on their entrepreneurial activities separately from the *pangaali* group, he fails to pin-point how such autonomy was supported. This model of their 'nuclear family' *(pulli)* is flawed because he fails to see how the decision-making power in the conjugal family was shared by the husband and wife, especially because the wife's property was not merged with her husband's. In my opinion, the Nagarattar conjugal family is economically more closely tied to the wife's natal family, a fact which heavily influences the decisions made about the family's economic strategy and alliance.

By allowing a married woman's property to be kept in her name and to be transferred to her daughter, the Nagarattars maintain a strong bond between the married daughter and her mother, since even after marriage, the daughter retains the right to inherit her mother's property when she has died. A strong preference for cross-cousin marriage as well as this bi-linearity are at the core of the Nagarattars' principle of caste endogamy, reflecting the fact that both the man and the woman hold equal ritual status as is implied by the rights of both to be given religious initiation (see Chapter 3). The bi-linearity of the caste membership is also reflected in the temple registration system of the marriage (see Chapter 2).

Nagarattar women bring a large sum of capital from their 'mother's house' *(ammaa viidu)*, and it is because of this, it is said, that *aacchis* dominate their home and their husbands. Though not always the case, the Nagarattars think of marriage as starting a new business: 'You cannot start a new life without any funds. Only when you have a stable fund, can you make a good family.' Therefore, establishing a new family needs capital from both sides, i.e.

husband's and wife's; while the husband's side looks after the family until they start to manage by themselves, the wife's natal family extends financial help after they have established an independent house. The *pulli* (the nuclear household), then becomes the symbol of the economic independence secured in the joint family.

1.5 Plan of the Nagarattar House

The ancestral house should face east, as shown in Figure 1.2, and the front entrance leads to an open space where a well is normally built. Then comes the veranda, usually occupied by men on ceremonial occasions and where strangers and business partners are entertained. If the joint family is wealthy enough, they can further extend this space and add a roofed hall to entertain guests and business partners. In such a case, this space may become the area used by accountants and clerks in transactions. If the house is fairly prosperous, the most senior male's quarters are secured in one corner of this area. In rich houses, this area is normally

Fig. 1.5. Front veranda of a *walavu viidu*

decorated in a Western fashion, with stained glass, chandeliers, desks and chairs, and Western-type wardrobes. There is a heavy door which separates this quarter from the interior and leads to the inner area called *walavu*. As seen in the second plan, the interior courtyard is called *walavu waasal*, and is the place where most of the ceremonial functions take place. It is in this area that they conduct auspicious rituals such as weddings and *saandi* (celebration of a male Nagarattar's sixtieth birthday. See Chapter 6). This is also the place where the corpse of a dead relative would be laid on a new mat to receive rituals from relatives. This *waasal* is surrounded by a corridor which faces several cell-like rooms *(ul viidu,* or 'a house inside the house'). *Ul viidu* is called *saami viidu* 'deity's room' where they place an altar and conduct *puja* (ritualistic worship of Hindu deities). When they have weddings, this room is referred to as the *kaliyaana viidu* (wedding room). In the past, when a man got married, he had this room as the starting-point: he would either have it built with the funds which he saved while he worked abroad; or nowadays, if he has several brothers, he inherits this room temporarily from his father. The room built with his own funds or inherited from his father is shared by him and any brothers he may have. After four or five generations, if the *pangaalis* still want to maintain the same joint household, the younger generation may build another quarter for rooms for their own nuclear family and their kitchens. If the father wants to build a new ancestral home to house his sons and his grandsons, he may ask for a contribution from those sons and grandsons. In any case, a Nagarattar man needs a ceremonial *ul viidu* for all ritual purposes. He does not live in this room, yet the room is ritually essential when he gets married and conducts important ceremonies for his family (see Chapter 3). It is usual for wives to keep their valuables in a safe and store provisions in this room. In the past, this was also the space where the newly-wed couple would consummate the marriage. When a wife gets older and becomes a widow she may sell her own house and live in this joint ancestral house, as was the case with a couple of widows that I saw in Chettinadu. There may be two or three widows living in the ancestral house in different *pullis*. However, even then, they would not share the same kitchen. They always cook separately and their financial concerns are strictly separate.

Another door leads to the kitchen. Usually, this quarter is where the servants sleep. There is also an open space for cooking. When big ceremonies are held, extra space is provided for drying things (such as chillies and large cooking utensils). Facing the open space, there are hearths *(aduppu)* which are allotted to each *pulli*. Once the newly married couple's training period is over, they are supposed to be independent, and have their own hearth and economic budget. Therefore, separate hearths as well as the *ul viidu* are a symbol of the autonomy of the nuclear household within the joint ancestral home. This kitchen quarter leads to the backyard of the house where the toilets are situated.

Usually, there are several toilets: if the family is rich the number of toilets is the same as the number of *pulli*. Usually, there are at least two toilets, because ceremonial functions require this. In a large house where very few people live, women use the back gate far more frequently than the front entrance. There are old widows who never open the front entrance for fear of burglars. The back gate is also used for informal visits and allows women more privacy. The building of such large, joint houses has been used as a tool to protect the economic welfare of family members: in times of poverty, they still have somewhere to live. It is relatively cheap and economical to share the cost and build a house in this way. According to some I spoke to, those who had worked as 'agents' abroad saved money and built ancestral houses at a relatively cheaper cost in the 1920s. Some of them, in reality, were living in utterly miserable conditions, but maintained their status as a Nagarattar because of their ancestral house.

1.6   Chettinadu Villages

Until the 1920s, Chettinadu was divided into several regions in the mind of the Nagarattars: West, East, South regions, the Karaikkudi area, and the Devakottai area. Since there was little means of transport, these areas made territorial, endogamous blocks. Nowadays, they intermarry, but cultural differences persist, which can cause difficulties among certain blocks of people when they marry people from other regions.

At the moment, the total population of the Nagarattars can be estimated to be around 130,000 to 140,000,[3] but most Nagarattars

[3] According to Chandrasekhar (1980: 45), the total number of temple registrations in their clan temple was 30,352 in 1950. The couple registers their marriage

Fig. 1.6. Deserted streets of Chettinadu

live in cities or in towns, so that a few villages out of the seventy-eight were deserted because of a decline in population. Yet the Nagarattars still identify themselves with the village *(uur)* where their ancestral houses are. 'Where are you from?' *('onga uur?')*, 'I am from Pallattur.' Such conversations are the norm between Nagarattars who meet for the first time. In this situation, Pallattur may not necessarily be the village he or she has been brought up in. He or she may have lived in cities, and only occasionally visited this village for functions as a child, taken there by his or her parents. He or she might have never lived in the village before or after marriage. The village *(uur)* mentioned is where his or her ancestral house is situated and patrilinearly transferred. Concerning the notion of *uur,* Daniel writes as follows:

---

at the groom's clan temple, so assuming that there are around four to five members in each family, I estimate that the total population can be around 121,408 to 151,760.

An *ur* is an entity composed of substance that can be exchanged and mixed with compatibility which are purely political and legal definitions of territory and which, therefore, do not summon forth in the Tamil the associations and concerns relative to substance exchange. It is the ideal of every Tamil to reside in his *conta ur* — that *ur* the soil substance of which is most compatible with his own bodily substance. Such compatibility can only be achieved when the *kunam* of the soil is the same as the *kunam* of one's own *jati*. (1984: 101)

Whether a Nagarattar lives in Singapore or in Los Angeles, he should come back to his *uur* in Chettinadu to attend ceremonies, as this is the place where he and his family see people who share the same 'substance', i.e. *jaati* (caste membership). Their ancestral house is inseparable from the *uur,* since it provides the identity of the caste status and proof of membership to the caste. The *viidu,* the house, is described by Daniel as follows:

To the Tamil villager, a house is a living being that is conceived in a sexual act, grows, is born, has a horoscope, goes through a formative period comparable to childhood, matures, and attains a stable nature, interacts in predictable ways with its human occupants and with neighbouring houses, and ultimately dies when it is abandoned. A house is a member of the village community. . . . Houses also assume the rank of the *jati* of their occupants. Hence, houses, too, must observe the rules of status and propriety which govern intercaste relationships. (ibid.: 149)

As I discuss in later chapters, the importance of the ancestral house is associated with the life-cycle rituals, e.g. pre-puberty, puberty, wedding, *saandi,* and funeral rituals. As Daniel mentions, procreative activities and death are shared by the *viidu,* especially by the ancestral house, for the Nagarattars. Chettinadu villages are full of grand mansions which are built side by side on the streets representing the close interwoven relationships between the members of the same caste.

The non-Nagarattars claim that the Nagarattar houses are conspicuously big whether they are *walavu viidus* or modern individual houses. One Nagarattar widow in her middle fifties who built a new house in Karaikkudi told me that it had to be large even though she lived alone, since her fellow castemen would not respect her unless the house was grand. Therefore, the Nagarattars equate their status with the grandeur of the house. Selling one's house is an obvious sign of economic decline; thus although they do not mind selling houses and land plots in urban cities, they do not sell the houses in Chettinadu unless they are extremely needy.

As I have already described, a number of such villages are deserted, and only the houses remain. However, the village does become animated when functions are held. The streets become full of people, music is heard everywhere, and rows of cars are parked on the streets. Wherever they live — Bombay, Singapore, America, or London — the Nagarattars come back to participate in the celebrations of weddings or *saandi*. Not attending leads to the loss of membership and status in the community. Chettinadu exists for them in an abstract sense even though it hardly functions as a village when no celebration is being held. The Nagarattars imagine their society to be the people of the Nagarattar community who own their ancestral house in Chettinadu even if in actual fact their people are dispersed all over the world.

At the centre of these social activities, are the *aacchis*, or the married Nagarattar women. Those who live in Madras and Madurai often come back to Chettinadu by train or by car. To them, coming to Chettinadu is an intrinsic part of their life. Some elderly *aacchis* constantly shuttle between Chettinadu and Madras, dealing with the social life and attending functions of other Nagarattars. If the *aacchis* did not return to Chettinadu they would have no real social life, and, without his *aacchi*, there is no social life for a Nagarattar.

1.7 Intercaste Relationships and the Nagarattars

According to Leach, within a caste in India there are two kinds of relationships. Those who belong to the same subcaste are bound by kinship while the external relations between different subcastes are economic and political. 'These relations stem from the fact that every caste has its special "privileges". Furthermore, these external relations have a very special quality since, ideally, they exclude kinship links of all kinds' (Leach 1960: 7). The intercaste relationships amongst the Nagarattars in Chettinadu are mostly transmitted through heredity. They have service castes who come to serve their life-cycle rituals, and have 'agents' (domiciliary stewards) who look after their property. The lower castes see the Nagarattars as aloof — they live in fortified mansions, and employ other castes such as the Kallars and the Brahmans as their 'agents'. Superficially,

Fig. 1.7. Well-structured *walavu viidu* from afar

this suggests that the Nagarattars appear to be one of the 'dominant castes', as the term is used by Srinivas (1987). Srinivas maintains the following:

Numerical strength, economic and political power, ritual status, and Western education and occupations, are the most important elements of dominance. Usually the different elements of dominance are distributed among different castes in a village. When a caste enjoys all or most of the elements of dominance, it may be said to have decisive dominance. (ibid.: 114)

However, the Nagarattars in Chettinadu do not fit exactly into this model of the dominant caste. As landlords, some of them may still have an eminent right over agricultural land, but this does not mean that they are willing to be involved in the local village politics of the non-Nagarattars. They want to be aloof and disconnected from village politics, although they have a number of village servants attached to them on a hereditary basis.

In that the Nagarattars are aloof, and of a high caste, they appear to be very similar to the Brahman communities. On closer examination however, it emerges that they are different from the Brahmans and highly Brahmanized castes such as the Shaiva Vellalars (Pillais) on several counts. Having village servants and agents, the Nagarattars can exercise physical power through economic power, if only indirectly while the Brahmans in Chettinadu cannot do so.

While I was in Mahamai Puram doing my first stint of fieldwork, I was told by one of the Pandarams (the village priestly caste), that one Pandaram who was serving in the Mariyamman temple had been attacked and injured one night by a local gangster, a Kallar, who was hired by a Nagarattar. According to him, the Pandaram who was attacked had been having an affair with a Scheduled Caste woman. Since he was a temple priest, he was told to stop the affair, as it was not 'good' for the status of a temple priest. The Pandaram ignored this and continued the relationship. The Nagarattar decided to teach him a lesson by hiring one of the local gangsters to attack the priest at night, and the priest quit the affair instantly.

What was striking to me was that the Nagarattars could effectively dominate the non-Nagarattars without using their own physical power, and that the Nagarattar had sent the local gang to the temple priest as a matter of temple honour. Generally speaking, the Nagarattars do not want to get involved with intercaste politics in the village, but if the matter turns out to be a temple affair, they will voluntarily get involved: if there is a charge of corruption in the temple management, the Nagarattars may even stop their donations. If they are asked to manage the temple treasury, they perform that task far more seriously than other castes.

The Nagarattars are different from both the 'right-hand castes' and the 'left-hand castes' which are described by Beck (1972) and Appadurai (1981). According to Beck, the dominant caste is defined as the subcaste community that controls a majority of the local labour force in a given area (1972: 15), such as the Gownder in the Kongu area. The Pillais are one of the high castes in the Kongu area, and are one of the 'left-hand castes', stressing ritual purity such as the elaborate dietary and interaction restrictions. They also prefer to stay away from agricultural labour, refusing, for example, to plough. Beck claims that the Pillais are not the dominant caste but they are viewed as being almost equal in rank to the Brahmans and hence are part of the 'head' (the highest caste) or neutral (i.e. apolitical) area of the social body, which stands above the rival prestige ladders of the right-hand dominant caste (ibid.: 9).

The Nagarattars are similar to neither the Pillai nor the agricultural Gownder caste type (as for the comparisons with the Gownders, see Chapter 5). They are non-agricultural, but do not imitate Brahmanic customs unlike the Vellalars or the vegetarian mercantile castes like the Komutti Chettiyars reported by Beck as not having any special tie to a landed group but trying to emulate Brahmans (ibid.: 12). As I shall describe in the following chapters, the Nagarattars' concept of purity and pollution also does not tally with the Brahmans' in many respects. Thus the Nagarattars are less dependent on Brahmanic value systems.

The Nagarattars employ the Brahmans to their own advantage in the same way as they use other service castes as part of their interactions with the village in Chettinadu. For the Nagarattars, their view of Chettinadu as the 'native village' *(sonda uur)* is not due to their holdings of agricultural land but because it is the site of their ancestral house *(walavu viidu)*. In any case, some Nagarattars nowadays have hardly any agricultural lands, even if they are rich, because they receive their income from other businesses. They regard society as a network of the Nagarattar community which has extended well outside the village boundaries: even kinship, their closest network, does not necessarily fit into the territorial boundaries of the 'village' in the sense meant by Srinivas or Dumont.

The majority of Nagarattars do not work in the fields, although they are landlords and make their labourers work in the field. Instead, they either engage in small businesses, or work as clerks, but are rarely agriculturalists. The most common occupation is that of moneylender. They are the prevalent moneylenders for the agriculturalists and various artisans in the village. And it is through this relationship that the Nagarattars in Chettinadu have been closely connected with the villagers.

As Fuller (1989) points out, until recently money power in the agrarian economy has been entirely neglected by major anthropological approaches. Money circulation in the revenue system of India both in the pre-colonial and colonial village economy has been crucial, and purchase of land and the title of *miras* and *zamindar* was commonplace as Fuller cites recent works done by historians (p. 49).

According to the historical analysis presented by Bayly (1983), for example, villagers were closely tied to the market economy and the supply of loans was essential for farmers to plan ahead for their business and family life in northern India. Merchants and money-lenders have also played important roles in the supply of money, the provision of loans, and the circulation of the products of both urban and rural economies. As for the Chettinadu area, dependence on the Nagarattar money by the local *zamindar* and peasants in the Ramnad region was quite acute (Price 1979).

This outlines more realistically the relationship between the Nagarattars and the non-Nagarattars in the village. As the landlord-cum-moneylenders, the Nagarattars lent money to farmers who needed capital to purchase seeds and manage their houses until the harvest was completed. However, since a good harvest depends on the climate and other unpredictable factors (e.g. natural calamities), the moneylenders have to take into account the risks involved when lending money to the farmers. One of the reasons why the Nagarattars are eager to patronize the local temples and village deities might well derive from the desire to prevent such unpredictable calamities from upsetting their scheduled recouping of money.

The local Parayas (the Scheduled Castes) who are normally employed by the Nagarattars as labourers, informed me that the Nagarattars used to give them chickens and other items when the Parayas worshipped their own lineage deity, Karuppa, whose shrine was situated in their quarter. According to them, whenever there was a drought, the Nagarattars asked them (through their agents) to worship their deities on their behalf, since the *kula deivams* of the Parayas were believed to be powerful.

1.8 Village Deities and the Nagarattars: Religion and Mercantile Morality

Such religiosity however, seems to be closely interwoven with mercantile interest as many scholars who work on mercantile communities have remarked (Bayly 1983; Mines 1984; Rudner 1994). A reputation for religious mindedness is an effective way to defend oneself and one's family. In other words, money spent on charity and village religious ceremonies can be considered as more of an insurance than employing guards and alarm systems. It is understandable why the Nagarattars who lived in an agrarian society surrounded by agricultural castes and the Untouchables had to 'keep them sweet' by spending money on their well-being. In other words, generosity is a prerequisite for becoming a 'big-man' in society (Mines 1994: 42) and necessary for maintaining a long-term business.

For example, while I was in Karaikkudi, I came across several renowned jewellery merchants in town who were reputed to be honest and trustworthy. The most renowned diamond merchant was a Jain who was famous for his honesty and generosity. People said that he built a shrine to worship deities, gave delicious festival food to the poor on *Deepavali* (autumnal festival), and was always generous to others. Although he had several large first-class diamonds in the safe of his house and had countless diamonds in his shop in town, there were no guards and no alarm system to protect them from burglaries.

I also met another diamond merchant in Tiruchi, a city near Samayapuram where there was a famous temple of Mariyamman. During the annual festival of this deity, he was believed to be possessed by this local goddess and put to work as a healer. He charged nothing for this service since it was the will of the goddess,

Fig. 1.8. Aduppu (hearths) in the *walavu viidu*

yet I could imagine that his business would have benefitted greatly from his reputation as a holy man.

The Nagarattars are much more conscious of the relationship between their religiosity and their prosperity than agricultural castes in general. Although they are renowned for their thrift, they do not grudge spending money on religious ceremonies and charitable activities to please the gods. They are renowned temple goers. In my opinion, they are rather 'addicted' to it. The women love to go to the local temples, especially on Fridays, which is the most auspicious day, offer *aacchanai* (offering through the medium of a temple priest), and maintain close relationships with the priests and the temple management. Even the Brahman temple priests (Gurukkals) admit that the Nagarattars, especially the *aacchis* are 'religious' in the sense that they love to go to temples and pray for the welfare of their family. The frequency of visiting temples among the Nagarattars in general is much higher than among other non-Brahman castes. For example, when I was conducting fieldwork on Mariyamman worship, I noticed that no villager visited the temple as frequently as the Nagarattars. Moreover, the Nagarattars patronize temples and give donations whenever necessary, or join the management itself by becoming trustees. However, the Nagarattars' love of temples is not restricted to the grand temples where Sanskritized deities such as Shiva and Vishnu are enshrined. In fact they worship local village deities more ardently than they worship the higher gods. They are fervent worshippers of goddesses, especially those who are the guardians of the village. Kaliyamman, Mariyamman, Selliyamman, etc. are deities who are believed to have especially ambivalent characters. If they are in good humour, they bring good rain and harvest, while in anger, they cause calamities and disease. Whenever there is a village festival of Mariyamman in a nearby village or in the village itself, the Nagarattars do their utmost to attend. If it is impossible for them to attend, then they give donations from the commonly pooled fund of the Nagarattars in the region.

In village life, both Brahmans and non-Brahmans worship *kula deivam* (the lineage god) which is located in the place where the family ancestry began. According to the Nagarattars, village gods, especially *kula deivams* are quite powerful and protective if they are pleased, while on the other hand, if they are not properly worshipped, they cause calamities and annoy people.

Kula deivams worshipped today, as well as those mentioned in the Puranic literature are mostly female (Das 1977: 82–3). The shrines devoted to them are usually small structures with thatched roofs, but sometimes they consist simply of stone markers. Although annual festivals are not held in a grand manner as the shrines for these deities are mostly small, they are believed to protect the locality for generations. Deities like Muni, Karuppan, Muttalamman, and Mariyamman are affiliated to particular villages, being worshipped as *kula deivams* by a single lineage or several lineages of different castes.

The Nagarattars, although Shaivites (worshippers of Shiva), are ardent worshippers of local gods and goddesses. In Kanadukattan, one of the Chettinadu villages, one elderly Nagarattar widow said that she could never start any auspicious function without first worshipping local deities such as Muni and Karuppan who were worshipped by local villagers (including the Nagarattars) as *kula deivam*. Therefore, even when she has a big function in Madras, she returns to Chettinadu to worship these deities offering *aacchanai* and sometimes a piece of cloth. Praying to such local deities is considered by the Nagarattars to be essential for a good start and auspicious for any venture. I was also told by local Parayas (one of the Scheduled Castes who are traditionally attached to the agricultural lands as labourers) that when there was a long drought, their Nagarattar landlord would give them chickens to worship their *kula deivams*. They would also make them carry out the humiliating custom of banging their drums on ceremonial occasions — a custom which has long since died out in non-Nagarattar villages.

The religiosity of the Nagarattars is closely interwoven with their hereditary profession as merchants. Although merchants are highly rational and live in a world of calculation and probability, the predictability of logic is contrasted with the unpredictability of natural disasters. Therefore, donations to the temples and expenditures to the charities are part of the cover or the insurance for the Nagarattars in this world, just as Rudner maintains that religious endowment has been a central component in Hindu business practice for a long time (1994: 134). While calamities may not be avoided even by being religious and charitable, the Nagarattars still enter into the world of the unequal relationship with the divine even if their daily life is based upon rational calculation and centres around the kinship relationship — a relationship which is based on the ideology of exchange and reciprocity, the germinator of auspiciousness.

In the following chapters, I shall discuss the mechanism which supports this ideology. In Chapter 2, I shall describe the conditions which support their strict moral code of caste endogamy, which assures the status equality within the caste. In Chapter 3, aspects in kinship terminology are extensively explored in order to explain the web of kinship which supports the status of married women. In Chapter 4, the married woman's relative economic autonomy is discussed in relation to the well-formulated contract papers concerning marriage. The detailed lists of bridal goods also shed light on the several spheres of complex gift exchange transactions between the bride's kin and her affines. Their unusual habit of hoarding bridal goods is discussed in terms of capital investment and the pooling system which is closely tied to their kinship. In Chapter 5, I shall compare wedding rituals between the Nagarattars and other South Indian castes, which clearly supports the argument to prove Nagarattars' ritual egalitarianism between the wife-giver and wife-taker. In Chapters 6 and 7, the two crucial stages of Tamil womanhood, i.e. married womanhood *(sumangali)* and widowhood *(amangali)* are dealt with, shedding light on the Nagarattar women's managerial position in their married house, which does not seem to diminish even in widowhood. In conclusion, I discuss Nagarattar egalitarianism as complementary between the wife-giver and wife-taker and between husband and wife, and which supports their ideal of reciprocity within the community.

Chapter 2

The Morality of Endogamy

WHEN I was staying in Karaikkudi in 1991, I started my research interviewing college girls in a nearby village called Pallattur. A Nagarattar entrepreneur built a women's college a few decades ago so that Nagarattar girls could get higher education while commuting from their own houses. When I asked for their views on marriage, they all rejected the idea of 'love marriage' and favoured arranged marriage. 'Marriage is a gamble,' according to them, since the true character of the groom would come out only after marriage. Yet if they follow their parents' opinions and choose their husbands accordingly, they are able to depend on their parents in time of hardship while if they choose their own husbands and marry against the wish of their parents, they lose that support. Moreover, if they marry someone from another caste, they would lose their caste membership. In South India, people are brought up to conform to society, i.e. to the family values, to the lineage and to the caste. The social pressure to preserve these values is extremely strong, especially for women, since they have no chance of keeping in touch with their natal families if they marry outside the caste. However, stray cases do occur and can cause a serious crisis of identity. In this chapter, I shall discuss how caste endogamy as a system forms a crucial part of the Nagarattar identity.

2.1 Caste Membership

In contemporary India, asking someone to reveal their caste is considered 'rude', since it can potentially cause embarrassment to those from the lower castes. Therefore, trying to establish someone's caste becomes a matter of deduction by other means and people often confessed that they did not have a clear idea of their friends' castes. When I discovered the caste of various people, their friends were often surprised as their assumptions proved to be entirely wrong. For example, a well-educated boy was believed to be of a non-Brahman caste by his friends who had deduced from his behaviour and educational level that he belonged to the Vellalar caste. In fact, he turned out to be a Vannan, or a washerman, which is considered to be a lower service caste ranked just above the Untouchables. Another boy who was a Vellalar Pillai, was believed to be either a Brahman or a Sawarashtran (one of the weaver castes of North Indian origin) because of his rather light complexion. An Aiyangar Brahman who had assumed this was surprised to discover his mistake.

Although assumptions of caste are often wrong, there are certain guidelines such as behaviour and speech usage, that can be fairly accurate indicators. In Tamil Nadu, Hindus are roughly categorized into three groups: Brahman castes, non-Brahman castes, and the Scheduled Castes (ex-Untouchables). Brahmans, according to the local people, are conspicuous, because of their light complexion and their tendency to use more Sanskritic terms in conversation than the non-Brahmans who tend to use Tamil terms.

Normally among the higher caste Hindus, it is said that behaviour patterns are different from those of the lower castes. Their lifestyle is seen as well organized: they rise early, keep their houses very clean, firmly encourage their children to study, and save money well. Their attitude, a religious mark on the forehead (worn when the person is a strict Shaiva or Vaishnava), the way clothes are worn, and caste dialect, etc. are all indicators that can be used to guess the caste of another party.

A further indication of caste is a person's name, which can imply broader categories — Brahman names and non-Brahman names are often quite distinctive. A Brahman would never have a name such as Karuppan, Muniyandi, Muttammal, or Nagamma, as these are the names of local village gods and goddesses. Instead they are more likely to have names frequently found in Sanskrit literature, e.g. Subramaniyam, Venkatesh, Chittra, Rajeshwari, etc. Again, this is not an absolute distinction, since the first set of names mentioned is used by both the non-Brahmans and the Scheduled Castes, and the latter names are used by both the non-Brahmans and the Brahmans.

However, when these names are used with a caste title, such as 'Subramaniya Aiyar', the caste is unmistakably detectable. In this case the person cannot be a non-Brahman, but must be a Smartha Brahman, since the caste title 'Aiyar' denotes this. Similarly, 'Aiyangar' is the caste title of the Vaishnavite Brahmans. In the case of the Nagarattars, a man whose name is Annamalai may call himself 'Annamalai Chettiyar', thus adding the title to denote that he belongs to a mercantile caste. It would be difficult to know which Chettiyar caste he is from: a Nagarattar, a Velan Chettiyar, a Vellalar Chettiyar, or a Komutti Chettiyar.

Adding a caste title at the end of a name is normally practised only by males. The example I gave was that of a man whose name is Annamalai, known as Annamalai Chettiyar.[1] For further clarification, he adds his father's and paternal grandfather's initials: LPL Annamalai denotes that his grandfather is Lakshmanan and his father is Palaniyappan (P and L are taken in this case). If his grandfather had built a house, it may be called LPL House in which the first shareholders would be his father and his paternal uncles. It would not matter that the house had been built by the grandfathers' ancestors; if the house is shared by Annamalai, his brother, and their father, i.e. by those who share Lakshmanan and Palaniyappan as their ancestors, the house would still be called LPL House. This would be the case for as long as Annamalai and his brothers' children remained alive, as it would make it much easier to refer to. However, the grandchildren of Palaniyappan would no longer keep the initial of LPL in their names, but would change it to PLA or just A, if they so desired, while someone who wished to keep initials from three generations may call himself LPLA Lakshmanan, for example. This method of identifying a male by the house name helps to differentiate between all those with the same name as there is very little originality in the naming of Nagarattars. As for women, the same method is applied, although they would change the initials after their marriage. This method is extremely useful when someone is making a telephone call, for example, since there are so many relatives who carry the same names.

The initials attached to the individual name imply the house to which a Nagarattar belongs and the social identity of a Nagarattar

[1] 'Chettiyar' is used when addressing a senior man from a mercantile caste in a respectful manner. The wife, servants, and house stewards would refer to a senior old Nagarattar as 'Chettiyar' when, for example, someone enquired as to his whereabouts. Thus, a married Nagarattar woman is called *aacchi* (elder sister), and an adult male Nagarattar is called Chettiyar.

partially consists of the house symbolized by this. The sharing of the ancestral home is made concrete in the form of a share holding of that house. A male Nagarattar is entitled to become a shareholder of an ancestral house which was built by his paternal ancestors. The inheritance is represented as a 'room' *(ul viidu)* and a hearth, although this is often divided when handed down to subsequent generations. Although the construction of new buildings has become rare, there are still some wealthier families even today, who can build a new house or add a new wing to an old house for male children to share.

2.2 Clan and Temple Divisions

The largest patrilineal unit among the Nagarattars is the clan, symbolized by the nine Shiva temple divisions.[2] These temples were given by the king when the Nagarattars settled in the Chettinadu area. They believe that the original members of the temple are also patrilineal relatives and that they thus share a common ancestry. Those who belong to the same clan division are called *pangaali*. The male co-sharers of the ancestral house, therefore, belong to the same temple division, and are also called *pangaali*.

The clan is exogamous. Sexual relations within the same temple division are considered to be incestuous, since the man and woman are believed to be brother and sister even if their connections are impossible to detect. The Nagarattars classify themselves through the clan and subclan system as *pangaali,* and the share of the ancestral house is passed down this line. Women do not inherit any share of the patrilineal ancestral house. They remain in their father's lineage before marriage and use their father's initial after their own. After marriage, they take their husband's name. They may also assume their husband's and his father's initials. LPL Lakshmi *aacchi* means that her father-in-law is Lakshmanan and

---

2 The nine temple divisions are as follows: (1) Ilayattakudi temple which has the following subdivisions: (i) Okkur, (ii) Pattanasamy, (iii) Perumarudur, (iv) Kinkanikkur, (v) Kalanivasal, (vi) Perasandur, (vii) Sirusettur (nowadays, marriages between these subdivisions are allowed); (2) Mattur temple — subdivisions: (i) Uraiyur, (ii) Arumbakkur, (iii) Manalur, (iv) Mannur, (v) Kannur, (vi) Karuppur, (vii) Kulattur; (3) Vairavan temple — subdivisions: (i) Sirukulattur, (ii) Kalanivasal, (iii) Maruttendrapuram; (4) Iraniyur; (5) Pillaiyarpatti; (6) Neemam; (7) Iluppaikkudi; (8) Sooraikkudi; (9) Veelankudi.

her husband is Palaniyappan. Like most Indian castes, she can also add her husband's name at the end: Sita Chidambaram, Meena Ramasamy, etc. Therefore, their initials and titles express their social identity, which is rooted in the joint house.

Among the Nagarattars, there were six territorial divisions, *wattahais* (regions) which were formerly endogamous units, probably until the 1910s. Since there were very few roads in Chettinadu until the 1930s, *pangaalis* used to come on foot to attend the ceremonies. Therefore, according to Somalay, it was the custom to contract matrimonial alliances with families of which they had first-hand knowledge who lived within such short distances (quoted in Rudner 1994: 168). This continued for quite some time. The regional endogamous blocks have since disappeared, although certain preferences in marriage alliances and slight differences in manners and customs remain. For example, people say that the richest families came from the east *wattahai*. It is said that their women always wear silk *sarees* and are culturally refined. On the other hand, those from the west region used to work for the eastern people as stewards. People from the south region in general are poor, sometimes the women work in the fields and thus they are darker than the eastern people. A middle-aged woman who belonged to one of the top families of the eastern region told me that her mother was quite upset when she heard that one of her granddaughters was going to be engaged to a man from Devakottai. A Nagarattar woman, one of her relatives, explains the reason for this,

It is not that we do not respect them. Those who want alliances with us may be extremely rich and may be highly respected in the region. Therefore, it is not the status or prestige but their lifestyle. Although we would welcome their daughters marrying our sons, we would not like our daughters to marry their sons. They would suffer if the standard of living differs. However rich they may be, their bathroom may not be as comfortable as ours. Our daughters may not enjoy freedom to come to Madras as often as we want. Marriage is a risk, and in order to protect our daughters, we want to avoid any possible risk.

As this remark shows, their regional differences do not seem to have created status hierarchies between different regions. The Nagarattars thus basically treat each other as ritually equal, whether rich or poor (cf. Chapter 8).

The nine Shiva temple divisions mentioned above, on the other hand, function as marriage regulators and those who belong to the same temple division should not intermarry as they are considered to be *pangaalis*. Each temple maintains a management board made up of elderly male members from the powerful families, and the trustees are replaced every three years or so. They make decisions about the budget, ceremonial functions, renovations of the temple and so on, but usually they have no moral authority over the clan members.

The temple trustee is a ceremonial position. Although the Brahman temple priests (Gurukkals) are the officiants at all the rituals, they cannot impose their opinion on the management to any great extent, since they are merely temple servants. However, the temple managers themselves do not have much moral authority except in their power to regulate marriage.

To be a pure Nagarattar, both parents must belong to any of the nine temples. Marrying someone whose parents are not full-fledged members means that the couple will fail to win the community's recognition of the marriage as authentic, and so the garland from the lineage temple will not be received by the bride and groom. The temple management, which consists of wealthy and powerful Nagarattars, objects to sending a garland and registering the marriage if the marriage is not between authentic Nagarattars.

As the wedding day approaches, the parents of both parties go to their respective temples, pay the temple tax, and ask the temple management to send a garland to their children's wedding. The temple of the male side registers the marriage in their registration book on this occasion. The temple trustees normally check the name of the parents in their registration book, and confirm whether their marriage was registered. If it has been, they acknowledge the marriage of their child and register his/her name as part of the authentic *pulli* (nuclear family).

Since the procedure of verifying the authenticity of the children is simple, few serious problems occur. However, I was told that there were some cases where the agreement of the trustees was needed. For example, a Nagarattar, who divorced his first Nagarattar wife and married another Nagarattar had to appeal to the temple trustees of both his and his new wife's temples after more than two decades: because he had married his second wife without a proper marriage ceremony, and had not registered his marriage with the temple, when his son was getting married, he faced a serious problem. His son was refused a garland because his father's marriage was not registered!

The trustees were called in to discuss this matter three days before the marriage ceremony. They unanimously decided that the man's son's marriage should be registered and the garland be sent, since his mother was an authentic Nagarattar. However, they demanded the temple tax which the man had neglected to pay at the time of his second marriage, with interest.

Another case which I heard, was more than a century old. A man had insulted the temple trustees by coming to a temple-meeting riding a horse. He did not get off the horse at the temple premises and his horse scattered dust over the trustees. The man was excommunicated because he had insulted the trustees, who were also the elders, in a public place, and he and his descendants were refused garlands upon marriage. Therefore, even though the descendants were all authentic Nagarattars, the garland simply did not come to the weddings of this man's descendants. I was told by one of the trustees that one of his descendants now wanted to apologize for his ancestor's mistake and regain the privilege of receiving the garland from the temple. The trustee I spoke to told me that this would be possible, since they were all authentic Nagarattars. So, the trustees were now thinking about the proper way to ask the man to express his remorse.

The clan temple system shows that as a first principle, the trustees, as the representatives of the clan group, should be respected in the temple. The temple institution bestows honour on the clan and the patrilineal structure which supports it. The garland which the clan temple sends symbolizes the couple's authentic membership of the community, honouring not only the man's patrilineal group but the woman's as well.

2.3 The Nagarattars and 'their' Purity Rule

The traditional value system based on the religious notion of the pure and the impure, is said to be deeply related to the social status among the Hindus in general. For example, Dumont (1970a) maintains that impurity is connected with biological processes: phlegm, blood, excrement, and especially the dead body, are all considered to be agents of pollution, and those who deal with such processes as hereditary occupations, are considered to be low in the social hierarchy — street-cleaners, undertakers, toilet cleaners, etc. are considered to be the Untouchables; washermen and barbers who deal with cleaning are considered to be engaged in lowly occupations, though not as low as the Untouchables. On the other hand, the highest status is given to the Brahmans who are the least engaged with the physiological processes of other people as far as hereditary occupations are concerned, and as hereditary priestly castes, they are allowed to touch the sacred idols and chant mantras (the sacred hymns). Therefore, even though most caste groups have discarded their traditional occupations, this value system attached to the stigma of pollution still classifies the castes in general, in terms of social status, according to Dumont.

The essence of Dumont's argument lies in his claim that Hindu culture in general is regulated by the single value system of hierarchical dichotomy of the pure and the impure, irrespective of caste, and this rule binds not only the external relationships between the castes but also the internal relationships, i.e. kinship itself. In terms of kinship, this purity rule differentiates the offspring from the primary (legitimate, in Dumont's sense) marriage and the ones from the secondary (illegitimate, or second marriage with a woman whose status is lower than that of the first wife) marriage, for example. In general, most castes give the first born son higher status than the other sons. Although it appears harsh to say that the first born son is 'purer' than the second son, the rule of hierarchy differentiates them, and the 'purer' sons, i.e. the legitimate sons are placed higher than those who are illegitimate, i.e. less pure, in terms of kinship, according to Dumont.

Rules of hierarchy are obvious in other crucial relationships, according to Dumont. Sons are far more appreciated and are given greater importance than daughters, and the paternal relatives (i.e. the wife-takers), are given a higher position than the maternal ones (the wife-givers). This relationship is expressed by the continuous flow of gifts given from the wife's side to the husband's family even after marriage. Dumont therefore claims that the hierarchical system, based on the pure and the impure, regulates not only the intercaste relationship, but also the intracaste relationship, i.e. the kinship system and the marriage alliance.

Discussing the regulation of marriage, Dumont claims that not only hypergamy but also endogamy is a corollary of hierarchy, rather than a primary principle (1970*a*: 113). If a man breaches the rule of endogamy and marries a woman from another caste, if it is a legitimate marriage, both the man and his wife and children obtain the status of his caste, although such irregularity is penalized by a loss of status within the caste of the man. Therefore,

Now the hierarchical principle which ranks castes and their segments does not stop at the bounds of the unit of endogamy, it permeates it, in a more or less effective way, and endogamous marriage does not necessarily unite spouses of equal status. (ibid.)

However, Dumont's claim that the hierarchical principle which ranks castes and their segments, prevails both outside and inside the caste group is difficult to substantiate, especially in the case of the Nagarattars. In other words, his argument of endogamy as 'a corollary of hierarchy, rather than a primary principle' (ibid.) loses its ground since the principle of Nagarattar caste membership is endowed bilineally. Whatever may be the caste of the mother, the child is not a Nagarattar unless both parents are from the Nagarattar caste. If a Nagarattar X marries a woman of caste Y, even if their marriage is legitimate, their children do not obtain their father's caste status. Only X remains as a full-fledged caste member until his death, and there is no chance of his offspring making alliances with his caste members. The concept of the Nagarattars' rigid endogamy therefore does not appear to resemble Dumont's hierarchical principle of the pure and the impure, since the Nagarattars' endogamous rule emphasizes the egalitarian exchange relationship as their basic principle while the Dumontian notion of the pure/impure depends on intercaste hierarchy. In daily life however, the Dumontian argument appears to be partially valid even for the Nagarattars as they refer to three divisions: high caste, low caste, and the Untouchables or the Scheduled Castes but this is more superficial and confined to limited areas as far as the Nagarattars are concerned.

Although the Nagarattars are proud of being Shaivites, they do not appear to be much concerned about the above-mentioned purity rules. They are in fact non-vegetarians. Although some families or individuals do prefer to be vegetarians, vegetarianism is not observed as a caste habit in general. As for marriage alliances, there is no status differentiation between a vegetarian family and a non-vegetarian family among the Nagarattars. Some Nagarattars, such as those from Devakottai are said to be traditionally vegetarians. However, such vegetarian Nagarattars which exist as a regional group do not enjoy any ritual privileges or a higher status than other Nagarattars, nor do they refuse to marry their daughters to non-vegetarian Nagarattars from different regions.

Moreover, the Nagarattars do not seem to respect the Brahmans for the latter's peculiar dietary habit. From the point of view of the non-Brahmans including the Nagarattars, the Brahmans' refusal to take food in the non-Brahman houses is taken simply as a peculiar, but orthodox Brahman custom. There are a lot of Brahmans who work for the Nagarattars as agents, clerks, and teachers at the schools run by the Nagarattars, and seem to be favoured for their loyalty and calm nature, and the fact that they are not able to eat together does not affect this close relationship. However rich the house may be and however good and clean the food is, strict Brahmans cannot accept it if the cook is a non-Brahman, and this custom can be taken as an expression of Brahmanic pride and so does not insult or humiliate the Nagarattars. The Nagarattars are happy to leave the cooking to non-Nagarattars, and both the Brahmans and the Nagarattars take each others' way of life for granted and so do not interfere.

All the cooks I met in the households of the Nagarattars were non-Nagarattars. They were either from Vellalar castes or from much lower agricultural castes such as the Vallambars, who would have been trained by the *aacchi* and whose forebears would have served the same family for a few generations. There were some families who even hired domestic servants and cooks from the Scheduled Castes claiming that these people were employed for their loyalty and obedient character. The few *aacchis* who chose to be vegetarians because of their devoutness did not mind leaving the cooking to the non-vegetarian lower caste cooks, either. Moreover, there are Nagarattar families whose members are both vegetarians and non-vegetarians, and the cook does the cooking for all. For the strict Brahmans, this would be unacceptable, since using the same cooking utensil to prepare both vegetarian and non-vegetarian meals would pollute their food.

The Nagarattars' flexibility about food preparation is demonstrated not only in their recruitment of servants but also in the preparation of the food itself. People joke about how *aacchis* are good at saving and storing unused things. A special delicacy called *'wattal kulambu'* is a good demonstration of the maxim 'waste not, want not'. For example, Brahmans use only a few fresh vegetables, and will not usually eat the same *kulambu* in the next meal, as they feel it would 'pollute' the body. The Nagarattars, on the other hand, insist that a three day old *kulambu* is the most superior. They also claim that this is true of fish *kulambu;* storing cooked food before eating improves the flavour in their opinion. 'When we have some left over *kulambu* after lunch, we give it to the servant. But I know an *aacchi* who orders her servant to sell it to poor people for 10 or 20 paisa per cup!', a middle-aged Brahman woman told me disgustedly. However, the Nagarattars will not be shamed by these critical comments made by the Brahmans. One Nagarattar said, 'Brahmans depend on us. Who gives them *daanam* (religious gifts for Brahmans) and jobs? Who supports the poor Brahmans? If we hadn't saved money and donated to the temples and the welfare institutions, who would have done so?'

The Nagarattars' economic rationality as well as 'taste' takes precedence over the Brahmanic purity rule. In addition, the Nagarattars consider feeding people to be an essential ritual which they have to practise, and they have to eat with their guest irrespective of their relative status. Although they may not eat anything in the house of a Scheduled Caste, for example, their concern in this case is directed towards 'hygiene'. I was convinced in Chettinadu that the Nagarattars would accept an invitation from a lower caste if the man's social status was high and the house was clean and neat.

This indifference to ritual pollution contrasts with that of the Shaiva Vellalars (Pillais) whose culture is more similar to the Brahmans (Beck 1972: 9) or of the Komutti Chettiyars (ibid.: 12). The Kontakatti Vellalars (a Shaiva Vellalar caste, hereafter referred to as KV) described by Barnett (1976) also clearly follow the Brahmanic purity concept. The purity concept of the KV has a clear alliance with local Brahmans, and they support a religious *madam* in Kanchipuram and claim that the Tesikars (vegetarian non-Brahman priests influential in certain Brahman temples) were once KVs (ibid.: 136). To the KV who are pure vegetarians, the Brahmanic purity rule is an essential guideline to regulate their daily conduct and the status hierarchy. Just like the Brahmans, they are meticulous in defining the group from whom they may accept water or cooked food. They also maintain their caste *madam* and patronize the temples of the Shaiva religion.

The contrast between the KV and the Nagarattars is also ap parent when the degree of dependence on the local service castes is analysed. While the Brahmanic purity rule means that they cannot hire service castes for purificatory purposes (the Brahmans' rule is that they must purify themselves) in any Chettinadu village, there would have been service castes such as Barbers and Washermen who served the Nagarattars. Only after serving them, would they serve other castes. The washerman and washerwoman launder the clothes, even though some of the Nagarattars may have servants or perhaps their wives themselves do the washing. The service of the washerman is necessary for clothes that are to be worn on special occasions such as weddings, festivals, Pongal (celebration of the new year), and Deepavali (autumnal celebration of good harvest). At these times the washerman becomes very busy, as ceremonial cleansing done by him is considered essential. The washerman's wife works for the women and she plays a crucial role when the girls reach puberty. She washes the *sarees* of the girl, and according to one Nagarattar woman, even lends her own *saree* to her during her first menstruation. She receives vegetables, paddy, some money, *adai* (pancakes) etc. which are used in the ritual. The barber also has additional work as the funeral priest in the cremation ground, shaving the chief mourner's head and helping him to conduct rituals over the corpse. His wife also works as a midwife.

As this shows, the relationship between the barber's wife and the Nagarattar women is casual and interdependent; thus, although there is a hierarchical relationship between the patron and the service caste, the concept of Brahmanic ritual purity does not influence the Nagarattar women as far as their traditional relationships with the two above-mentioned service castes are concerned. This tendency is consistent with their acceptance of women's menstruation as an auspicious symbol of reproduction rather than the Brahmanic concept of pollution.

2.4 Endogamy as Caste Morality

Although the Nagarattars may sometimes pay lip service to the ritualistic purity rule observed by the Brahmans, they largely dismiss it in real life, nor do they follow it in terms of food intake. However, their kinship orientation and caste membership is strictly endogamous, and it is quite different from the concept of ritual purity *(suttam)*. However rich they may be and however many generations are born, the Nagarattar line is not authentic if there has been a marriage with a non-Nagarattar member. For example, if A's father is a Nagarattar and mother a non-Nagarattar, he may claim that he has inherited his father's temple membership, as would be the case with regard to the Brahmanic *gootra*. A male Brahman's marriage to a non-Brahman, if she is from a high caste, is mostly accepted and his children are assimilated into his caste eventually, and children take up their father's *gootra* as their identity of caste membership.

In the case of the Nagarattars, if the offspring of such an alliance marries a Nagarattar, he or she will nevertheless remain a non-Nagarattar. Even if the partner's father were a Nagarattar and the mother a non-Nagarattar, the children thus appearing to be full-fledged members as they would have inherited temple A and B from their fathers, would not be considered authentic, since a pure Nagarattar should inherit membership of the caste from both parents. In other words, the clan temple membership is inherited from their father but the caste membership is based on a bilineal inheritance.

The temple garlands for the bride and groom come from their fathers' temples on the wedding day, and the implicit rules are that the couple's parents' weddings must have been registered in the books kept in the respective temples. The consequence of marrying someone who is not a Nagarattar is as follows: (1) if a male marries outside his caste, his membership as a Nagarattar will be maintained until his death. He can attend ceremonies and functions as a Nagarattar if he wishes to do so, but he would not be accompanied by his wife and children, since they would not be regarded as pure Nagarattars. The relationship between his family and his kin would gradually diminish in successive generations. His offspring would never be able to merge back into the Nagarattar community. Instead, they would belong to the diverted line which is formed out of the endogamous tendency; (2) if a female marries outside her caste, she immediately loses membership in her community and instead acquires temporary membership of her partner's caste and her children belong to her husband's community.

Whether a Nagarattar marries a higher caste or lower caste, the offspring is separated from the mainstream. Such offspring used to be denied any right to claim their father's property until recently;

and although nowadays, the legally married non-Nagarattar wives and their children may claim their share of the property under modern law, they are still not entitled to make alliances with the pure Nagarattars. Marrying a non-Nagarattar is considered to be detrimental, not because it creates 'impurity' in the Brahmanic sense, but because it allows property to flow out of the caste and breaks the reciprocal relationship of marriage alliance between the wife-givers and wife-takers. Complete isogamy is based on the compatibility between these two. The garlands sent by the paternal clan temple of both sides thus represent a strict membership based on the ideology of equality of status among the members, since the garland cannot be bought, however rich a man may be.

Divorce is permissible among Vellalars and non-Brahman castes if it is unavoidable, but it very rarely takes place among the Nagarattars, since it is taken as a violation of customary law and the man's status is diminished. Marrying a Nagarattar woman after divorcing the first wife is permissible whereas intercaste marriage is not. However, divorce cannot be effected without paying compensation to the first wife and returning the dowry and other property which were brought by her. Bigamy, in the sense of a man having two authentic Nagarattar wives is unacceptable, although having a concubine from another caste is another matter entirely.

As this is the case, how would the Nagarattar woman look upon her marriage especially when she is young? Would she accept that she can marry a man she hardly knows and would she accept the fact that some men are promiscuous and have extramarital affairs?

When I started research in Karaikkudi, I asked such questions of college girls who were mostly Nagarattars. They generally answered that love marriage is not acceptable, since it would jeopardize their relationship with their families. Instead, they claimed that their parents were quite understanding and would try to accommodate their wishes. They also ruled out the possibility of tolerating extramarital affairs by their future husbands and maintained that they would seek a divorce if their husbands committed adultery. In this sense, the present Nagarattar women, just like other young women in India, seem to believe in an affectionate bond being crucial in the conjugal relationship. They also stress their own choice of husband within the limited range of an arranged marriage system.

We would discuss it fully before my parents start to seek an alliance. I would not marry someone I didn't like even if my parents insisted. My parents would know this and would search for someone who is suitable for me. Since I have little experiece in life, I trust my parents' judgement. They would also ask my opinion when they proceeded with the alliance.

Cross-cousin marriage is one of their possible choices even today, since it is still an advantage for the boy's and the girl's families to come to know each other very well before marriage, ensuring that the groom is not a total stranger to the bride. Unless she has any particular reasons to dislike her cross-cousin, he would still be preferred by her and her parents, although other options such as distant relatives or non-relatives may have become more frequent choices than in the olden days (see Chapter 3).

2.5 Intercaste Marriage: 'Love Marriage'

According to the South Indians, a 'love marriage' (they use the English term) is regarded as eloping and considered shameful (Caplan 1984). Most Nagarattar women college students I inter-viewed would not consider such behaviour, since it would mean disconnection from their natal families and the loss of support from their kin and relatives. 'Love marriages' however do take place sometimes, though not too often in this community, and are legal, and from the point of view of property inheritance, children have the full right to inherit from their parents nowadays. However, as the following cases show, there are still problems in securing caste membership for their children, since most 'love marriages' are intercaste marriages.

Case 1.   Meena, female Nagarattar, late twenties, married to a pawnbroker, has two daughters.

Meena married a pawnbroker of the Servai caste after she became a widow at nineteen. Meena's mother died when she was fourteen, and her father remarried. Her stepmother was unkind and wanted to marry her off as quickly as possible. Meena was forced to marry her stepmother's nephew at seventeen, although she did not like him at all. He was a middle-aged bank clerk, working for the Bank of Madura.

He was very fat and very dark. I really didn't like him and said 'no' to my parents. But my stepmother forced me to marry him because she wanted to get rid of me as soon as she could.

He died suddenly two years after she had had a daughter. When she became a widow, her mother-in-law took away her jewellery saying that she no longer needed it since she was a widow, and later Meena had to fight her step-mother in court to retrieve it. She was forced to live with her mother-in-law and her sister-in-law for a while, who would speak ill of her whenever her husband's former colleagues came to mourn her husband's death. 'My in-laws said that I had had affairs with my husband's colleagues. It was unbearable.' She left the house with her daughter as soon as she got a job in the same bank where her husband had worked. According to law, the widow of a former employee is automatically given a position in all public and semi-public organizations in India.

In her aunt's house, she met a pawnbroker, Ramasamy, who was a Servai. He fell in love with her and, rejecting all other good alliances, he married her.

He was offered many good alliances. One of the girls' fathers even begged him to marry his daughter offering him a car and a house. But my husband said that he wouldn't marry his daughter because he had already promised to marry me, and didn't give in to such sweeteners.

Ramasamy's father and his brothers objected strongly in the beginning, but finally gave in, respecting his choice. After all, Ramasamy was quite successful as a pawnbroker and he did not depend on anyone financially. Meena was accepted by Ramasamy's family as his wife. 'It was easier because I was a Nagarattar, a higher and more refined caste than the Servais.' It was a gain for them, but, according to Meena, if it had happened to one of Ramasamy's sisters, none of his brothers would have accepted it:

They would have rushed to their sister's husband's house, and would have dragged her back. They would have beaten her husband to death, whatever caste he may have been. To them, it is unbearable to lose a woman of their caste. It is a humiliation for them.

Meena's parents have severed all communication with her, but, unlike the Servais or Kallars, the Nagarattars would not use physical force. 'They just frown, and show signs of rejection when I see them.' She was cast out by almost her entire family; only her maternal uncle is still friendly and welcoming. As her maternal uncle, he still feels that it is his responsibility to think about her happiness, even though he would not be able to assist her much after her marriage. 'All the Nagarattars stopped talking to me. Although I attend some weddings of friends, nobody talks to me.' She said she did not mind, since she was happy with Ramasamy, adding that, if she were still with the Nagarattars, she would not have been able to remarry, and would still be living as a poor widow. Nowadays, she feels like a Servai. She has had another daughter by Ramasamy who believes that she is a Servai, since she was brought up in a 'mixed' culture, and even her first daughter has come to regard herself as a Servai.

I don't think that the men of the Nagarattars are 'real men'. They will do whatever their *'aacchis'* say. My husband may beat me if I say something wrong. But I married him, and I have to bear it because he is my husband. I don't like the way of the Nagarattars. Their marriage is only for convenience. The *aacchi* goes this way and her husband goes that way — leading separate lives — that is not a real couple.

In expressing this sentiment she may well have been thinking about her father, who was dominated by her stepmother. Meena said that her first daughter could marry a Nagarattar if someone suitable came along in the future.

I do not reject that possibility, since she is a pure Nagarattar. I know Nagarattars like wealthy families. Since we have money, they may want to come to us for an alliance. I don't mind which caste she marries into.

As for the second girl, Meena said, 'She will most probably marry a Servai, because her father is a Servai.'

Even if Meena hoped to return to the Nagarattar community by marrying off her first daughter to a pure Nagarattar, it would in fact be impossible. Although her first daughter has authentic Nagarattar parents, the next generation would not be able to have any contact with Meena's present husband. On the other hand, as a custom, the Nagarattar who married her daughter would expect affinal relationships to continue with her former husband's relatives, which would, of course, be unacceptable to Meena.

CASE 2. Meenakshi, female Nagarattar, thirty-five years old, married to a non-Nagarattar Komutti Chettiyar, lives in Madras, has no children.

Meenakshi married a man who was a Komutti Chettiyar and the

owner of the factory where she had been working. The Komutti Chettiyar divorced his wife and married Meenakshi because his wife did not look after him well. (I met both Meenakshi and her husband at the wedding of a relative of Meenakshi's.) After they married, they were disowned for a few years, but since the Komutti Chettiyar was a rich man, Meenakshi's relatives started to invite her and her husband to their ceremonies.

They are childless. When I asked about the possibility of adoption, Meenakshi's relative sighed, 'Who would come to them? After all, they do not belong to any caste, it is a mixed union!'

The Komutti Chettiyars are a caste of Telugu origin who often call themselves 'Aarya Vaisyas'. According to a Telugu Brahman priest, they are even richer than the Nagarattars and stricter in ritual matters.

Unlike the Nagarattars, they are strict vegetarians, and wear the *puunal* (sacred thread) all the time — the symbol of the twice born. They diligently observe the annual rituals such as *Varalakshmi noombu*. They are even better than some Brahmans!

When I was attending the wedding of a boy who was a relative of Meenakshi, another relative told me that Meenakshi's marriage to a Komutti Chettiyar had affected their status.

The groom could not get a good alliance. Moreover, he was forced to marry quickly because of a misfortune. His sister had eloped, and was subsequently taken back home. In addition, Meenakshi made an odd marriage. People say that the family background is very bad if you have such stray cases. They are not well disciplined. I would never offer my daughter to such a family.

Meenakshi's story illustrates the kind of factors that affect family status, and the consequent alliance possibilities. 'Bad' relatives strongly affect an individual's status in the community, which explains why strict endogamy is maintained as a matter of morality.

CASE 3. Alagappan, male Nagarattar, late forties, married to a non-Nagarattar lawyer, and has one son.

Alagappan is a politician and was a minister in the central government. When he was practising as a lawyer twenty years ago, he married Kamala, who was his colleague. She was from another caste, but had a good family background. Her father was a

Supreme Court judge, and her mother a poet and philanthropist, and Kamala herself was one of the best lawyers in Madras. In spite of such a background, Alagappan faced strong opposition to his marriage. Nobody in his family attended their wedding, and they had a registered marriage in which his close Brahman friend was their legal witness.

His younger sister told me,

When he announced that he would marry Kamala, my father had a heart attack. He was carried to the hospital. For my father, it was an unbearable shock. My father was a hard-working man, modest and virtuous, respected by all. He was adopted into a rich family from a moderate background and worked hard to enrich his adopting family. My maternal grandfather liked him so much that he wanted to marry off his youngest daughter, that is, my mother, to him. So he promised the L M House, the family who adopted my father, that he would give his daughter if they adopted my father. My father was such a sincere and hard-working man who was appreciated by people. Even after he was adopted and became the only son of a rich family, he never wasted money. He always felt that it was bad to waste money, so he worked hard and saved well, donated money to the temples and welfare institutions. He was respected by all the Nagarattars and nobody spoke ill of him. Such was his character that he could not bear a blemish to his family. He even refused to see Kamala, but Alagappan didn't give in saying he didn't like the idea of keeping Kamala as his mistress, and taking some other Nagarattar girl for his wife. He was very firm on this point — he wanted to marry only Kamala.

Their marriage caused a sensation. It was reported in a newspaper as a scandal, since the family was well known. They were not only rich but also related to an aristocratic line: Alagappan's family was related to the Nagarattar's topmost lineage through his mother. According to Alagappan's sister, her mother was so ashamed that she did not set foot outside her house for more than a year.

After Kamala had a child, the parents gave in and Alagappan and his parents reconciled and started to communicate again, but other people still continued to speak ill of them for several years. Only after Alagappan became a Member of Parliament did people stop.

Alagappan's sister said that in spite of the scandal, they could not stop him from marrying Kamala, since he was a 'man'.

Because he is a man, he wanted to show his will and strength. So he married Kamala. What could we do? We had to give in because we did not want to lose him. We are now very close and Kamala often comes here. Their son comes here and stays with us while his parents are away. But it will be very, very difficult for him to marry a Nagarattar. He now studies in America. He may even marry an American. I don't think any Nagarattar would offer their daughter to the boy even though my brother is a politician and rich. Moreover, my brother and Kamala do not think their son should have to marry a Nagarattar. They had a love marriage. How can they insist on a caste marriage for their son? Their son may marry anyone. But I can't allow it for my daughter. When she became fourteen, I told her not to fall in love. A love marriage is not possible for us. Because she is a girl, she should stay with us, in this community. If she falls in love and marries someone outside the community, everyone suffers. She understood and said that she would marry whomever we chose for her.

This story shows how the morality of the present Nagarattars has changed in the past twenty years. The public morality has changed and having a concubine has become a far more expensive business nowadays. Under the modern law, children of the concubines can claim a share of the property if they want; the male Nagarattars can no longer dispose of their extramarital wives and their children with a meagre sum of money. Some Nagarattars who are in the middle income group also maintain that concubinage was never the norm for the Nagarattars with a modest income. Only those who had lived abroad for a long time and could afford to spend money at home used to have them. For average Nagarattars, monogamy used to be the norm, since running two houses was in any case costly for average Nagarattar males and since there was no chance of bringing up their illegitimate children as their heirs.

2.6 Half-Nagarattars

Since no Nagarattar would marry offspring from an intercaste marriage, a line has been formed called the 'Second House Chettiyars'. This naming itself is a humiliation, given probably by the non-Nagarattars, since no Nagarattar ever mentioned this term to me. When I talked with them, they called themselves 'Chettiyar'. Offspring from these intercaste marriages have already turned up among the richest and most prestigious families, but they also tend to opt for the title of Chettiyars rather than Nagarattars.

The half-Nagarattars can be divided roughly into two: those of South East Asian origin and those of South Indian origin. The Nagarattars who had 'local wives' in South East Asia, mostly abandoned them with their children in those countries, leaving them behind with only meagre compensation. Their descendants still engage in mercantile activities in South East Asia, and call themselves 'Chettiyars', but not Nagarattars.

Some Burmese women who were taken to Tamil Nadu by the Nagarattars have created another group. I came across some of their descendants (their sons, daughters, and grandchildren) in Madurai, and they were working as maids or three-wheeler auto-drivers.[3] In general, they remain manual workers and marry among those from similar status chosen from the mother's side. They sometimes call themselves Burmese, since they can gain status if they claim a 'foreign origin' and they live with their mothers in the fatherless families.

Another group of Second House Chettiyars are of local origin. Many of the Nagarattar concubines come from the Isai Vellalars (devadaasi, the temple dancers' community). There are also concubines who are Mudaliyar, Vellalar, or Asari.[4] Amongst these there are some who are well-educated and rich, and because of the close connection with the Isai Vellalar caste who are talented in dancing and music as their caste tradition, they may have close access to the movie industry.

However, they have realistic expectations for their children's marriage prospects. Although they envy the pure Nagarattars and hate their own illegitimate origin, they feel it is better to marry among themselves. If a man of Second House origin is rich, he would want to find an alliance for his daughter from an equally rich family of similar origin. He may fear that even if he is rich enough to marry off his daughter to a poor Nagarattar, she may be bullied by her husband's relatives because she is not a 'pure'

[3] Three-wheeler scooters are called *rickshaws* or autos, and used as a cheaper version of four-wheeled taxis.

[4] According to Somalay, a Nagarattar writer, *vellaacci*, is a term used by the Nagarattars which has three meanings: (1) a female domestic servant, especially from the Vellalar caste; (2) second wife; (3) mother-in-law. The term nowadays means 'second wife'. Somalay assumes that in those days (before the 1940s), a lot of the maid servants used to come from the Vellalar caste, and probably became the concubines of their masters as well. (1953: 21)

Nagarattar. In marrying among themselves, they avoid such problems altogether.

It is extremely rare for a Second House Chettiyar to marry a pure Nagarattar, since it requires enormous wealth and power to coax the other party to give up part of their sense of caste authenticity. As far as I know, there is only one such case at the moment; Mala, who is a successful entrepreneur and a widow of a rich Nagarattar businessman, married off her two children (a male and a female) to pure Nagarattars who lived abroad. Her daughter married someone who is in Malaysia, and the son married a girl who was brought up in England. Her success in making these alliances was due to her wide contacts with authentic Nagarattars at the top of the line. However, she is said to have serious problems with her daughter-in-law and her son-in-law.

The Nagarattar who told me about her said that these two families abroad were a good 'catch' for her. No Nagarattar who lived in Tamil Nadu would accept such an alliance, and so she had to search for families who were abroad and who were less concerned about caste authenticity. Everyone who knows her accepts that the wealth of the two families is not equivalent. The Nagarattars who made the alliance with Mala's family were lower in status and it was said that she had 'bought' a bride and a groom for her children (Purchasing of a good bridegroom with huge dowry occurs in most of the alliances among the Nagarattars, yet this fact was conveniently forgotten in this case). This was the only time I heard of a case in which an authentic 'arranged marriage' took place between the Half-Nagarattars and the pure Nagarattars, demonstrating just how difficult it is for the Nagarattars to give up their caste purity even if they are offered money.

CASE 1. Mother, Savittri, a Brahman, and her daughter, Rada. Savittri became a concubine of a Nagarattar at sixteen. Her father, a Smartha Brahman, was a scholar and a renowned poet. When her father died, one of her sisters took her to a rich Chettiyar in Devakottai, since there was no one who could look after her financially. The Nagarattar was forty-four then, and his *aacchi* was several years older than he. According to Savittri, in those days, wives were much older than husbands among the Chettiyar (Nagarattar). 'Naturally, men prefer younger women and so have a "side wife" (concubine).'

The Nagarattar died after nine years, leaving five children behind with Savittri. Since his *aacchi* did not have any children, she adopted a son from her husband's temple division who conducted the funeral as an authentic son. Consequently, the adopted son inherited all the property. Except for the house in which she lived, Savittri had very little property. The *aacchi* took pity on her and gave her 2 acres of land so that Savittri and her five children could survive and, perhaps more importantly, so that people would not criticize the *aacchi*. Savittri's eldest son became a three-wheeled scooter driver since he was not interested in studies. At present, her second son is studying at a local engineering school to become an electrician. Her eldest daughter married a Chettiyar of mixed origin who lived in Malaysia. Savittri gave her daughter Rs 100,000 dowry, twenty-five gold sovereigns, and a few kilograms of silver vessels.[5]

Her youngest daughter eloped with someone from a low caste. Savittri did not talk about her to me. When I asked her if she had only two daughters, she said yes. Her worry was about her second daughter, Rada, who was thirty-two years old. She had an M.Phil. in commerce and was teaching at a women's college.

Rada was very sensitive about her birth and suffered from a sense of inferiority because of it. She wanted to marry only an authentic Nagarattar, who was well-educated. If this was impossible, she did not want to marry at all. She hated Brahmans, since she felt that her relatives were responsible for her misery. From her point of view, they put her mother into trouble by sending her to the Chettiyar as a concubine. Savittri, her mother, was only sixteen then and was very naïve, and so Rada did not blame her mother but shared the misery with her. Rada refused all alliances offered by her mother's friends, since they were either from the Brahman community or from mixed castes.

Savittri said that the boys of the half Chettiyars were mostly ill-educated. Her daughter did not want to marry a rich boy, but a well-educated one. However, Brahman women who became the concubines of the Nagarattars were few and far between and it was extremely difficult to find a boy with a similar background, i.e. with a Nagarattar father and a Brahman mother, or vice versa.

---

[5] As shown in Chapter 4, the amount of dowry and gold she gave to her daughter is of the lower middle-class standard amongst the Nagarattars.

Savittri lamented her lot. She wondered why she was being made to suffer like this.

I was born into a Brahman family. Brahman is a religious caste, renowned for their accumulation of merit, having lived in austerity for many years. What mistakes did I commit in my previous life such that I should suffer like this?

While her 'husband' was alive, she was not happy. He treated her cruelly, beating her every day. She would go to her Brahman friend's house to weep. She said to me that she had never felt happy for even a single day although she was living in a nice bungalow with all amenities and servants. Since her husband's death twenty-four years ago, she has been living as a widow, and she feels that her suffering continues because of the marriage problems of her children. She feels that intercaste marriage has negative effects: 'It creates a lot of sins, and tortures the offspring for generations.'

She is critical of the Nagarattars in general. She says that they are simply money oriented and cold-hearted.

If a Nagarattar finds a flower, he will pluck it, saying it may be useful for some purpose. He will use it for a *puuja* or for something else, and immediately throw it away after that. He never feels for the flower. The *aacchis* are very calculating and stingy. They protect their property and they never give shares to the concubines.

For the past ten years or more, both Savittri and her daughter have repeatedly made visits to Satya Saibaba's *ashram*[6] for spiritual relief. They go to see Baba whenever Rada gets long holidays from the college where she is teaching. Recently, she got a post in Satya Saibaba Women's College. Savittri has found relief in this. Although the salary is less than the present college, she feels it would be better for her daughter to spend her life there. Savittri even feels Rada does not need to get married if she does not want to. If they live close to Baba, they may be relieved from their agonies. She has decided to live with her daughter in Anandapuram where they can see Baba regularly, renting out her house in Devakottai.

I made my elder daughter marry happily. She is happy in Malaysia, and has a child now. My second daughter does not need to get married if she does not want to. She can live to serve God if she wants. Baba will look

---

[6] *Ashrams* are Hindu religious institutions which are open to both world-renouncers and lay people as religious retreats.

after her. It may be less painful than having a lot of problems in marriage. After all, intercaste marriage is a bad thing, and we have had to suffer for it. I feel sorry for her and for myself. My daughter does not need to create another unhappy child by marrying someone.

Savittri is a good friend of Mala, and, on visiting her, Savittri talked about her daughter's marriage. Savittri was surprised when shown the large collection of bridal 'saamaan'(goods) in her house.[7] Mala said that she would only marry her two children to pure Nagarattars. 'How can she do that? She is a non-Nagarattar, and no Nagarattar would come to her children for alliance!' But Mala succeeded, and Savittri was quite upset.

She is a non-Nagarattar, isn't she? She was also a 'sidewife'[8] Nobody talks about it because she is a rich entrepreneur. I thought that there was no way she would be able to marry off her children to Nagarattars, but she succeeded. Unfortunately, I do not have that much money for my daughter and that's why Rada has to suffer.

CASE 2. Mani, male, mid-forties, and his daughter, Lakshmi, twenty-three years old, married.

Mani is a doctor working for a hospital in Tanjore. His father is a Nagarattar, and his mother is an Isai Vellalar from Coimbatore district. In the beginning, Mani's mother was a concubine, and lived in a separate house with her children where his father used to stay. Mani was engaged to a woman of the same background (father was a Nagarattar and a rich pawnbroker-cum-landlord, and her mother an Isai Vellalar). Before the wedding ceremony, Mani's father took his concubine (i.e. Mani's mother), Mani, and his sister to his ancestral house. The Nagarattar knew his *aacchi* was dying and he wanted to conduct his son's marriage in his ancestral house, since Mani was his only son. The *aacchi* and the concubine lived under the same roof for six months until the *aacchi* died. After her death, Mani's father married Mani's mother. However, when his father died, Mani had to fight with his paternal relatives for the traditional right to the ancestral house.[9] He won the case, and he

[7] The Nagarattars in general, provide an extraordinary collection of bridal *saamaan* for their daughter. Concerning this, see Chapter 4.

[8] The conversation was all in Tamil, but she used this English term in order to signify 'concubine'.

[9] As I described earlier, according to the tradition of the Nagarattars, the right to inherit the ancestral house is shared by the offspring of the brothers who

lives in half of the house, while his paternal uncle and his family live in the other half. There is no communication between them, and they belong to entirely different alliance groups. Mani has two daughters. He recently married one of them off to a man whose background is similar to his; the groom's father is Nagarattar and his mother is Isai Vellalar. The groom is a successful computer engineer, who is well-educated.

Mani is modestly rich. Aside from his salary, he has a business and property which he inherited from his father. The business was originally started with the money his wife brought as a dowry. Most of the income from his business is not reported to the tax office, but is placed in a fund for his daughters' marriages. Out of this income, he spent around Rs 800,000 on his first daughter's marriage. This amount places him in the upper-middle level income group even among the Nagarattars.[10] Because of the problem with his paternal uncle, he had to hire a wedding hall for his daughter's marriage. He also spent a lot of money on gold jewellery and silver vessels for his daughter.

Despite expensive jewellery and silver vessels, his list of bridal goods was simple and his taste more urban than that of traditional Nagarattar families, and this lifestyle was maintained by his daughter and her husband. The names of his two daughters are Brahmanic and he tends to move within the circle of urban professionals, especially Brahmans.

His ease with the Brahmanic customs is rooted in his maternal ancestry: since his mother was an Isai Vellalar, she maintained the *devadaasi* tradition which was half Brahmanic. (As I shall explain in the following case study, the *devadaasis* took up some of the Brahmanic customs through their interactions with temple Brahman priests.) Both he and his wife are pure vegetarians. He goes to the Vinayaga temple every morning, visits *madams,* and sees the *swamis* (the religious head of the *madam*) regularly.

---

jointly built the ancestral house. The 'share' of the house is handed down to the brothers' children but only to the male children of authentic lineage. This unwritten law is still maintained by the Nagarattars as custom.

[10] According to one person I talked to, the relationship between class and the amount spent on marriage is as follows: 1.5 lakhs (Rs 150,000): very poor (below this, marriage is not possible); 3 lakhs (Rs 300,000): not poor, middle class; 5 lakh to 10 lakhs: moderately rich; more than 30 lakhs: rich.

However, he also tries to present himself as a pure Nagarattar and stresses their positive aspects.

The best aspect of the Nagarattars is their hospitality. Since many of them have spent much time abroad, they know how to make foreign guests welcome. They extend their hospitality thinking that they may be able to gain something in return either in business or by making contacts abroad.

He also laments that some of the good traditions of the Nagarattars have now disappeared.

During the British colonial period, they were willing to take risks, engaging in long-distance trade and finance. Nowadays, the boys want to be well-educated, become white-collar workers, and avoid taking risks. The good traditions are gone.

Describing himself to me as a Nagarattar, Mani however occasionally talked about the Nagarattars with resentment.

They earned money in Burma and in Malaysia, and took everything from there. They never thought about the prosperity of the host country, but only about themselves. They should have become citizens and contributed to that country but they didn't do so. They only cared about bringing everything to Chettinadu. It is quite understandable that the local government became angry and drove them out. Although the Nagarattars were not able to get any compensation when the government confiscated their assets in Burma, they had already brought an enormous amount of their property from there in kind and in money. There can be no complaints about the confiscation of the local property. They exploited the local people, deserted the local wives, leaving them meagre sums of money. They took away the wealth from such countries and never thought about looking after the local people.

Mani's criticism of the Nagarattars' actions in Burma is consistent with the account given by Mahadevan (1978), who claims that they exploited the Burmese rather than helped them. However, Mani's criticism was largely coloured by his own experience. As an unauthentic Nagarattar he had been discriminated against. Although he was critical of the Nagarattars, he never mentioned his non-authentic origin. When socializing with authentic Nagarattars and attempting to behave like a genuine one, he does not mention his relatives who are Isai Vellalars. According to Raj, a dance teacher and an Isai Vellalar, Mani's mother is related to her family, though she never mentions this to others.

CASE 3. Raj, female, dance teacher, from the Isai Vellalar caste, sixty-five years old.

Raj was legally a concubine of a Nagarattar and she lived with him for thirty-three years until his death, and even supported him financially. She was seventeen when she started to live with him. When Raj came to Devakottai for a performance at seventeen, TR, a young Nagarattar, approached her mother to ask for her daughter as his concubine. He was already married but said his wife had had a hysterectomy and was not fit for married life (he already had two daughters from his wife). Eventually Raj's mother agreed. He left his family, built a house in Karaikkudi, and started to live with Raj. He lived with her for thirty-three years, had one son, and died at seventy-five.

Unlike ordinary concubines, Raj had her own means of support as a dancer. She started to dance at age five and became fairly successful. Later, in her fifties, she won the All-India national award as one of the best dancers of Bharatanatiyam. Throughout her life, she continued dancing and supported herself even when there was no money coming from TR, her husband.[11] During World War II, he became a freedom fighter for the Congress and was put in jail. Raj often went to visit him and supported herself with her own income. After Independence, when TR wanted to start a business, she offered to add her savings towards his business fund. Because of actions such as these, TR's wife did not show any animosity towards Raj, indeed, she even treated Raj politely in functions where Raj appeared with TR. The wife's children, too, would visit Raj's house, calling her 'aunty'.

However, their relationship suddenly turned sour when TR was about to celebrate his *saandi* (the anniversary of the completion of his sixtieth year; see Chapter 6). In the beginning, he wanted to celebrate with both wives, in Raj's house where he had lived for nearly twenty years. However, his wife insisted that he come and celebrate in the ancestral house and only with her as his legal wife. TR refused, and did as he intended, inviting friends and relatives. His wife then stopped sending her children to their house so

[11] In fact, she continued to talk about him as her 'husband', since according to the tradition of Isai Vellalars, women can never start cohabitation without a proper marriage ritual. Therefore, even though the man may have another family elsewhere, from the point of the Isai Vellalar woman, cohabitation is a 'marriage' because a ritual will always have taken place.

that when he died at seventy-five, their relationship was cold. While praying, he collapsed and died in the temple of which he was a trustee. His body was carried to the ancestral house by fellow Nagarattars without informing Raj. The *aacchi* and her relatives immediately cremated the corpse, denying his illegitimate son's right of kindling the funeral pyre. They did not invite Raj or her son to the funeral.

While Raj was mourning for her husband in her house, the wife's brother came to her on the third day after the cremation to talk about the property partition. She refused to talk about it as she was in mourning. However, he told her that a quarter of the share of TR's property should come to her. She said she did not care how much she got, and in the end, she received nothing.

At that time, her son was a lecturer in an engineering college. After his father's death, he claimed his share of the property from his mother. He took most of Raj's property given by TR, and from the money built his house in Madras. He rarely comes to see his mother these days.

He married twice. The first time was a 'love marriage' to a Christian girl in Bombay. Without informing his mother, he married her and brought her to Raj's house. The wife was left there when she was about to have a baby. After the child was born, the wife left him, leaving the baby girl in the custody of Raj. Later, he married a girl from the Isai Vellalar community. He neglected the daughter from his first marriage, leaving her with Raj.

Raj's granddaughter became a dancer and married her maternal uncle who is a *nadaswaram* (traditional musical instrument) player. There was no dowry, but her married life is a happy one. Raj now brings up her great-granddaughter in her house, still earning money as a dance teacher. She says her great-granddaughter will also become a dancer. She does not mind whom her great-granddaughter marries.

Unlike Savittri, the Brahman woman mentioned before, Raj does not regret her life with her lover, TR. In effect, she was his wife and helped him in times of need. Although her first daughter-in-law disappeared after giving birth to a daughter, Raj did not consider the child a burden. In her community, girls are able to support themselves as dancers.

Raj's father was a Smartha Vadama Brahman working as an accountant in a temple. He came forward to cohabit with her mother although he was already married. According to Raj:

It is not so easy to find a husband for *devadaasis*, as their husbands have to be able to maintain two houses without trouble. It is a difficult thing for most men although sometimes a girl and a priest who met every day might fall in love and start living together.

According to Raj, girls of the Isai Vellalar community were divided into two categories. Those who married an Isai Vellalar were not supposed to take part in any kind of performance. They were called *kudumba peeru*, and their status was higher than the mixed breed, although they never performed. Those who became *devadaasi* came from the mixed breed. Only those who married into castes such as the Brahman or Chettiyar were allowed to enter the fine arts. The custom of giving the *pottu* (the symbol of the *devadaasi*) was abolished eighty-five years ago and the *devadaasi* disappeared.

In terms of manners and customs, Isai Vellalars are largely influenced by Brahman temple priests with whom they have had much contact. While the Isai Vellalars are mostly non-vegetarians, those *devadaasis* who were concubines of the Brahmans also became vegetarians. However, according to Raj, as far as the status in their caste is concerned, the former's is higher than the latter's. Such distinction does not seem to have created any substantial discrimination, since children from the intercaste marriages may marry freely into those of *kudumba peeru*.

Sixty years ago, if a girl who was born to a *kudumba peeru* wanted to perform, it was possible only in the temple where her father was performing music. No other temple would allow her to dance. If a girl from a mixed marriage, i.e. whose father was either a Brahman or a Chettiyar, wanted to become a *devadaasi*, she had to go to the temple where her mother was dancing. Even if her Chettiyar father had a temple of his own or had a temple under his custody, the temple management would not allow her to perform, since there would always be a dancer hereditarily attached to the temple. The hereditary tradition was strictly followed because they were serving the gods.·

Compared to the Chettiyars, Brahmans are more affectionate to the women of the Isai Vellalar caste, according to Raj. The first wife, i.e. the wife of the Brahman priest, treats the concubine of her husband as a relative. She is called 'aunty' by the first wife's children. But if the husband is a Chettiyar, there would be no relationship between the wife and the concubine. Nothing would be given to her.

According to Raj, children of Nagarattar fathers are richer, but in terms of culture, children of the Brahman fathers are more refined. Brahmans also treat Isai Vellalars more respectfully because of the long-standing relationship between the two communities. The family of the Nagarattars denigrate the second wife from the Isai Vellalar community saying 'the concubine has come' *(waicci wandaval)*.

In the Brahman's house, my mother was treated with respect, and the Brahman's wife used to say, "aunty has come." The first wife would call the concubine's daughter "my daughter", and my sister's husband was called "sister's husband" by her. Nowadays, even the pure Brahmans marry women whose parents are Isai Vellalar and Brahman. Or, even if both are Isai Vellalars, Brahmans will still marry them. Those whose parents are Isai Vellalar and Mudaliyar, or Isai Vellalar and Chettiyar are accepted as well. But none of the Nagarattars accept such combinations.

2.7 Why 'Love Marriage' Cannot Replace Caste Endogamy

The Servais, Kallars, and Maravars, who together form the Mukkulatoors, are renowned for their 'masculinity', and membership of their caste is inherited patrilineally. They are very pleased if a man of their caste manages to marry a Brahman girl, for example, since their own women are normally very dark, and women of fair skin are considered attractive.

Brahman women do not work in the field, and eat only good vegetarian food full of *ghee* (purified butter) and milk, which cools down their body, so their skin is quite fair. However, we are angered if a Brahman boy has married a girl of our caste. We'll ask where the fellow is, and go with a group to beat him and get back our girl!

However, among the high castes such as the Shaiva Vellalars and Shaiva Mudaliyars, the tendency is to accept Brahmans or those of an equivalent high caste as marriage partners if there are not many options open to them. If a 'love marriage' takes place, as long as the partners are of the same caste status, then it will not be frowned upon. Offers of marriage alliances are often advertised in newspapers these days and several mention that they do not discriminate against subcaste distinctions.

Those who know both Savittri and Raj say to me,

> People who originate from intercaste marriages tend to be unstable. They suffer from psychological problems, and their children often make arbitrary marriages too. Therefore, it is better to avoid intercaste marriages altogether. It creates the potential for a lot of problems in the future.

This point of view, however, ignores the fact that nowadays even in South India, 'love marriages' as well as arranged intercaste marriages have become more widespread and acceptable among the Vellalars and the Brahmans. The 'dowryless marriage' is quite advantageous for the girls and the cases of love marriage are more predominant among the professionals such as doctors since they have more chances to meet during their medical training period as colleagues. For example, a middle-aged doctor who lives in Tiruchi, an oculist and a Vellalar (he admits that he is not sure what kind of Vellalar he is), says that he has married a woman from the Soliya Vellalar caste for love.

His two brothers also had love marriages. One of them married a Mudaliyar girl, and another married a Brahman. Both brothers were non-vegetarians and their wives have begun to cook some non-vegetarian dishes for them, though they themselves still eat only vegetarian food. The oculist's parents had a 'love marriage' as well. Their father was a Vellalar and their mother was a Mudaliyar. No dowry transaction took place in his family.

> My wife did not bring anything except a few cooking vessels she needed. She did not have her own property, either. Now she spends from the joint account in which I deposit the regular income.

He says such love marriages are quite common especially among the Vellalar community. Although his statement cannot be seen as general opinion among the Vellalars, it is nonetheless true that a Vellalar (both a man and a woman) whose parents are from another caste can marry a pure Vellalar if both sides agree.

'Vellalar' is a broad category which combines dozens of regional castes, and they have come to accept varieties of subdivisions to be intermarriageable. Intercaste marriages often take place between the Vellalars and the Brahmans without destroying the parent–child relationship. Marriage to a Vellalar is especially advantageous for Brahmans from the point of view of educating their children; a Brahman is a 'forward' caste, and as such does not get a 'reserved seat' in colleges and public institutions. Since the political situation is at present quite negative for Brahmans in southern India, they use alliances with 'backward' castes as a means of survival. Even after marriage, the parents maintain their relationships with their daughters, according to the oculist. They continue to visit their daughter's family just like other Brahman parents who married their daughters to Brahmans. It is often a relief for Brahman girls whose parents cannot afford to pay a dowry. In most cases, the children take on their father's caste. Yet if the girl's side is more powerful and dominates the groom, both the groom and the children may adopt the bride's culture.

The oculist added that failure in marriage will happen whether it is an arranged marriage or a love marriage. He says, 'Therefore, you cannot say that love marriage alone creates problems. It happens just as frequently in arranged marriage.'

The Nagarattars have a quite different attitude: 'You can get respect only if you marry a Nagarattar. We will never make alliances with people whose family have married non-Nagarattars in the past.' This comment came from a nineteen year-old housewife who recently gave birth to her first child; even among the young Nagarattars, the idea of authenticity continues to exist. Her view was shared by other college girls I interviewed.

However, it is also true that 'stray' cases are on the increase. One middle-aged Nagarattar said,

If you've established your base abroad, it's unavoidable. Say, for example, the XX family. They have three sons and three daughters. One son married a German, another a North Indian, and one girl is married to a mixture (an unauthentic Nagarattar). Even TS's first wife's grandson married an American. What can you do? Nothing. Boys and girls fall in love and marry. I would guess that this happens to about ten per cent, and their marriage is not registered in our clan temple. We may lose some of our authentic population in this way, but the majority do not want to marry in that way.

The present law orders them to give property shares to children of unauthentic origin as well, provided their parents were legally married, thus even the Nagarattars cannot entirely stop the outward flow of their caste capital. However their ethic of endogamy acts as a breakwater, i.e. marriages between cross-cousins and through affinal ties do stop this flow to a great extent.

Thus, it is evident that subtle discrimination is still practised. The temple garland, the symbol of the morality of the authentic Nagarattars, was not sent to the weddings of Mala's children mentioned by the Brahman woman, Savittri. Nowadays however there is a way to insist on the legitimacy of the union even if the man has a wife and a concubine. In a recent case, the concubine, who was from the Isai Vellalar community, was admitted as an authentic wife in the court and inherited most of the property of her deceased 'husband'. According to the story, when her husband died, she tactfully refused to give the corpse to his relatives. And with the help of her relatives, she conducted the funeral ritual in accordance with the Isai Vellalar style. Since the *devadaasis* start cohabitation with their 'husbands' after conducting proper rituals of 'marriage', the court admitted her claim as she was the woman with whom he had lived for most of the time. The *aacchi* who was the authentic wife from the point of view of the Nagarattars was not admitted as the legal wife in the court and she only managed to get the ancestral house in which she lived, while the Isai Vellalar 'wife' managed to get most of the property of her 'husband'. This offended the *aacchis,* since among the Nagarattars, only the *aacchi* is the authentic wife whether she has had a child or not.[12] Mala at least succeeded in marrying off her two children to authentic Nagarattars, yet even she cannot influence the course of her son's children.

Among the Nagarattars, a child whose father or mother is not a Nagarattar immediately loses the chance of inheriting the property which is of Nagarattar origin. Although this prohibition of intercaste union is the norm in most parts of southern India, the rule is particularly strict among the Nagarattars. As Tambiah describes (1973b), the laws of Manu take a liberal attitude to the absorption of the diverted line (i.e. the offspring from the caste mixture caused by accepting brides from the lower castes). As a

---

[12] This is a version I acquired from the Isai Vellalars and this explanation has a slight problem under the present Hindu law. Under the Hindu family law, the Hindu marriage is monogamous, thus the second marriage is valid only when the first marriage is cancelled. Therefore, it is unlikely that the Isai Vellalar woman was considered to be the legal wife while the first wife was not yet divorced. Since the present Hindu law endows inheritance rights to all the children including the illegitimate children, it is more likely that the Isai Vellalar woman claimed her share of the property through her children.

means of enforcing hypergamy, after three to seven generations depending on the caste of the wife, even the Brahmans acknowledge the offspring derived from such intercaste marriage. Thus the Brahmanic ideology is basically hypergamous, as a device to accumulate wealth at the top of the *varna* hierarchy.

Dumont (1986: 177, 294–5), highlighting the case of the Piramalai Kallars in South India, refers to the offspring which derived from the union with a woman of lower status, which was later reintegrated into the caste with equal rights. My fieldwork data too, confirms that among the Chettiyar castes, Veelan Chettiyars and Vellalar Chettiyars intermarry nowadays, and Kallars, Maravars, and Ahamudiyas recognize one another as equals and intermarry. Moreover, in the area near Tiruchi city in Tamil Nadu, I found that the Brahmans, Mudaliyars, and Vellalars intermarry quite often as a result of 'love marriages', and indeed the direct interaction between the male and the female is allowed because love marriages do not involve the risk of severance from the natal families of both sides.

In comparison, the Nagarattars are extremely strict in maintaining their endogamous principles. By marrying into another caste, a Nagarattar, whether man or woman, loses the caste membership of the Nagarattars for his or her offspring for good. The stigma of marrying a non-Nagarattar is so strong that even if parents cannot find a partner for their daugher, they may prefer the daughter to remain unmarried or marry her off to a man whose qualification and salary are lower than hers. However, as I discuss in the following chapters, such strict endogamy partly supports married women's status. Women circulate within the caste along with their capital, which is generally inherited through the matriline, and this makes the women and their capital inseparable: for a male Nagarattar, both the kinship network and the capital attached to his wife are essential to maintain his identity as a Nagarattar. Divorce means not only to break himself off from the kinship network of his wife, but also from the capital attached to her. A Nagarattar wife, on the other hand, rarely claims an official divorce, yet as a last resort she may claim a separation from her husband. In this case, she may stay with her parents or live separately along with her children, using the capital given to her upon marriage. Although both her economic and social status may suffer a setback due to separation, she is not cut off from the network of the community as long as she is married to a man of the Nagarattar caste. Married women also maintain their 'marital power' (decision-making capacity in the conjugal relationship) due to the network they inherit from their parents. In other words, Nagarattar women do not get separated from their natal families after marriage but are encouraged to exploit the relationships both they and their parents have cultivated within the caste before marriage. As I discuss later, such a web of relationships works to their advantage in times of need. Therefore, even though women's property share in general is much less than men's, the Nagarattar women may obtain unaccounted resources when they need them. For example, they can still express their strong opinion in marriage alliance. Although women play more crucial roles in arranging marriages in most castes in India, the Nagarattar women can enjoy far more influence in this field politically, since marriage among the Nagarattars is crucially the centre of their political alliance which binds the two families for several generations.

On the other hand, a wrongly married line has to opt for alliances with families of a similar background, i.e. those who are called Half-Chettiyars. They may even marry other castes and merge into them. By marrying a non-Nagarattar, the relationship between brother/sister and cross-cousins in the subsequent generations eventually disappears, as communication becomes less and less until the diverted line is severed from the trunk of the Nagarattars.

For the Nagarattars, endogamy is essential to pool capital within the community and by closing the circle of exchange, they strengthen the reciprocal (egalitarian) relationship among themselves. Women's status and their property rights are protected as a result of the importance placed on women's work after marriage. They have to cultivate their own network while their men work outside their hometown and the core of such networking is created out of kinship closely interwoven by cross-cousin marriage. Through this they enhance their own prestige and status. In the following chapters, I shall explain how cross-cousin marriage creates a web to support women.

Chapter 3

Kinship and the Internal Structure of the Nagarattar Caste

3.1 Kinship Classification

As discussed in the previous chapter, the caste boundary is strictly protected by endogamy among the Nagarattars, so that there is no recruitment of new members from the offspring of intercaste marriages. Their nine Shiva temple clan divisions regulate marriage as the exogamous group. Descent is patrilinearly transferred as is the membership of a clan temple division. The bride and the groom should belong to different Shiva temple divisions, and their children inherit their father's temple division. Men remain members of their father's clan temple division but women change their clan membership after marriage.

In using the term 'descent', I shall follow Dumont's definition. Dumont uses this term exclusively to refer to the transmission of membership in the exogamous group. The terms 'patrilineal' and 'matrilineal' are applied to descent only in that sense, and not to succession and inheritance (Dumont 1983: 38). Therefore, when talking about property transfer, I shall not use terms such as patrilineal or matrilineal, and shall discuss property transfer separately from descent, e.g. property is transferred from father to son, or from mother to daughter, etc. Similarly in using the terms 'patrilateral', 'matrilateral', and 'bilateral', I shall also follow Dumont and use these terms only when discussing cross-cousin marriage.

In South India, among the non-Brahmans, one cannot marry someone who belongs to the same *kula deivam* group, since *kula deivam* is transferred unilineally and functions as the descent marker to regulate marriage. Among the Brahmans, although they have *kula deivams*, this group is not the marriage regulator. If one party in the marriage belongs to a different *gootra*, it does not matter whether he or she worships the same *kula deivam*, and those who share the same *kula deivam* may marry if they belong to different *gootras*.

Similarly, as I have already mentioned, the Nagarattars have nine clan Shiva temple divisions which are patrilinearly transmitted, like the Brahmanic *gootra*. Therefore, as long as the husband and wife belong to different Shiva temple divisions, they follow descent exogamy. Marrying (or having sexual union) with someone who belongs to the same temple division is considered to be incestuous and is scandalous. However, although this is a rule generally accepted, an occasional 'incestuous' sexual union may still occur. If it does happen, attempts are made to hide it to avoid a scandal. For example, I was told that a male Nagarattar who belongs to a wealthy family fell in love with one of his cousins who belonged to the same temple division (i.e. she was his parallel-cousin). They eloped, went to Kerala, and married there. Since descent is traced differently from caste to caste and Muslims in Kerala practice parallel-cousin marriage, they encountered no problem in getting married there. However, the eloped couple's families could not come out in public because of their shame and other Nagarattars made the parallel-cousin marriage into a scandal.

Although the Nagarattars feel that liaisons like the above are not as unacceptable as other incestuous relationships (e.g. father–daughter or mother–son), their normative rule nevertheless forbids such relationships at least formally. Of course, it is in the nature of any rule to be broken, yet, as the above case shows, when it happens, people try to conceal it from the public.

Such prohibitive rules of sexual union between certain relatives exist in kinship systems to regulate marriage. For example, in South India, the majority of castes treat cross-cousin marriage as some sort of preferential marriage pattern (either matrilateral, patrilateral, or bilateral), although it does not mean that all marriages follow this pattern. In order to discuss the marriage alliance and kinship of the Nagarattars, following Good (1991), I shall distinguish between three analytical levels.

(1) the statistical-behavioural level consists of the aggregate consequences of the behaviour of members of the society or group in question. In the case of kinship, this level is exemplified by demographic data on residential, marital, and other observed patterns.

(2) the jural level comprises the normative, legal, moral, religious, and analytical statements of the group's members . . . jural data consists of ideals and justifications made explicit by group members themselves, though not always verbally. . . .

(3) the categorical level comprises modes of classification and systems of nomenclature. The relationship terminology is the archetype of data at this level. Categorical data generally differs from jural phenomena by being implicit. (Good 1991: 54–5)

Although cross-cousin marriage may exist as a preferential pattern of alliance in South India, not all alliances follow this pattern. In other words, the statistical level may not always reflect the preferential cross-cousin marriage of the caste. According to one senior Nagarattar, cross-cousin marriage was quite common until the 1950s, since it was the most convenient way to find a suitable partner in a nearby area. There was very little transport connecting the different regions of Chettinadu, thus cross-cousin marriage was more practical as this kind of alliance needed only a small amount of cash dowry and enquiry about the other party. On the other hand, according to the same Nagarattar, a drastic change has taken place recently. As people became more urbanized, the men with good qualifications started to seek alliances with girls from richer families, thus not following the traditional cross-cousin marriage pattern.

His explanation cannot be proven statistically, as time and locality, demographic situation, etc. affect the real pattern of marriage alliance, and the choices of cross-cousin marriage or non-relative marriages are a matter of individual choice for each family. In other words, marrying a cross-cousin is not an obligation or a 'rule'.

The jural level, which gives the normative, legal, or moral aspects in the kinship system, on the other hand, expresses the rules and statements which are often referred to by the members verbally: one should not have sexual union with Ego's parallel relatives, e.g. his parallel-cousin or his sister. This is a breach of the moral code among the Nagarattars (and also among most South Indians). Although such normative rules are sometimes broken, transgressions are to be concealed, since they are performative statements intended to direct, justify or rationalize the structure observed by the group.

The kinship terminology followed by the group belongs to the categorical level mentioned above in (3). The terminology, unlike the jural level, works as prescription. Thus a man can marry any woman who is marriageable, i.e. who is or is not his cross-cousin, yet the terminology defines the relationship. His wife may start to call him 'attaan'(elder cross-cousin brother) following the prescription of the kinship terminology which classifies the age difference.

The kinship terminology of the Nagarattars expresses preferential bilateral cross-cousin marriage. As Good's diagram (ibid.: 61) clearly shows, the consequence of repeated bilateral cross-cousin marriage can create the terminological identifications. Following Good, I shall use the following abbreviations in this chapter for kinship notations. B = brother, F = father, Z = sister, S = son, M = mother, W = wife, H = husband, D = daughter. Thus the terminological identifications are as follows: Z = FBD = MZD, B = FBS = MZS, MBD = FZD = WZ = BW, MBS = FZS = ZH, D = BD = WZD, S = BS = WZS, ZD = SW, ZS = DH, F = FB = MZH, FZ = MBW = WM, M = MZ = FBW, MB = FZH = WF, FF = MMB, MM = FFZ, FM = MFZ, MF = FMB. The kinship terminology among the Nagarattars is shown in Table 3.1. These people as a whole are called relatives (sondakaaran).

Table 3.1: Kinship terminology of the Nagarattars

Relationship term	Genealogical referents	Level
1. aiyaa	FF, MF, FFB, MFB, FMB, MMB	+2
2. appattaal	FM, FFZ, MFZ, FMZ	+2
3. aayaa	MM, MMZ	+2
4. appacci	F	+1
5. periyappacci	FeB, MZH (older than F)	+1
6. cittappa	FyB, MZH (younger than F)	+1
7. aataal	M	+1
8. periyattaal	MeZ, FeBW	+1
9. cinnattaal	MyZ, FyBW	+1

Table 3.1 (contd.)

Relationship term	Genealogical referents	Level
10. *ammaan*	MB, FZH, WF, HF	+1
11. *attai*	FZ, MBW, WM, HM	+1
12. *maamiyaar*	HM	+1
13. *maamanaar*	HF	+1
14. *annan*	Be, FBSc, MZSe	+0
15. *aacchi*	Ze FBDe, MZDe	+0
16. *tambi*	By, FBSy, MZSy	+0
17. *tangacchi*	Zy, FBDy, MZDy	+0
18. *attaan*	MBSe, FZSe, WeB, H, eZH	+0
19. *aittiyandi*	MBDe, FZDe, WeZ	+0
20. *maappillai*	DH, FZDH, MBDH	+0
21. *kolundaan*	HeB, MBSyws, FZSyws, HyB, yZHyws	+0
22. *koludunar*	HyB	+0
23. *naattinaal*	HeZws, HyZws	+0
24. *kolundiyar*	WZe, WZy	+0
25. *sammandi*	MBDyws, FZDyws, HyZ, yBWws	+0
26. *sammandi*	DHF, DHM, SWF, SWM	+(−)0
27. *mahan*	S, BSms, ZSws, HBS, WZS	−1
28. *mahal*	D, BDms, ZDws, HBD, WZD	−1
29. *marumahan*	BSws, ZSms, WBS, HZS, DH	−1
30. *marumahal*	BDws, ZDms, WBD, HZD, SW	−1
31. *peeran*	SS, DS, BSS, ZSS, BDS, ZDS	−2
32. *peetti*	SD, DD, BSD, ZSD, BDD, ZDD	−2

Relationship notation: F father, M mother, B brother, S son, D daughter, H husband, W wife, P parent, e elder, y younger, ms: man speaking, ws: woman speaking.

In Table 3.1, there are several interesting features which illustrate the Nagarattar kinship. First, *aattal (attai)* connotes not only FZ, MBW, WM, HM but also mother herself. Secondly, there are three terms to distinguish a +2 generation female, while there is only one for a +2 generation male. Although it is possible to argue that terminologies cannot always explain preferences and both are 'independent variables' (Good 1995: personal communication), the Nagarattars' case can still be discussed as the one which shows some logical relationship. In other words, in my opinion, terminological features seem to explain their preferences.

Preferential bilateral cross-cousin marriage pattern may make FZ and WM or MBW the same person as is the case for several other South Indian castes. The strong preferential bilateral cross-cousin marriage pattern suggested by terminology also indicates strong attachment to the maternal grandmother. In the generation +2 level, instead of only two terms, the Nagarattars have three: while they identify father's father, father's father's brother, mother's father and mother's father's brother *(aiyaa)*, mother's mother *(aayaa)* and father's mother *(appattaal)* are distinguished. Therefore, the terminology does not create a completely symmetric structure since while there is only one term to signify all the males of the +2 generation, the paternal and maternal side of women of +2 generation are divided into two. The paternal grandmother shares the stem of *'appa'* with other paternal male relatives, e.g. *periyappa, cittappa. Aayar,* the maternal grandmother on the other hand, is completely different. The term may thus imply the fact that the maternal grandmother is much more closely associated with the children's nurturing, since the term *aayaa* also implies nanny or child-minder in Tamil, implying that the maternal grandmother is a frequent visitor to the house. Although this term is used to refer to a nanny, it is never used to address her directly. Except when she is highly respected, almost like one's own maternal grandmother, a nanny is never addressed *'aayaa!'* in person. For example, a young Nagarattar man I know always calls one senior old Nagarattar woman *'aayaa!',* since according to him, she looks after him when his mother is absent. He maintains, 'She is almost like my grandmother, so I call her *aayaa.* Somehow, I do not feel like calling her *appattal* because it does not fit to our relationship.'

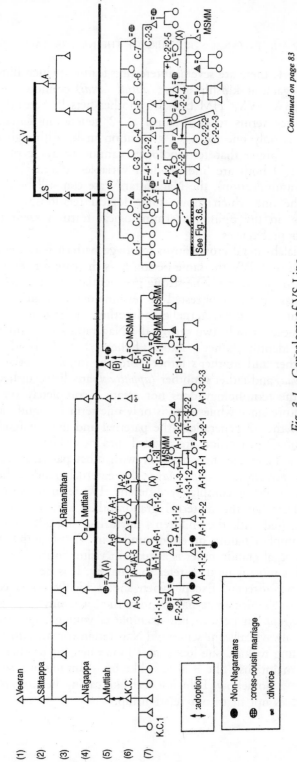

Fig. 3.1. Genealogy of VS Line

Continued on page 83

(1) Veeran

(2) Sāttappa

(3) Nāgappa

(4) Muttiah

(5) K.C.

(6)

(7) K.C.1

Rāmanāthan

Muttiah

:adoption

● :Non-Nagarattars

⊕ :cross-cousin marriage

✘ :divorce

See Fig. 3.6.

Continued from page 82

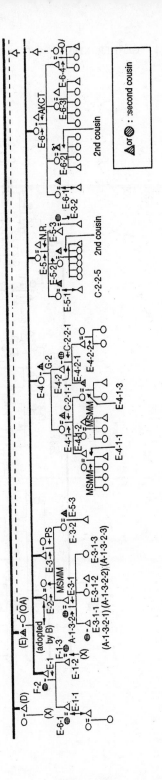

Continued on page 84

Fig. 3.1. Genealogy of VS Line

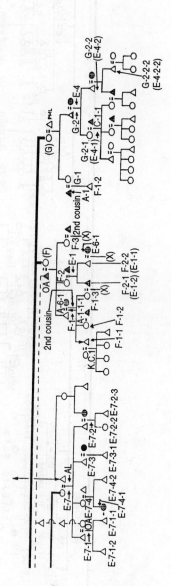

continued from page 83

Fig. 3.1. Genealogy of VS Line

Table 3.2: The structure of Nagarattar relationship terminology

level	Parallel		Cross	
	Δ(M)	O(F)	O(F)	Δ(M)
+2	*aiyaa*	*appattaal*	*aayaa*	*aiyaa*
+1 (e)	*periyappacchi*	*periyattai*	*periyattaa*	*periyamman*
(y)	*appacchi*	*attai*	*attai*	*ammaan*
+0	*annan*	*aacchi*	*aittiyaandi*	*attaan*
−0	*tambi*	*tangacchi*	*kolundiyal (sammandi)*	*kolundiyar (sammandi)*
−1	*mahan*	*mahal*	*marumahal*	*marumahan*
−2	*peeran*	*peetti*	*peetti*	*peeran*

The two kinds of relatives, parallel and cross, are distinctively different in several ways. As seen in Table 3.2, Ego's relatives are divided according to relative age, into senior and junior (elder brother = *annan,* younger brother = *tambi,* etc.), but the cross and parallel relatives in each level maintain different naming. There is classification by terminological levels: the terminology distinguishes six levels, i.e. three senior to Ego and three junior: [(+2, +1, +0) levels: grandparents, father, and elder brother], and (−0, −1, −2) levels: younger brother, son, grandson). The distinction prescribed in the terminology classifies marriageability when it is applied to the gender of the opposite sex: a man could marry his cross-cousin who belongs to the (−1) generation. A female Ego may marry one who belongs to her own generation but who is older than her, i.e. *attaan.*

Although this is a generally accepted rule among the South Indians, the Nagarattars seem to break this rule quite often (case study of Savittri in Chapter 2). Both the Nagarattars and non-Nagarattars admit that the Nagarattar males may marry women who are slightly older than them which is quite unusual as an Indian custom. In other words, the Nagarattars prefer bilateral cross-cousin marriage to maternal uncle–niece marriage far more than other castes in South India; so much so that they do not mind breaking the rule of age seniority of husbands over their wives. Before I discuss this issue, I shall explain several crucial kinship relationships of the Nagarattars.

3.2 Kin and Affines as Business Network

The most essential part of the Dumontian argument is the relationship between Ego's father and his mother's brother based on the alliance. This alliance relationship defines the mother's brother by reference to the father, but the father himself is defined by reference to Ego (1983: 10). Father and mother's brother are similar in generation and different in kin, as these two classes of people created by marriage creates two kinds of relatives, i.e. kin and affine. However, according to Dumont, there are no special terms for affines, since 'my mother's brother is essentially my father's affine' (ibid.: 12), and 'we have in fact taken the two oppositions as a way leading from Ego to the father and from the father to the mother's

Fig. 3.2. A girl standing beside her paternal grandmother

brother' (ibid.). In other words, Dumont maintains that the relationship with Ego's mother's brother is not through his mother but through his father, since his mother's brother is essentially his father's affine.

This point, however, is questionable, as, in the case of the Nagarattars, there are two distinct categories which distinguish cross and parallel relatives surrounding Ego. *Pangaalis* are equivalent to the parallel relatives discussed above and the *dayaadi* are translatable as the cross-relatives. What the Nagarattars call 'mother's people' *(dayaadi)* includes not only mother's brother *(ammaan)*: for a married woman, it is her natal family members, i.e. her parents, her brother, who become the gift-givers for her. For her children, 'mother's people' means both their grandparents and maternal uncle and his children, who are their cross-cousins. Although the affinal relationship between a married man and his wife's brother is essential, this depends on the stronger relationship between his wife and her natal family, since it is his wife who is the official gift-receiver. His children also become gift-receivers from his affine, yet this is again through his wife, as his children call his affine 'mother's people'.

However, Dumont is still correct in distinguishing the two classes, i.e. kin and the affine (or parallel and cross relatives), as the core of the South Indian kinship system. In the case of the Nagarattars, these two classes of relatives have conspicuous differences not only in terms of marriageability/non-marriageability, wife-givers/wife-takers, gift-exchange relationships, but also in the life-cycle rituals in which they participate, and the very distinction of these two relatives marks the essential part of the ritual life of the Nagarattars. It also works in their business alliance as is clearly seen in the alliance network of VS line.*

This case study explains how the strategy of maintaining the business group works through the cooperation of the *pangaalis* and the transgenerational link with bilateral cross-cousin marriage and clearly contradicts Rudner's argument. According to him, the Nagarattar kinship does not follow most models of marriage alliance in Dravidian kinship, as the latter's marriage alliances were not automatically renewed but rather 'one-shot' alliances (1994: 163). Yet according to the data I collected, Nagarattar

* See section 3.3.

kinship conforms to the Dravidian kinship system perfectly in all three levels that Good listed (1991: 54–5): in other words, the statistical-behavioural level (the frequency of cross-cousin marriage), the jural level (ideals and justifications), and the categorical level (classification). Thus contrary to Rudner's statement, that 'there is no evidence that Nagarattars were constrained by any marriage rule'(1994: 188), the data shown in section 3.3 clearly illustrates the strong preference for bilateral cross-cousin marriage. I shall strongly argue that the Nagarattar business acumen used to be strongly linked with the bilateral cross-cousin marriage alliance which maintains the ideal of egalitarian marital exchange relationship and has effectively strengthened married women's position. Because of this closely interwoven kinship network, women's activities involve important networking inside and outside their household. While marriage is the most important occasion to transfer property for women, for men, this is the occasion to expand social alliances: his social status, credibility, and even his character is assessed at this occasion, and marriage even affects his share in his ancestral property. For the Nagarattars, to be in touch with their relatives is extremely important and the influence of a particular *aacchi* can be easily measured by the number of the people she associates with. In order to be well informed, she should not confine her association only to the richest and the most powerful group. Not all of her relatives are well-off, yet the richer she is, the easier it is for her to attend weddings and ceremonies at her own cost. In order to acquire a good reputation, she is expected to associate with as many people as possible.

This also gives the Nagarattars a strong incentive to consider their business as a comprehensive economic activity: attending ceremonies, gossiping, and visiting each other on small errands are an all-important part of economic activities. In other words, money earned should not only be saved but also be spent effectively in order to lubricate the kinship network. Only through socializing can the pooled capital be circulated, and the major part should not leave the caste community.

This system expresses the Nagarattars' egalitarianism which is strongly based on kinship within the caste, as compared to the North Indian model of hypergamy and non-kin oriented marriage alliances. The system is reminiscent of Papua New Guinean and Trobriand societies in which cross-cousin marriages are predominant e.g. (Strathern 1971; Weiner 1976). These societies have a distinct hierarchy between the chiefs and the commoners, and express their statuses through elaborate gift-giving ceremonies through which the circulation of wealth within the community is encouraged. Such a model of egalitarianism is based on endogamy and is in sharp contrast to the Brahmanic model of hypergamy in a hierarchical society. In the following section, I shall describe how the Nagarattars strategically use bilateral cross-cousin marriage and support endogamy. Although the following case study deals with the richest line in this community, the basic principles are the same throughout the caste: frequency of cross-cousin marriage. When there is no child, they adopt a male child whose family is not so well off, from the husband's Shiva temple group.

3.3 The VS Line

The VS[1] line was originally set up by two brothers (Arunachalam and Satappa) who settled in two villages in Chettinadu in the late eighteenth century. The villages were adjacent and the brothers started to engage in mercantile activities. According to their legend, one of the brothers had a stomach ache when he went to see his married sister who was residing in Kanadukattan. His sister looked after him well and after he recovered, he decided to live in his sister's village, marry, and settle there, as he felt more comfortable living near his sister. The other brother continued to live in Pallattur, another Chettinadu village where the two brothers had originally settled. This story therefore implies the continuation of cross-cousin marriage between the brother's and sister's children.

The line is now split into several prestigious families called Raja's family who are the topmost 'aristocratic' families among the Nagarattars. They have become the top group because of the prosperity of the members in the fifth generation, especially Raja Sir Annamalai Chettiyar. He was awarded the titles of Raja and Sir by the British because of his contribution to the colonial economy as merchant-cum-banker. The VS line has so far had three MPs (Members of Parliament).[2] There are also two honorary

---

[1] I use this nomenclature after the initials of the founders, i.e. Veeran and Satappa who are earliest ancestors the people of this line can remember.

[2] Raja Sir Annamalai became the first MP, the second was M.C.T. Chidambaram, and the third is P. Chidambaram who is currently a Member of Parliament.

Fig. 3.3. Girls standing at the *walavu viidu* courtyard
before leaving to collect vegetables from neighbouring houses

Consul Generals appointed by foreign governments from this line.
With their wealth combined, the VS line as a whole is the biggest
business group in South India. The AMM group, on the other
hand, is often discussed as the TI group in several Nagarattar
papers. Although these papers do stress the cooperative nature of
pangaalis in their business, it is obvious that they are also closely
interwoven in the affinal web created by bilateral cross-cousin
marriage.

At the moment, the VS line has several *pangaali*-based business
combines: (1) the MCT Chidambaram group (founded by M.C.T.
Chidambaram who was a businessman and an MP), which is
mainly based on moneylending; (2) the AMM group has interests
in electrical manufacturing; (3) the MAM group has industrial
interests such as construction, chemicals, cement manufacturing;
(4) the A.C. Muttaiah family and CVCT family which is a newly
sprung joint group, renowned for chemicals, fertilizers, radiators,

etc. and is joined by cross-cousin marriage alliance. Other smaller families run businesses like pulp manufacturing, textile and yarn business, as well as moneylending.

With the money they acquired in South East Asia during the British colonial period (especially in Burma), the VS line started the first banking business in India, but lost a considerable part of the property when the Burmese government closed the door to foreign investors. Nevertheless, they survived as indigenous business firms, becoming manufacturers themselves in India after the 1950s, and established their ground as middle-scale business entrepreneurs.

Two *pangaali* lines sprang out of Sattapa's and Arunachalam's lines, and although they are established in two different villages and worship different *kula deivam* attached to each village, they are none the less *pangaalis*. (Thus, I call them VS line and VA line, respectively. See Fig. 3.1. For convenience, I shall give them in alphabetical order and indicate female lines with bold initials.)[3]

The man in the fifth generation, Muttaiah, had seven children, i.e. (A), (B), (C), (D), (E), (F), and (G). Cross-cousin marriages took place in this generation: A, B, C, and G, married their cross-cousins. (B)'s and (C)'s spouses are brother and sister, so are (E)'s and (F)'s spouses. (See Fig. 3.1). As this example shows, the basic pattern of sister exchange and cross-cousin marriage take place more easily if they have more children.

(A) had two sons and five daughters yet none married cross-cousins. Two cross-cousin marriages took place in the next generation, although in one of the marriages (A–7)'s, the son was adopted. In the seventh generation, two cross-cousin marriages took place and one alliance took place with the MSMM family, a family which occasionally makes alliances with this group. These cross-cousins are the children or grandchildren of the sibling of (A). In the eighth and ninth generations, two intercaste marriages took place. As a consequence, two male members disappeared from the kinship network.

(B) had no children, so he adopted one of (E)'s children. The

---

[3] I have listed brothers and sisters neglecting the senior/junior order, since this makes the figures much simpler and more compact in explaining the cross-cousin alliances. The part of senior/junior among the brothers is not crucial in this part of the discussion.

adopted son married a woman from the MSMM family, and had one son. As was the case in (A)'s line, the MSMM family has made alliances three times with this line, maintaining the closely intertwined relationship with this group.

(C), who married her maternal cross-cousin, had seven children. Some married their cross-cousins,[4] yet this line did not maintain alliances with the mainstream of the VS line. However, one of (C)'s daughters, (C–2), married her second cousin, and had nine children. There were three sons among the nine children, and they jointly started a business (the AMM group). This turned out to be successful, and the business was transferred to the next generation without any split. They maintained cross-cousin alliance relationships within the (C) line itself. They also took partners from (E) and MSMM families. (E), who married his cross-cousin (paternal aunt's daughter) from the OL family had seven children. Two of these married first cross-cousins and one married a second cross-cousin. As I mentioned before, one son was adopted by (D)'s brother, thus the share of the ancestral house was divided between two brothers, and formed the Raja group business combine. Among (E)'s seven children, two married cross-cousins, but others such as (E–2), (E–6), and (E–7), married members of the family with which they had previous affinal relationships. (E–1) married his cross-cousin, who is connected to (F) and OL family, and his two sons, i.e. (E–1–1) and (E–1–2) respectively, married their cross-cousins. The former married an offshoot of (F–1) and (A–6–1), and the latter married (E–6–1), who is an offshoot of (E–6) and another powerful family, AKCT. (E–3) married a non-relative from PA, but their two children married their cross-cousins from (A) and (E) group, respectively. (E–3)'s grandson married a girl from (A) group.

Although these two were once combined and called Raja's group, they split their property when their father died, and now they run separate businesses, although their unity and co-operation is often expressed in business partnership when they have common interests. Amongst women, (E–5) and (E–6)'s descendants married into either the AMM, Raja's *pangaali* line, or the OL. However (E–7), who married an adopted son of a family which did not have any alliance relationship formerly, did not make alliances with this group in the

---

[4] I could not find out the actual number of cross-cousin marriages which took place in this generation.

next generation. Yet she made her first son marry a woman who is from the OL line, maintaining the alliance with the fringe of the VS line. (E–7) also had her grandchildren marry each other recently, forming another alliance line among themselves.

Among the VS line, at present, the most integrated big joint business organization is the AMM group. This joint business property is also relatively recent (dating from the sixth generation), and there is a possibility of its disintegration in the forthcoming generation. However, by the time such disintegration takes place, the shareholders of the joint business will have already established their own businesses with their sons and grandsons. This shows how several new *pangaali* businesses can come out from the older business firms, replacing the older structure. In this sense, the *pangaali*-based joint business is flexible enough to reorganize its structure within three to five generational cycles.

Another feature appears in the VS line with respect to the alliance. Occasional alliances take place with specific families like MAMM or OL families who have had conjugal relationships with the members of the VS line before. These families occasionally supply partners and strengthen the aristocratic trunk, and through a medium such as this, even the *pangaali* lines (i.e. VS line and VA line) can exchange partners indirectly.

On the other hand, cross-cousin marriages still take place in spite of the fact that the number of children is decreasing, and it is getting more difficult to find a suitable partner within a limited number of families.

Among the descendants of the VS line, four families come up as the major trunk, i.e. MCT, AMM, MAM (Raja group 1), and MA (Raja group 2). If there is no child or no male in the family, they adopt a son. In the history of the VS line, at least nine adoptions have taken place, and there are a few cases which are pending in the present seventh generation, although they are not shown in the chart. For example, KC in Fig. 3.1 is an adopted son, and his adoptive father is related to the VS line in the third generation, i.e. the founder of the VS line. KC's daughter, KC 1 eventually married the son of F 1 whose mother (F) is the daughter of KC's adoptive father. This case significantly shows how the *pangaalis* exchange women via another lineage after a few generations.

Adoption takes place even if there are two daughters. (F–1–1), who is an adopted son, has been sending gifts to his two sisters.

One of them is F–1–3 whose husband, F–2–1, is Raja Sir Anna-malai's grandson, who celebrated the grandest *saandi* in 1991 (see Chapter 6).

As seen clearly, there is no case of maternal uncle/niece marriage although the South Indian cross-cousin marriage often prescribes this marriage as part of their combination. I asked the Nagarattars why they do not have maternal uncle/niece marriage as often as cross-cousin marriages. They could not give me any positive answer, since according to them, maternal uncle/niece marriage is allowed and can happen. One of the reasons why such a marriage does not take place so often could be, as I reported earlier in this chapter, that the Nagarattars can marry slightly older female cross-cousins. This practice would limit the chance of maternal uncle/niece mar-riage since the age gap is likely to be much wider than that between the cross-cousins.

The case study of the VS line proves how the Nagarattars tend to prefer cross-cousins even these days, although they now stress that too many such marriages should be avoided within one or two generations. An *aacchi* (E–7–4) who married her daughter (E–7–4–1) to her cross-cousin maintains that this is all right, since neither she nor her own mother (E–7) did marry a cross-cousin. Therefore, cross-cousin marriages are still preferred even though they may not take place due to other considerations.

3.4 *Pangaalis* and their Ritual Importance

The term *pangaali* literally derives from *pangu*, the share, and means that they are the sharers of ancestral property transferred from father to sons. Among the Nagarattars, those who belong to the same Shiva temple division are believed to be descended from the same male ancestor, so they are brothers and sisters, i.e. *pangaalis.* In daily usage, '*pangaali*' denotes more immediate kin, i.e. Ego's siblings, F, FF, FBs, FFBs and their families, i.e. those who used to live under the same roof in the ancestral house and are normally termed as such. *Sondakaaran* on the other hand means relatives in general; thus both the kin (parents and parallel relatives) and the affines (cross relatives) are all covered by this term.

If a Nagarattar does not have a child, he is only allowed to adopt a son from his own clan temple division. In other words, whether

Fig. 3.4. The girl makes 108 holes on a *doosai* cake
assisted by her maternal grandmother and her maternal uncle

the adoptive son is a close kin or not, *'pangaali'* both in a distant
and a closer sense, appears to have some sense of shared common
blood which David claims to be intrinsic to the Sri Lankan Tamils'
ideas about the *sakootarar* (David 1973: 524).

The *pangaalis,* when it came to business, would act co-operatively.
The close *pangaalis,* who shared the expense of building their joint
household, used to live under the same roof for a certain period.
And the *pangaalis* were the ones who would take care of the death
ritual. If a man did not have a son, and failed to adopt one, then
the role of chief mourner would be taken up by one of the *pangaalis*
— in most cases, either a nephew or a brother. Death involves the
heaviest ritual pollution, and the role of the *pangaalis* in the funeral
is essential, since there is no other group to take up this role (see
Chapter 7 for this discussion).

The core of the *pangaali* category are Ego's male parallel relatives, with their wives and children subsumed under this category.

Pangaalis are sometimes the co-operative workforce. Among the landholding families, brothers share the land, as is the case with most agricultural castes and landholding higher castes. Among the Nagarattars, *pangaalis* used to own business property jointly, including the ancestral house which was used as the business headquarters.

In terms of business, business credit was shared by *pangaalis*. The Nagarattars created a credit instrument called a *hundi,* which is discounted with the Imperial Bank by a Nagarattar businessman when he needs cash immediately. For this purpose, his brother will also sign, as, for *hundis,* two signatures are required (Gandhi 1983: 407). The Nagarattars were renowned for having their own funds, which were pooled into a joint fund among the close *pangaalis.*

The relationship among *pangaalis* can become strained however, because of shared property and joint business. One middle-aged Nagarattar said to me that his relationship with his deceased father's uncle turned sour as his uncle wanted to divide their joint property in his own favour. 'Because of this, we did not invite him to *padaippu* (ancestral worship) in which we worship our common ancestors as well as my deceased father.'

Another Nagarattar also lamented, 'In the past, people used to send good managers if their brother's companies were in difficulties. Nowadays, no brother and no *pangaali* help each other.'

Although such strains are found especially among paternal uncles and brothers, since they are supposed to compete with each other to gain profit, *pangaalis* are still an essential group for life-cycle rituals.

3.5 *Padaippu* — Ancestral Worship Ceremony of the *Pangaalis*

Padaippu is held to commemorate the patrilineally related ancestors. There are two different types of worship. One is the worship of *kula deivam* (lineage god) who is normally enshrined in the place (a village) where the ancestry began, usually five or six generations back. Families congregate once a year or once every several years, and hold a grand *padaippu* in which the eldest male member of the oldest family officiates over the ritual. Sometimes, if the participating families are large, they may hold the officiant's position in turns, each family providing an officiant once every ten years.

The other type of *padaippu* is much smaller in scale. At these

Fig. 3.5. The girl heading for a nearby
Shiva temple led by her maternal uncle

times, it is not the *kula deivam* who is worshipped, but those
ancestors who are specially remembered by the family and whose
photographs are hung on the walls of the ancestral house — a
deceased father, mother, aunt, uncle or child may be remembered,
for example. Only the close kin among the *pangaalis,* such as family
members and joint family members, i.e. Ego's father and his spouse,
father's brothers and their spouses, their children and their spouses
and children, may attend. Or it may be even smaller in size with
only the father, mother, sons and their spouses and children. Even
so, holding a *padaippu* is essential before any auspicious ceremony
such as a wedding or *saandi.* Special clothes such as *sarees* and *veetti*
are presented to their favourite ancestor and are kept in a special
box. After the worship, the participating male members wash and
dry them before returning them to a box or a chest.[5] Cooking

[5] According to Dumont (1986: 375), a chest *(petti)* is often treated as a sacred
object in the village temples. The priest officiates over the ritual offering which

vegetarian meals and sacrificing a chicken are also strictly male tasks on such occasions.

The area specially reserved for the sacrifice is the *walavu waasal*. Sweets, snacks, and vegetarian food are the commonest items offered. Freshly-sacrificed chicken and mutton are offered if the ancestors are non-vegetarians. Clothes that have become torn are taken out from the box and worn by the members who congregate at the *padaippu*, and new clothes replace them as offerings to the ancestors.

Since ancestors are supposed to be already pure and auspicious, everything for the ritual must be fresh and new. New buckets are used to scoop water, and the participants are expected to bathe and wear new clothes, or at least clothes washed by the washerman. Women, especially married women who have become members of the family as in-marrying affines are also crucial in this ritual. Since the occasion is a pure and auspicious one, they should not be menstruating when attending. It is said that women sometimes take pills to postpone their menstruation for this reason.

In order to worship the pure ancestors, the *puja* room should be extra clean, and this job is assigned to women. It is mostly left to the most senior woman, i.e. either the widow of the deceased or the wife of the eldest in the family takes the initiative and instructs her sons. Clothes kept in a box for the ancestors are to be washed only by men and hung on the washing line by them.

The order of worship starts with the males who prostrate themselves in front of the *ul viidu* where a pot filled with water and a box containing clothes for the ancestors are also placed, as are food offerings. First come the eldest males followed by the younger ones who may be their sons or brothers. Children follow next, according to seniority. The wives follow their children and the order is again decided according to seniority. If daughters get married, their lineage changes and they cannot participate in this ritual in their natal family.

As the prohibition of participation by married daughters from the worship as well as the order of worship show clearly, full participation in the worship of the patrilinearly inherited ancestors is given to the males and their children — and, in spite of their

---

is kept in a *petti*, placed in the intramural temple. In the period between festivals, the chest is identified with the entire temple.

seniority and authority over their children, the wives as the in-marrying affines are regarded as more distant from their husband's ancestors than their children are.

Padaippu is particularly essential before a wedding, since the marriage must be reported to the ancestors so that they may send their blessings to the marrying couple; so both the bride's and the groom's sides hold the ritual separately. *Padaippu* is also essential after someone in the family has been deceased for over a year. In order to mark his/her status as an ancestor, the family members should hold the *padaippu*, but, unlike the funeral, the ceremony is auspicious and pure as the deceased is already purified. To the Nagarattars, *padaippu* expresses ritual purity but the generators of this purity are the kin, the closest family members and the *pangaalis*. On the other hand, the Brahman priests are associated with purificatory rituals which involve pollution, such as funerals (I shall return to this point in Chapter 6).

When a Nagarattar dies, it is only the *pangaalis* who help the chief mourner to conduct the rituals held both at the cremation ground and in the ancestral house. Even when a wife dies, it is her husband's *pangaalis* who organize the funeral. In this way, for a married woman, full membership of her husband's lineage comes only after death. By becoming one of the ancestors who are worshipped by her sons, she can truly become the guardian of the house.

Among the Tanjore Brahmans described by Gough, a man propitiates his deceased parents, grandparents, paternal great grandparents, and then his maternal grandparents every month, but his deceased father (and his mother, if she is also dead) is separately propitiated on a particular day of the month (Gough 1956: 838–9). However, among the Nagarattars, the 'ancestors' are those who are closely associated with the officiants, and this relationship does not go beyond their grandparents' generation. In addition, the Nagarattars do not worship the maternal line. The mother's parents are simply not propitiated as they are affines to the man.

A contrast can also be found between the Nagarattars' ancestor worship and the Brahmanic one; in the former there is no chanting of the names of the deceased while among the Tanjore Brahmans, they chant the names of all the propitiated male ancestors, but not the females (ibid.: 839). They are only associated with their husbands as sets, while among the Nagarattars, wives are still considered to be essential ancestors in their own right. However, while among the Tanjore Brahmans, the ancestral propitiation is done both for paternal grandparents and maternal grandparents, the Nagarattars do not worship the maternal side at all. This also shows that they separate the *pangaalis* and *dayaadis* clearly in terms of rituals. When a wife dies, especially as a *sumangali*, she is to be worshipped as the guardian of the family, and she would be called *periyaacchi* (big *aacchi*).

3.6 *Dayaadi* (Mother's People) and the Ritual Role of the Maternal Uncle

The Nagarattars, like most South Indian castes, think that the maternal grandparents, and the maternal uncle and his family, are more affectionate and less formal than the *pangaali*. They call those who are related to their mother 'mother's people' *(dayaadi)*, with

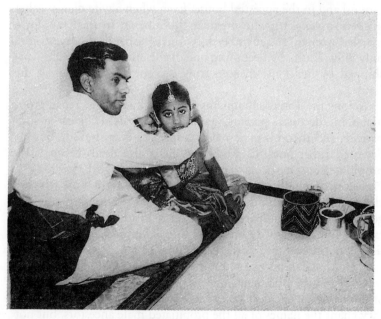

Fig. 3.6. The girl is given a small *taali* by her maternal uncle in the *ul viidu*

more affectionate implications. In terms of kinship terminology, mother's brother *(ammaan)* is identical to father's sister's husband and wife's father, and mother's father is father's mother's brother. What the Nagarattars normally mean by mother's people are those like mother's parents, mother's brothers and their children, who are more likely to live under the same roof or nearby. The possibility that the mother's brother and father's sister's husband and wife's father (or husband's father) are all different people is greater than that of these three being the same individual. Among these three categories, the most crucial one is the mother's brother, to whom ritual roles are assigned on ceremonial occasions. Similarly, mother's father and mother's mother are the important figures for Ego rather than father's mother's brother or father's father's sister, even though, terminologically, they can be identical.

The role of mother's people is closely associated with the gift-giving which takes place as a result of the marriage alliance. The distinction between the wife-givers and wife-takers exists when the actual marriage takes place, although preferential cross-cousin marriage maintains isogamy in principle. One of the most essential obligations of the wife-giver is continuous ceremonial gift-giving to their daughter's family. When a woman gets married, she is given part of her share of property from her parents in the form of *siir danam* (the gift from the 'mother's house').

Among the Nagarattars, a woman's property comes from two sources: first, she is entitled to inherit all the property of her mother. If she has sisters, she should share it with them. Secondly, her father gives her part of his property as an inheritance on her marriage, although the amount she receives may not be as large as that of her brother. If she is the only daughter or if she has no brothers, she is entitled to receive all of her father's property, unless her father adopts a son. It seems to be the custom among the well-to-do Nagarattars to adopt a son only after getting their daughters married so that their adopted son would be useful for ceremonial purposes and remain as a protector to their married daughter. If possible, there could even be a cross-cousin marriage between their children. A married Nagarattar woman can also expect to get her share of the inheritance in instalments in the form of gifts. According to Dumont, 'the most conspicuous feature of alliance as an enduring marriage institution which defines and links the two kinds of relatives, consists in the giving of ceremonial gifts and functions' (1983: 79). He goes on to say that in societies with 'male predominance' (I shall rather say patrilinearly organized descent groups), property is transmitted from one generation to the next in two ways: by inheritance in the male line, and also by gifts to in-laws, namely from father-in-law to son-in-law (ibid.). A married woman will receive a regular flow of gifts from her parents on Deepavali, Pongal, and at the birth of her children. This role is later taken up by her brother, i.e. her child's maternal uncle, until the woman is dead.

The ceremonial role of the maternal uncle thus represents a continuation of the gift-giver of Ego's mother's generation, i.e. the function of gift-receiving has come down one generation after the birth of the child. The child's grandparents give gifts such as gold and silver ornaments at the birth, and on several other occasions such as a birthday, or the puberty ceremony for a girl, and then again at marriage. As the above case of gift-giving clearly shows, gift-giving follows the cycle of the growth of the family, i.e. reproduction. On the other hand, among the Nagarattars, 'mother's people' do not give any gifts when death takes place in their married daughter's family, unlike the Kallars and Maravars in Tamil Nadu (ibid.: 93–104).

When a child has no mother's brother, his role may be taken by the father's sister's husband, or a relative of equivalent position, at least during ceremonial occasions like a wedding. With regard to this point, Dumont explains that a man inherits his father's property with the obligation of supporting his sister, not only with marriage gifts but also with other gifts which are to be given in the future, including the presents to be given to the sister's children.

These are provided or compensated for by the fact that the sister had no formal share in the heritage, her share consisting precisely in such presents. If she has no brother and if no special arrangement is made, she will exceptionally inherit her father's property, but, as a negative counterpart, nobody will be there to make the customary gifts to her children. If she wishes her cousin to assume the role of a brother, she has to give away to him precisely the same property or at least a part of it as would have gone to her brother if she had one. (ibid.: 90–1)

If there is no maternal uncle to take the groom or the bride to the marriage platform at marriage, their paternal uncles might take the role, not as *pangaalis* but as a surrogate (although I never came across this situation during my fieldwork). As a matter of courtesy, if this takes place, the bride's parents have to give special gifts to the surrogate maternal uncle who assumes such a role. The transmission of property takes place in the form of gifts, and this explains the affection towards the 'mother's people' from the married woman's children.

From the point of the gift-receiver, i.e. the married woman's family, this constant flow of gifts also suggests dependence on the 'mother's people'. Among the Nagarattars (and also among most South Indian Hindus), what they call 'mother's house' *(ammaa viidu)* is in fact the married woman's father's house. Yet when a woman talks about 'mother's house' affectionately, she means the gift-giving house from which she can expect constant economic support. It is especially so among the Nagarattars, as I explain in the latter part of this chapter.

If cross-cousin marriage takes place, this dependence on the 'mother's house' becomes much stronger. For example, if a girl marries her mother's brother's son, she may regain the privileges of her mother's natal house after marriage. A young Nagarattar girl once told me, rather regretfully, showing me her maternal grandparents' grand house, that she would not be able to use the facilities available there as frequently as her cross-cousins who were born there. However, she said that she would be able to do so if she marries one of her cross-cousins, who live in her maternal grandparents's house. She appeared to be quite optimistic about this possibility, although the decision to claim the traditional right *(urimai)* to marry one of the cross-cousins is reserved for boys, not girls.

The maternal uncle, as I explained before, is supposed to be economically responsible both for the male and female children of his sister, and the ceremonial role of the maternal uncle is more explicit if the child is a girl. As Good (1991: 5) maintains, the role of controlling the reproductive capacity of a woman is partially shared by the affine in the group where preferential cross-cousin marriage is practised. Among the Nagarattars, as the potential supplier of spouse of the girl, in the classificatory sense at least, the affines represented by the maternal uncle endow the girl with a *kaluttiru*, the necklace which is given at the wedding.

3.7   *Tiruvaadirai:* Celebration with the Maternal Uncle

According to Fuller (1992), *Tiruvaadirai,* when young women pray to win a divine husband, is held in homes on *ardra* star day in Madurai, Tamil Nadu, especially among the Brahmans (ibid.: 197). The festival particularly involves young girls, because traditionally — although never today — Brahman girls were married before puberty (ibid.).

The Nagarattars had pre-pubertal celebrations not only for girls but also for boys. For a five year old boy, there was a ritual called *pudumai* in which the role of his paternal aunt was crucial. He would be dressed up and sat on a large lacquer plate which was held by his mother, his grandmother, and his paternal aunt. The plate would be swung several times as the women sang songs. He would be taken to the nearby temple and meals would be served to the gathering. This custom however was stopped as the financial condition of the Nagarattars worsened. The girls' celebration, *Tiruvaadirai,* continued to be celebrated for some more years.

Among the Nagarattars Tiruvaadirai was held as the celebration for a girl when she was around five to ten years old. She was decorated with jewellery, dressed in a grand *saree,* and was given a small *kaluttiru* around her neck as ritual protection.

In this ritual, the maternal uncle was the person who was responsible for tying the *kaluttiru* around the neck of the girl. This ritual died out in the 1950s, but the important role of the maternal uncle remains in several crucial life-cycle rituals such as the puberty rite and the wedding. A man should give *sarees* and gifts of provisions when his sister's daughter attains maturity. He ties a string called *kaappu,* a ritual protection, around the wrists of his sister's children. Both the bride and the groom receive this protection from their maternal uncles respectively at their wedding ceremony. Both the groom and the bride are guided by their maternal uncle at the wedding and he becomes one of the key ritual performers at wedding ceremonies (see Chapter 5 for details). But the maternal uncle as the ritual officiant is more important for girls than boys.

A senior Nagarattar explains the history of *Tiruvaadirai* as follows:

When the girl was around five to ten years, her parents presented her to the neighbourhood. She was decorated with a grand *saree* and jewels, and visited the neighbourhood from house to house, asking for vegetables.

Her maternal uncle, mother, brothers and sisters, and her friends of about her age, all accompanied her. She sang a song in each house while begging for vegetables. She carried a silver basket to collect vegetables, singing a verse, and she visited all the Nagarattar houses nearby accompanied by her friends and her maternal uncle. She never visited non-Nagarattar houses, since "neighbours" and "public" meant only the Nagarattars. However, their non-Nagarattar friends were welcome to the feast, as was always the case for their celebrations.

The food was cooked with the vegetables the girl collected, in addition to the vegetables her parents bought the previous day. The number of guests varied from between a hundred to three hundred depending on the status of the family. These guests had to be served breakfast, lunch, and tea. In the evening, the girl cooked a sweet *doosai* with the help of her maternal uncle, and put 108 holes in it. On the morning of the ceremony, she was given a small version of a gold *kaluttiru* (a necklace decorated with hand-shaped gold pieces, only worn at a wedding ritual) by her maternal uncle in the ancestral room of the joint house. *Kaluttiru,* as I describe in Chapter 4, is an essential part of a woman's property, and is given before a *taali* (marriage necklace) is tied around her neck. *Kaluttiru* itself contains a *taali* at the centre, and while the *taali,* on a gold chain, is kept around the neck all the time, the *kaluttiru* is kept in a safe. In one house, I saw some photographs of *Tiruvaadirai* which was celebrated when the girl was five and a half. Uma, now a middle-aged woman in her early forties said

People removed the *kaluttiru* from my neck when I fell asleep that night. I quite liked that ceremony and felt sorry that it would not be around my neck any longer the next morning.

The small *kaluttiru* was the one kept in her father's house for this purpose, and unlike the real *kaluttiru* which is given to the daughters on their marriage, it was not supposed to be given away, but shared by girls who are born in the family.

A similar ritual was observed among the Nayars until the 1920s, according to Gough (1956: 49). *Taali* is an indispensable pendant made of gold, worn on a string around the neck, and for most South Indian women, this indicates their married status. The unique aspect of the *taali* rite of the Nayars was that it was to be held not at the wedding but before puberty. Discussing this rite, Fuller (1976: 101) maintains that this rite was not a recognition of physiological puberty, since a separate rite *(tirantukuli)* marked a girl's first menstrual flow.

According to Fuller's description, each Nayar *taravad* (matri-lineal joint family), was linked to other local lineages, known as *enangan* lineages. A girl's *taali* was tied by a male member of one of her lineage's *enangan* lineages, and the person who tied the *taali* was known as the *manavalan*. The *taali* rite was held in a group, assembling pre-puberty girls of a *taravad* or several *taravads* nearby, and attended by every member of the *enangan* lineages, and also by representatives of all other Nayar households in the village. The *taali* rite lasted four days, and the girls worshipped the goddess Bhagavati in a lineage shrine, and feasts were given to those attend-ing. And on the fourth day, the girl and the tier of the *taali* visited the temple. After the ritual, the *manavalan* and the girl would take a meal together separately in the inner loggia, and the rite was finally closed with an elaborate feast for the participants (ibid.: 101–3).

Fuller's argument on the *taali* tying rite sheds light on the meaning of *Tiruvaadirai* among the Nagarattars, as they do appear to share symbolic meanings in a few crucial respects. First, both rites are pre-pubertal rituals for a girl. Secondly, the *taali* (in the case of the Nayars) and *kaluttiru* (the Nagarattars) were worn temporarily and not necessarily as the eternal emblem of marriage worn by South Indian women. For Fuller mentions that the *taali* worn by the girl was not necessarily worn continuously but in some areas the custom was that she removed it shortly after the ceremony (ibid.: 103). Thirdly, the *taali* tier was the maternal uncle of the girl in the case of the Nagarattar, and *enangan* in the case of the Nayars, both of which are categorically affines to the girl's lineage, thus symbolizing the affine as the 'connector' (David: 1973) to the girl's family, the relative related to the future reproductivity of the girl. In both cases, the girl and her children do not undergo the official death pollution at the time of the death of the man who tied the *taali*. (If the man is a husband, as a wife and his children, they should undergo a mourning period.) The Nagarattar girl's *kaluttiru* tier is her maternal uncle. The maternal uncle, being her cross relative, does not play any role in the funeral ritual of her family, nor is she expected to undergo a ritual mourning period upon his death. Although the *taali* tier at the 'real' wedding should be the groom, both cases show that the *taali* tiers are not the 'husband' of the girl either in a real sense or in a symbolic sense. As Fuller maintains, the *taali* rite is not the 'marriage' for the Nayar girls but the first stage (first marriage, in Fuller's words)[6] which endows the girl with social status, a rite of passage for the girl, marking her progress from the social category of girl to that of woman, i.e. a female initiation rite. Among the Nayars, it is to be followed by the *sambandham* ritual, the sexual union, after puberty, during which a girl is linked as a sexual partner to one or more men with whom she is expected to bear children (Fuller 1976: 105). The second stage (secondary marriage, in Fuller's words) is the consummation, and what constitutes 'marriage' is the whole process including both the first and the second stages. In the case of other South Indian castes, instead of a pre-puberty ritual, a puberty ritual becomes the significant marker that endows a girl with social identity before the wedding ceremony.

Fuller argues that the *taali* rite is crucial in the pan-Indian context of marriage, i.e. crucial to secure the 'purity and legitimacy' for the girl's offspring (ibid.: 114) and that makes the status of the man who ties the *taali* very important for that family's girl (ibid.: 115). Following Fuller, Good, discussing puberty rituals and weddings among Tamil Nadu non-Brahman castes at Terku Vandanam, maintains that the puberty ceremony and the wedding are in fact two stages of the same process (Good 1991: 198).

Following Fuller's scheme however, Good further stresses the significance of the puberty rite in relation to the control of female sexual activity in the pan-Indian scheme. Before discussing this point, I shall briefly discuss the puberty ritual of the Nagarattars.

3.8 *Sadangu Waruhiradu* (Puberty Ceremony)

During the puberty rite of the Nagarattars it is not the maternal uncle but the grandmother (either paternal or maternal) who gives a ritual bath to the girl.[7] The girl, after purification, is taken to a certain spot and is made to sit on an auspicious *koolam* (floor

---

[6] Fuller calls this stage 'first marriage' (1976: 105), but since this name is quite misleading and rather confusing, following Good's terminology (1991: 184), I shall simply call it the first stage.

[7] However, this varies from caste to caste. For example, among the Daasari caste which I studied in 1985, it was the maternal uncle who gave a ritual bath to the girl.

decoration), and her grandmother places *adai* (pancake) on seven spots of the girls' body: head, shoulders, arms, and thighs. Then, while she touches each spot with *margosa* leaves, the girl should shake off the adai onto the ground. Ceremonial offerings such as rice, banana, coconuts, and aubergine, are given to the washerman's wife with *adai* in exchange for the services she gave to the girl during her first menstruation. The washerman's wife washes the girl's clothes, and may even lend the girl her own *saree*. (This is still practised today in some places.)

According to Good's detailed accounts of the puberty ceremonies of the non-Brahman castes (e.g. Maravars, Paraiyars, Konars, Velars, etc.), the social identities of the participants in the puberty ceremonies clearly indicate cross relatives as the role players. At Terku Vandanam, the girl who has come of age participates in a mock wedding in which the role of a 'groom' is played by her female cross-cousins and the *saree* gift almost always comes from the maternal uncle (Good 1991: 211).

In the case of the Nagarattars, the ritual officiant who gives a ritual bath is either the girl's grandmother or an older woman who lives with her (but not her mother), and although the *saree* should come from her maternal uncle, her grandparents (both maternal and paternal) should also give presents such as a *saree* and ornaments. The ceremony is exclusively for women — no men are present. The 'female bridegroom' who is present at Terku Vandanam is absent in the Nagarattar ritual. Therefore, the puberty rite of the Nagarattars involves their affines less conspicuously than Good describes. The Brahman priest who is present at the puberty ceremony as a purificatory ritual officiant for Terku Vandanam is absent in the case of the Nagarattars, although the washerman's wife's role is considered essential to express auspiciousness during the ritual: her involvement in the puberty ceremony is associated with her role as the ritual 'cleanser' who washes the polluted clothes of the girl. Although the girl's garments need not be washed by a washerwoman after the first menstruation, the clothes should be washed by her for the first menstruation period. This role leads to the question of the purity and auspiciousness of the menstruating girl which has been extensively discussed by Good (ibid.) in relation to women's sexuality. That is, the series of women's rites (i.e. *taali* tying ritual, puberty ritual, seclusion, and the weddings) are all concerned with regulating and controlling sexuality, purity, and reproductive capacity, which are crucial to the maintenance of caste identity (ibid.: 232).

Among the Nagarattars however, the wedding ritual rather than the puberty ceremony is more conspicuous as the marker of a woman's transitional stage. The puberty rite of the Nagarattars is focused more on the 'sealing' of the virginity of the menstruating girl (as is shown in the offering of *adai* to the guardian goddess, and the iron bar set beside the girl symbolizing the protection of her chastity). No cross-cousin is present at this ceremony as the officiant, while the *puuram kalikkiradu*, which is a preliminary ritual held before the wedding, marks the removal of such a protection and the maternal uncle plays a key role in this. His blessing in the ritual appears to be the symbolic acknowledgement of his giving away the right to take the girl as the bride of one of his sons, since this role is not played by her father-in-law even if he happens to be her 'real' maternal uncle (see Chapter 6 for this ritual). *Puuram kalikkiradu* takes place before the wedding to remove the protection of the girl's virginity and thus to make her a marriageable and mature woman. Thus, as Good maintains, 'this girl–woman transition is the social counterpart of the folk-biological change implicit in the immature–mature transition' (ibid.: 196).

Good contends that a sexually mature but unmarried female is an anomalous creature and the ritual relieves her natal family of some of the burden imposed by this anomaly, and that the affine of the girl's natal family will eventually resolve it by accepting her in marriage (ibid.: 197). The puberty ceremony represented as the pseudo-wedding (in the case of the Terku Vandanam) initiates both the social process of removing the girl from her father's jurisdiction, and the physiological process of transforming her blood or body from that of a girl to that of a mature woman, and then at the wedding, to that of a wife. It achieves both these aims by linking her with the family of her ideal future husband (her cross-cousin), so that she ends the ritual identified more with her cross-relatives and less with her father (ibid.: 200).

Therefore, the purity of the girl is a concern of both her natal family and her future affine, and this is symbolized by her maternal uncle in the ritual, as it affects the status of both her natal family and her future affine. The maternal uncle plays a key role for the girl. By being her maternal uncle, he is a protector who belongs to her mother's people. By being a cross relative, he also symbolizes her future affine, as the kinship terminology for the maternal uncle *(ammaan)* also signifies the father-in-law. The kinship terminology is not coercive, unlike the jural rules, but it represents one of the idealized patterns of social relationship. Even if the girl marries her non-relative in the future, her father-in-law is still expected to behave as if he is her maternal uncle by becoming her protector, as is the case for her maternal uncle.

On the other hand, as the boy's ritual *pudumai* shows, the relationship between the girl and her maternal uncle is not over-stressed, unlike other cases such as the Nayars, since in order to keep the balance of their bilateral principle of cross-cousin mar-riage, the Nagarattars also express the importance of the relation-ship of the paternal aunt and her nephew, although this is not as conspicuous as that of the maternal uncle and niece.

3.9   'Mother's House' and the *Pulli*

As I discussed at the beginning of this chapter, the nuclear family household is economically tied to the wife's natal family, and by being so, it is economically independent from the husband's natal family. However, this is not a phenomenon unique to the Nagarat-tars but by and large shared by other South Indian castes as a result of cross-cousin marriage, equal status between the wife-givers and wife-takers, and the constant flow of gifts from the wife's natal family to the wife's nuclear household. For example, Dumont describes the general case of South Indian castes as follows.

If, two years after my marriage, I decide to leave my parents' household and establish a separate one, my father-in-law will conclude the series of marriage gifts (a part of which has gone, not to myself, but to my parents) by sending to me, as the head of the new household, the necessary pots and pans. Then, if a child is subsequently born to me, we are told that it will be presented with gifts by its maternal uncle on each ceremonial occasion. (Dumont 1983: 87)

Kolenda (1984: 103) reports that the Nattati Nadars in Tamil Nadu, like the Nagarattars, also follow patrilineal descent organiza-tion, but the residence is fairly flexible, so that rather than overall adherence to patrilocal residence, some opt for uxorilocal residence but live mostly in nuclear family households, possibly supplemented by a grandparent. A newly married couple may briefly reside with the groom's parents, but otherwise they live in nuclear or supplemented nuclear households (ibid.: 104).

Therefore, the Nagarattars' combination of the patrilocal residence with neolocal residence, and occasional cases of virilocal residence, does not seem to conflict with the general pattern of South Indians. The flexible residential system is supported by the close relationship with the wife's family, especially among the Nagarattars. Generally speaking, a contrast seems to exist between the North Indian type of patrilineal descent groups whose system is combined with a hypergamous tendency, and the South Indian type of patrilineal descent groups, which are based on an isogamous tendency. In North India where hypergamy is considered to be ideal, as Parry (1979) reports in the case of Rajputs in Kangra, the patrilineally organized joint family does not tolerate the couple creating their own economic unit in the joint family economy and the wife as an in-marrying affine who comes from an unrelated family, as a stranger, occupies a lower status than that of her husband's family; thus the wife tends to create the fission and tension between the nuclear family and her husband's natal family, eventually dismantling the structure of the joint family household.

Among the prominent mercantile castes (such as the Marwaris and the Komutti Chettis) I have come across so far, I have been told that the joint family household is the norm and so both the economy and the domestic labour should be pooled together. The Nagarattars however, choose residential patterns in accord with the economic circumstances and the size of the family. Formerly, when the Nagarattars sent their men abroad, the newly married couple used to have an *ul viidu* built either by the groom or his father. According to a senior Nagarattar, a newly married couple lived with the groom's parents for some time until the bride was trained in household management.

In those days, the couple married young. So the bride did not know how to manage the house well. Therefore, until the first child was born, the couple would live with the husband's family and the household expenses would be met by the husband's natal family. If they felt they could manage by themselves, they were encouraged to become independent and have their own house.

As *ul viidu* means internal house, it is a nuclear household where the couple sleep and store their own goods. They have a separate hearth to cook for themselves. When the couple becomes financially separated from the husband's natal family, it becomes a *'pulli'*, a nuclear family of its own. *'Pulli'* in Tamil means a dot, and expresses the basic unit of society, i.e. a nuclear family. It normally consists of a husband and wife with or without unmarried children. If a man becomes a widower with children, he is still regarded as a *pulli*, since he is expected to get married. If the wife loses her husband and maintains a household with unmarried children, she is regarded as a half-*pulli*.

This unit is used for the collection of tax for festivals and ceremonies. For example, in a festival of the village goddess Mariyamman, all the castes collectively meet the festival expenses, and the money collected for this purpose as festival tax is based on the unit of the *pulli*, although the amount collected from each *pulli* differs from caste to caste. Normally speaking, in a joint household where a son lives with his wife, his widowed mother, and unmarried siblings, the festival tax collector would count them as one and a half-*pulli* — a widow with children is half *pulli*, but if she has a married son, this is a full *pulli*. Therefore, it is not only the Nagarattars who regard the nuclear unit as based on the *pulli*.

People regard a *pulli* as a relatively autonomous unit which is responsible for contributing to social activities. When a Nagarattar gets married, he forms a potential *pulli* with his wife, as he normally does not become independent immediately. According to a senior Nagarattar, the young couple need a little training before doing so and are coached by the husband's parents. Financially, they are under the umbrella of the joint family. While the husband works outside, his wife gets training at home under her mother-in-law. Such a systematic way of coaching seems sensible, especially when people marry young — a girl would hardly have time to get proper coaching before she marries at around twelve years of age.

When they have a child, it is normally considered to be the right time to separate their economy from that of the joint family. They may still stay in the same joint household where they keep their own room *(ul viidu)*, and a separate hearth *(aduppu)* in a big kitchen space where the couple cook separately and eat separately from the other *pullis*. The housewife would have the keys to her own storeroom and the safe in which all her assets, such as daily provisions and jewellery, are kept. If they are rich enough, they may establish their own household and parade their independence. However, the place where they started their married life remains a sacred space. It is in this space, which has been handed down from father to son, that the important auspicious rituals are held. A young girl is given a small *kaluttiru* in this room by her maternal uncle; at the wedding, both parents sign the marriage contract in this space; the bride stays in this room to preserve her auspicious condition until her *taali* is tied; the wedding couple should enter this room before the groom ties the *taali* for his bride, and in some areas, the ritual of tying the *taali* takes place inside this very room. Ancestors are supposed to be worshipped here as auspicious and pure spirits.

When the young couple build a house of their own, the wife's mother's people almost always give financial help of some sort, and the wife may even sell some of her jewellery, if necessary. Even if her mother dies, the married woman still calls her natal house 'my mother's house' and she gets financial help from it in the form of the occasional gift. For example, an old woman in her early eighties pointed to one mansion and said 'that's my mother's house'. The house she pointed to was the ancestral house of her father where she was born. Although her parents are both dead and even her brothers are dead, she still calls it 'my mother's house' even though it was legally her father's property to which a woman had no right. In a man's case on the other hand, his natal family is not 'mother's house'. The man, after marriage, would build a house of his own, thus his natal family is where his parents would live. He and his family go back to his natal house after his parents' death. He may not do so if he is not the only son. Therefore, even though he establishes his own house, his visits to his natal house become less frequent than his visits to his wife's family.

This reveals the different relationships that exist between a son and a daughter, in terms of their natal house. The married woman will visit her natal family more frequently, calling it 'my mother's house' and get whatever she wants from her mother. Her husband is also welcome in his in-laws' house. To him, his wife's family is a place where he can relax and get financial support in times of need. And the father-in-law would always give gifts and be indulgent with his daughter's family, while he may not be so with his son's family.

Part of the reason for this differing attitude is that the sons are expected to get everything from the parents after their death, while the daughters can only make a claim before the death of the parents. Therefore, in addition to the dowry, parents are expected to supply substantial financial support both in kind and in money every now and then.

Since a couple establishing a house of their own is a sign of independence from the husband's house, a man consciously separates from his father's household economy and keeps his distance. Promoting the autonomy of the nuclear family is the job of the man's wife's family. If a man wants more help from a source other than his wife's, it would be from his parents' house. Asking his father-in-law directly for immediate financial help is said to be below a man's dignity, as this is taken as an indication that he is not capable of managing his own family. Since the husband can utilize his wife's dowry and may use it as part of his business fund, he would do so if the matter is urgent. However, his wife may go and ask for help directly from her father, and it is through his wife that the son-in-law can get financial help from his father-in-law. If he wants to borrow from his own father, he may, but because ancestral property should not be partitioned, he has to return this money with interest. A senior Nagarattar in his early eighties said to me that he and his brothers used to borrow from their common fund pooled in their joint business when they wanted to build their own houses. 'We borrow money, and after working hard for several years, we return it with interest by several instalments.' Nobody is allowed to take money without returning it to the joint business.

The following case explains how the nuclear family is tied to the wife's side and the wife's dowry is managed by the groom's father-in-law, while the nuclear family still enjoys responsibility for managing their own income. The pattern of residence also changes from virilocal to neolocal, as they acquire managerial skills and become economically independent from the husband's family.

CASE STUDY

Nacchiammai is twenty-three years old and married to a university professor in his early thirties. She was just fourteen when she married, having barely finished the nineth standard, while her husband, already a lecturer, was twenty-six. She gave birth to a girl at fifteen. In spite of her age, her parents wanted her to marry, since the alliance was 'very good'. Her groom was related to her distantly. Her husband was the son of her mother's elder sister's husband's nephew.

In fact, since Manickawasagar was already twenty-six and was reaching the upper limit of the ideal marriageable age for a male, he wanted to marry as quickly as possible. In South India, people do not like to marry their daughters to a man substantially older for fear of early widowhood. Having been busy with his academic studies, Manickawasagar lost the chance to seek alliances in his early twenties. If Nacchiammai's parents had asked him to wait for one or two years, he would have opted for another girl. Therefore, Nacchiammai's parents had no other choice but to marry her off. There was no assurance that they would get a better alliance in the future.

When Manickawasagar got married, he borrowed money from his mother to purchase some items for his wedding, and returned it a few days later. She would lend money if one of her sons needed it. Although she charges her five sons no interest, no son gets such a fund from her as a 'give-away'. According to Nacchiammai, her mother-in-law is affectionate enough to all her daughters-in-law and Nacchiammai received a present of five gold sovereigns from her, but her mother-in-law still takes interest from Nacchiammai's father when he borrows from her as part of his business fund.

When Nacchiammai married at fourteen, she had to live in Madurai where her husband's natal family lived. Manickawasagar's father was a pawnbroker. He was well-organized at running a business and he educated all of his five sons well. Aside from the moneylending business, the family also kept several cows. The work of looking after the cows had been done by Manickawasagar, the third son. As soon as Nacchiammai was married, this job was assigned to her. Nacchiammai felt miserable about this, but her husband did not want to continue doing it any longer, preferring to leave the tedious job to his young wife. Getting up early in the morning and milking the cows was quite difficult for a young girl of fourteen who had had a protected upbringing.

I missed my natal family a lot in those days. In my mother's house, we had a servant to do such work, and I never did any work at home. Since I was an only daughter, they spoilt me. My mother did not even teach me how to manage the house. When I married, many of the domestic chores were assigned to me and I felt it to be a big burden.

Manickawasagar's elder brothers were already married, and lived in separate houses, so she was the only daughter-in-law living with her in-laws at that time.

Her ordeal, however, was over after six months, as Manickawasagar acquired a post in a university in Karaikkudi, Chettinadu. That was much closer to her mother's house, and since she was then pregnant, she was allowed to stay with her natal family for six months until the child was born. Her husband often visited her there and stayed there at weekends, enjoying talking with his brother-in-law. Nacchiammai felt much happier being away from the husband's family. Although her mother-in-law was kind to her, she still preferred to live close to her natal family, since she would have more freedom. She came back to her husband a month after her daughter was born.

She now regrets having stopped her own education at the ninth standard, and feels she cannot even teach her seven year old daughter. Her husband coaches their daughter every night and saves the private tuition fee. Luckily, her daughter is doing quite well at school, so both Nacchiammai and her husband hope to send her to a medical school eventually, although Nacchiammai would not send her to a far away place to be educated.

'A good education and a good job will help her to make a good alliance,' Manickawasagar says. 'To have a respectable job as a career woman may help her gain a good husband.' Although they have only one girl, they do not want any more children for financial reasons.

If you have a girl, you want to give her a good education and marry her off to a well-educated man. I cannot afford to have any more children. I may adopt a son after marrying her off, but that is not so essential.

Manickawasagar tries to save as much as possible in anticipation of his daughter's wedding. He is also saving up to build his own house. After all, this would become his daughter's asset on his death. His salary is around Rs 4,000 per month. Out of this, Rs 1,000 is automatically invested in company stocks. In addition, part of the Rs 10,000 dowry Nacchiammai brought in had been invested in her father's pawnbroking business and now it has accumulated to around Rs 40,000 to 50,000.

Nacchiammai's mother-in-law, who is a widow, invested part of her share of Nacchiammai's dowry which was given as the *maamiyaar siir danam*[8] a money gift. It was Rs 21,000 and she invested it in some stocks. Nacchiammai's mother-in-law spends the interest on herself, keeping the principal untouched. According to Nacchiammai, some of the mother-in-law's money is also lent to Nacchiammai's father who is a pawnbroker. The interest charged by Nacchiammai's mother-in-law to Nacchiammai's father is around 1.5 *wadi* (18 per cent). Nacchiammai's mother-in-law says she charges a special rate for her son's father-in-law as her interest rate is slightly lower than the market rate (22 per cent). From Nacchiammai's father's point of view, he gets part of the capital necessary for his business from his son-in-law's mother, at a rate cheaper than the normal rate. Since the interest is paid to his own relative, i.e. an affine who is his daughter's mother-in-law, that eventually benefits the family of his daughter. Therefore, rather than paying interest to an unrelated person he is happy to pay it to her. From the point of view of Nacchiammai's mother-in-law, it is better to lend money to her affine who gives her far better interest than the banks. Moreover, her affines are reliable debtors. (Nacchiammai's mother privately lends money to some local people and earns pocket money as well.)

As this case shows, the merging of capital exists among the kin and affines as a common fund, while they are still engaged in their own profit-making. From the point of view of both families, the profit made by lending money to each other is not immoral, since all the properties will eventually go to their children. This kind of merging while taking a profit sometimes also takes place between a husband and wife. A wife from a well-to do family told me that she sometimes lends money to her husband and receives interest. 'That's for a mutual benefit. My husband gets a lower interest rate from me than when he borrows from the bank. And I would get a better interest rate than the market rate.' After all, it is better to pay interest to one's own kin or affine than to the outsiders. In this way, the money circulates within the kin and affines, benefits both parties, and serves their common aim of saving for the next generation. What they are expected to do is to utilize the money provided by the relatives and earn more by hard work, and pass it on to the next generation.

---

[8] *Maamiyaar siir danam* is the cash given to the mother-in-law *(maamiyaar)* upon marriage, from the bride's natal family. For detailed discussion, see Chapter 4.

The notion of common property always exists among the family members although they insist on a strict business attitude in money matters so that the gain should be mutual. By alliance, mutual investment in each other's business becomes easier.

When I asked Manickawasagar whether he could trust his father-in-law in money matters, he said he could. 'Of course, I do. Who would doubt his father-in-law? He knows that all our money will go to our only daughter who is also his granddaughter. In a way, he knows that he is multiplying our money for Uma.' Even in his mother's case, he claims that she thinks only of the welfare of her five sons and their children.

After all, all her money comes to us after her death. Even though she saves money by charging interest from my wife's father, it is going to be our money, and therefore, it should go to my daughter. Until then, she enjoys herself spending the interest and saving the principal.

In this way, the accumulation of property for a daughter is part of the family business which involves not only her parents but also her grandparents, especially those on her maternal side. Even after marriage, the daughter may expect constant financial back-up from her 'mother's house'. As for daily provisions like rice, wheat, flour, dhal, dried chilli, sweets, etc., Nacchiammai obtains these from her 'mother's house', so that she does not need to buy anything. She says she can claim anything from her 'mother's house' except a broom and cooking oil which, for Nagarattars, are forbidden gifts for anybody, even their daughters.[9]

Nacchiammai regularly pays visits to her 'mother's house' and gets provisions, in addition to items such as kitchenware and plastic buckets. She also gets cash as a gift from her mother's house. Nowadays, the Nagarattars are extremely fond of plastic plates and plastic buckets, as well as stainless steel goods, and so Nacchiammai asks for these items whenever she wants one. She says, 'It is better to be a woman. You can keep on getting things from your mother's

[9] They explained this as follows: the broom sweeps 'everything'; thus people anticipate that the daughter may take everything away if they give away a broom. Oil, on the other hand, is not good to give away, since it is ritually a staple material. Cooking oil is treated the same. It should be supplied by oneself, and not given by others. Although the explanations were not entirely satisfactory, I could not obtain any further explanation from my informants concerning this.

house.' She spends money regularly from her husband's salary approximately as follows: *dhal* Rs 238, vegetable Rs 75, meat and fish Rs 80, fruits Rs 80, house rent Rs 40, electricity Rs 75, milk Rs 150, newspaper Rs 60, stationery and school tuition fee Rs 60. Thus she estimates that the monthly total expense could be around Rs 1,218.

In addition, Nacchiammai buys books, school uniforms (two per year), and shoes for her daughter which cost about Rs 500 per year. She now keeps a part-time servant who receives Rs 40 per month in addition to food. As her husband has a scooter, they buy gasoline for approximately Rs 200 per month. They also visit relatives quite often, and transport by bus amounts to approximately Rs 100 per month. They have to contribute money for the weddings of relatives which may cost about Rs 200–300 per year or more. Therefore, she spends approximately Rs 2,000 per month keeping another Rs 1,000 for emergency expenditure and to save, in order to purchase electric gadgets.

Their tight budget is solely directed towards saving for their daughter's marriage, since that will be the most important achievement in their lives. It will even decide their lives later on, because it is essential to have their daughter happily married to a well-to-do husband in order to gain respect in their community. In such circumstances, the financial assistance of the wife's mother's house is crucial. Her mother started to send provisions to help Nacchiammai when she and her husband set up a house in Karaikkudi and it made a big difference.

Although the household economy is said to be pinched if the food budget exceeds 30 per cent of the total income, most families in India still spend a large proportion of their income on food. Entertaining guests with good food is the commonest treat in India, and since food is still expensive, it is natural that it should be treated as a part of an exchange of gifts.

In the case of Nacchiammai however, the expense both for food and other consumables is extremely low. The clothes that the family members wear come mostly from her mother's house as well. These two items save a lot of money for a young couple bringing up children.

A Brahman girl who is a friend of Nacchiammai laments that her father has to prepare for her wedding jewellery, saving money for this purpose.

My father's family is not well off, and we have to help them. Even though my mother is the only daughter, after getting married, my grandparents could not help her much since married daughters are disconnected from their natal family on marriage in our caste. They cannot go back to their parents' house and demand things. My mother's jewellery would go to my mother's brother's wife after her death.

In the case of the Nagarattars, the preparation of jewellery would partially come from the mother's house, especially from the grandmother of the marrying girl. Being an only daughter, Nacchiammai would certainly receive gifts from her maternal grandmother on her marriage, while among the Brahman communities, giving gifts to their married daughter is not as frequent as it is among the Nagarattars.

When I went to see Nacchiammai on the day before Deepavali, her brother was visiting her with a gift of a set of diamond earrings. In exchange, she returned a ceremonial gift of betel leaves and areca nuts on a small plastic plate, an expression of ritual honour. This ritual gift given by the wife to her brother shows her respect to her natal family who would constantly support her and her children, and cannot be equated in value with the gift from her natal family. Formalized ceremonial exchanges between the two parties are meant to solidify their relationship not only economically but also in ritual terms.

When I asked whether Manickawasagar did not feel sorry about having only one daughter, he said,

What can I do about it? Of course, I wanted a son, but I cannot resist my fate. A girl is born, and I have a responsibility to marry her off. After all, my father had five sons, and when I married I took a dowry from my wife's family. Now it should become the reverse. I should give whatever I can to the groom's side. Things which are given to me may be given away some day. That is life. You cannot keep on getting without giving anything.

In 1994 they built a house on a nearby street with the help of Nacchiammai 's father. It is a two-storey house and they rent the first floor out in order to reduce their mortgage. However, Manickawasagar did not get any financial assistance from his mother, since if she helped him she would also have to help the other four brothers and this would be bad for her finances. At the moment, neither Nacchiammai nor Manickawasagar discount the possibility of having a son and marrying his child to their daughters' child in the distant future.

3.10 Women as Tribute, Women as Cross-Cousins

As the above comment of Manickawasagar shows, the Nagarattars have the idea that things taken should be given away and things given come back to the family in due course. Reciprocal exchange represented in the preferential bilateral cross-cousin marriage is implicitly connected to such an idea, since wife-givers and wife-takers are replaceable in the same generation (sister-exchange) or in the next generation (bilateral cross-cousin marriage).

Comparing the weddings of Rajputs in North India and Nadars in South India, Kolenda (1984) argues as follows. Although both give a dowry when the daughter gets married and the wife-giver is obliged to keep on sending gifts on important ceremonial occasions, the hypergamous relationship of subordination of the bride's kindred to the groom's among the North Indian Rajputs maintains the role of the bride as 'tribute' offered to the groom's side. In the South however, as represented in the case study of the Nadars, the husband and wife are considered to be a pair, as 'the seed and the earth' (ibid.: 114), or god and goddess, in which the wife-giver and the wife-taker's statuses are equal, and hence isogamous, which is well represented as the ideal of cross-cousin marriage.

An *aacchi* in her early eighties recollects the time when her marriage with her cross-cousin was fixed.

We were both eleven years old. I was a few months older than he, though. That time, when we were being photographed with other cousins, my uncle made us sit together for the first time. He did it because he knew we were going to get married.

In the case of the Nagarattars, the independence of the *pulli* or the nuclear family is more systematically secured than most of the South Indian castes, and the traditional notion of *stridhana*, i.e. the female property line from mother to daughter follows the traditional Hindu type of dowry system (dowry as the woman's property, and not to be given to her husband's family). This reduces the chance of the husband's family exercising authority and control over their daughter-in-law. When the family does not have any daughter, the son's mother's property goes directly to her grand-daughter, and not to her sons.

I had only sons, and didn't have any daughter. It was a pity since I had carried all the *saamaan* (bridal goods) from my mother's house, and there was no one to give them to. My elder son married last year and his wife brought a lot of *saamaan* as well — even though I told her family that everything was available here. They still gave a lot to their daughter!

The middle-aged *aacchi*, who had her first granddaughter, told me excitedly that both she and her daughter-in-law were delighted to have a girl child and were looking forward to giving their property to her and maintained that the property given to the daughter came more from 'affection' rather than the 'obligation' which they feel for the son (I shall go back to this theme in the following chapter).

When there are only sons, the property of the mother would be kept until the day a daughter is born to her sons since under no circumstance is it possible to keep the *saamaan* and the wife's jewellery in the family for good. As Manickawasagar correctly maintains, people cannot keep on receiving without giving. People cannot keep on having sons indefinitely. When they marry their sons, some of them have daughters, and the daughters will inherit both their mother's and grandmother's property which come from both the paternal and the maternal side. With the property they are given, the daughters will be married off. Therefore, whether it is immediate or delayed, the exchange takes place, and the wealth of the caste circulates within the caste through marriage alliances.

If that is so, what would be the relationship between brother and sister? In the case of matrilineally organized societies such as the Nayars, until the joint family system started to be dismantled in the early twentieth century, the woman sometimes was faced with the dilemma of locating her membership in two institutions: her own *taravad,* which is organized by a brother–sister relationship as her brother (or maternal uncle) manages the house as *karanavan,* and her relationship with her 'husband' and child which may tend to keep her in the husband–wife relationship and, as a consequence, split her loyalties (Gough 1961: 360–1; Moore 1985: 536–7).

When it comes to the North Indian type of patrilineal organiza-tion, the hypergamous tendency makes it difficult to make a co-operative relationship diachronically between the brother and sister. There is no sister exchange, as there is no repetition of marriage between two families, and the natal family of the bride is regarded as lower than that of the groom and that the continuous flow of gifts to the groom's house from the bride's natal family is an expression of 'tribute' rather than the expression of continuous gift-exchange relationship between these two families.

On the other hand, in the South Indian type of patrilineal descent, which is combined with an isogamous tendency, it is much easier to create solidarity between husband and wife based on their neolocality. This does not conflict with their patrilineal descent orientation, as the South Indian type of patrilineal descent orientation tends to tolerate nuclear families, or rather encourage them in order to activate their economic activities (as was the case of the Nagarattars).

Under such a system, a woman can be practically freed from obligations to her natal patrilineal descent group (as is also the case of the North Indian type of patrilineal groups). Her ties to her husband can be maximized to the point where they take priority leading to the establishment of their own nuclear family. Where a woman's tie to her own unit is greatly weakened, as in North India, her severed or weakened tie to her natal family does not allow her to return to her natal family once divorced. But in patrilineal descent groups where preferential bilateral cross-cousin marriage is practised, she is not so totally severed from her natal family. The gifts which she receives regularly from her natal family are the expression of such a tie which stretches to the next generation, and which may materialize in the form of marriage between one of her children and one of her brother's. The control over an in-marrying woman by the groom's family is certainly restrained when she has her own economic assets, especially when they are still under the management of her natal family, in which the preferential cross-cousin marriage pattern organizes the relationship between kin and affine both in the present and the next generation. Transfers of goods and services establish rights for the wife, and yet the continual sending of gifts by her natal family combined with the prescribed cross-cousin marriage does not make a hierarchical relationship between the wife-giver and wife-taker; rather the gifts work to make the co-operation between the two groups advantageous.

On the other hand, economic co-operation between father and son gives the father advantages in terms of authority, as well as in creating a strong emotional bond. The bond between the father and son accords with the co-operative patrilineally organized group system, as seen in the business enterprise amongst the Nagarattars. The son looks after his father's ancestral property after the latter's death and keeps sending gifts to his sister. In return, he gets most of the property left after the death of his father. The son becomes the chief mourner for his parents, and worships them after death as ancestors, which is included as part of the obligations he has to observe in exchange for a larger property share.

From the point of view of advantageous alliances, brothers and sisters are dependent on each other: if either fails to make a proper marriage, the other's alliance also fails (see Chapter 4 for a detailed discussion). Daughters should get married quickly, since having an unmarried woman of marriageable age is definitely a minus in getting a good alliance for her brother: the bride's party take into consideration the expenses which are involved in the wedding of the unmarried daughter. If the sister is already married, and if she is married to a reliable partner, this brings benefits to her brother as well. Preferential cross-cousin marriage being practised, future alliance with their children may be also taken into consideration. Such a long-standing co-operative relationship between the brother and sister is represented in the chain of gifts sent by her brother to her family after marriage. Even if her parents are dead, the relationship between them does not disappear because the co-operative relationship between the brother and sister is already extended to their children's generation.

3.11 Cross-Cousin Marriages and Older Wives

Another peculiar aspect in relationship terminology is the dual usage of *aacchi* which originally denotes elder sister and elder parallel sister and is also the term to refer to wife or a married woman (see Table 3.1). As I argued before, the property preserved for the married women is secured because of preference for bilateral cross-cousin marriage. As Tambiah (1973*a*) maintains, a woman's property right is more protected in southern India and Sri Lanka where there is a strong tradition of isogamy in which wife-takers and wife-giver's positions are interchangeable. In the case of the Nagarattars, this tendency is further stressed because rather than choosing the maternal uncle and niece marriage, they opt for cross-cousin marriage even if the bride is older than the groom, an unusual practice among Indians as a whole

This strategy not only ensures the equality of status between the wife-giver and wife-taker but also the sharing of decision-making power between the husband and wife, especially to the advantage of the wife's side. It is also possible to assume that under these circumstances, the Nagarattars consider the seniority of the husband over his wife to be less important, since the conjugal family receives economic advantages by being tied to the wife's natal family especially if the partition of the husband's and wife's property is secured under the supervision of the wife's natal family. The Nagarattars also maintain that it is important not to give the entire share of the daughter's property on marriage but rather to give it in instalments for decades, as she would be far better treated by her husband in such a case (I shall go back to this point in the following chapter). Therefore, her brother acts as her custodian who sends her share of property little by little in order to maintain her high status in her conjugal relationship. The seniority of the wife is also important in improving her married status, since she is less subservient to her husband in terms of life experience.

Although South Indian Hindus generally used to opt for cross-cousin marriage and even maternal uncle–niece marriage, it was necessary for the male to be older. Thus, even if there were a good match of cross-cousins, if the woman were older than her cross-cousin, the alliance would be avoided. Thus, Good maintains that among the Maravars he studied, marriage was only prescribed between cross-relatives of the same terminological level, with the additional proviso that a man must be older than his bride (Good 1991: 74). The man's seniority is absolutely a necessary prerequisite for the Brahmans as they strongly maintain the ideological gender hierarchy between the husband and wife. One Brahman explained:

According to the *shastra*, both the mental and the physiological maturing of men and women is different. The groom should have at least five years' seniority over his bride in order to offset the imbalance. These days compromises are made so that even four years' difference is acceptable, but it shouldn't be less than that. Of course, we never accept a marriage in which the bride is older than her husband. This is a significant difference between us Brahmans and the Nagarattars.

Even other castes, such as the Mudaliyars insist that the age

seniority of the husband is essential in order to take the initiative
in conjugal life.

However, the Nagarattars dismiss such Brahmanic beliefs as
groundless and an *aacchi* told me,

We still do not mind if the girl is one year older than the boy. If the
alliance is good in other respects, and if the couple like each other, the
girl's slight seniority is not a problem even if they are not cross-cousins.
In the old days, we used to prefer cross-cousin marriage much more than
today so that it was completely acceptable for the bride to be a few years
older than the groom. For example, my mother-in-law was married at
nineteen to her cross-cousin, my father-in-law, who was then thirteen:
she is six years older than her husband! My maternal grandmother was
also one year older than my grandfather. She was even one inch taller
than him, and so he used to wear a turban when he had photos taken
with his wife! In this way, if a couple were cross-cousins, the wife's age
seniority did not matter at all. We no longer place such great importance
on cross-cousins and so we would not marry our son to his cross-cousin
if she were much older than him. Yet we still do not mind if the bride
is slightly older. If they like each other, whether they are related or
unrelated, the bride's slight seniority (eg. one or two years) does not
matter at all. I know many couples in which the wives are either the same
age or one year older than their husbands.

In other words, the custom which allows a Nagarattar male to
marry an older female gives primary consideration to his cross-
cousins over his niece and supports the egalitarianism between the
wife-giver and wife-taker. Marriage to his elder sister's daughter
ultimately makes hierarchy between the wife-giver and wife-taker.
As Yalman neatly describes in the case of the Tanjore Brahman,
consistent marriage practices to the sister's daughter is structurally
identical with cross-cousin marriage, expressing the hierarchy or
the 'desired asymmetry between the god-husband and the consort-
wife' (1971: 351). In the case of Terku Vandanam in south Tamil
Nadu which was studied by Good (1991), marriage to the elder
sister's daughter is prescribed in the kinship terminology and the
requirement that 'the husband must be older than his wife is built
directly into the terminological prescriptions' (ibid.: 68).

3.12 *Aacchi* as the Honorific Title

Aacchi literally means 'elder sister' and refers both to one's elder
sister and a female elder parallel cousin only among the Nagarattars.

In the Nagarattar context, it also means 'a respectable married woman'. However, no caste-specific term of reference has been given to the Nagarattar male. He is usually called 'Chettiyar', or simply 'sir' (the English word), especially after he has married. Yet any man in any Chettiyar caste can be addressed or referred to as 'Chettiyar' and any man of a respectable family may be addressed as 'sir' in Tamil Nadu. If he is quite old, he can even be addressed as *'Aiyaa'* (an elderly gentleman, also a term of reference to denote grandfather), as is the case with elderly men in other castes. A Nagarattar married woman, on the other hand, is always addressed and referred to as *'aacchi',* or *'periyaacchi'* (big *aacchi*), if she already has a grandchild. However, *aacchi* is a specific term which implies more than mere wifehood.

Nagarattar married women would consider it shameful to be addressed as *ammaa* (lady), which is a common Tamil usage which denotes any married or respectable woman in general. The Nagarattar women also refuse to use the term *aacchi* for any non-Nagarattar woman married to a Nagarattar man, however closely they may associate with the woman in private. Their pride in the term *aacchi* was exemplified for me by the following episode.

I was talking to a Nagarattar man in his mid-fifties on the phone in the presence of several *aacchis*. When I said, 'I was just talking with your wife,' the *aacchis* expressed displeasure and corrected me, suggesting that I should use *'aacchi'* and not *manaivi* (wife, in Tamil). Although I changed the word and said 'wife' (the English term is quite commonly accepted in modern Tamil), and then *ammaa* (lady, or wife, in this context), they refused to be satisfied until I corrected myself and said *'onga aacchi'* (your *aacchi*) to the Nagarattar man on the phone.

When a Nagarattar man marries a non-Nagarattar woman, she is never called an *aacchi* even if she is legally married. A non-Nagarattar woman with a highly respectable job who is married to a wealthy Nagarattar may be addressed as 'such and such *ammaa*' but not *'aacchi',* since she lacks both the alliance network within the Nagarattar community and the back-up from the female kin and affines. The ritual of *saandi* described in Chapter 6 is closely interwoven with the alliance relationship between them, also involving the woman's husband and her children.

Chapter 4

The Economics of Marriage

4.1 Marriage as a Contract, Marriage as a Sacrament

As Leach claims (1961: 107–8), varieties of what we call 'marriage' can be brought together and roughly defined as a 'bundle of rights' which involves both the legitimation of offspring and access to the spouse's sexuality, labour, and property.

Among the Nagarattars, marriage is a much more well-defined contract than Leach's 'bundle of rights', and the following documents and contract papers are provided in every marriage.

(1) The *muraichittai* (contract paper) is exchanged by both parties on the day of betrothal in which these detailed mutual promises are listed:

    (a) the amount of dowry *(siir danam* and *maamiyaar siir-danam);*

    (b) the quantity of jewellery and gold;

    (c) what the bride's party should do for the groom's party;

    (d) what the groom's party should do in return;

    (e) how much money is to be paid to the groom's party by the bride's party;

    (f) how much is to be paid to the bride's party by the groom's party;

    (g) what the bride's party should do on the first Pongal, Deepavali, in the fifth month of the first pregnancy, and on the birth of the first child;

    (h) the list of *saamaan* (goods) carried by the bride.

(2) The *moy panam eludal* (the attendance record) is signed by all the relatives as soon as the *muhuurtam* (the major ceremony of the wedding) is over and those attending the occasion traditionally pay 25 paisa (¼ rupee). *Moy* means payment,

Fig. 4.1.a. Displays of bridal *saamaan*

Fig. 4.1.b. Displays of bridal *saamaan*

and according to the Nagarattars, its collection is quite commonly practised among other South Indian castes for weddings, puberty rituals, and funerals in order to cover the the expenses incurred by the function (cf. Dumont 1983: 231; Good 1991: 105–7, 120). However, among the Nagarattars this collection of money does not have real economic meaning, but is merely treated as token money.

(3) The *'Isai padimaanam'* (mutual agreement) is signed by the fathers of the bride and the groom as soon as the *muhuurtam* (the auspicious moment, i.e. tying the *taali*) is over. The form is fixed and is written in a special notebook: '____'s son whose lineage Shiva temple is ___, married to ___'s daughter whose lineage Shiva temple is ___, on the date of ___.'

Until the early 1960s, the *moy panam eludal* and the *isai padimaanam* were recorded on palm leaves, but nowadays, special notebooks are used that are sold in Chettinadu. However, this document is signed not because the Nagarattars consider marriage as a pure contract but as a supplementary aspect to support marriage as an institution since they consider marriage basically non-dissoluble. Marriage, if considered as a pure contract, such as among the Muslims, is regarded as a 'civil contract' (cf. Rao 1995: 393; Pant 1995: 3) which can be easily dissolved. Although the Nagarattars maintain the contractual aspect in marriage, they still consider marriage a sacrament or a bond, which binds two families for generations. In the following, I shall describe how the marriage is arranged.

4.2 How to Arrange a Marriage

4.2.1 Going to See the Girl

It is usual among the middle class and upper-middle class Nagarattars for alliances to be offered either through relatives or friends. When a potential candidate arises, information is passed through the family and friends network, and the larger the network, the more likely the family is to make a good alliance. It is acceptable for the boy's or the girl's side to suggest the possibility of an alliance, and then the two sides will acquire information about family background, education, qualifications, etc. and whether the girl is physically attractive. Some members of the family go to see her in a gathering without letting the bride's party know. Temples, relatives' or friends' houses are the commonest places for this to occur especially when a function is being held. Once the offer of an alliance is made, it becomes difficult to reject it.

If the girl's side takes the initiative, her elders visit the boy's house to gain information and begin negotiations. In addition to giving a detailed account of the girl's background, they also discuss the amount of dowry (cash, gold sovereigns, and diamond jewellery) they are prepared to give her. In addition, the girl's property in terms of gold sovereigns and diamond jewellery is discussed.

Fig. 4.2. The grandmother of the bride sorts out the *saamaan*

According to an elderly informant, showing photographs is becoming common nowadays because of the lack of opportunity for public meetings between a prospective couple. Among the upper- middle class Nagarattars, attending relatives' weddings is a good opportunity to search for suitable alliances for their children, since almost all the relatives and affines come together for the ceremony.

When an offer of marriage is made, the boy's family considers several factors, and after comparing the offer with any others given, they decide whether they are prepared to accept it. If the boy's family are satisfied, they start the negotiations. According to my research however, it is rare among the upper class to find a completely unknown suitor because people become well acquainted with one another during functions such as weddings. I was also told by a middle-aged, middle class Nagarattar: 'The top group do not use intermediaries, but prefer to negotiate directly among themselves.'

4.2.2 Pen paakka (Seeing the Girl)

One of the families will visit the others' house for the *pen paakka*. At this stage, the alliance is almost fixed and although the boy can still refuse, it is very rare for him to do so. The relatives and the boy visit the girl and usually the boy's mother asks her what she is studying, whether she can cook and whether she can sing. Tea and snacks are provided but no meal is served to the boy's party because this would symbolize an intimate relationship between the boy and the girl which is only allowed after marriage. (If the girl's party want to entertain the groom's party by offering food, they may eat out at a restaurant.)

A middle-aged woman explained these pre-marriage precautions to me. She said that intimacy ought to be avoided until the *taali* is tied in case the marriage is suddenly cancelled because of a change of heart or a calamity befalling either side:

If the boy dies, or something goes wrong, it is always the girl who suffers. It is a pity if she loses her partner before she is even married. Who will then marry such a girl even if people know that she is pure?

The boy's party is given a room in the bride's house, where they discuss whether they approve of the girl. If they do approve of her, they fix the date of the wedding then and there, but if they do not like her or cannot decide immediately, they say that they will write a letter informing the bride's party of their decision in a few days. This process is very similar in both Brahman and non-Brahman castes.

4.2.3 *Betrothal:* Peesimudittal *or* Nicchaittal

The marriage date is fixed at this ceremony which should fall on an auspicious day. Both parties bring a plate of betel nuts and betel leaves with lime as a formality. A middle-aged Nagarattar said, 'The exchange of this plate is a symbol of "fixing up" the marriage and once it is fixed, neither party should go back.'

At this point, the detailed contract *muraichittai* (marriage contract paper) is exchanged and the groom's family bring a piece of gold for the *kaluttiru* to the bride's house. (If the girl is not going to bring a *kaluttiru*, this piece is included in her *taali* later.) It is only one gold sovereign but has an important symbolic significance as a gift from the groom's side. Fruits, betel leaves, areca nuts, tamarind, and bananas with a two rupee note should be given in a plastic bucket to all the relatives who attend the formal giving of the *kaluttiru* piece. Half or one-third of the fruits, betel leaves, and areca nuts given by the groom's party to the bride's party should be returned to the groom's side with some money attached as not reciprocating is considered bad manners because it is an ominous sign. Fruits given by the bride's party are distributed among the relatives. The elders of both parties have major roles, yet neither the bride nor the groom attend this transaction.

4.3 Does a Bad Marriage lead to a Divorce?

Only after such a formalized process of marriage transaction, can women get married and acquire the status of *sumangali*. Yet according to most Nagarattars interviewed, marriage is extremely difficult for women from poor families especially among the Nagarattars. Although most women I interviewed said that however difficult it may be, it is still preferable to get married and acquire the status of a married woman. *Sumangali* or 'the married woman' is the highest status of womanhood. A girl commented,

A woman is treated like a street dog unless there is someone to protect

Fig. 4.3. Nacchiammai with her Malaysian-made table fan

her. After her parents die, only her husband can protect her. He protects her from other men as it is a matter of his honour. The woman who does not belong to anybody is in danger because she falls prey to men.

The girls I met said that they did not want their grooms to have bad habits such as drinking, gambling, smoking, or womanizing. However, there is of course a chance of having a husband who has such vices. The following case study tells of the disaster that befell a married woman, although she still speaks in favour of arranged marriages because of the financial support a woman can get from her natal family.

CASE STUDY: Muttammal, twenty-five years old and married, has a child, and is presently taking an undergraduate course in a women's college at Chettinadu.

Muttammal is in her final year of a Master of Commerce course. Ten years ago when she married, her parents gave her Rs 50,000 in cash, out of which Rs 25,000 was her *siir danam* (her own property which is given from her natal family)and another Rs 25,000 was *maamiyaar siirdanam* (cash payment to her mother-in-law). The money deposited in her name has been managed by her father. She brought twenty sovereigns of *kaluttiru*, forty gold sovereigns, 1.5 kg. of silver, and two *nahai* of diamond jewellery to the marriage as part of her own property. These amounts show that she is slightly above middle class, like Nacchiammai who is married to a university lecturer.

Her husband did not prove to be worth the dowry as he had all kinds of vices. Soon after marriage, he started to live with another woman, and spent money on gambling and drink. He had a good job as a bank employee and so he had some money to spare. She could not bear his ways and so she returned to her parents' house with her daughter, taking her jewellery and gold with her. Now she lives in Karaikkudi with her parents who objected to her leaving her husband and tried in vain to patch things up. She had not actually divorced him, as her parents were still against it. Her husband sends her Rs 1,000 only once every three months which is of course, far from sufficient for her and her child to manage on and so most of the money still comes from her parents.

After she returned to her parents' house, she started a course at a college that she hopes will lead to a job in a bank. If this proves difficult, she wants to go for higher studies and become a lecturer. Muttammal regrets her early marriage. She was young and did not know the possible consequences. She was fifteen at the time and so her opinion was not considered important by her parents, but she feels that a girl should wait until she is twenty-one before she gets married so that she is more mature. Although she admits that her marriage was a failure, she still supports the idea of arranged marriages, as she believes that if her parents and relatives had been more careful to check the character of her husband, this mistake would not have happened. This case actually demonstrates one of the advantages of arranged marriages: if the man has been chosen by her parents, the woman can return home to her parents whenever she wants, because they are to blame for the failure of the marriage, and she can even stay there with her children. If, however, she chooses her husband herself, she loses the support of her family and so has no back-up if her marriage fails.

The girls I spoke to almost invariably disliked men with any of the four vices that they had singled out (womanizing, drinking, gambling, and smoking). I asked men of other castes and almost invariably they said that these vices were common, especially among the men of the Nagarattars. One Brahman professor who was teaching in a college in Karaikkudi even said that quite a few Nagarattar boys were addicted to narcotics.

Since their parents have money, they do not bother to lead a disciplined life. They feel they can spend money as they wish. Most Nagarattar boys I have met have had this attitude.

People who criticize these vices in the Nagarattars attribute them to their wealth since if they did not have an excess of money, they would not be able to cultivate such lifestyles and this view does indeed appear to have some validity. 'Unlike the Brahmans, the Chettiyars have acquired money. It is not unusual for some of them to cultivate such habits.' At the same time, another young professor who is a Nagarattar said,

People tend to tolerate vices if the man is rich. If he is not, people tend to be critical. Who cares if he has a concubine, or if he drinks, or gambles? People tolerate him if he is a rich man, because he can help others, donate a lot of money to the temples and build schools and hospitals.

Even if the wife is dissatisfied with her husband, the marriage contract rarely breaks down, as divorce is not regarded as a solution for women. Since remarriage is not customarily permitted among the Nagarattars, women who do divorce their husbands usually remain single for the rest of their lives. The worst prospect for a Nagarattar woman who divorces is the loss of her prestigious status as *sumangali* and the shame it causes her natal family, while by accepting her and providing help, the woman's natal family can at least save the worst situation. Marriage as a social contract is unbreakable for the Nagarattars, and the women clearly understand the aspect of 'contract' in marriage as much as anthropologists do.

4.4 The Economic Differences of Marriage

When I began this research in January 1991, one pound sterling was worth approximately Rs 25 to 26. The Indian rupee was devalued by around 25 per cent in July 1991, which led to an acute price rise. While wages in semi-urban and rural areas remained almost

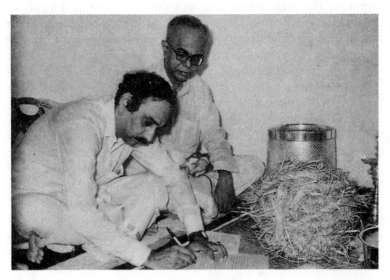

Fig. 4.4. Fathers of the bride and groom sign the marriage contract

unchanged, the cost of goods in these areas rose by up to 30 per cent. During 1991 I stayed in Karaikkudi one of the large towns in the Chettinadu area. At that time in Karaikkudi, a chauffeur earned Rs 750 to 800 per month, a schoolteacher earned around Rs 1,500, and a college professor earned Rs 4,000 to 7,000 per month.

Although the middle income group would regard a college professor's salary as more than adequate, it would still be difficult for a family on this income to provide the necessary amount of dowry for their daughter. Anxiety over dowries was expressed by parents everywhere. Unless the daughter inherits most of the jewellery from her mother,[1] the father has to make extra provisions. The situation could

[1] Although most of the mother's jewellery is given to the daughter on marriage, a few items, such as *taali* and *kaluttiru*, which are associated with her status as *sumangali*, cannot be relinquished until the mother's death. To lose them would signify the loss of her own auspicious status and so new ones are made for the daughter.

be quite difficult even for a well-to-do, middle-class Brahman family and of course, amongst the poorer sections, the problem is even more acute. I was told that a good number of unmarried girls are kept at home in Chettinadu, and that this practice was particularly prevalent amongst the Nagarattars, although this statement is difficult to prove. The Nagarattars are generally regarded as a rich caste, but in reality this is not always the case. The standard amount of dowry among the Nagarattars is high, and this can create difficulties in finding partners especially amongst the poorer sections. The following stories were collected during lengthy interviews while I was staying in Karaikkudi. They mostly originate from lower-middle class Nagarattars, who spoke of the difficulties they encountered when they were getting married. When I saw the vast discrepancy between their monthly income and the money required for a proper marriage, their problems became apparent and this went a long way towards explaining their parsimony in everyday life: it would be difficult to marry off a daughter unless money had been saved over several years. The Nagarattars believe that money should only be lavishly spent on important functions, such as marriages, funerals, *saandi*, etc. If they are poor, they eat cold rice with salt in order to save money for their daughter's marriage.

CASE STUDY 1.   Sala, twenty-two, unmarried and the sixth daughter out of seven siblings

When Sala's mother married Nagappan forty-two years ago, he was unemployed and they survived on her dowry. Later they started a small 'mess'[2] using money from her dowry but any profits they made were lost through her husband's gambling. She brought one diamond *taali*, a *kaluttiru*, some other gold jewellery, and cash to the marriage. Sala did not know how much they had cost, but most of them were lost through her father's weakness.

Sala's mother had seven children. The second daughter worked as a nurse for central government but is currently employed as a typist. She started work at seventeen and helped all her sisters acquire an education using her own income and money borrowed from her office and moneylenders. In this way she provided an education, food, and clothes for Sala and managed to raise enough money for the third daughter to be married.

[2] Locally, people commonly use terms such as 'hotel' or 'mess' to signify a restaurant or an inn.

None of Sala's brothers and sisters are married to relatives because they are too poor. They found partners either through friends or 'brokers'. Those who go to brokers are usually poor, and are unable to find anyone to arrange marriages for them. If the broker manages to create an alliance, he charges Rs 500 to both parties. The brokers do not make a profession out of finding people partners; all of them are Nagarattars and the job is only part-time.

In Sala's family, whenever one of the daughters got married, they received Rs 1,000 for Deepavali and Rs 500 for Pongal as a gift from the mother's house during the first year. The first, second, and third daughters received this money from their mother, but by the time the fourth and fifth daughters got married, their mother had died and so the money was sent by their sisters.

Sala is very pessimistic about her prospects of marriage.

Nowadays, even a boy who earns below Rs 1,000, who is a temporary worker and without a degree, demands at least Rs 40,000. If he has a degree, he will demand between Rs 60,000 and 100,000. Even if a girl can raise Rs 40,000, there is no guarantee of a happy marriage. Yet people talk about marriage all the time in the village. If a girl is not married, people gossip about her. In the city, people do not care. If a man is not able to make a woman happy, why should she marry? Even after marriage, the groom orders his wife to get things from her mother's house. Rather than being miserable in this way, I would ideally prefer to remain unmarried, and help my sisters, although I realize that it puts a woman in an untenable position.

She has been depositing money into the Life Insurance Corporation every month for four years, and her sister Valli also deposits Rs 1,000 annually. They plan to continue saving for fifteen years so that they can live on the interest as their pension. They also deposit Rs 54 per month in the Provident Fund. Sala, who has a Bachelor of Commerce degree, earns Rs 650 per month working at the school where she has been for four years. She is also currently studying for the B.Ed. (teacher's training course) and MA by correspondence and if she manages to complete these courses, she will be able to earn Rs 800 per month. Sala manages to save Rs 237.30 in total (Rs 100 is deposited in the bank, Rs 83.30 in Life Insurance and Rs 54 in the Provident Fund). She is financially independent and Table 4.1 shows her monthly expenditure out of an income of Rs 650. She adjusts the deficit by cutting some expenses each month. For example, she manages without entertainment or purchasing sweets and if her relatives bring her some wheat or rice, she manages without purchasing it for a few days.

Table 4.1: Sala's monthly expenses[a]

Expenditure	Rs
Rice	43.20
Coffee and tea	15
Sugar	10
Vegetables	40
Kerosene	30
Wheat and gram (chickpeas) (4 grams, ½ kg each)	40
Cooking oil	40
Milk	100
Fruit and sweets	20
Electricity	12.50
Loan (debt)	nil
Gift-exchanges	nil
Education (correspondence course)	83.30 (× 12)[b]
Clothes	83.30 (× 12)
Transportation (bus fare to visit relatives)	41.60 (× 12)
Savings	
Bank	100
LIC	83.30 (× 12)
PF	54
Total Expenditure	796.20
Monthly Income	600.00
Deficit	196.20

[a] Since Sala lives alone, the expenses are only for her.

[b] The Nagarattars calculate some of their finances on a yearly basis and so where I have had to divide the amount of money by twelve for the average monthly expenditure, I have placed '× 12' in brackets.

After having seven daughters, Sala's mother at last had a son. He went to school for ten years and now at twenty years old, works in Madras. He has health problems and finds it difficult to cope with night duties. However, Sala expects him to marry someone quickly and to receive at least Rs 100,000 on his marriage from the bride's side as *maamiyaar siir danam* (cash payment to the bride's mother-in-law before marriage). Out of this money, she would purchase *pattu sarees* (silk *sarees*), one gold sovereign for the bride, and give a feast on the night of the wedding. In addition, she wants to give her second sister a large share of this money, as she has spent a great deal of money on her other sisters and she would also like to buy sarees for each sister. Any money remaining would be kept in the joint account of the couple.

Sala's maternal uncle is rich, but he has five daughters and so is unable to help Sala's family, which she understands. As maternal uncle, he gave each of his nieces Rs 51 when they came of age, and at each Pongal, he still gives them Rs 11 each. N, the owner of the school where Sala works, gave her sisters Rs 500 when they married.

N's wife's father, who was related to Sala's father, would regularly help Sala's family financially, but since he died, N's family has not continued their support. Sala's mother has two friends who also helped by giving Rs 2,000 on the sisters' marriages. However, they do not help out as much now as they used to. Sala understands that it is difficult for poor women to find marriage partners, but she still hopes to get married some day. It is necessary for a woman to be married in order to protect herself from scandals. A single woman is placed in the same category as divorcees who are likely to be a topic of gossip and who are shown little respect.

CASE STUDY 2. Umayal, thirty-five, unmarried and lives alone

Umayal's parents died several years ago, and she now lives alone in a quarter in her father's ancestral house. The quarter in which she lives has no electricity but the other side, occupied by her relatives, does, and she manages with the light which comes from their side at night. She has sold all of her mother's silver vessels and most of her other vessels, but she has set a few brass vessels aside in case of emergency. Her elder married sisters suggest that she marry at around Rs 50,000, but Umayal does not know how she could possibly come up with so much money. A nearby Nagarattar *Sangam* (a caste association for the welfare of the community members) may give her around Rs 30,000 to 40,000 if she is lucky enough to be selected from a large number of candidates.[3] But she will still need another Rs 10,000 to meet the expenses of a wedding.

Umayal is a tailor and earns around Rs 300 per month. She still hopes to get married and has asked a marriage broker to find her a partner in Coimbatore where her relatives live. None of her relatives are willing to make the effort of trying to find an alliance for her because she is poor, and it has been suggested that her family depends on 'donations' from rich Chettiyars. Couples and relatives sometimes visit rich Chettiyars with printed invitation cards asking for help. They take the cards with them to prove that their marriage is finalized because they cannot obtain any money before this.

Table 4.2: Umayal's monthly expenses

Expenditure	Rs
Rice (10 kg)	54
Sugar (2 kg)	10
Kerosene (5 litres)	15
Milk	30
Vegetables	35
Clothes	50 (× 12)
Dhal (¼ kg)	30
Oil	20
Wood (collects her own)	free
Coffee	6
No electricity	
Total monthly expenditure	300

CASE STUDY 3. Janaki, twenty-seven, unmarried and works as a part-time teacher

Janaki is her parents' third child. She teaches part-time in a higher secondary school, and earns Rs 800 per month. She gives all her

---

[3] Nagarattar *Sangam* offers to help poor Nagarattars marry by offering money as the dowry. However, there are many candidates and so the chance of getting assistance is slim.

wages to her mother taking no pocket money for herself. There are eight members in her immediate family and they live in one-half of a room in her father's ancestral house. She has nearly given up all hope of marrying because of lack of money.

Table 4.3 shows the monthly expenditure of Janaki's household. The amount is almost the same every month and so she was easily able to give me a detailed account. It is unusual for her family to spend anything extra unless there is a special function.

Table 4.3: Monthly expenses for Janaki's household

Expenditure	Rs	Expenditure	Rs
Rice	350	Coffee, tea, sugar	150
Dhal (wheat, chickpeas, etc.)	160	Salt, pepper	50
Cooking oil	200	Milk	175
Vegetables, fruit	175	Fish (twice a week)	150
Sweets	25	Gas	10
Electricity	nil	Kerosene and wood	80
Education	100	Transportation	50
Clothes[a]	125	Entertainment	30
Gift exchanges	30	Repayments on loan	1,000

[a] One piece of clothing for everyone per year. They usually spend Rs 1,500 on the day of Deepavali.

Note: Total income in Janaki's household: Rs 3,100. Seven members eat together.

At present, they are Rs 35,000 in debt. They hope to repay the loan in one and a half years, as they expect Janaki's salary to increase and also to obtain a dowry on her brother's marriage.

Janaki's household has a few electric gadgets including an electric grinder, an electric mixer, and a black-and-white television set, which is typical of a moderately modernized household of the lower-middle class. However, despite the fact that Janaki works, she has not saved any money for her marriage, even though she feels that marriage is essential for a woman.

After a certain age, an unmarried woman will suffer. Even if she is "pure", people will say she sleeps with men to explain the fact that she cannot marry. A woman should marry — it is better to be married and suffer hardships than remain a spinster. If she behaves properly and bears the hardships, the whole community will be sympathetic.

As mentioned, Janaki says that she has not saved anything for marriage.

How is it possible? she says. A husband should be able to support the family, but if I want a well-qualified boy with a degree, the dowry is far too expensive. A boy with a similar qualification to mine would demand at least Rs 75,000 in cash, in addition to gold. Nowadays, Rs 40,000 is needed for a 10th standard education, Rs 45,000 for a 12th standard, Rs 55,000 to 60,000 for a degree holder. For a postgraduate, Rs 75,000 is required. In addition, *kaluttiru* is required as the status goes up. Diamond jewellery is also needed. As the cash payment increases, the number of gold sovereigns I should bring with me also increases.

When people criticize the dowry system, they often cite the greediness of the groom's party who 'demand' cash payment for his family. Yet in this case, this confuses the two problems which are different: the money which is demanded by the groom in order to be paid to his parents and the money which becomes the conjugal fund for the couple. In the case of the Nagarattars, the basic capital asset which is assumed to be necessary to start a marital life is higher than in other castes, and the girl's family who fails to meet this standard cannot marry her off. This standard of basic minimum is set higher than in castes such as the Komutti Chettiyars among whom fewer women are said to remain unmarried. A well-to-do *aacchi* thus laments, 'I can easily marry off four or five servants with the money I give to marry off a poor Nagarattar girl.'

However, once the woman gets married, the Nagarattar system of property-holding protects her property rights more than that of other castes. In other words, Nagarattar mercantilism controls the number of marriages not only by imposing a strict endogamous system but also controlling the number of people who can afford to marry. In some Chettinadu villages, I was told that there were some Nagarattar women who married Muslims and disappeared from the Nagarattar community.

If the girl is too poor to get married, marrying a Muslim is much easier since it is the man who pays the money. Of course, if this happens, she disappears from the Nagarattar community and her family loses face.

4.5 Is The Dowry System Undesirable?

According to some commentators of Hindu Law, the section on *stridhana,* or the woman's property is said to be the most difficult branch of Hindu Law (cf. Desai 1990: 157). Different schools give different definitions of *stridhana.* For example, Manu Smritis include gifts made before the nuptial fire, gifts made at the bridal procession, gifts made in token of love, gifts made through affection by her father-in-law and mother-in-law, and those made at the time of her making obeisance at the feet of elders, gifts made by the father, the mother, the brother, although other commentators agree that they are not the complete enumeration of *stridhana* (ibid.).

During my research, I also found out that in practice, different perceptions exist among different communities in terms of *stridhana.* In Madras, it was explained to me by women who were Gujarati Jains, Modh Banyas, and the Marwaris who were the Jains

Fig. 4.5. Kaluttiru (above) and diamond *taali* (below)

from Rajasthan. According to them, there exists a considerable difference between the Gujarati Jains (and Modh Banyas) and Rajasthan Jains in terms of acknowledging women's property. Gujarati Jains and Modh Banyas claim that cash payment to the groom's family used to be non-existent, and the *stridhana* used to be given mostly in kind, i.e. jewellery. Yet this comes both from her natal family and from the groom's family. In the case of a woman in her mid-fifties who was a Modh Banya married in 1964, her in-laws presented her thirty gold sovereigns in addition to thirteen *sarees* and some bridal goods.

In our community, parents do not give lavish gifts for marriage. On marriage, my parents gave me a nose-ring, a pair of earrings, one ring, and a necklace. In total, it was around thirty gold sovereigns, almost equivalent to the gift from my in-laws.

According to her explanation, only after marriage, can parents give gifts to their married daughter in her own name, since they feel lavish expenditure on marriage should not cause acute inequality between the rich bride and the poor one. In this community, the married woman's property comes from both the conjugal family and natal family, since, according to their explanation, mercantile households should hedge the fund to several members of the family, including the daughter-in-law and the wife.

Even if you keep some property in your wife's name, she is not going to divorce you. If things go wrong in your business, it is better to keep some property in her name since it would not be taken away by your business partners.

On the other hand, none of these practices exist among the Marwaris, another mercantile Jain community in Rajasthan.

In our community, the bride is expected to bring in a large amount of property on marriage only to be handed over to her mother-in-law. While she can claim almost nothing as her own, including her own jewellery and bridal goods and vessels, her natal family is expected to keep on sending her everything including a hair brush or toothpaste, supporting her financially till her death. As a bride, I have to live with my husband's natal family. Even my *sarees*, my food, and my pocket money should all come from my natal family so that I do not become the liability of my husband's family. Whenever I visit my natal family, my in-laws expect me to bring a lot of presents from them. On my return, I should report whatever I was given and hand over everything to my in-laws.

This status continues until she becomes the eldest woman in her husband's joint family. In other words, the patriarchal mercantile system of the Marwaris is strongly supported by the immediate and complete amalgamation of in-marrying women's property into the patrilineal joint family property. Thus *stridhana* as the married woman's property seems to be almost non-existent.

In-laws would feel that if the bride were given some property share of her own, she would immediately divorce and get freedom. Therefore, she is expected to have a son as soon as possible and wait until the day when she gets her own daughter-in-law. Ironically, only when she has her, can she have something to call her own.

The Komutti Chettiyars, another prominent mercantile caste in South India, have a patrilineally organized joint family system similar to the Marwaris. Yet to a certain extent, they acknowledge the *stridhana* as women's property which should be handed down from mother to daughter. While men share the patrilineally organized joint business property mostly undivided for at least several generations, in-marrying women's properties are jointly held under the custody of the eldest female. Unlike the Marwari joint family system however, the custody of women's property right is temporary, since the mother-in-law is expected to keep a separate safe box for each daughter-in-law and is expected to hand over each female member's property either when the joint family property is partitioned or when the daughter of the owner is getting married.

Until then, all the female members of the family can share the property. In other words, if the mother-in-law decides that a particular piece of jewellery of a particular daughter-in-law should be lent to another daughter-in-law, so be it. In this way, we can share all the jewellery as part of the family asset and display it at public functions. Even if we have to pawn the jewellery in order to get some loan for business, we can combine the entire jewellery together and offer it as pawn.

As these cases show clearly, in order to discuss modern 'dowry', it is necessary to differentiate the three situations; 1) the ownership belongs to the bride completely and should not be entrusted to others (the Nagarattar case); 2) the bride temporarily entrusts it to the eldest female member of the family (Komutti Chettiyar case); 3) the ownership itself is immediately transferred to the mother-in-law (Marwari case).

In the case of the Nagarattars, the ownership of the *stridhana* is

well protected so that every single piece of bridal goods is regarded
as part of her assets. In addition, what she acquires after marriage
through her savings, earnings, or by gifts given by relatives, are all
considered to belong to her, which are to be handed down to her
daughter.

Now I shall separately discuss the 'dowry evil', the cash payment
directly paid to the mother-in-law. This practice greatly differs from
caste to caste and from region to region. Srinivas discusses this cash
payment as a modern type of dowry, differentiating it from the old
type. In his discussion of dowry in modern India, he claims that
there are two types — traditional and modern types of dowries.
While the traditional type of dowry is regarded as the property of
woman, as Tambiah (1973a: 62) also maintains, the latter one is a
payment to the groom's family (Srinivas 1984: 14). While the richer
and higher strata of hypergamous castes paid huge sums by way of
dowry to obtain desirable grooms, the poorer members of the lower
strata even had to pay bride price, or have recourse to marriage by
exchange, either direct or indirect (ibid.: 14).

Srinivas denounces modern dowry as a disease and deterioration
as the groom's kin regard the wedding as an occasion for securing
the 'many and much-desired products of modern technology' (ibid.:
15). The reason why this 'disease' started, according to Srinivas, was
that young men who had salaried jobs, or careers in the professions,
were 'scarce commodities' at the turn of the century, and their
scarcity was exacerbated by the rule of caste endogamy and the need
to marry a girl before she came of age (ibid.: 11). Although Srinivas's
argument about the 'modern evil of dowry' corresponds to the
stories widely talked about in modern India, his definition of old
and new dowries is still confusing since, in a real setting, both appear
simultaneously.

According to Beck, 'dowry' can be differentiated from the property given to the girl by her natal family. She maintains that 'dowry'
refers to an actual sum of money demanded by the groom from the
bride's family, as *warata Tacanai'* (her spellings) while the general
household gifts the girl receives are simply *'kuTukka veeNTiya
murai'* (her spellings) 'that which she has the right to receive' (Beck
1972: 327).

Discussing the urban setting of Madras Christians, Caplan also
differentiates between two types of dowry, groom-price and the
woman's asset, i.e. *dowry* (his italics) and dowry (*stridhanam* or *siir*

danam) (Caplan, L. 1984: 217). Caplan maintains that in general, in South India, the practice of making cash offerings to the bridegroom's family is a comparatively new phenomenon.

This supports Srinivas' observation that this practice started at the turn of the century due to scarcity of eligible men in white-collar and therefore prestigious jobs with the British colonial government. This has become almost a pan-Indian phenomenon, although in the North, as Parry's Rajputs in Kangra exemplify (1979), a hypergamous tendency in the region is the basis for cash payments to the groom's side from the bride's natal family.

In South India, the tendency to pay cash is said to be not as predominant as that in the North, as both the bride's and the groom's sides tend to share the expenses incurred at the wedding (cf. Beck 1972: 326). According to Caplan's Christian informants in Madras however, they still have to pay groom-price (what they call *dowry*, using the English term) because if they do not, their daughters will remain unmarried, and the endogamy restriction means that there are simply not enough suitable boys to marry. In addition, they maintain that the groom's side should demand cash payment because they have to recoup the investment in their son's education (Caplan, L. 1984: 220). Thus those who are in enviable positions are the ones who can afford to give some property to their daughters on their marriage, and parents from up-coming families try to make such arrangements in order to enhance their status. Ifeka, also discussing the Christian communities in Goa maintains that her data shows obvious signs that economically less privileged peasant families have been shifting to marriage with dowry and withdrawing their women from field labour since the 1930s (1989: 267). Among the up-coming Christian toddy-tappers in Goa which she researched, none of the daughters or wives worked for others outside the home though one wife assisted her husband in selling locally brewed alcohol (toddy) (ibid.: 269).

Such a dramatic change in the marriage market suggests that while women's labour as cheap field labour is despised as a sign of poverty, men's wage earning capacity is excessively valued. Therefore, the scarcity of highly qualified grooms has made them an attractive and sought after merchandise in the marriage market, which goes a long way towards explaining the development of groom-price. Groom-price can thus be considered as a compensation in exchange for the economic dependence of the bride after marriage as both Srinivas (1984: 17) and Beck (1972: 230) maintain, since after marriage, both wife and children should be a man's dependents. Therefore, groom-price becomes the real 'dowry evil' in the case of poorer women who are deprived of earning a low wage as agricultural labour or factory worker or do not have the means to earn their own money, or to have their own assets. The argument on dowry however is not yet complete unless we discuss the point of the transformation of women's earning power in the money market economy.

For example, discussing the Moroccan case, Maher (1984) also discusses the transformation of women's earning power. After the introduction of a money economy, work relations and even the work itself attached to women underwent considerable change. Women's work is composed of repetitive activities such as the care of animals, the cultivation of crops, food processing and cooking, cleaning and care of the household members (ibid.: 120–1). These works do not give access to money and confine the woman's sphere of social relations to the domestic area which is distant from sources that could endow women with prestige and status (ibid.: 123). Women do not sell products which derive from their own agricultural work but leave this work to men and are therefore left as pure consumers in the money market (ibid.: 125).

Just staying at home does not mean that women are deprived of earning power or lack economic and social power. This happens only when they do not have access to the money market where they can convert their labour into cash. Rather than earning meagre wages by day labour, the Nagarattar women may use the assets given to them by their parents for moneylending, or pawning when they need instant cash. Women may help in looking after the land, even paying periodical visits from cities to their villages (cf. Sharma 1984), they may manage the family business or keep a cow or bullocks to earn some cash. Indeed, lending money to relatives and neighbours and pawning their jewellery when the family needs instant cash are essential means of enhancing the decision-making power of the wives in their in-marrying families.

What is described by Srinivas as the 'dowry evil' in the money economy resembles the situation which Maher describes as the case of Moroccan women since Srinivas criticizes the introduction of cash-oriented money economy introduced in the British period. Prestige is given to the white-collar Brahman groom who has power to earn money while Brahmanic women and urbanized middle class women lost the means to maintain their own economic autonomy.

Compared to the Nagarattar women, Brahman women used to have less opportunity to earn money. Rather, they looked down upon Nagarattar women for getting petty cash by selling jasmine from their gardens or by selling milk from their cows. Yet the Nagarattar women were far more exposed to the money market through their savings, and property in goods and kind. When things went wrong, they were ready to sell their bridal goods to make ends meet. Small-scale moneylending, sale of small goods and services are still part of their commonest activities, the income from which women keep in their own name.

In other words, the Nagarattar ideology makes the *siir danam (stridhanam)* the business principal for women, which is to be handed down from mother to daughter. Marriage is part of their business activities which require the principal. Therefore, dowry demands become 'evil' for those who cannot afford it since without this principal, the Nagarattars refuse to let women get married and so get endowed with the title of *aacchi*. The title, after all, is given to women who are married. I shall now discuss the 'business principal' which belongs to the Nagarattar women.

4.6 *Muraichittai* (Contract Paper)

Nowadays, the average amount used for a *taali* is sixteen gold sovereigns (128 g) among the Nagarattars. It is unacceptable to give less than ten sovereigns as a *taali* to a daughter. One Nagarattar lamented that because of inflation and the increase in the price of gold, giving *kaluttiru* to their daughter had become more and more difficult.

Nacchiammai married in 1981, and her *muraichittai* was as shown in Table 4.4.[4]

Nacchiammai's mother who married in 1968 followed a different measurement system for the calculation of gold and jewellery, and

---

[4] For convenience, I did not follow the method of Nacchiammai's father who uses both g and mg to note down the gold jewellery. Although it is conventional to write 31 grams and 600 mg as 31.6 g, he wrote it as 31 g. 600 mg. Among some families, gold is not mentioned in the *muraichittai* at all as a tax evasion policy.

old Nagarattars say the system has changed several times. In Nacchiammai's case, the future promises and obligations of both parties
were not listed in the book although it was supposed to be included
in the *muraichittai,* as I mentioned before. Nacchiammai's father
made the *muraichittai* much simpler and allowed it to be omitted.

Table 4.4:   Nacchiammai's *muraichittai*

Items	Weight (g)
Kaluttiru 32 pieces[a]	22
Small *taali* chain	31.9
Puuchalam (diamond *taali*)	529.6
Bangles (8 items)	91.2
Ring (1)	6.4
Old diamond earrings (1 and ¼ carat)	6.8
New diamond earrings	4.2
Bead earrings	6
Small chain for the groom	23.9
Watch strap (for the groom)	32
Diamond ring (for the groom)	6.5
Tombu (small gold piece for *kaluttiru*)	42

[a] *Kaluttiru* is a necklace which consists of thirty-two small pieces of gold.

The gift-exchange record starts on the day of the marriage, when
a piece of gold is brought by the bride's party as part of *kaluttiru.*
At that time, the groom's side should give some money to the
bride's relatives. Those who are given money are both the paternal
and maternal close relatives of the bride, i.e. her parents and
grandparents. Forgetting to give money to them is a sign of dis-
respect, although the amount given to each member is minimal.
As shown in Table 4.5, the money is considered to be a token used
as an essential ritual item rather than money itself.

As is the case of *moy panam eludal* (small amount of money
given by close relatives at the time of their signing up as marriage
witnesses), money is handled mostly as an auspicious ritual item
among the Nagarattars. *Moy* collection on ceremonial occasions is

quite common among South Indian castes (Dumont 1983: 81–3; Good 1991: 105–7) where it makes up a substantial part of the ceremonial expenses, especially among the poor sections, as Good recorded (Good 1991: 105–7).[5] However the Nagarattars do not regard the *moy* as a money collection, but as an attendance token, since 25 paisa or 1 rupee does not have much value by itself especially to the middle class Nagarattars. Similarly, the payments to the relatives shown in Table 4.5 may be seen as a ritual payment of money in the same way.

Table 4.5: Money gift-exchanges at Nacchiammai's wedding

Receivers of bridal gifts	Amount (Rs)
Bride's father and mother[a] (Rs 5 × 2)	10
Grandfather and mother of the bride[a]	21
Bride's grandfather's brother[a]	7
Bride's paternal uncle[b]	4
Bride's maternal uncle[b]	4
Three brother-in-laws of the groom[b] (Rs 2 × 3)	6
To the bride's maternal grand-uncle a plastic bucket with a lid	7
Gifts from the groom's house to his pangaalis	
To the groom's maternal grandfather one plastic bucket	7
To his son, i.e. the groom's maternal uncle one plastic bucket	4
To the groom's father-in-law one plastic bucket	4
His bride's sisters' husbands (two people), two plastic buckets (Rs 2 × 2)	4

[a] In addition, they receive some buckets of fruit, betel leaves and areca nuts.
[b] In addition, the party receives a brass bowl, a plastic box, one *kottaan* (a small bamboo basket, seven small plastic buckets, and two plastic plates.

[5] For example, when I was studying the Mariyamman festival in 1985–6, the *moy* collection added up to a substantial amount especially among the Scheduled Castes, even though the amount donated by *pulli* was around Rs 1 to Rs 2.

As another example, I cite the marriage record of Janaki's brother which took place in 1981.

Table 4.6: Money gift-exchanges at Janaki's brother's wedding

To thirty-one *pulli* (close relatives, both maternal and paternal) with 31 plastic plates   62

Items	Amount (Rs)
siir danam from the bride	2,001
In exchange for *kaluttiru*	2,001
In exchange for *maamiyaar saamaan*	10,501

Bride's party should do the following

When the boy comes and sees the girl *(pen paakka),* the girl's party should give one plastic bucket

2 bunches of bananas

4 mangoes

Rs 16

When the groom's relatives come to see the girl, they are given

6 plastic buckets

Rs 30

After tying the *taali* to the bride (at the wedding), the groom's party is given one big plastic bucket

For the mother-in-law's ritual

This is called *manaavalai sadangu* (Chapter 6 for detail)

mother-in-law: one plastic bucket

Similarly, as Good's case shows, lower castes seem to collect *moy* from most of the people attending the occasion, including neighbours and friends both at the weddings and funerals in order to cover their expenses.

Table 4.6 (contd)

4 daughters: one plastic bucket each. In addition, they all receive one bunch of bananas and 10 oranges

The 5 relatives (as above) who perform the ritual are given Rs 31 each

To those who fix the date of *muhuurtam,* 2 members (i.e. the parents), are given 2 plastic buckets and Rs 10 each

When the bride takes leave of her natal house to go to live at the groom's house

6 people are given one plastic bucket and Rs 5 each

At pen alaippu *(inviting the bride to the groom's house)*

The bride's house give the groom's parents the following

2 plastic buckets

2 bunches of bananas

4 oranges

Rs 22

To thirty-one *pulli* (close relatives, both maternal and paternal) with 31 plastic plates   62

When the groom is invited to the bride's house, the following are given to the bride's relatives in return for the gifts given to the groom

One aluminium box

One bag

One box

9 aluminium boxes

3 stainless steel containers

Note: The elders from the bride's side meet the groom in the temple and he is given a gold chain, a watch, a scarf, and a ring from the bride's party then and there. See the next chapter for details to this ritual.

Table 4.6 (contd)

When the taali *is tied, the following is given by the bride's side to the groom's relatives*

Groom's grandfather	10
Groom's father and mother	31
Betel nuts and betel leaves	10
Groom's 3 younger brothers (3 × Rs 7)	21

When the bride is invited to the groom's house (pen alaippu), *the groom gives the following to the bride's relatives*

Groom's father and mother-in-law	31
Groom's father-in-law's father	10
Father-in-law's grandfather	10
Father-in-law's father's three daughters' families (to 3 *pullis*) (3 × Rs 10)	30

From the bride's side to the groom's relatives

Groom's eldest brother	10
Bride's maternal aunt's husband, i.e. groom's brother's wife's father	10
Groom's paternal uncle	10
Maternal uncle	10
Two other close families	20
Given instead of fruit	21
Goldsmith (given as a token of *kaluttiru*)	4
Betel leaves and areca nuts	4
To the female relative who does the *aaratti*	2
For the *padaippu*	2
To a servant	7
Another servant	16
Fruit	21

Table 4.6 (contd)

Vegetables	4
Areca nuts	4
Food	7
Groom's maternal grand-aunt's husband	10
Maternal grand-aunt's sons and daughters (Rs 7 × 7)	49
Grandchild of maternal grand-aunt	5
To another grandchild	5
Ditto	5
Paternal grand-uncle	10
Paternal uncle	11
Groom's brother's father-in-law	29
31 *pullis*	155
35 *pullis* (Rs 2 × 35)	70
Eldest brother's father-in-law	31
Second brother's father-in-law	31
Third brother's father-in-law	31
Maternal grandmother	101

Promises for the first Pongal

Buckets (for salt and tamarind)	7
Cylindrical-shaped containers (stainless-steel) with lids and handles	3
Plastic plate	1
Iron stoves for *Pongal* preparation (for the first *Pongal*)	2
Pots	2
Stainless-steel vessels	2
Small vessel	1
Big spoons	2
Small spoons	2

Table 4.6 (contd)

Sackful of rice (50 kg)	1
Half a sackful of paddy (25 kg)	
Plastic buckets	21
Cylindrical vessels for oil	2
Aluminium oil container	1
Rs 10	
shikkaai powder (kg)	1

Janaki's family is middle class, and so the above wedding list is not spectacular, but is fairly average among the Nagarattars. Included on this list are the promises of the first-year Pongal, and according to Janaki's mother, the items listed above are already given on the day of marriage. In addition, the items listed in Table 4.7 are given to the groom's side in the basket carrying ritual *(Veevu[6] Irakka)*. As I explain later, the *Veevu Irakka* ritual is supposed to be done after one year of marriage, the idea being that it should be a gift of provisions carried by the bride's maternal uncle and her brother to her house. 'We do it on the day of the marriage now since we live in a busy world where the couple can not be sure whether they'll be able to receive the gift in the traditional manner.'

Table 4.7: Record of wedding money transactions (1)

When the groom's family say that they accept the daughter *(peesim-uditu),*[a] the bride's party gives

The first instalment to her dowry	Rs	1,001
Maamiyaar siir danam	Rs	10,501
To the groom's house	Rs	1,001
For the veevu irakka *basket carrying ritual*		
Money	Rs	25
Coconuts		10

[6] *Veevu,* is a word from a caste dialect of the Nagarattars which means *veelvu,* or marriage presents (cf. Fabricius 1972: 906).

Table 4.7 (contd)

Sugar (kg)	1
Pumpkin	1
Bundles of 50 banana leaves	10
Bunches of bananas	2
Betel leaves and areca nuts on a plate	
Sugar cane	
A bunch of turmeric with Rs 5 note	

These are given to the groom's party in a basket
In exchange, Rs 31 is given to the bride by the groom's side

From the bride's side to the groom the following should be given

Small chain	1
Gold ring	1
Gold watch	1
Table fan	1
Radio	1

[a] *peesimudittu* is the ceremony of betrothal in which the groom's side formally states that they will accept the girl as the bride, thus the payment must have been over before the wedding. However, Janaki's family notebook recorded this payment here.

Table 4.8: Record of wedding money transactions (2): Janaki's brother's wedding (groom's side)

26th April 1981
Rs 6,000 is handed to the groom
The remaining Rs 3,500 is to be given on the day of the marriage[a]

Murukku (snack)	151
Measures of sweets	7
Cylindrical vessel to make *biriyani*	1
Close relatives were given Rs 25 each	5

Table 4.8 (contd)

When the bride performs the ritual of holding the idol[b] in the *pallu* (the flapping part of the *saree*), Rs 16 is given to her by her parents

---

[a] As this record shows, they paid the *siir danam* and *maamiyaar siir danam* by instalments.
[b] This is a ritual to symbolize the birth of a child.

As seen in Janaki's brother's record, there are two noteworthy things about the gift transaction. First, the exchange takes place as a mutual gift-exchange, but the gift from the bride's side to the groom's side is excessive and the money and goods are always accompanied by ceremonial gift items such as fruits, betel nuts and betel leaves, plastic buckets, and sweets. On the other hand, the groom's gift to the bride's side is more ceremonial, and even simpler, signifying the fact that the gifts given to the daughter on marriage are part of her share of her father's property. Therefore, the immediate need of the couple is catered for mainly by the bride's family while the groom's share of his father's property comes much later after his father has died.

The money is an auspicious token in the ceremony, as the amount given to each member is always a number considered to be auspicious such as 31, 7, 21, etc. (Even a large sum of money such as the dowry should be an auspicious number such as 2,001, 101.) Those who participate in a ritual (e.g. the goldsmith, a female relative) receive a small amount of money (two to four rupees), with betel leaves and areca nuts. The money given to the relatives is not a substantial amount, but used as an auspicious ritual object, since money itself is the symbol of wealth. The Nagarattars also believe that sending the participants and relatives away empty-handed is not good, since the host should show his respect to the participants and return their goodwill in the form of gifts. The giving of gifts at the wedding assures the continuation of gift-exchange for several generations. Those who are given money and gifts should reciprocate by giving gifts on their children's marriage. Children who were given money at this time will invite their uncles and aunts to their wedding feasts. In this way, reciprocal gift-exchange extends the social relationships based on kin and affinal networks.

A daughter and her dowry become vehicles for setting up a

relation of affinity between the bride's family and the husband's family and this relationship of affinity is accompanied by gift-giving which persists long after the marriage rite.

While the man's ancestral property is traditionally pooled in his natal family which is patrilineally organized and cannot easily be divided from the main line, the woman's property forms a large part of the conjugal fund. Ideally speaking, it should be kept untouched until their daughter gets married. However, if the husband needs funds immediately for his business, he can utilize it with the consent of his affines. However, the transaction in marriage is based on reciprocity and even the groom's side should spend a large sum, although this is normally not as much as that spent by the bride's side.

4.7 Cash Payment and Its Increase

As I maintained already, when the English term 'dowry' is used in a modern context, it has a rather negative connotation, since it is considered to be the obligatory cash payment made to the groom's family. It is said that the mother-in-law of the bride will use it for her own purposes; in particular, to marry off her daughter. Therefore, money which is given out of 'affection' *(periyam)* is not generally considered to be a 'dowry' by the South Indians. 'Please give whatever you want to your daughter. It's completely up to you,' would be considered a very generous attitude on the part of the girl's future father-in-law if expressed to her father during negotiations on the amount of dowry before betrothal. Yet people say such an attitude is becoming very rare nowadays.

For most families, it is traditional for the parents to make known the amount of 'cash' that will exchange hands at marriage during preliminary negotiations. For example, when the girl's father or a relative goes to the boy's house to make an offer, he should present the amount in this way. 'The girl will bring a dowry of Rs 10,000, and forty gold sovereigns.' After considering other factors such as the girl's family background, her physical features (her complexion etc.) and her qualifications etc., the boy's parents decide whether they believe it to be a good alliance. If they are happy with the offer, they may agree to go and see the girl *(pen paakka)*, and at this point the betrothal is nearly fixed, although the boy is still given the opportunity to reject the girl after seeing her.

Among the Nagarattars, there are two kinds of cash payment from the bride's house. One is the conjugal fund given to the daughter as her own property *(siir danam)*. Among the middle class and lower-middle class, this is pooled in a joint bank account which needs the signature of both the husband and the wife. The other payment is the *maamiyaar siir danam,* which is made to the mother-in-law, as a sign of goodwill. Traditionally, Nagarattar women's main property consists of jewellery and gold, although other items such as cash, various kinds of vessels and household utensils are also common. However there has been an acute rise in the phenomenon of cash payments since the 1960s. One senior Nagarattar remembers that when he got married, people never paid cash immediately. Instead, the groom was given papers, somewhat like a draft check by his father-in-law, and in time of need, he could go to his father-in-law and get the cash. However, the Nagarattar laments, 'Nowadays people do not trust each other and if the money is not paid before the wedding, the mother of the groom would think nothing of cancelling the wedding!'

Concerning this relatively recent development of cash payment, a wealthy *aacchi* recalled that her family was partially responsible.

Formerly, cash payments had never exceeded 3,500 rupees. In 1961 when I got married, my mother gave me one lakh in cash along with other assets such as stock bonds and jewellery, etc. This started the competition of cash dowries, although cash carried by the bride remains with her, and her husband's family cannot touch it, but her husband can increase it. Six months later, when one of my relatives married, she carried one and a half lakhs with her. Nowadays, a lakh has become the common denomination of cash payment.

This *aacchi* belongs to the upper class, and from the information she gave, it is possible to deduce that this kind of competitiveness amongst the upper class may also have affected the upper-middle class, and gradually might have involved the lower economic groups too.

However, the payment made to her by her parents of one lakh was hers alone, since in the upper class, there is no money transaction between the two parties, and everything the bride brings to the marriage is regarded as her property. Normally, wealthy families make a separate 'file' for each member of the family and thus the bride's property as a whole is in her name. In this group, the payment to the mother-in-law does not normally take place. According to them, they are not interested in monetary gain but in getting an alliance with a good family with a good reputation. Another reason could be that a daugher is regarded as the representative of her natal family, and the chances of her own assets still being in control of her natal family are large. Therefore, demanding some cash payment may be considered to be a disgrace. Moreover, as the bride carries a large sum of assets as her own, her contribution to her conjugal family may be considered to be far larger than the immediate cash payment to the groom's family. On the other hand, the *mammiyaar siir danam* which is paid in cash, seems to have originated in the 'goods' given to the mother-in-law *(maamiyaar saamaan)* as an expression of goodwill, since there are some *muraichittai* which still record goods for the mother-in-law. If goods are given to her, no cash payment is made. In other words, payment replaces the exchange of goods.

Siir danam remains as the bride's fund. This fund remains in her name or sometimes is put in the joint account she shares with her husband. The groom has no access to the fund if he divorces her, nor does he have any right to the bridal goods or jewellery she carried with her. According to Manickawasagar, the husband of Nacchiammai, the amount for *siir danam* and *maamiyaar siir danam* has been increasing for the past two decades. The records for five brothers including him is shown in Table 4.9.

Table 4.9: Dowries received by five brothers

	Year of marriage	siir danam *(Rs)*	maamiyaar siir danam *(Rs)*	*Amount of gold and jewellery*
1st	1969	3,000	6,000	55 sov. +2 *nahai*
2nd	1973	3,000	6,000	60 sov. +2 *nahai*
3rd	1975	10,000	11,000	60 sov. +2 *nahai*
4th	1981	10,000	21,000	60 sov. +2 *nahai*
5th	1991	10,000	65,000	50 sov. +2 *nahai*

The records of their mother (married in 1946) and Nacchiammai's mother (married in 1962) are shown in Table 4.10.

Table 4.10: Dowries brought in by two brothers

Year of marriage	siir danam (Rs)	maamiyaar siir danam (Rs)	Amount of gold and jewellery
1946	5,000	3,000	100 sov. +3 *nahai*
1962	3,000	2,500	75 sov. +2 *nahai*

The economic status of the bride is judged by the amount of gold and diamond jewellery she can bring to the marriage. (*Nahai* literally means 'jewellery' in Tamil, yet in Table 4.10, it is used as a unit to count sets of diamond jewellery.) The mother of Manickawasagar must have been from an upper-middle class income group, since she carried three *nahai* and one hundred sovereigns. Her husband, on the other hand, would not be able to place all five of their sons in such a good financial position.

As I mentioned before, the status of the groom is affected by the family property. The father of a daughter takes into consideration the number of sons and daughters in the groom's family when he arranges his daughter's marriage. Having five sons in a family would not be favoured by the bride's party, as the ancestral property would be divided equally among the five.

However, Nacchiammai's mother managed to give sixty gold sovereigns and the same amount of diamond jewellery that she received on her own marriage to her daughter, because she is the only female child.

4.8 Importance of Jewellery and Gold for Women

As the above case clearly shows, the status of the bride's family is clearly assessed by the amount of cash and jewellery she brings with her. While cash payment is a relatively recent phenomenon, jewellery used to be the most important asset for Indian women throughout history; thus, its peculiar position as a status carrier is understandable.

In August 1991 the price of gold per sovereign was around Rs 3,192. One sovereign was 8 g. Therefore, fifty sovereigns were worth approximately Rs 159,600. At that time, the cost of silver was approximately Rs 74 per 10 g. Although I got such information through newspapers, I was amazed by the fact that most women

(unless they were below marriageable age) did know the approximate market price of both items without even checking the newspaper. Thus this fact would clearly show the importance of these
items for women.

In most Hindu families, the major part of a woman's property
consists of gold jewellery. Among the Nagarattars, it has even
more importance. As soon as a girl is born, the parents start to
collect gold jewellery. Gold is most favoured, as it is a safe
investment against inflation, or so it is thought. If a woman wants
instant cash, she may take her gold ornaments to a jewellery shop,
where the shop owner will weigh it, and pay her according to the
day's price for gold. Thus, it is the weight of each ornament which
counts.

In South India, the *taali* is the symbol of married status, and
no woman removes it until the death of her husband, as it is
considered to be bad luck. There is only one *taali* for every woman.
However, rich Nagarattar women change *taalis* sometimes, since
they have a few. Normally, the woman wears one *taali* which she
will have worn on her wedding day. It is also called *tiru-man-
galiyam,* since it is the symbol of auspiciousness *(mangalam)* with
the image of Lakshmi (the goddess of wealth) in the centre and
a very small ruby on it. In addition, another *taali* such as an oil
bath *taali (ennei taali)* is given along with *kaluttiru,* a necklace
with several large hand-shaped gold ornaments. Both the oil *taali*
and *kaluttiru* have the centre-piece of Lakshmi with a red spot,
since this is the most essential part of the *taali.* The idea of the
oil bath *taali* is that when they take an oil bath every week, they
wear the oil bath *taali* first and remove the normal *taali* since not
wearing any *taali* even momentarily is considered a bad omen.
According to one middle-aged *aacchi,* the oil is not good for the
gold, and so a simpler and smaller *taali* is worn to bathe. This is
obviously wrong, since gold is not affected by oil. According to
one senior Nagarattar man, the *taali* suffers wear and tear because
the women wear them constantly, so that the erosion of the *taali*
(normally it is around 0.5 g or so) should be recovered at least
every four or five years: 'The *taali* should be maintained at the
same weight, but some will ask for more gold to be added when
it is sent to the goldsmith.' In the meantime, the women are
supposed to wear something around their necks and so a replacement or another *taali* is a practical way to be consistent with the

ideal that a married woman should always wear a *taali* with a gold chain around her neck[7]

In our caste, *taali* has always been put on a gold chain, since we feel that it's necessary to protect it with this chain. At the wedding, the *taali* is already set in a gold chain and hung around the neck by the groom after the *kaluttiru* is tied around the neck.[8] Among other castes, the yellow thread of the *taali* is changed into a gold chain later.[9] Therefore, women of non-Nagarattar caste would wear their *taali* with yellow thread until the chain was ready. Setting the centre piece into the chain takes only a few minutes at the shop, and in the meantime, the woman merely wears the yellow thread. We don't like it. A woman should never remove her *taali* once she puts it on while her husband is alive. That's why we provide other *taalis* so that she can leave her main one at the goldsmith's for a few days. Among other castes, *taali* was only three small gold pieces which were placed into a mere yellow thread, and they used to change the thread once a year. It is only recently that other castes have started to use gold chains, too. But we do not like to remove the *taali* for even a single moment. A wife should also wear the *taali* with its original weight, which should always be the same, or even more.

However, as I describe in the next chapter, the most important ritual item at the *muhuurtam* is not the *taali,* but the *kaluttiru.* The *kaluttiru* is a special ornament used only by the Nagarattars as a symbol of a woman's wealth. It is customarily taken from the bride's house to the groom's house one day before the wedding. The gold for the *kaluttiru* is handed over to the goldsmith in the bride's house, and the goldsmith hits the gold with his hammer symbolically before he takes it to his house to make it into a *kaluttiru.*

Even if there is no *kaluttiru* to be handed over, the Asari (goldsmith) is still called in and a piece of gold is hit by his hammer, and then added to the gold of the *taali.* The role of the Asari is thus crucial for women. However, the Asari is considered to be inauspicious. This may be because he appears either for making a

[7] According to a Smartha Brahman woman, they have two *taalis* one piece is given by the groom's family and the other by the bride's family. However, in their case, both are set on one thread for the wedding, and are worn together, or one of the pieces is kept in a safe.

[8] As I explain in the next chapter, the *kaluttiru* is tied around the neck with yellow thread, and tying this is the major ritual of the wedding.

[9] Those who are not well off keep on wearing their *taali* with yellow thread. However, since it gets dirty, the thread is changed every year, just like the *puunul* (white thread of Brahmans which signify the status of the twice-born, a high caste).

gold ornament or melting it, i.e. when a woman becomes a widow. Another explanation may be the sacred thread *(puunul)* he wears. A middle-aged Nagarattar man told me: 'Asaris are inauspicious since they wear the *puunul* like the Brahmans.' I could not pin down the specific reason for the inauspiciousness of the Asaris. In any case, whatever the reasons, for him to be the first person or thing a man sees on leaving his house is considered a bad omen. A middle-aged woman asked her Asari not to come before four o'clock one day so that her husband who was leaving on a business trip would not see him on his way out.

Seeing a black cat crossing on your way is very ominous. Similarly, seeing the Asari when you are away from home is bad. Brahmans like black cats and keep them at home. But we do not like cats. They are inauspicious.

The groom's party collects the unassembled *kaluttiru* from the bride's family on an auspicious day. The assembling of the *kaluttiru* is strictly a job for a man on the groom's side, and can only be done by the elderly males of the groom's family. The *kaluttiru* pieces are joined together with strong white thread. Two elders unravel a length of about the width of the outstretched arms, fold it into three, and weave it into a chain. The thread is soaked in turmeric water, and should be strong enough to sustain the weight of thirty-four gold pieces. It is then folded in half, making a length of twenty-one *paahai,* which is about the length of an outstretched arm. The gold pieces are threaded onto it, and it is then knotted at both ends. Each elder applies the turmeric (yellow paste, and symbol of auspiciousness) many times until the thread becomes unbreakable.

Since *kaluttiru* includes the *taali,* the symbol of *sumangali,* breaking the cord is an inauspicious omen. Both *kaluttiru* and *taali* are associated with *sumangali,* and consequently even an elderly woman who is over eighty would never part with her *taali* or *kaluttiru.* If she dies as a *sumangali,* both the *taali* and the *kaluttiru* would be handed down to her daughter or granddaughter. If she becomes a widow, both the *taali* and the *kaluttiru* are melted and the gold is given to her daughter.

The severing of the cord is extremely inauspicious, as it symbolizes the death of the woman's husband, and an accidental break of the cord before marriage becomes highly significant for both parties. Leaving the job to the males of the groom's side is believed to be the safest way for both parties. First, by being the groom's party, they cannot hope for the bride to become a widow. Secondly, by being elder males who are responsible for the prosperity of the house, they have every reason to protect the groom, and are thus protectors of the *taali*. Thirdly, because they are males, they would not be jealous of the wealth and happiness of the bride. Both parties are afraid that the women of the groom's side may unknowingly cast the 'evil eye' upon the *kaluttiru* if they are dissatisfied with their lives. Since it is to be worn by the bride, a woman of the other party, the women of the groom's side prefer to leave the job to their men in order to avoid misunderstandings. The ritual significance of the broken thread is grave; the *kaluttiru* is worn only by the *sumangalis* and the breaking of the cord is highly inauspicious. Since the welfare of the bride depends on the life of her husband, it must never be allowed to break.

The *kaluttiru* is very rarely used. After the wedding, it is kept in a safe. Traditionally, it is worn in the wedding ceremonies and *saandi* of close kin and affine. For the *saandi* of a woman's husband, the wife would wear the *kaluttiru* along with a new diamond *taali*. One middle-aged Nagarattar woman said to me,

Other castes criticize the *kaluttiru* as a vulgar ornament, but to view the *kaluttiru* as an ornament is a mistake. Its significance lies in the fact that it is a woman's property, and she only wears it on very important ceremonial occasions.

Along with gold, the most valuable items amongst a woman's property are her diamonds. Although almost all married women above middle class wear diamond studs and sometimes a nose decoration *(mookkutti)*, these are taken for granted and do not count as sets among the Nagarattars. Because diamonds are the most valuable assets of women, their selection is considered to be of the upmost importance. The size of a diamond bought is dependent on the budget — obviously, larger stones tend to be more expensive and so people choose smaller stones and ask the goldsmith to set them in traditional designs.

Diamond jewellery is considered, in general, an essential for South Indian women above the middle class and at least one piece of diamond jewellery is given to a marrying daughter unless the family is extremely poor. In Tamil Nadu, a diamond is particularly associated with Brahmans and Chettiyars, since these two castes used to be more affluent than others. The stone is believed to have strong powers and so special precautions are taken when they are purchased. One Brahman woman said to me,

We always buy our diamond jewellery from a jeweller who is well known to us. Even if they are very tiny pieces of jewellery such as a pair of studs with small diamonds, we would not purchase them straight away, but inquire into the history of the diamond. If it was ever in the possession of another family, we need to know what kind of family they were. If the diamond has been worn by an unhappy woman, we would never take it, no matter how beautiful it may be. When we are not sure about the history of the diamond, we borrow it, we put it under our pillow and sleep for three nights or so. If you do not have bad dreams, the diamond is acceptable. If you have bad dreams, you return it.

A diamond is the most precious of stones and has been so for centuries. Therefore, a piece of good diamond jewellery may not necessarily be a new one. Because a diamond is the hardest material in the world and outshines other stones with its purity and clarity, the stone is believed to have *shakti*, power. Thus a diamond can work positively, making the owner prosperous, or it can work negatively because of the unhappiness of the previous possessor, and may cause the new owner harm. Even if the stone is new, people still prefer to buy from a jeweller who has had a long-standing relationship with the family. If a man wants to be successful as a diamond merchant, he must also be pious and honest. For the local people these qualities are almost synonymous with the quality or worth of his diamonds. In estimating the value of the diamond, the cut, colour and clarity are taken into account as is the resale value.

According to the Brahman woman, the people of her caste care for the 'spiritual' aspect of a diamond, while the Chettiyars only consider its commercial value.

Each diamond has a history, in our opinion. Even if the stone is new, it has to undergo a long process before it becomes a piece of jewellery. Since it is more valuable than other stones, people take care of it more in the process. That is why it acquires more power and has been important throughout history. Beautiful diamonds circulate from person to person. Normally, if the family is well off, jewellery is handed down from mother to daughter and then to the granddaughter. If it is diverted from this line, there is usually a good reason.

Jewellers buy diamond jewellery and then sell it to their clients. Even if it is second hand, this jewellery is traded at the price of

gold and diamonds in the current market. But of course the
purchase of the jewellery depends on the taste of the client who
may prefer the design and size of old jewellery and choose it for
this reason rather than for its value on the 'antique market' in
Europe (cf. Spooner 1986: 225). A diamond is very expensive, but
because it retains or increases its value, it is a highly favoured
investment.

According to the Brahman woman who gave me this information, one renowned English jeweller used to visit her mother every
year to hear stories about diamonds.

He used to listen to my mother's stories about famous diamonds and
even said to me that if someone wants to know about diamonds, it is
best to ask a South Indian Brahman woman.

From this woman's point of view, however expensive a particular
piece of diamond jewellery may be, it is worthless if it has a sad
history. 'The Chettiyars do not consider the spirituality embedded
in the diamond. They will simply take one that has a good value.'

However, borrowing jewellery and sleeping with it underneath
the pillow seems to be the accepted custom among the Nagarattars
as well. I often saw the Nagarattars taking jewellery from the
jeweller and then returning it after a few days. One middle-aged
aacchi once said to me that she returned one set of jewellery after
a few days because she did not like it. It seemed that she took the
custom of 'testing' the jewellery for granted, and I discovered that
this custom was even practised in Madras.

While I was visiting a Nagarattar family, they called a jeweller
whom they knew and asked him to leave a pair of diamond earrings.
The jeweller obliged and the family returned them after two or
three days. In the meantime, the aacchi and her family members
had discussed if they liked and wanted to keep them.

This kind of relationship between a jeweller and his customers
is possible only after they have developed mutual trust over a long
period of time. Similar relationships occur between clients and
goldsmiths. People tend to buy from a particular merchant and
employ a particular goldsmith in order to avoid mishandling and
cheating. This strong bond comes about because a woman's property may contribute to what the Brahman woman called the 'spirituality' of the diamond.

Davenport (1986: 108) discusses the difference between ordinary commodities (of economic value only) which are exchanged at markets and items which can only be exchanged in restricted ritualized contexts (i.e. those which have spiritual value). He shows that among the Eastern Solomon islanders, the spiritual value of an item has a dual association. First, it is associated with human life itself (among the Eastern Solomon islanders, human sacrifice takes place in a very important ritual transaction). Secondly, the intensive labour and time invested to make the object refined and beautiful, which are thought to be the fruits of an inspired aesthetic accomplishment, is associated with the supernatural.

Yet as Davenport demonstrates, the spiritual value of an item cannot be separated from the intrinsic value which results from the material out of which it is made and the labour that went into forming it. These commodities are then invested with spiritual value through either the application of aesthetic skills or the taking of human life, and it is only after this that the object (or activity) can become a representation of the sacred and spiritual (ibid).

For the South Indians, religiosity (*bhakti* or devotion) is equivalent to their hard work in creating something. The difference in the relative statuses of goldsmiths, silversmiths, and blacksmiths in South India can be explained by the value of the commodity they handle and the amount of labour they subsequently put into transforming that commodity into an item. Thus, because diamonds are the most expensive precious stones, and hence people put in more effort and labour into making them 'fine', they are believed to be the most powerful. This is the explanation behind the Brahmans' claim that each diamond has a 'history'.

Concerning the artistic workmanship of jewellery, a Brahman woman told me about a ring which was given to her by her maternal uncle. It was made of gold and small rubies, but since it was very delicate, one of the fine lines of the decoration was broken, and their regular goldsmith was called in to repair it.

When he saw my broken ring, he was struck with amazement, and whispered, clasping his hands: Oh God, this was created by a person with strong *bhakti*. Nowadays, nobody would be able to make such a fine ring I can mend this for the time being, but I would not recommend you to repair it anymore if it breaks again, because nobody can repair this completely and it will damage the fine work.

This Brahman woman regards jewellery, especially diamonds,

as essential items among a woman's property because of this spirituality. However, this spirituality does not exclude the economic value, as Davenport correctly argues.

Merchant-bankers view investments in jewellery, especially in diamonds, as very sensible. When the Indian rupee was devalued in the summer of 1991, the shop of a renowned diamond merchant in Karaikkudi became very busy because people were eager to purchase diamonds before they suffered from sharp inflation.

Bayly (1983: 402–3), discussing eighteenth to nineteenth century North Indian mercantile activities, cites the hoarding of gold and jewellery as a means of sensible investment in those days. When a merchant of Meshed in Iran decided to retire to Benares in 1786, for example, he carried his capital in the form of eighty pearls. For similar reasons, high officials at the Indian courts bought jewellery, as it made it more difficult for the ruler to confiscate their property if they lost office.

The Nagarattars count diamond jewellery in sets when they are given to their daughters as their property on marriage. *Nahai* usually refers to jewellery in general, but among the Nagarattars, one *nahai* means a diamond necklace set in gold. Two *nahai* means a gold necklace with diamonds and a set of diamond bangles set in gold, and three means the addition of one *ennei taali*. Giving one's daughter three *nahai* would demonstrate that the family is upper-middle class.

The gold is referred to in terms of the number of gold sovereigns given to the girl on her marriage. In general, the minimum a woman would receive is thirty sovereigns. Middle-class women receive between thirty and fifty, upper-middle-class women receive between seventy to a hundred, while those from the upper class receive more than a hundred sovereigns in addition to other property.[10] The

[10] This rate is higher than those found in other castes. For example, a Brahman woman who married in 1986 said that she had brought fifty gold sovereigns in her dowry. However, she is constantly annoyed by her father-in-law who tells her that another of his daughters-in-law brought one hundred and thirty gold sovereigns. Since she said she used to be called a 'rich girl' by her classmates while she was at school, and her wedding attracted three thousand guests, the amount she carried may not be especially low. However, according to her, even though her father-in-law is rich and does not need her jewellery, taking a lot of jewellery is a status symbol for both sides, and that is why her father-in-law is concerned about the amount of jewellery that his daughters-in-law have.

richest families can give a very large number of gold sovereigns —
one woman told me that her *kaluttiru* alone weighed a hundred and
one sovereigns.

The more jewellery they give the better, although the upper class
does not seem to be so keen on jewellery nowadays. One upper
class Nagarattar woman said,

My daughter told me that she doesn't want much jewellery. She says she
won't often have the opportunity to wear it when she goes abroad. So
we gave her only a hundred sovereigns and three *nahai*. However, she
plans to run a computer company, so she was given some of the fund,
real estate, and stock bonds from several companies for this purpose.

However, most other Nagarattars still think that an increase of
jewellery is equivalent to increasing their property. They invest in
gold because it is the easiest commodity to sell in times of need.
The meagre amounts that are saved daily are spent on jewellery as
soon as enough is acquired because it is a simple and dependable
way of beating inflation. Historically, gold and silver has also been
credited with the power of transforming and enhancing the human
body, as witnessed by their use in various forms of traditional
medicine (Bayly 1986: 291).

Aside from the collection of gold and silver items, the Nagarattars also collect other metals such as brass, copper, stainless-steel,
etc., and the heavier metals are considered better. Shop-keepers
price their silver and brass, and even their stainless-steel goods, by
weight. Jewellers handle even the tiniest fragment of gold with great
care, and a delicate scale is used to weigh amounts as small as
0.01–0.03 g. Each piece of gold jewellery is carefully priced according to weight, and it is this rather than the design that affects
the price.

The jeweller records the weight of the gold used for the jewellery
on a slip of paper in front of the customer in addition to the current
price of the gold on that particular day of purchase. If the customer
wants to exchange the item for something else, the jeweller is happy
to oblige. If the customer wants to return the goods, they will be
bought back at the market value of that particular day.

The care taken with tiny fragments of gold has to be understood
within the context of the customer's attitude: gold may well form
a large part of his assets. Gold jewellery is useful because it can be
sold at any time at the current market price and it can be worn

and enjoyed in the meantime. If a man loses his money through business, as a last resort he can fall back on his wife's assets in the form of jewellery. It is for this reason that husbands are well informed and consulted prior to the purchase of jewellery. Stock bonds or even bank notes are ultimately seen as nothing but paper which may lose value due to inflation, but jewellery and precious metals can be instantly converted into cash and are relatively strong against inflation. In addition, any item made from these metals (whether it be a bangle, a chain, a ring, a plate, or a bar), can be displayed as 'property' and demonstrate the status of the family, and as such would be considered 'useful'. The Nagarattars' value-system is largely contingent on usefulness. Their love of jewellery is rooted in their belief that it is a good investment. People say the best diamonds are available only in Chettinadu because they will only invest in the highest quality and are only interested in the best quality as an investment.[11] Yet it is rare for people to say that the Nagarattars have good taste. Talking about themselves, one Naga-rattar scholar said to me, 'People say sarcastically that the Nagarat-tar women decorate themselves just like the Koravas, a Gypsy caste, who wear rugs but always decorate themselves with many gold ornaments.'

Each Nagarattar house in Chettinadu has a particular goldsmith (tattaan) who is called to their house for making jewellery. When they call him to their house, he weighs the gold there, and weighs it again when he comes back with the finished jewellery. An elderly Nagarattar woman told me that in the olden days, when the Nagarattars wanted a number of trinkets made for their daughter's marriage, they would employ several goldsmiths, give them food, and make them work in their own house for a few weeks until they had finished all the jewellery. On leaving, the goldsmiths were submitted to a body search. This is a normal procedure which has probably been practised for centuries. Nagarattars try to prevent the gold from being stolen by the goldsmith while he is making the jewellery. As another precaution, the Nagarattars always make jewellery with 22-carat gold so that they can identify the genuineness by its colour. When I asked a goldsmith to make

[11] According to Brahmans, the Nagarattars are not interested in 'coloured stones' such as rubies, garnets, emeralds, and sapphires because they are not such a good investment. It is customary for the Brahmans, on the other hand, to give their daughters several pieces of jewellery containing coloured stones.

a ring for me with 18-carat gold, he flatly refused. He said that no goldsmith would do this in Chettinadu as it would ruin his reputation.

4.9 *Saamaan* as Female Property

Saamaan (bridal goods) is also the essential property of Nagarattar women. Everything is carefully counted and checked off on the list of *muraichittai* before being carried to the groom's house. After or before the wedding, at whatever time is convenient for the bride's party, several people come to check the items against the list. (There are two copies of the list of *saamaan,* one for the bride's parents and the other for the groom's house.) A senior Nagarattar commented: 'It normally takes two or three days to check the list. Yet we get used to it. It is not difficult to differentiate varieties of *saamaan.*' The major goods are placed in store-rooms of the groom's ancestral house, the key is given to the bride and they should not be touched by anyone without her permission.

Saamaan can be useful especially if the Nagarattar women are uneducated. A middle-aged *aacchi* said,

I remember one widow of my relatives survived for a few years by selling her *saamaan* until her sons grew up. She took them one by one to the shop, asked the shop owner to weigh them and was given money in exchange. Uneducated *aacchis* cannot handle difficult documents so they may be cheated and lose money. Selling *saamaans* is the easiest way to avoid being cheated. You can sell them on the spot without any complications.

The custom of counting the *saamaan,* and leaving the wife in charge of the store-room's key is in keeping with the economic autonomy of the nuclear household.

When the bride gets married, she lives with her in-laws until they set up a new family. A family is usually set up when the wife gives birth to the first child. If her husband is an only son, it may not take place, but even so, they will either build a new house nearby or set up their own independent kitchen and quarter for themselves somewhere in the big compound.

Until then, the bride is not supposed to use the goods she brought from her natal family. The couple's immediate needs are provided for by her mother-in-law who purchases things for her daughter-in-law either from her own pocket or from the money she was given as *maamiyaar siir danam*. While the newly wedded couple live with the groom's family, they are under the custody of the groom's family.

I shall now go back to Nacchiammai's *muraichiitai* record again and discuss the detailed list of *saamaan* carried by her. The list of goods is divided into several categories: (1) silver items, (2) bureaus, (3) stainless-steel items, (4) brass items, (5) items for the groom, (6) items for the bride, (7) *sarees,* (8) miscellaneous items.

4.10 Why is Hoarding Necessary?

This is a meticulously detailed list of goods, and supports the impression other castes have gained of the Nagarattars. It is said that Nagarattar parents give their daughters everything they will need when they get married, so that they will not have to buy anything else for the rest of their lives!

The goods can be divided into consumables and durables. Items such as toothpaste, soap, detergents, as well as the clothes (suits, *sarees,* towels, etc.) are for the couple's own use. Silver, stainless-steel, brass, and wooden goods are to be kept for following generations, although some of them are essential items for ceremonial occasions.

This detailed list of bridal goods also demonstrates the Nagarattars' tendency to accumulate goods without using them. For example, when Nacchiammai received her elder brother, who had brought her a gift of diamond earrings on the day before Deepavali as a *siir* from her 'mother's house', she gave him a plastic plate with betel nuts and leaves as part of the ritual. Her brother carefully put the plate into his cloth bag. When I asked him how he would use the plate, he said that he would store it somewhere until it should be needed. He would probably keep it for the marriage of his daughter.

Similarly, empty jars of Horlicks are used for storing pickles and cooking ingredients. Toys, furnishings, and other items given as gifts (e.g. pencils, clips, soap, paperweights, knives, nail clippers), are all carefully stored for the marriage of the daughter or granddaughter if a family does not have a daughter. Indeed, in several Nagarattar houses I saw a number of old Western dolls which must have been handed down for generations.

Table 4.11: Nacchiammai's list of *saamaan*

Silver items

1	Lamp (about 3-feet tall)	1	Silver match box	1	Container for the lamp wicks
1	Small lamp (about 2-feet tall)	1	Ice tumbler	1	Wooden cover for the flour grinder
1	Lamp for *Pongal* (large)	6	*Metti* (toe rings)	1	Vessel with a sharp edge
1	Pot (small)	2	Serving spoons (big and small)	1	Small milk feeder for a baby
1	Slate lamp	1	Comb	1	Anklet
1	Idol of Vinayaga	1	Very fine needle	1	Tumbler
1	Conch shell	1	Mysore vessel	1	Tray for sweets
1	Arrow (*kilikki*)	1	Tray for coconut and fruits	1	Stand for *kunkum* and spoon for *ghee* (oil)
1	Pot for *Pongal*	1	Sandal paste container	2	Plates
1	Mysore vessel (small)	1	Box to keep sacred ash	2	Dinner plates
3	Small vessels				

Bureaus

1	Bureau	1	Cupboard	1	*Pattanam* bureau
1	Bureau with a mirror	1	Bureau to keep mattresses	1	Kitchen cupboard

Stainless-steel items

1 Lamp	2 Items Tekkalur pots with lids	1 Big pot
2 Sets nested Mysore vessel (10 items)	4 *Pongal* pots with lids	1 Rice cooking pot
1 Vessel for ground flour	1 Set of nested tall vessels	1 Set of nested milk containers
6 Buckets (big and small)	3 Tiffin carriers	1 Ice tumbler
7 Cylindrical-shaped vessels	2 Milk containers	2 Vessels with lids to keep lamps
3 Sets of nested serving vessels (15 items)	2 Vessels with two handles	1 Cylindrical vessel with lid (lunch-box type)
2 Tekkalur pots	1 Pot to keep butter milk	1 Chindamani pot
24 Tumblers	1 *Puri* box	2 Sets lunch plates (4 items)
1 Lunch plate	8 Plates with small cup for ritual	1 Vessel with a handle
4 Coffee filters	3 *Ghee* containers with a handle and a lid	2 Oval-shaped plates
3 *Dosa* plates	2 Trays to keep fruits and coconuts	2 Square plates
2 Plates with four small legs	1 Kasi plate	2 Seven-holed *idli* plates with lids
3 Five-holed *idli* plates with lids	3 Small containers to cool the coffee	1 Betel leaf plate

Table 4.11 (contd)

1	Pumpkin shaped vessel with lid	3	Lids	10	*Donnai*-shaped containers
6	Small *ghee* spoons	3	Small *ghee* spoons with deeper scoop	1	Tin spoon
2	*Sambaa* serving spoons	1	Coffee spoon	1	Spring for a baby's cradle
1	Playing instrument	2	Cups and saucers	1	Tea filter
1	Knife to prepare *halva*	2	Knives to cut vegetables	1	Screw driver
1	*Donnai*-shaped big vessel	1	Pot stand	4	Trays for betel nuts
4	Trays (large and small)	1	Cylindrical oil container	1	Cylindrical container with a handle
2	*Karttigai* lamps	2	Small containers	2	*Sangu* (conch-shaped feeder)
2	Flour scoopers	1	Needle to prick the fish	4	Spoons to prepare fish (large and small)
1	Scissor-shaped instrument to remove vessels from the stove	1	Spoon stand	1	Box for *paan* paste
1	Box for areca nuts	1	Oval-shaped box to keep calcium paste	4	Amber boxes
2	Spoons with holes				

Brass vessels

2 Tall lamps (big and small)	2 Tekkalur pots with lids	3 Tekkalur pots without lids
5 Copper pots	1 Pot for sandi	1 Tiruwoni pot
1 Tekkalur pot	2 Kumbakonam pots	2 Kasani pots
1 Large vessel to boil rice grain	1 Large vessel	1 Extra-big, tall vessel (cylindrical)
2 Cylindrical vessels with lids to keep rice	2 Vessels bought for Rs 100	5 Mysore vessels (big)
4 Mysore vessels (small, sets 20 items)	1 Set of large cylindrical-shaped nested vessels (5 items)	2 Barrels
5 Round-shaped vessels for butter (large and small)	2 Rice keepers	1 Set of 19-holed *idli* plates (3 items)
3 Seven-holed *idli* plates	3 Four-holed *idli* plates	1 Vessel to keep the lamp
1 Mysore bucket	6 Bucket-shaped vessels	1 Small container for *ghee*
6 Vessels to keep vegetable *birriyani*	6 U-shaped vessel	7 Cylindrical vessel with handles (large and small)
1 Flower bucket with lid	1 Barrel with lid	1 Small cylindrical vessel with lid
2 Cindamani vessel	1 Karahani vessel with lid for sweets	7 Round-shaped vessels with handles
1 Round screw type lid	2 Coffee filters	3 Tiffin carriers big and small

Table 4.11 (contd)

5	Plates	4	Kasi plates	4	Coffee coolers
3	*Pongal* makers	2	Pots for washing (Tekkalur pot)	1	Pot for washing hands
2	Kasi pots	1	Vessel for boiling milk	1	Vessel for boiling milk with lid
1	Milk pot	1	Container for *dosa* flour	1	Tumbler
1	Pair of bellows	1	Torch with cloth wick	1	Basket-type vessel
3	Vessels for boiling milk (small and large)	4	Mysore vessels	2	*Donnai*-shaped vessels
1	*Idi-appam* maker	1	Set of scales	1	Big spoon with a very long handle
3	Kasi plates	3	Rice servers	9	*Halva* cutting spoons
3	Kasi pots (big and small)	1	Milk pot	1	Set of vessel and grinder for making betel powder
2	Set of measuring cups (4 items)	2	Sets of plates for scales	1	Plate to serve vegetables
1	Mysore vessel	2	Tumblers (large and small)	2	Poona plates
1	Small cup	2	*Pongal* pots and lids	4	Mysore container (small)
1	Oil pot and lid	1	Kasi pot with lid	1	Bell
3	Water jars with lids	5	Spoons with holes	2	Spoons to stir milk

5	Kartigai lamps	1	Betel nut cutter	1	Spoon to prepare fish
1	Small plate	1	Comb	3	Small cups
1	Music instrument				

Things kept for Nacchiammai

1	Lady's Citizen watch	1	Wrist watch strap	1	Cane hand-bag
1	Leather purse	2	Bead purses	2	Leather cases (large and small)
1	Suitcase	1	Aluminium vanity box	1	Silver powder box
1	Plastic soap box	1	Umbrella	2	Mirrors (large and small)
3	Combs	1	Lice removing comb	1	Hair brush
1	Tube of Signal toothpaste	12	Toilet soaps	1	'501' soap
1	500g of Surf powder	1	Oil bottle	1	Powder tin box
1	Sopiar face powder	1	Snow brand face cream	1	Shampoo
1	Comb for shampoo	1	Shaving kit	1	Washing brush
1	Pair of slippers	1	Key chain	1	Lock
1	Powder sponge				

Bride's sarees

2	Pattu sarees	12	Polyester sarees	2	Cotton sarees

Table 4.11 (contd)

Miscellaneous items

16 Saree blouses	6 Underskirts	1 Naidu Hall brassiere
5 Ordinary brassieres	16 Ribbons	2 Towels
2 Turkish bath towels	2 Cloth cradles	1 Embroidered cloth bags
2 Long cloth bags	5 Embroidered bags	3 Embroidered cloth bags
1 Baby cloth	1 Towel cloth to cover the baby	1 Net bag for keeping fruits
1 Dindikkul pillow cover	1 Embroidered towel cloth sugar bag	1 Satin baby cloth
3 Rice bags (large and small)	2 Bags for chickpeas (small)	1 Cloth for banana leaves
2 Bags for rugs	2 Ordinary bags	2 Kuttalam bags
1 Kanmark mat	6 Mattresses	31 Pillows
6 Burma mats	1 Baby mat	5 Ordinary mats
1 Plastic mat	1 Square carpet	2 Large carpets
2 Long carpets	1 Mosquito net	1 Baby mosquito net
1 Silk rug	2 Burma mats (small)	1 Malaya mat
1 Square mat made of cigarette packets	1 Hand fan	

Things kept for the groom

Qty	Item	Qty	Item	Qty	Item
1	Citizen watch	1	National Panasonic 'two-in-one' (radio/cassette player)	1	National table fan
4	Cassette tapes	1	Alarm clock	1	Table lamp
1	Vijay company iron box	1	Suit case (Ecola's)	1	Small plate
1	Suit case (ordinary)	1	Rubber-cane bag	5	Plastic bags
1	Foldable basket	1	Toothbrush	1	Table
1	Chair	1	Goldridge chair	1	Mirror
3	Sandalwood soaps	3	Lavender soaps	2	'501' soaps
1	Bottle of lavender face powder	1	Sopiar soap powder (Malaysian made)	1	Bottle of liquid foundation
1	Jar of vaseline	1	Bottle of Tata hair oil	1	*Bindi* bottle
1	Bottle of ordinary oil	1	Oil bottle	1	Powder box
1	Soap box	1	Sponge	1	Comb
1	Tube of Colgate toothpaste	1	Toothbrush	1	Gillette shaving set
1	Shaving brush	1	Bottle of shaving foam	1	Surf powder packet (large)
1	Bundle of writing paper	1	Writing board	1	Diary
1	Pilot pen	1	Hero pen	1	Ball point pen

Table 4.11 (contd)

12	Pencils	1	Paper weight	1	Foldable knife
2	Idols of elephants	1	Paper clip	1	Key ring with bottle opener (1 set)
1	Cigarette lighter	1	Sharpener	12	Plastic clips
1	Snuff box	1	Photo album	1	Mouth organ
1	Scrubbing brush	1	Pair of slippers	2	Brushes
1	Bottle of perfume	1	Bottle of Queen Rose scent	4	Coat stands
1	Belt	1	Washing line	1	Rope (to tie around the hips of men)
1	Purse made of palm leaves (*oolai*)	7	Pieces of underwear	2	Coloured undershirts
5	White undershirts	1	*Veetti*	7	Towels
1	Thick cloth bag	1	Bath towel	2	Face towels
1	Hand towel	1	White hand towel	1	Muffler
1	Woolen shawl	2	Shawls	2	Pairs of socks
1	*Vibudi* (sacred ash) bag	1	Umbrella		

If a couple has several daughters, they divide the goods brought by the wife and add newly-purchased goods, so that all the daughters have an equal share and they accumulate more possessions in accordance with the status of the groom. If items brought to the marriage by the daughter are not used, they may be handed down to her daughter as part of the mother's property. Since this has become their tradition, the original concept of the 'usability' of the goods is no longer applicable: people tend to be more interested in preservation than use.

One explanation for the enormous variety of items that are hoarded is that the market price for each commodity differs according to the economic climate, e.g. the price of silver may go down while brass goes up. The Nagarattars consider the security of a daughter's finances to be essential and they believe that it is dangerous to put all their assets into a single commodity. Even though a daughter from a rich family will nowadays own stock bonds, company shares, real estate, bank accounts, etc., her parents do not abandon the tradition of accumulating goods. The purchase of a house, a coffee estate, or stock bonds is based on the same principle as the collection of Horlicks jars.

Hoarding itself, therefore, is based on their rational calculations as merchants, and is not particularly unique to the Nagarattars. There are a few techniques employed to avoid financial risk and to spread their assets so that all their eggs are not in one basket to guarantee the future. And moreover, even among the North Indian mercantile families, hoarding was one of the practices taught early to children (Bayly 1983: 402). Bayly continues by saying that court cases from the early nineteenth-century suggest that relatively small concerns in the villages deposited sums as large as Rs 1,000–3,000 in the form of bullion or jewellery, and banking firms from the 1880s through to the 1930s appear to have maintained between 15 and 25 per cent of their total assets in the form of jewellery, bullion, plate and government paper, and this acted as a reserve fund only to be called into play in an emergency or in case of partition (ibid.). Therefore, hoarding is not peculiar behaviour and has a practical application rather than being a waste of unusable capital (ibid.).

In his discussion of hoarding, Bayly distinguishes between the following six types:

(1) Distress hoarding, which is a technique of survival, as different

from the hoarding that occurred as part of the regular running of businesses.

(2) The deposit of family jewellery. This had a ritual and social significance, as it was closely connected to the family's honour and status. The wife's jewellery was thought of as insurance at the time of the death of her husband.

(3) The purchase of jewellery and pearls as liquid capital. They were superior to money because they were universally negotiable and not subject to money changers' discount.

(4) Gold pieces and jewellery as collateral. This was particularly important to the merchant community as this could be an easily transferable heirloom.

(5) Silver, as the family firm's basic reserve. It acted as an insurance against sudden demands.

(6) Gold and silver for savings. They continued to be the commodities traded most frequently, and peasants, for example, would sell off smaller quantities of gold and silver, in order to buy bullocks or provide for marriages (Bayly 1986: 402–3).

These six kinds of 'hoarding' were quite common among the North Indian mercantile families in the late eighteenth to nineteenth centuries, according to Bayly, and are still practised by the Nagarattars to this day as a caste tradition of accumulating assets in various forms. However, the Nagarattars hoard a much wider variety of items than those mentioned by Bayly, and so the question remains as to why they hoard 'junk' items such as nail clippers, toothpaste, plastic buckets, etc. Of course, items like toothpaste, soap, detergents, as well as clothes such as suits, *sarees,* etc. would be used by the couple in the future. Clothes, towels, etc. are not durable and do not last until the next generation.

The Nagarattar teaching of parsimony encourages the marrying couple to use these goods as long as possible. When the mother buys dozens of pillows for her daughter as part of the *saamaan,* she is taking her daughter's future children into account and also the necessity for pillows when a function is held and guests come to stay. If she has more pillows than she can use, the daughter might give some to her servants on an occasion when she is required to give a gift. In any case, according to the Nagarattars, buying consumables in bulk makes good financial sense because, for example, if they were to go to the market in a hurry to purchase one pillow, it would be expensive, while if they buy dozens for their daughter's marriage, they are able to get a large discount.

Therefore, in the case of the Nagarattars, conspicuous parsimony is not manifested in a simple lifestyle but in their custom of purchasing excessively in order to add the items to their hoard. *Aacchis* love shopping in general, but consumption of the goods they buy is restrained by their habit of conservation and parsimony. I was often struck by the inconsistencies between their economic ethic and their collecting habits. For example, a wealthy old Nagarattar woman used to go to a bazaar in Karaikkudi in an air-conditioned car, driven by her servant. She was well-informed about the prices of the vegetables and provisions, and told me that a particular vegetable was 10 paisa cheaper here than in Madras as was a bath mat made of coconut fibres. She said that she was well-versed in prices, and very particular in collecting the exact change from her servant. 'I would count each paisa and ask my servant how much each item cost, and if he did not give five paisa change, I would ask him why he didn't.' This attitude is very different from that of women of other castes. A young Vellalar woman told me, 'I don't mind even if my servant does not give back ten or twenty paisa change.'

This habit of thriftiness encourages them to hoard. Children are taught to be thrifty and frugal and when a woman gets married, she tries to save money, spending as little as possible. This is partly because of her upbringing but also, as a housewife she is given autonomy to manage her own nuclear family and her purpose is to pass on her property to the next generation. The silver, stainless-steel, wooden and brass goods are kept for future generations, although some of the items are used in daily life and on ceremonial occasions. Goods can also be categorized according to their purpose: they can be used for rituals performed at auspicious events, or can be handed down from generation to generation without specific use. Some may be used for ceremonial cooking or in daily life.

During my fieldwork, I managed to read about twenty-five–thirty lists of bridal goods and observed consistent similarities between them, although a few items may be omitted or added according to the status and convenience of the families.[12] One

---

[12] It is not widely known that the Nagarattars draw up these lists. They are considered to be extremely personal and are not discussed with non-Nagarattars.

woman told me that the system of list-making had remained the same for generations.

If you do not have a list at home, you may go to a house of similar economic status, borrow it from them and follow their system. It is normally the father who makes the records, but it may be an accountant (domiciliary manager) if the family has one.

I compared a list written in 1906 with the modern lists, and found that a few modern items have been added as essential items (e.g. electrical gadgets, plastics, and stainless-steel goods). Although traditional goods (silver, wood, ceramics, enamel-coated items, stones, *sarees*, etc.) are still carried by the bride, they are outnumbered by the modern items.

4.10.1 Silver Items

Silver has been one of the essential items as an asset that can be easily liquidated on such occasions as when money is needed for tax payment or purchase of bullocks, and it works as the pan-regional and international trading currency. In addition, both gold and silver are used to make ritual instruments (e.g. lamps, trays) and food containers for ceremonial occasions because they are believed to be the most immune to ritual pollution.[13]

Silver is a versatile asset, along with gold, as it can be sold immediately in time of need. Its economic value goes hand-in-hand with the 'auspiciousness' and 'purity' of the material and silver goods have become essential for the bride. Even if the family is not well off, it is necessary to provide at least a few silver items (such as a cup, a plate, and one or two lamps) for the daughter's wedding.

As the use of silver in a ritual is auspicious, it is well represented at a wedding most commonly in the form of a lamp and a *kottaan* (basket). Among the silver ritual items, lamps are important for most Hindus. Lighting is one of the most essential parts of a Hindu ritual, and the Nagarattars especially favour using different varieties of lamps for different rituals. At the wedding ritual, the transfer of

---

13 To be ritually pure or ritually polluted is an abstract notion and is often a temporary state. Thus ceremonies are held to produce a ritually pure state (e.g. before getting married) or to 'cleanse' someone from the state of being ritually impure (e.g. the last day of a mourning ceremony).

a candle lamp (which is referred to as a *'sleit vilakku'*) symbolizes the transfer of the bride to the groom's house. As a symbol of auspiciousness and prosperity, the lamp is held by the bride's female relative and is then passed on to one of the groom's female relatives (see Chapter 5).

For Hindus, lamps symbolize goodness and auspiciousness. Even if the family cannot afford a *puja,* they have to light a lamp in a *puja* room as soon as evening comes so that the auspicious goddess Lakshmi will enter the house (Lakshmi is considered to be the goddess of wealth as well as auspiciousness). It is a woman's job to light a lamp in the evening so that the house can be wealthy and happy. *Sumangalis,* auspicious married women, are identified with lamps, and they should bring luck to the family into which they marry.

Kottaan (basket) is also an important ritual item as seen in the next chapter, although a lot of middle class families have started to use stainless-steel ones. In addition, the *sangu* (conch shell) which is blown during weddings, *padaippu,* and funerals to announce that a significant ritual is to take place, should be made from silver.

4.10.2 Wooden, Stone, and Enamel-Coated Items

These are mostly old-fashioned, traditional items which would have been made prior to the arrival of stainless-steel or plastics. Although the Nagarattars use only some of these items (stone grinder, wooden grinder, etc.), they still pass these items on to their daughters. There are some items which are traditionally used in rituals, such as the wooden pounder. Although they no longer pound husks with a wooden pounder, this is still necessary for the funeral ritual, since the daughter of the deceased should offer the pounded rice to the deceased.

4.10.3 Bureau (Wardrobes, Chests, Desks, etc.)

When there were still a large number of Nagarattars in Burma, they made wardrobes and chests in teak and rose-wood, and sent them by ship to Chettinadu. These items, just like chandeliers from Europe, were costly and exotic and became the symbols of rich Nagarattars. These Nagarattars brought about a fashion which created a demand for these bureaus in Chettinadu until the early twentieth century, but the South Eastern trade zone was closed to the Nagarattars when British colonialism collapsed, and these wooden items have become very expensive. Nowadays, most of the Nagarattars (like other Indians) use stainless-steel chests and wardrobes (see photographs), and modern furniture with vinyl and plastic covering has become popular and fashionable among the middle class and the upper-middle class.

4.10.4 Stainless-Steel and Brass

Stainless-steel goods are cheap, convenient replacements for traditional goods made in silver, brass, or coated in enamel. They have become quite popular in modern Indian households, including those of the Nagarattars. The Nagarattars like to use stainless-steel goods partly because they are lightweight and unbreakable. The 'auspiciousness' that is seen as integral to this new substance has made it the commonest gift among the Nagarattars. A young woman told me that during auspicious and important events such as *pen paakka* or *peesi mudittal,* i.e. the betrothal rituals, guests are served using new stainless-steel vessels because they are shiny and unbreakable. To serve coffee in a china cup on such an occasion would be considered an insult because it is breakable. I also noticed the frequent use of stainless-steel goods at funerals. Even I was given a gift of a stainless-steel vessel as a gift at a funeral I attended, along with all the others who attended. It has become very common for stainless steel goods to be given on all ceremonial occasions, and I presume that this is because of its highly durable quality. It rarely gets scratched or blemished, and so is considered appropriate for symbolizing the termination of mourning (a new start) and also auspiciousness.

Brass items are still important in spite of the popularity of the stainless-steel goods because large brass vessels are considered to be essential for cooking on ceremonial occasions (see photographs). They are expensive and represent the Nagarattar's rich 'material culture'. For example, 'Mysore vessel', 'Kasi plate', 'Kuttalam pot', etc. represent certain characteristics of the design of the vessels. They distinguish their materials using special names as these, and also name them according to their convenience. One of the *aacchi's* most important tasks is to go to the ancestral house once a year or so to polish these vessels.

4.10.5 Electrical Gadgets and Vehicles

Electrical gadgets are now an intrinsic part of the bridal goods in all Indian communities. They are quite accurate indicators of the groom's status, according to Nacchiammai's husband, Manick-awasagar. A couple of people informed me of the present price range for prestigious electrical gadgets as seen below. Although individually they are not too expensive for the middle class, it is costly when several items have to be purchased at once. Neverthe-less, most Hindu (and Muslim) grooms nowadays claim that the bride should bring such modern items as part of the bridal goods: they are essential household items, especially among the urban middle class.

Table 4.12: Approximate prices of 'modern' bridal items

Items	Approximate prices (Rs)
Refrigerator (medium size, for a nuclear family)	6,000 – 7,000
Radio/cassette player	1,500 (+)
Television: (black and white)	4,000 – 5,000
(colour)	12,000 – 13,000
Scooter	14,000 – 18,000
Table fan (varies depending on the model)	500 – 2,000

The groom will demand such items in accordance with his status as an essential part of the bridal items. Such modern gadgets are sought after for utilitarian purposes, and not for mere col-lection like vessels and jars, most of which may not be used. In addition, possession of those gadgets classifies the family as middle class, and so they serve as a distinct marker, especially of urban lower-middle and middle class. However, in this respect, the modern gadgets are solely indicative of the groom's economic status and have no ritual or aesthetic value unlike some of the other commodities (such as silver, gold, jewellery, carpets, etc.).

Thus, however costly electrical gadgets and vehicles may be, they are regarded as commodities and are not included in the valuables which are exchanged in ritualized contexts.

4.10.6 Carpets and Mats

Again these are necessary for big functions. When the Nagarattars hold a wedding, the bride's family spreads a large auspicious carpet to cover the *walavu waasal* on which the rituals are held. Small auspicious carpets on which the bride greets her relatives before she takes leave of her father's ancestral house are also very important. They are decorative and are embossed with the family initials. Special Burmese mats which are softer and thicker than usual mats are offered to important relatives who come to stay in the house during large functions. However, these mats are no longer available on the market and so are often bought from antique shops. When someone dies, the corpse is laid out on a new unused mat, in honour of the dead. Although the mat is to be washed as soon as the corpse is taken away to the cremation ground, the Nagarattars do not feel that it is polluted and are quite happy to use the same mat on other occasions. The use of carpets on auspicious occasions is definitely not a South Indian custom, and is probably a Western influence or a North Indian Muslim legacy, as I have not come across any other caste in South India which uses them in traditional ceremonies. Carpets tend to be used in colder climates and are alien to South Indian culture. The Nagarattars, while engaging in the long and tedious ritual procedures of a wedding, would be very hot in the ancestral house where the open roof of the *walavu waasal* is sealed with a decorative cloth and paper, and a thick carpet all over the floor would appear to increase the discomfort. However, the Nagarattars insist on carpets being spread on any auspicious occasion. This custom probably originated during their interaction with the West, where since the Middle Ages, 'oriental' carpets have been popular items for palaces as well as ordinary households (cf. Spooner 1986), or they might have adopted it during their interaction with Mughal royals in North India.

Along with the Burmese mats and other foreign items, carpets were picked up by the Nagarattars as 'exotic' and this gradually led to the demand by all Nagarattars for these items to be an integral part of the property of the bride.

4.10.7 Sarees

Literally, *pattu saree* means simply 'silk *saree*'but in Tamil it refers to the Kancheepuram *saree,* which is distinguished from an ordinary 'silk *saree*' which they pronounce in English. While a 'silk *saree*' would refer to either a non-Kancheepuram silk *saree* or a synthetic *saree* made in Japan or Malaysia, i.e. an expensive 'foreign' item, *'pattu saree'* signifies a higher grade of silk *saree.* It is made of silk, usually handwoven, is thick and heavy in weight, and is embroidered with *jari* (silver thread) of golden colour. An authentic *pattu saree* is heavier, because it contains genuine silver thread with embroidery on the wide borders, while the cheaper *pattu saree* is lighter.

The giving of *pattu sarees* is essential on important ceremonial occasions. People assess the status of the host of the function by noting the quality of the *pattu saree.* Since women are normally well versed in the quality and price of *sarees,* any woman who gives cheap *sarees* will suffer ruthless criticism behind her back. Watching a video of her relative's *saandi,* one middle-aged woman says, 'The *sarees* are all only embroidered on one side and are, all in the same colours — they won't have cost more than Rs 1,500 each — cheap ones.'

If a *saree* is embroidered on one fringe, it costs around Rs 1,500–2,000, but if both fringes are embroidered, it costs more than Rs 2,500. For the wedding of a rich girl, her mother-in-law would purchase a much more expensive one which may cost as much as Rs 6,000, in order to express the family's 'affection' for the girl. For example, at a grand wedding I recently attended, a girl wore a *saree* which cost Rs 4,800 at the reception on the day of the wedding, two more *sarees* of around Rs 6,000–7,000 on the day of wedding, and one *saree* of an equivalent cost at another reception which was held later in Madras. (These *sarees* worn by the bride are provided by the groom's side and so they are careful in choosing exquisite *sarees.*) Because of the popularity of making video films of such functions, relatives and friends can assess each other's *sarees* easily. Wearing an expensive-looking *saree* is therefore a matter of showing status. A woman from North India who runs a *saree* shop in Madras said,

Here in southern India, people think of nothing but *pattu sarees,* but it's rather boring. It is like a uniform. The pattern is very simple — all have either one or two borders. Unfortunately, South Indians do not appreciate the delicate and complicated patterns of other *sarees* such as the Benares *saree,* and see it as an insult if *pattu sarees* are not worn at weddings.

On ceremonial occasions, men are given cheaper gifts such as a *veetti* (loin cloth), shirt, and a pair of trousers which will probably not cost more than Rs 250–500, while their wives receive a *pattu saree* or at least a silk *saree.* Since the gift should be given to a couple, even if a man has only male children, he should still buy *pattu sarees* for his daughters-in-law. Thus the most expensive aspect of gift-giving is the necessity of giving these *sarees* to women, whether it be the groom's or the bride's side. The demand for *sarees* is rapidly increasing. It is a major currency in the Nagarattar's gift exchange market. Special gifts are delivered from the wife's 'mother's house' often in the form of *sarees* for weddings, *saandi,* and puberty cere-monies. In addition, annual celebrations such as Pongal and Deepa-vali are also occasions when sarees should be given. However, it is at Deepavali that the sales of *sarees* sharply increase when the *saree* shops are packed full of customers. One Nagarattar woman who lives in Singapore lamented, 'Our female relatives in the villages will only have *sarees* as their gift. They don't appreciate perfume or chocolates. I cannot afford to go back to India as frequently as I would like because they expect a *saree* gift on each occasion.'

The life of a *saree* is short-lived when compared to the lasting nature of gold and silver. *Pattu sarees* will last between ten to fifteen years nowadays. In the past, they would last for up to twenty to thirty years because the materials were well-woven in comparison to the modern machine-woven ones. When the *saree* is worn out, the *jari* is melted and the gold and silver is sold. Nowadays, there are few *pattu sarees* that contain much gold and silver. The golden thread is not made of *jari,* but of metal threads.

Silk *sarees* last around five to ten years, and synthetic and cotton *sarees,* four to five years. *Sarees* do not have a long life because the tropical climate in India means that people often sweat excessively so that *sarees* need to be washed frequently. In addition, the *sarees* are not looked after particularly well — they are usually folded in piles and stored in a steel bureau with other materials, which has a detrimental effect on the silk. Girls often wear their mother's old *sarees* when attending a wedding in which they do not play an important role, but if the wedding is that of a close relative and a girl does have to play a major role, then she should wear a new one. A young unmarried girl told me:

If I wear my mother's *saree* it will look really old and shabby, and so I should not wear it on an important occasion as it would cause my parents shame. For my parents' sake, especially for my mother's, I should wear a gorgeous *saree* and glittering golden bangles and earrings. These days, I mostly wear imitation gold since it looks more gorgeous. Otherwise, people would say, "What is her mother thinking of? She looks so shabby!"

Despite the fact that the life of a *saree*, unlike jewellery, is very short, the purchasing of *sarees* has increased. It is considered to be a status symbol to wear different, good quality *sarees* on several important occasions, as it reflects not only the woman's status but the financial status of her whole family.

Clothes are part of a person's identity. Clothes imply the social category to which he or she belongs. They define age, sex, and occupation, for example. In India, they can imply purity or pollution, auspiciousness or inauspiciousness, and illuminate the relationship between two parties if they are exchanged as a gift. Historically, from the symbolic point of view, transactions in clothes widely imply a pledge of future protection (Bayly 1986: 288). Village women reserved particularly auspicious *sarees* (i.e. colourful silk *sarees*) for important days, and the king used to accept clothes on particular days as special tribute (ibid.: 292). Silk is considered to be a far purer and more formal material than cotton because of the former's rarity and economic value.

Bayly claims that transactions in clothes took place quite commonly and just as grain, could transfer value and honour in a way money could not. Clothes in comparison with grain or cooked food were considered to be a safer medium of transaction as they lasted longer but did not create the same immediate bond as sharing a meal would (ibid.: 302). For a man and a woman to exchange pieces of cloth does more than symbolize an act of marriage, it is a central part of the ritual of marriage. For most central Indians and southern Brahmans in the last century, silk was essentially the dress for ritual and worship, and this practice extended to other ritualized cultural performances. Since silk was considered to be much purer ritualistically than cotton, it was not considered necessary to wash silk clothes before ceremonial use, although for a cotton cloth, washing was necessary (ibid.: 289).

Weddings are the most important occasions for the giving of clothes as gifts. The bride's side give a number of gifts to the groom's side in the form of clothes (to the groom, his parents, sisters, brothers, etc.) and the groom's side also gives *sarees* and other clothes to the bride, for her use after marriage.

Even after marriage, the wife's family give clothes to the newly married couple, and this custom continues after the birth of children. Although this would appear to imply that the party of lower rank always gives gifts to the party of higher rank (in the same way as the king accepts a tribute in the form of cloth from his subjects), this is not necessarily the case, since during *Deepavali,* employers are expected to give their servants a new set of clothes for the next year.

4.11   *Siir danam* as Auspicious Property, 'Dowry' as Curse

According to Tambiah, female property is largely confined to moveables both in classic Hindu law and also in most parts of present India (1973a: 68). Women are given cash, jewellery, and household goods which constitute *stri dhanam* (i.e. female property, in Sanskit), while men are given immoveables, particularly land.[14] Although women are not entitled to inherit the ancestral property, dowry is still the woman's property which gives her security after marriage.

Mercantile castes in general tend to give away a large proportion of property to their daughters. Bayly, for example, cites as an example a family where approximately 20 per cent of their entire capital assets was reserved for the marriage of the daughter (Bayly 1983: 376, fn. 16). As Bayly claims, this is a significant amount but it was seen as an investment in social relationships which might have definite financial advantages on occasions when the family had to fall back on resources to raise cash speedily (1983: 376). This is in fact a rational expense, since, as I demonstrated before, the asset given in the daughter's name is not wholly given away but is still part of the business fund of the father. A grand wedding ceremony for the daughter is also an advertisement of the mercantile house, which is comparable to the companies of

[14] However, as Tambiah says, this is a generalization and in southern India and in Sri Lanka, women are sometimes given agricultural land and a house by their parents, and their husbands move in so they can look after the land and cooperate in agricultural work with their wife's brothers.

the capitalist West spending a large proportion of their profit money on advertising.

Grand weddings are regarded as necessary to 'advertise' the house and those who cannot marry off their daughters through lack of funds face shame and are seen as failures. Detailed lists of *saamaan* and their display are part of the demonstration, although the detailed contract form also protects the right of a woman as a member of her natal family: if she is divorced or if she returns home voluntarily, all the *saamaan* and dowry have to be returned with her to her natal family. Although this may not always happen in practice, the well-defined marriage contract makes divorce extremely difficult (and therefore rare) particularly for men who would lose a lot of money and advantageous business relationships. By divorcing his wife, a man and his *pangaalis* lose not only the moral support of her natal family but also the 'economic support'.

Among the Mukkuvars who are Christians, the custom is of giving the *siir* as the property of the marrying daughter (Ram 1992: 188–9), yet Ram maintains that if the family is not well off, the gold once given as *siir danam* to a marrying daughter may even be transferred to her own sister's dowry or her sister-in-law's. Therefore, the gold jewellery can be borrowed so that it is part of another's bridal asset and is then returned to the woman who was originally given the jewellery by her mother. However, this does not happen among the Nagarattars, since the property given to the daughter is regarded as a fund to protect her in times of need, so that even if her husband throws her out, she can support herself. The Nagarattars make arrangements for each of their daughters and their assets cannot be transferred to anybody except the woman's daughter or her granddaughter. However, the mother still retains some part of her property until her death and thus a large part of the bridal property for her daughter is made up by the father of the girl as well as her maternal grandparents. The woman who is marrying into the family carries property of her own: it is economically valuable, but property as 'commodities' is not the only significance it has. Such a sense of woman's 'individuality ' is quite strong among the Nagarattars compared with other castes. For example, among the Komutti Chettiyars, although a similar custom of recording the property is followed, the property of the bride is merged into the asset pool of the groom's joint family property until the time of partition of the joint family property.

As the term *siir danam* (the gift from the woman's mother's house) signifies, they are originally regarded as not mere marketable commodities but 'gifts' which are 'valuable'. Gold, silver, diamonds, cash, lamps, carpets, etc. are all highly 'auspicious' items. Even the money given to the daughter has the significance of a gift with affection: auspiciously valuable.

Like the traditional valuable items (decorated necklaces and armshells) which circulate among the restricted members of the Trobrianders, the valuables carried by the Nagarattar women as part of their *saamaan* and dowry acquire what Weiner calls the 'historicity' of the valuables (Weiner 1981: 211). These items, passed on from mother to daughter and then to granddaughter, become a symbol of the 'authenticity' of the Nagarattar who possesses them, and gives her status and power. For a woman, they are the symbol of her reproductive power, i.e. auspiciousness, and for a man, they symbolize his social status — without marrying an authentic Nagarattar woman, i.e. an *aacchi* , his social status is non-existent.

However, this raises yet another question. Are these *saamaan* to be regarded as valuables i.e. 'inalienable' objects or possessions which are invested with a significance for the possessor (cf. Weiner 1985) or should they be regarded as 'property', i.e. alienable objects which are thought of in terms of their practical use only (cf. Hirschon 1984; Strathern 1984)? As I have already pointed out, gold and diamond jewellery are inalienable objects not only because they are scarce commodities in the market economy, but also because they gain 'cultural and social biographies' (Davenport 1986), as they are handed down through the generations. (Jewellery should not leave a family as this would be indicative of declining wealth.)

Citing the cases in Melanesia and among the American Indians, Gregory (1980) uses the terms 'quantitative measure' and 'qualitative measure' of money depending on the context in which an exchange is made. In a Nagarattar context, if money is exchanged for goods in the market-place, then the money and goods are quantitative. Although diamond jewellery as the woman's asset should not be sold except in financial difficulty (i.e. qualitative measure), it is sold in the market as commodities (quantitative measure). Money is also used as a gift on specific occasions when it is given ritualistically such as *moy* (money which accompanies the attendance record on the wedding), and in this case the money is qualitative as the auspicious ritual agent. Thus the same item, e.g. money, can have different implications and so can create either a 'gift-debt' or 'commodity debt' depending upon the context, distinguishing gift-debt from commodity-debt (Gregory 1982). The commodity exchange, according to Gregory, establishes a relation between the objects of a transaction, gift exchange establishes a relationship between objects, which is why I argue that the *saamaan* create a gift-debt, and are therefore inalienable.

The *saamaan* collection is regarded as a qualitative measure within the Nagarattars' complex system of gift-exchange, as it is not acceptable to give money instead of the items on the list. Thus, even if there is little chance of practical use for wooden things and porcelain goods, or even a large number of plastic goods, they are not convertible to cash. Cash is given in a ritualized context as *siir danam*, but this differs from the money given to the kin and affines as a gift on ritual occasions.

Among the Nagarattars, even money which is given as the cash part of the dowry can in fact create a gift-debt if the bride is not given her mother's dowry with added interest, as it would be an overt sign of a decline in the family's wealth or a loss of 'symbolic capital' (Bourdieu 1990). This gift-debt can be paid off by subsequent generations if they can regain wealth and status. It is at weddings that gift-debt and gift-credit in terms of symbolic capital of the family are assessed.

According to Mauss (1990: 46), any transaction is basically reciprocal. Among the Maoris of the Trobriand Islands, for example, valuable items *(tonga)* are believed to contain *hau* (spirit). This spirit is identified with the original owner of the valuable, so that if someone is given a *tonga* but fails to give the owner another *tonga* in exchange, the spirit which is embedded in the valuable harms the receiver. Therefore, Mauss stresses the principle of reciprocity in gift-exchange, as the notion of *hau* alone can force valuables to circulate among the closed circle of members.

According to Sahlins however, *hau* among the Maoris should not be regarded as a spirit which forces the receiver to give in return, but as spiritual quality associated with fecundity and productivity (1972: 167). When a gift is given, the receiver takes great care of the item so that when it is returned it has accrued a spiritual interest:

the *hau* is stronger. When gifts are given as symbols of alliances and solidarity, they are symbolically associated with fecundity.

Sahlins's explanation of the way the *hau* of a valuable item is increased in an abstract sense on reciprocation corresponds with a more concrete notion of interest in the gift-exchange of the Nagarattars. Gift-giving is regarded as a reciprocal activity, forming what Sahlins might refer to as a 'political' alliance, and the auspiciousness intrinsic to the gift-exchange of the Nagarattars is not only closely connected with increased production, but also with reproduction. Women, as auspicious agents, are the central figures in the Nagarattars scheme of gift-exchange. They are producers of future progeny and as such are the most auspicious valuables exchanged between two lineages because without marriage, the lineage can no longer maintain an exchange relationship with the rest of the Nagarattars. As with the Trobriander's exchange of valuables, the Nagarattars marital exchanges only take place within a limited circle, and women, along with other valuables and commodities, are carefully exchanged only within those boundaries.

Thus, the Nagarattars do not regard the handsome dowry which accompanies the woman on marriage as something that is given away, but as an investment for the future, and so the woman's role as mediator between her natal family and her husband's family is crucial. The exchange of women is a reciprocal gift which is the equivalent to forming an alliance between the two families. Because of the Nagarattars' preference for cross-cousin marriage and complete caste endogamy, the wife-giving side is more or less guaranteed that it will have the wealth (and a woman) returned in the future with the accrued interest. Therefore, the kinship system of the Nagarattar generates wealth in two ways. First, it encourages motivation among the individual nuclear families to increase their wealth so that it can be passed on to their children. Secondly, the nuclear family is supported and continually given gifts by the affines in the hope of an alliance, i.e. cross-cousin marriage.

The Nagarattars' work ethic is motivated by the desire to increase their families' prosperity, and to pass enriched property down to the next generation of sons and daughters. Property is handed down but still remains in the caste pool maintained by strict endogamy, which creates capital for larger investment. 'Correct marriages' are essential for this kind of rational economic strategy as the profit-seeking motivation derives from the ethic of caste endogamy and isogamy, which is shared by women, and ultimately benefits the married woman by endowing her with high status as the generator of wealth. It would be misleading however, if Nagarattar women are discussed as the mere agents exchanged as the property, since the identity of a Nagarattar man is inseparable from the wealth and kinship of his wife.

Yet one cannot also deny another aspect attached to the women's property, i.e. 'dowry as the curse of our caste', which was expressed by a well-to-do *aacchi*. I heard some 'Cinderella' type stories such as a son working in the USA, who was from one of the top ranked families, chose a girl of sixteen whose complexion was the lightest among all the candidates in spite of the fact that her family could offer only a moderate dowry. Obviously this would not happen to those poor women like Sala and Umayal who are mentioned in the beginning of this chapter. They are too poor to even be qualified to get married within their own community. In other words, auspiciousness attached to *siir danam* exists because of the existence of such poor women. Just like the auspiciousness of married women *(sumangali)* is fragile, so is the auspiciousness of *siir danam,* as they are both two sides of the same coin. In order to retain the caste membership for their offspring, both men and women should be able to create wealth without which the community loses its means of existence.

4.12   *Siir danam* as 'Affectionate Gift'

As has been already mentioned, the traditional property of men and women is different in kind: while men keep immoveables (land, house), women are given moveables (jewellery, household utensils, and money). While sons' property mostly has an ancestral origin and to inherit it is treated as a right, the daughter's property as *stri dhanam* (i.e. *siir danam*) is called the gift of 'affection' even in traditional Hindu Law. In other words, women's share is always fluid and can fluctuate at the will and wish of the donors, i.e. parents, close relatives etc.

Although the daughters' share of their parents' property is also said to be far less than that of the sons who inherit the majority of the land, house and businesses, women's property has the advantage of being relatively easily liquidated while the immovable property given to the sons may not be as easily liquidated — at least until the father dies. Therefore, although the son has got married, it is unlikely that he can treat his father's property as his own. In the meantime, the money and property which have been brought by the wife can be utilized for various household purposes provided the wife gives her consent. In that respect, both the cash and jewellery tied to women are extremely useful in keeping the family economy afloat.

Cash can be deposited and can yield interest, or it can be used for everyday purposes. The Indians in general still value jewellery more than cash: it can be used as status preserver (ornaments for women) on important occasions as well as property which can be mortgaged. In time of need, it can be sold at the current market price of gold.

Another advantage of gold jewellery exists in terms of credit networking. For example, Ram reports how jewellery circulates through women's 'credit network', created by the affinal relationships (1991: 150). Married daughters are expected to help raise the dowry for their younger unmarried sisters — by using their own jewellery, or by drawing upon the jewellery of their female associates, if necessary. Thus the jewellery given to the previous generation helps finance the marriages of the present generation of unmarried girls (ibid.: 150–1).

Such credit business is more or less a help-line which only creates a negligible hierarchical relationship between the lender and borrower: while financing the poorer relatives, it helps to enhance the prestige of the lender. The women's credit network created by their dowry property acutely differs from what the men create from their business and economic transactions. Ram claims that credit available to men in the workplace is mostly from merchants and middlemen, and its economic purposes and outcome tend to perpetuate the power relations and dependency between creditors and debtors. In such relationships, high interest rates are a crucial way in which the relationship of indebtedness is reproduced in men's credit. According to Ram, women's credit economy, on the other hand, does not lead to a concentration of economic power in the hands of creditors, since as the obligations of the debtors are distributed over a very wide range of people, all owe relatively small amounts (ibid.: 153–4).

Although Nagarattar women in general are not as deprived as the Mukkuvars who even offer their own jewellery in order to marry off their sisters, the credit network still operates among the closely interwoven women's circles which also work to find marriageable partners. For example, senior women from relatively well-off families are connected to Nagarattar women from various economic strata and are known to be extremely helpful. They find partners for girls of marriageable age, and even help finance dowries. When children grow up, they may be asked to find money for education, as well as job vacancies. However, such a women's network does not create tensions between the debtors and the givers as these activities are more or less attributed to the givers' philanthropic inclinations.

Banks and co-operatives, when lending money, define the purposes for which credit may legitimately be given. Business and purchasing or improving the means of production, are considered to be suitable cases for credit. Because the criteria for obtaining credit are so narrowly business-oriented, most people's needs of borrowing money for marriage, education, or day-to-day expenses cannot be catered to and people have to find other ways of getting money. These activities are not classified as 'productive' or production-oriented from the point of view of banks and co-operatives, thus people have to seek other means of borrowing, and turn to the women's credit line.

The women's credit network provides much smaller amounts but for a greater number of day-to-day needs and is also closely intertwined with marriage alliances, especially in the South. As Ram maintains, 'where credit flows between villages, it tends to follow the channels already carved out by marriage exchange' (ibid: 150). It is important to remember that the principal money for such credit networks comes from the *siir danam* given to the woman on her marriage, and the money which the woman has saved since her marriage.

Although neither a married woman's household work nor her credit network are accredited as productive or as economic activities, and they may be categorized as 'jobless' or non-working housewives, their activities are in fact extremely productive. The so-called non-working housewives are able to use their assets to enhance their family status and expand networking with relatives and neighbours. In other words, rather than working as cheap labourers in somebody else's fields, they tend to opt to use their assets to engage in their own economic activities however small the scale may be. Lending money to their relatives with low interest enhances their family status. Therefore, the role of housewives who are not working outside their house may be more important than of those who are (cf. Ifeka 1989), and such married women are also more economically independent than women who carry out field labour (Epstein 1962: 236).

In comparing between the dry-land village Wangala and fertile village Dalena in South India, Epstein clearly shows that

women in Dalena are not working outside their homes but earn income in various ways, and hence are economically more independent and have more access to travel afar than women of Wangala' (ibid.),

which is reminiscent of the activities of the Nagarattar women. The process of earning income through the operation of *siir danam* itself paves the way to create women's network's, as is already discussed, which also serves the purpose of both finding marriage partners for their children and kin, and creating a support system.

In addition, in the case of the Nagarattar women, management of the household economy, as well as the majority of their own property, used to be left to them because of their husbands' long-term absences. This must have played a role in securing greater economic autonomy for them than for the women of other mercantile castes. With the economic autonomy in her hand, the senior *aacchi* exercises more power by playing an important part in devising marriage alliances, as well as being part of the small-scale credit economy which connects families and villages. Although today the middle-class income group among the Nagarattars tends to stress women's wage-earning power in the white collar job sector as an important factor in the conjugal relationship, the community as a whole tends to stress the non-working wives' power which is acquired through networking; and as a whole, the Nagarattars are not ready to discard the tradition of close networking activities carried out by women, as they consider this a crucial part of maintaining their caste identity. Under the guidance of their natal family members, they may acquire the way to manage the fund when they grow old. It is much easier if the fund of a married woman is managed by her natal family. This custom is taken for granted by the Nagarattars, and most of the informants did not mention this fact unless asked by me. For, they insist that the married woman's natal family does it on the behalf of her conjugal household for practical reasons and not because they are following a custom. Yet the fact that the assets given continue to be supervised by her natal family after marriage is a crucial part of the 'protection' provided for a young married woman by her natal family. They know well that handling of property by her natal family would benefit both sides as was the case for Nacchiammai whom I discussed in Chapter 3.

One senior Nagarattar, Veerappa, who belongs to the upper class also manages his married daughter's property. Her dowry money is invested in several funds, her house is let, and the rent is collected by his agent. Her gold, silver, and jewellery are kept in the safe unused, and he awaits the day on which they will be handed down to his daughter's children at the time of marriage. If necessary, he says, his grandchildren or great grandchildren may sell them in the future for reinvestment or to purchase real estate.

He employs eleven accountants and manages the assets of his wife, his two sons, his daughter, his son-in-law and son-in-law's parents, as well as his own. He has three offices in India, and three in Malaysia, but the headquarters of his business are still in Chettinadu where he has his ancestral house and where he set up two primary schools and one college. 'It is better to set up the headquarters in a small town. The fees of accountants are cheaper there.'

According to Veerappa, his son-in-law does not interfere with his father-in-law's management, but entrusts his own savings to him as well, which is also the case for Nacchiammai's husband who belongs to the middle-range income group of this caste. The accumulated income from her property is in the hands of Veerappa and if he ever needs to borrow money for business development, he uses his daughter's fund and returns it at a higher interest rate than the bank's. In this way, he scatters his capital in several channels which are closely connected through kinship and affine networks. In other words, he runs a business which combines the property of his sons, daughter, wife, and his own property forming a limited partnership.

Although they tend to opt for cross-cousin marriages far less than before, the Nagarattars still follow this pattern over a longer time span: even if there is no cross-cousin marriage between their daughter's and son's children, their childrens' descendants may marry in the future and the wealth circulates anyway. This web supports his daughter's status, since a large part of her conjugal fund is still under the protection of her natal family. A similar idea of 'protection' for the married daughter works when the Nagarattars maintain the custom of giving a sum to the married daughter in several instalments on various occasions, such as childbirth and *saandi.*

A senior Nagarattar male maintains, 'You should give big presents in instalments so that your daughter is well looked after by her husband.' In addition, unlike women from most of the other castes, the Nagarattar women are endowed with the right to inherit their mother's property even after their marriage. Such protection goes hand in hand with the interest of the Nagarattars as a mercantile caste. Their strategy clearly aims at hedging a large part of their caste capital as women's property. Thus, the system as a whole also works to eliminate poverty-stricken families by barring poor women from marriage. Both the Nagarattar married woman's high status and the egalitarianism between the wife-taker and wife-giver are secured by such a drastic measure. In other words, 'affection' as expressed in the form of gifts has been well arranged so that capital does not go stray from the caste pool.

Chapter 5

Gender Hierarchy in Wedding Rituals

5.1 The South Indian Wedding
as an Expression of Hierarchy

L EACH argues that rituals are the means by which it is possible to mark the move from one social status to another (1976: 77). Thus, one of the crucial aspects of the wedding ritual is the chance for the bride and groom to express the acquisition of their new statuses. It is also an expression of the bond which unites not only the two individuals, but also the two groups to which they belong and marks the couple's status in the newly established kinship of both the bride's and the groom's side. The woman's capacity to give birth to a child is to be used in order to bring prosperity to two families.

The wedding ritual thus first focuses on the legitimation of offspring. Rituals as 'statements' (Lewis 1981) claim that the child who results from this alliance is given legitimate caste membership. Yet the person who endows the child with his or her status may differ from caste to caste. In castes which express a strong patrilineal-hypergamous ideology, it is the groom who becomes the status-transmitting parent, while in matrilineal castes, the bride's status is of primary concern (Bernard and Good 1984: 113). Among the matrilineal avanculocal Nayars, the pre-pubertal ritual, *taalikattu* is stressed and the role of the maternal uncle is most conspicuous in the ritual. The rite of symbolic consummation between the bride and groom *(sambandham)* is far less important (Gough 1959; Fuller 1976). The patrilineal-virilocal Nambudiri Brahmans, by contrast, maintain that the child's status carrier is the bride. Only an authentic Nambudiri Brahman wife can give birth to a legitimate Nambudiri heir. Yet her acquisition of reproductive power is not marked with any kind of puberty ritual. Instead, it is the marriage union which is celebrated in a grand manner, and importance is given to male

sexuality as is expressed by the exclusively male thread-tying ceremony (Good 1991: 239).

On the other hand, among the South Indian castes who practise
cross-cousin marriage, the role of the bride's mother's brother is
ritually highlighted in women's rites of passage. The puberty rite
and the wedding ceremonies are the most important occasions in
which the maternal uncle plays a ritual role because he symbolizes
the ideal affine who shares the responsibility with the girl's parents
towards the girl's children. In other words, even if a bride does not
marry her maternal uncle's son, the maternal uncle's offspring are
still very important relatives whose line could produce marital
alliances with her children in the future. These affinal relationships
are expressed through ritual gifts sent both to a bride and her
mother by her maternal uncle whose role is taken over by his son
after his death.

However, having seen the wedding rituals of various castes, I
have noticed that even among the patrilineal-virilocal castes who

Fig. 5.1.   Puuram kalikkiradu

prescribe cross-cousin marriage, the role of the maternal uncle is not always equally crucial. Instead, among some high castes, particularly the Brahmans, the wedding focuses on the hierarchical relationship between the wife-giver and wife-taker. Sometimes the importance of the hierarchical relationship between the bride's brother and the groom is also stressed more strongly. Therefore, to gain an understanding of South Indian wedding rituals, it is first necessary to understand the broader context of kinship relationships. Parkin (1992), for example, proposes that two levels of comparisons are needed for the study of rituals: internal comparison and external comparison. Each level involves a study of the hierarchy of values. The former involves the study of each ritual in relation to all of that caste's rituals (i.e. how the rituals express their hierarchy of values). The external comparison examines value hierarchies among collective identities (ibid.: 9).

In my discussion of the ritual roles assigned to the participants, the internal comparison shall focus on the hierarchical relationships between the affines and the husband/wife of the respective castes. The external level of comparison involves the comparative study of hierarchical expressions among different castes (e.g. comparison of the ritual roles of relatives). I shall be stressing the egalitarianism of the Nagarattars between the wife-giver and wife-taker as well as the gender egalitarianism between husband and wife which is relatively stronger than among the Brahman castes. Their bilineal property transfer system, preference of bilateral cross-cousin marriage, and their isogamy which is based on strict caste endogamy, are used to demonstrate their ideology. By contrast, I argue that the strong gender hierarchy between the husband and wife is ideologically stressed in the Brahmanic-vedic wedding ritual. I shall maintain that the strong hypergamous ideology which places the wife-taker in a higher position to the wife-giver is noticeable even among the Tamil Brahmans who tend to prefer cross-cousin marriage.

Hypergamous ideology stresses gender hierarchy. In general, the stronger the tendency of patrilineality, the stronger is the collective ideology, as control is exercised over women's fertility (Good 1991). In a patrilineal system, women's fertility poses a potential threat to that system: by giving birth to a child whose father is not from her status group, she can lower the status of her natal family and if she gives birth to an illegitimate child after marriage, it can have dire consequences for her husband's lineage. Various patrilineal castes therefore express their collective ideology of controlling the fertility of women in rituals and also impose various notions such as pollution on women. The weaker the patrilineal ideology, the less the castes express their ideology of pollution during the process of women's maturity. In addition, during the wedding ritual, the expression of ritual control over women's fertility is also weaker. On the other hand, among the strongly patrilineal groups such as the Brahmans, gender hierarchy is strongly expressed and the notion of women's pollution during menstruation is strong.

South Indian Brahman castes such as the Nambudiri Brahmans and the Tanjavur Tamil Brahmans express a strong patrilineal ideology (Gough 1956; Mencher and Goldberg 1967; Yalman 1971). A bride's connection with her natal family is terminated, and she is cut off and has to adopt the completely new married status of a Nambudiri Brahman woman (Mencher and Goldberg 1967). She uses the same kinship terms as her husband when addressing her in-laws, and her property right is not acknowledged, as her dowry is completely merged with the property of her husband's natal family. As a bride, she has no economic autonomy in her conjugal family and in the patrilineal joint family system, she is under the control of her mother-in-law. Therefore, the bride's unstable status (because she is an outsider) remains until she bears a child (particularly a son). In the case of the Tamil Brahmans, the bride's isolation from her natal family is not as complete as the Nambudiris, as they used to practice preferential cross-cousin marriage, which means that her father in-law or mother-in-law is her father's or mother's sibling. However, as Gough (1956) reports in the case of Tanjavur Brahmans, the separation from her natal family is ritually complete, as she is not supposed to come back to her natal family under any circumstances. She also lacks the right to claim her share of property from her natal family after marriage, and even on divorce, she cannot return to her natal family. When she marries, her dowry falls into the hands of her husband's parents. Thus the in-marrying bride is still considered a partial stranger to her husband's lineage, but to balance this, the husband's lineage needs her reproductive capacity to produce an heir.

The ambivalence surrounding her fertility is clearly observable in the strong notion of the menstruation taboo: while menstruating, she is believed to be a pollutant to her husband and affines. I was also told by a Tamil Brahman priest that the first menstruation after the wedding is believed to be particularly polluting when she stays with her natal family until her period is over, demonstrating that she is still regarded as an alien even after her marriage. Even during subsequent menstruations, married women are to stay either in a hut separated from the main house or at least in a room where she is expected to stay unbathed until the menstruation is over: she is given food by her mother-in-law or sister-in-law who treats her as a pollutant. The menstruating woman is not supposed to touch anything except her own goods, nor is she supposed to cook. Cooking can be done by other women who live under the same roof. In emergencies, the cooking can even be done by her husband. Menstruation is also the justification for the prohibiting of Brahman women from receiving ritual initiation (i.e. the wearing of a sacred thread and the chanting of a *mantra* by the *guru.*) During menstruation, women cannot chant *mantra* or enter the *puuja* room, and so they cannot follow the routines of meticulous *puuja* which an initiated person is expected to do every day. Therefore, *shastric* teaching maintains that women are the equivalent of Shudras even if they are born as Brahmans (Kane 1973: ii/1. 594). This notion of menstrual pollution deliberately prohibits a Brahman woman from being placed on equal ritual footing with her Brahman groom, even in the wedding rituals.

Bearing these points in mind, I shall first describe the Nagarattar wedding so that I can contrast this with those of other castes.

5.2 Wedding Rituals and Expressions of Woman's Life-Stages

In Tamil culture, women's lives are classified into five stages (Reynolds 1980: 36). A female is classified as a girl *(kanni)* before menstruation and becomes a mature woman *(pen)* after puberty. When she reaches puberty, she loses the pure status of a girl, as the menstrual cycle ritually pollutes her body, although this is necessary if she is to become a fertile woman *(pen)*. A virgin is auspicious because of her potential reproductive capacity, although she has to suffer from menstrual pollution every month. On the other hand, a female's natal family has to arrange marriage for her as soon as she has attained maturity, because as an unmarried female, her reproductive capacity poses a threat to her natal family. Her natal family should 'protect themselves from the consequences of any sexual activity she may engage in' (Good 1991: 5) and control her sexuality. It is a great concern for her family, since any sexual activity in which she may engage, particularly with partners of unsuitable status, may lead to loss of status for her family in their caste group (ibid.). From the point of view of her future bridegroom and his family, her virginity should be protected until she marries, since it is a prerequisite for the endowing of proper status for the offspring of his family.

Therefore, some castes prefer to engage in child marriage and transfer the girl before puberty (as was the case among the Brahman castes) to the groom's side. Others segregate a mature woman at home under strict surveillance until she gets married. The pre-puberty ritual of the Nagarattars involves the maternal uncle tying the small *kaluttiru* on his niece. This is intended to symbolize the transfer of part of the responsibility to the future affine, i.e. the maternal uncle. The second stage, i.e. the puberty rite, which

Fig. 5.2. Ritual after the *puuram kalikkiradu*

symbolizes the sealing of the virginity of the girl is officiated over by women only.

The sealing of virginity is symbolically removed on the morning of the wedding, again by one of her woman relatives (e.g. her paternal grandmother), and her maternal uncle gives her the first blessing as the representative of her affine. The wedding ritual transforms her into a wife *(sumangali)*. With this new status acquired at the wedding, she is expected to engage in sexual activities with an authorized partner and to give birth to a child. After giving birth to the first child, she becomes a mother *(ammaa)*, and as both a *sumangali* and a mother, she reaches the peak of the status of womanhood. Her status suddenly changes however, if her husband dies and she becomes a widow *(vidavai,* or *amangali)*. She has to remove her *taali* and live a life of religious austerity. She is considered to be inauspicious on ceremonial occasions because, being a widow, she has already renounced her reproductive capacity. Therefore, as Good maintains, there is no substantive distinction between 'puberty rites' and 'weddings', since all rituals deal with different stages of controlling female sexuality. The major theme of the wedding ritual, therefore, is focused on the transformation of a woman from a virgin to a wife: removal of protection of her virginity is followed by a symbolic sexual union with her husband. The marriage ritual also focuses on affinal ties. The maternal relatives are directly related to reproduction, as the classificatory affine, and they play crucial roles in the wedding, blessing the couple, giving gifts, and representing auspiciousness.

5.3   Rituals of the Nagarattar Wedding

5.3.1   Padaippu: *Ancestor Worship*

The ritual of the wedding starts from the worship of the ancestors, as I explained in Chapter 3. *Padaippu* is a form of ancestor worship performed only by the close *pangaalis*. While the worship of the dead is extremely inauspicious, *padaippu* always takes place prior to any important auspicious ceremony. It should ward off evil by appeasing the dead and asking for their protection. Therefore, the dead, already appeased by their funeral, become benevolent protectors, especially when the living continue to worship them. For this

Fig. 5.3. Brahmanic wedding

worship, Nagarattars (and most non-Brahmans) do not summon a Brahman priest. According to the Nagarattars, since *padaippu* is an auspicious occasion, a Brahman priest is not necessary, since the ancestors are already pure and auspicious.

5.3.2 Muhuurta Kaal *(Auspicious Pole)*

Padaippu should be held before the installation of the *muhuurta kaal* (auspicious pole or auspicious pole-erecting). Good describes the installation of the auspicious pole among the non-Brahman castes such as the Pillais (Vellalars) as follows. A hole is dug at the south-western corner of the courtyard three days before the marriage takes place, and the Ooduvar (a non-Brahman agricultural caste) priest sprinkles coconut water and waves incense and burns camphor over all the items on the banana leaves, and the guests take turns pouring cow's milk into the hole (1991: 111–13). Beck also reports this ritual as a necessary beginning for all auspicious life-cycle rituals (1969: 564–5).

Among the Nagarattars, the hole is not dug in the *walavu waasal*, since it is paved with concrete material, nor do they use a branch with milky white sap. Their ritual is much more simple. Either seven, five, or three days before the marriage, both the bride's and the groom's families tie a long bamboo stick to the roof of their respective ancestral houses at the north-east corner of the *walavu waasal*.

The modern version of *muhuurta kaal* which I saw was simplified, but the emphasis was the same. They prayed to the ancestors and the local spirits for the welfare of the house. When I attended the house ceremony of a groom who was marrying a cross-cousin, before starting the ritual of installing a pole, the paternal grandmother of the groom, an elderly widow who is also the maternal grandmother of the bride, prayed at the *puuja* room in her house, and then went out to the nearby shrine of Muni (a local guardian deity), and prayed again. This demonstrates that the Nagarattars give priority to the local deities who are appeased before all important life-cycle rituals take place.

A man whose title was *Kottahai kaaran* (a man who installs *kottahai*, a marriage pavilion) had been invited and he installed the pole at the corner of the *walavu waasal*. *Kottahai kaaran* was a man of the Pandaaram caste, whose family was hereditarily in charge of this work in the village. 'Kottahai' signifies the temporary hut which is set up for the wedding.[1] The Kottahai kaaran comes alone, and, as an auspicious figure, he is welcomed by the family, making a striking contrast with the lone Brahman priest who is considered to be an inauspicious figure at otherwise auspicious occasions.[2] He turns up alone for another auspicious ritual (arasani kaal) on the night before the wedding. Among the Nagarattars, the distinction between auspiciousness and inauspiciousness is clearly based on the difference between the wedding and the funeral. Therefore, the same hut is given different names according to whether it is being used for a wedding or a funeral. According to Beck, all auspicious rituals begin with the tying of a branch with a milky white sap (muhuurta kaal) to a pillar of the house (1969: 564–5).[3] However, the Nagarattars do not use the branch with a milky sap, but use instead a bamboo pole, and mango leaves and flowers are tied to the upper end of the pole, in the same way as that of the Vellalars described by Good (1991: 111–13). The participants were given milk and betel leaves and areca nuts as the auspicious prasaadam, and in a similar ritual the arasani kaal was installed on the eve of the wedding, using milk and coral as the key symbols of auspiciousness and fertility.

5.3.3 Arasani Kaal

On the eve of the wedding, a wooden plank for the marriage was placed on the walavu waasal, and a koolam was drawn at the entrance and in front of the walavu waasal in the bride's house. Simultaneously, with arasa malam (neem leaves) twined around, a pole was inserted upright into a hole in a concrete block. Inside the hole, small pieces of coral were put with milk, which should never be allowed to dry. At the muhuurta kaal, the white milk combines with the red coral to symbolize sexual union and fertility. The block was then placed in the centre of the platform by the kottahai kaaran who also installed the pole for muhuurta kaal with

[1] A similar type of hut used for funerals is called 'pandal'. But the Nagarattars do not use the same term for wedding and funeral huts, the latter being inauspicious.

[2] The Pandaarams work as the priests of the village deities, and, by caste, they are non-vegetarians.

[3] In the temple festivals I observed, a similar ritual was held at the beginning of the festival. A flag was hung on the pole, and milk was poured on it (cf. Nishimura 1987: 70).

the assistance of the bride's male kin and the washerman brought a red silk cloth and tied it around the beams of the *walavu waasal,* signifying auspiciousness. The block with the hole combined with the pole, represents a symbolic sexual union.

5.3.4   The Symbolism of Red and White

As Beck argues, red is the colour of blood, the source of energy, a substance which is essential to all life processes, but its connotations become negative when it is linked with the spilling of blood, i.e. death, and so it becomes a pollutant (1969: 553).

Red, according to Beck, also symbolizes heat. While body heat is associated with life and fertility, excess body heat is believed to create problems, as it is the energy which can both activate and nullify life. For example, while heat warms the body, excessive body heat kills; the funeral fire burns the body, but at the same time, it purifies the body, and sends the soul to the heaven.

However, Beck argues that heat has to be consumed and controlled and then it can be used as a source of power by humans. Without this control, heat is considered to be dangerous. Red substances symbolize a 'heated' state and white substances symbolize coolness. White, like red, changes its meaning depending on the context: it symbolizes both coolness and death and is considered to be the colour of milk and water. Red, on the other hand, if used in the temple and at weddings, is a sign of auspiciousness and purity. In South India, both water and milk are cooling agents, and in this context coolness represents auspiciousness as cool weather brings rain and leads to a good harvest. Milk and water have a close association in temple rituals: *abisheka,* the purifying and cooling ritual of the deity, involves these two cooling agents.[4] People are given a little milk to drink by the priest at the ritual for purification, and it is also recommended for diseases which are supposed to be created by heat, such as boils. White, the cooling colour, is, however, also the colour of death. A widow's *saree* is white and symbolizes death and infertility. White is auspicious when stability, well-being, and the absence of evil are primary concerns, especially when it is combined with red, as is the case in the temple and at a wedding. A red cloth is often

---

[4] Normally, for this purpose, fresh water taken from a well or sacred river by temple servants is used, but for further purification, they add cow urine and rose-water, and chant *mantras* (esoteric verses) into it.

tied around the major ritual participant who wears a white shirt and a *veetti* at the wedding, puberty ceremonies, and *saandi*. In the temple festival, a red cloth is tied around the pole, from which hangs a white flag representing the image of a deity.

Beck claims that white is desirable when one wants to indicate the end of some climax or disturbance, while red, on the other hand, supersedes the ordinary. The combination, therefore, of red and white is desirable when people want to symbolize the extraordinary (red) surrounded by purity and stability (white).

In the case of the wedding ritual of the Nagarattars, milk (white) and coral (red) fits into this combination, representing auspiciousness and fertility; white as the stability and purity surrounds the red which represents the life force or procreation. The coral, by its red colour, represents new life, while the milk represents semen and also the seed (Shulman 1980: 103). The combination of the pole (phallic symbol) and the concrete block depression (female organ) also represents procreation, and the hope for progeny. This combination is also repeated when the bride receives the *taali* at the *muhuurtam*. The bride wears a red *saree* while the groom is in a white *veetti* and shirt.

5.3.5 Puuram Kalikkiradu

The *puuram kalikkiradu* ritual[5] is held early in the morning on the day of the wedding, before sunrise, as soon as the bride has taken her first bath. She wears an ordinary *saree* and a small garland sent by her father's lineage Shiva temple *(koovil maalai)*, and sits on the plank which will be used for the wedding. The ritual is linked to the puberty ritual discussed in Chapter 2, in that the protection of her virginity is sealed at the ritual of puberty. This protection is now to be removed as the preparatory stage of marriage, as she is transformed from an unmarried girl *(kanni)* to a marriageable woman and then to a wife *(sumangali)*.

After the bride prays with the guidance of the Brahman priest of a local Vishnu temple,[6] her paternal grandmother puts *margosa*

[5] *Puuram* means 'fullness' or 'completion' (Facricius 1972: 733), and *kali* means 'to pass' (ibid.: 214). Therefore, the ritual is meant to mark the maturity of the girl.

[6] Although the Nagarattars are Shaivites, i.e. worshippers of Shiva, they do not mind using a Vaishnava Brahman priest (worshippers of Vishnu) for ceremonies

leaves on the seven spots of the body which were touched during the puberty ceremony. Using a longer margosa twig, the grandmother touches each spot three times, and after that, the bride shakes the leaves from her body. Margosa leaves are believed to be auspicious and are used for medical purposes. Margosa is also associated with the virgin goddess, Mariyamman, and is believed to ward off evil effects and purify the atmosphere.[7]

The ritual is assisted by one of the maternal uncles of the bride.[8] He wears a red silk cloth around his hips, and a spotless white shirt and *veetti* washed by a washerman.[9] Thus the symbol of auspiciousness predominates in this colour combination as the white surrounds the red. He takes the hand of the bride, and guides the bride to the platform and assists her until she sits down.

The maternal uncle is crucial in this setting. As Good points out, the maternal uncle becomes an intermediary between the bride's natal family (her father's lineage) and the family of her future husband (1991: 200). As a cross-relative, and as the classificatory father-in-law of the bride (*ammaan*[10]), the maternal uncle initiates the social process of removing her from her father's jurisdiction, and assists the process of the transfer of her social identity from her natal family to that of her husband. Therefore, he plays a key role both as an initiator and a gift-giver to the couple in the ritual.

As a symbol of purification and auspiciousness, the maternal uncle sprinkles rose-water and petals on seven spots of her body, symbolizing both the removal of the protection of her virginity, and a blessing. This act of blessing is followed by the bride's *pangaalis,* all of which are males, an unusual aspect of the Nagarattar wedding,

---

such as this, which again represents the relative indifference of the Nagarattars to the sectarian differences concerning religious doctrine.

[7] When someone has contracted boils, smallpox, or chicken pox, people hang *margosa* (neem) leaves at the entrance of their house or room in order to ward off heat and contamination. It also symbolizes faith in the goddess Mariyamman who is believed to protect the patient (see Nishimura 1987: 12–13).

[8] In one of the weddings I attended, the bride had three maternal uncles, one of whom happened to be her father-in-law, and so did not play the role of the maternal uncle in the ritual, leaving the other two to play the role by turns.

[9] He should wear the clothes specially washed by the washerman, who is believed to remove ritual impurity from the clothes.

[10] I have explained the kinship terminology in Chapter 3; the Nagarattars call their maternal uncle 'ammaan' while, according to standard Tamil, it is 'maaman'.

since unlike other castes, they do not have the ritual of *nalangu* (anointment of the bride and groom before the. wedding ritual) performed by the *sumangalis*. Even the prayer to gods performed by the bride is a symmetrical performance which is going to be repeated by the groom later. According to the Nagarattars, the bride has the right to start the prayer to gods before the groom since the wedding is held in her *pangaali's* house.

Therefore, the announcement of the bride's marriageability (representation of her fertility) is combined with the expression of egalitarianism in terms of ritual status.

5.3.6 Maappillai Alaippu *(Inviting the Groom)*

In his ancestral house, the groom takes a bath, dresses for the wedding, and proceeds to the Vinayaga temple (or Shiva temple) closest to the bride's house, accompanied by his relatives and parents, where the whole group waits to be served breakfast. Vinayaga is an auspicious god who is worshipped to secure a good beginning. Waiting for the bride's party at the Shiva temple is less common, but still an acceptable beginning, since Shiva is the god of resurrection.

The food is sent to them from the bride's house, as everything is on their account until the evening. Eating food at the bride's house has a symbolic significance for the groom. In Hindu culture, food nurtures the body, and so accepting food from the other party is a sign of accepting an equal ritual status.[11] In marriage, eating together is a sign of mutual assimilation, since the husband and wife are going to eat the same food throughout their lives.

The bride's party go to the temple to fetch the groom with a band of musicians at an auspicious moment. Entering the temple at an auspicious time is important, as is the music which wards off evils. The father and the paternal uncle (or some old senior *pangaali*) of the bride accompanied by a group of people selected from. their side, bring a garland and several presents to the groom. These presents include not only the gifts for the groom but also for his natal family members, yet gifts for the groom himself almost always

[11] For example, Parry stresses the special importance of food intake in Hindu culture both as a source of life and a key symbol of nurture and kinship as well as a source of danger and contamination (if one eats improper food) (1985: 613–14).

consist of a gold chain, a gold watch, a ring, a set of *veetti,* a towel, a shirt, jasmine flowers, lime fruits, *kunkum* (red powder which is worn on the forehead to signify auspiciousness), *manjal* (dried turmeric), and a big garland. The groom is also given a silk turban when he greets the party.[12] When the groom walks from the temple to the bride's house, the townspeople come out from the houses to see him.

The groom, along with his male relatives, enters the *walavu waasal* of the bride's house,[13] and *aarati* is performed by an old woman who is a relative of the bride. At the wedding I attended, it was the bride's paternal grandmother who did this. The paternal grandmother also applied sacred ash to the forehead of the groom.

Procession of the groom along with the troupe is important (Good 1991: 174). According to the Nagarattars, it is intended to show the groom to the bride's villagers. The introduction of the groom to the villagers is also a demonstration of the status of the bride's house.

5.3.7 Praying to the Gods:
Bhagavadyaanam *and Tying the Yellow Thread*

The groom enters the *walavu waasal,* which is now covered with an auspicious carpet, and sits on the platform *(manaavalai).* The *puroohita,* i.e. the Brahman priest,[14] starts the ritual of *bhaga-vadyaanam,* the prayer to the gods, before the important part of

---

[12] According to the Nagarattars, wearing a turban at the time of wedding was a privilege allowed to them by a Chola king.

[13] When the groom is about to enter the house, in some regions, he waits for the bride to welcome him first at the entrance. The bride comes to the entrance with her uncle or aunt (either paternal or maternal). The uncle or aunt lifts the chin of the girl three times so that the groom may see her face. I saw this custom still being observed in the villages of southern Chettinadu. I was told by the people of the eastern region that this custom was practised on the eve of a five-day marriage function, when the groom would ride to the entrance of the bride's house on horseback to catch a glimpse of the face of the bride.

[14] At the wedding I attended, the priest who officiated over the rituals at the wedding, including the *bhagavadhyaanam* on the *puuram kalikkiradu,* was a Vaishnava Brahman priest. Since the Nagarattars are supposed to be Shaivas, this shows that they do not attach much importance to the difference between the Shaiva Brahmans (Shiva temple priests, also called Gurukkals), Smartha Brahmans (home priests), and Vaishnava Brahmans (Vishnu temple priests).

the ceremony. Following the guidance of the Brahman, the groom pours yellow rice on the ground. He sprinkles it on his head as well, and knocks both temples of his head with his fists to beg the gods' forgiveness for any mistakes before he starts the ritual, and also to pray that the function goes well. A large plantain leaf is spread on the ground on which a mound of white rice and a pot with a coconut and mango leaves are placed. A red spot of *kunkum* is smeared onto the coconut and the pot as well, and the groom sprinkles yellow rice over these too.

In front of the groom are five cups which are used for *muraip-paali*. *Muraippaali* is a mixture of five grains soaked in water and sprouted before the wedding. It is a symbol of auspiciousness, fertility, and growth[15] which is also used in temple festivals and in auspicious rituals.

After the *muraipaali* is carried in, the groom mixes the rice in the bowl. The priest places betel leaves and areca nuts in the groom's hands as an auspicious gift. Holding these auspicious things, the groom has a yellow thread dyed with turmeric and a red silk cloth tied around his right wrist by his maternal uncle. They are called *kaappu* and symbolize the protection of the groom to ensure that nothing inauspicious happens to him until the ritual is over. When the *kaappu* is tied around the groom's wrist, he should not be empty-handed, as it is a bad omen. The Nagarattars say that empty hands are a sign of poverty.

The groom places a coconut on top of the yellow rice in the bowl. Coconuts are a symbol of fertility and an essential offering to deities in expressing one's devotion, since the white colour inside the shell is supposed to represent the purity of the devotee's heart. Both the groom and the bride should hold a coconut smeared with yellow-coloured turmeric, with both hands when they tie *kaappu*.

Another pot which contains milk, water, and flower petals is carried in for the ritual of purification and the flower blessing. As the initiator, the groom's maternal uncle soaks his fingers in the pot, and sprinkles the water over the groom, symbolizing his blessing and purification. This is repeated by other male relatives.

This is a preparatory stage of purification given both to the groom and the bride before they tie the *taali*. After the groom sits in front of the priest and goes through this process, he leaves the

[15] Growing *muraippaali* is also practised in the village festival (cf. Nishimura 1987: 71).

platform and sits with his relatives. The bride then comes to the platform and repeats the same process.

As for the colour combination of the whole ritual, the white and red, auspicious and purifying colours, are combined with green and yellow. As Beck explains, yellow is the colour of saffron and turmeric, both of which are cooling substances (1969: 559). Green, as represented in the bunches of leaves, expresses growth, and thus future prosperity. The auspicious colour symbolism of the ritual, especially that of red and white, is strongly expressed by the clothes of the bride and groom. While the groom's clothes are always white, the bride normally changes her *saree* three times. For example, at one wedding I attended, when the bride entered her father's ancestral house, she wore a yellow and green *pattu saree* with gold embroidery, changed to a red one with gold embroidery before the *muhuurtam,* and wore a light blue one with silver and gold embroidery when she attended the rituals in her groom's ancestral house at night. Fuller and Logan, discussing the colours associated with the Goddess Meenakshi at the *Navaratri* festival, maintain that the red colour which Meenakshi wears on the eighth night symbolizes her full sexuality and union with Shiva while the white one which she wears on the succeeding night symbolizes her state of penance (1985: 91). A red *saree* is a symbol of a *sumangali,* i.e. married woman, who is at the peak of her sexual capacity, while a white *saree* is a symbol of a widow, an inauspicious and infertile woman, though she is pure. Similarly, at the wedding of the Nagarattars, the colour of the bride's *saree* symbolizes the state of auspicious fertility. She changes her saree from a modest, auspicious colour to a very auspicious red one, and then to a cooler colour.

5.3.8 Mangaaliyam Puujai

After the purification ritual of the bride and groom, the *kaluttiru* and *taali* are carried in on a plate with limes, jasmine, betel leaves, and areca nuts, and the groom applies *kunkum* to the *taali* and the *kaluttiru (mangaaliyam pujari).* The groom puts *kunkum* on the *tiru mangaaliyam* and *kaluttiru. Kunkum* is a red powder which is always used as an auspicious symbol whether it is in a temple or a house ritual.[16] Lime, jasmine, betel leaves, and areca nuts are all

---

[16] The red colour is mainly associated with fertility, and while in the temple of the goddess both *kunkum* and sacred ash are given to the devotee, *kunkum*

cooling substances while the *kaluttiru* and *taali* are made of auspicious gold (yellow) and there is a red spot at the centre, symbolized by a small ruby.

The plate is carried by the bride's maternal uncle and his wife to all the elders, who assemble around the *walavu waasal* for blessings. Elders, both male and female, touch the *taali* as an indication of their good wishes for the marriage. After this, the groom leaves the platform and sits with his male relatives and friends in a seat near the *walavu waasal*. While he waits for the most auspicious moment to come, the bride is taken into the *kaliyaana viidu* by her female relatives to change her *saree*. The seclusion of the bride at this stage is symbolically important as it is meant to protect her purity until the climax of the wedding. As discussed by Good, the seclusion of a woman symbolizes an intermediary stage: at this point, she is not yet married, since the *taali* has not been tied (1991: 197–9).

According to Good, the women are secluded on two distinct occasions, i.e. during menstruation and at weddings. When a woman is secluded in a hut during menstruation, the liminality exists between the hut and the house, since she is not in a ritually pure state but she is neither wholly excluded nor included in the house which represents 'normal purity'. The hut where the menstruating woman stays demonstrates the intermediary stage a person is in when they are ritually impure, while the house where her family stays represents normality, i.e. it is ritually not impure, and thus shows 'normal purity' (ibid.: 197). On the other hand, at the wedding, the marriage pavilion *(pandal)*[17] represents positive, pure liminality in relation to the other areas where normal life takes place (ibid.).

Good's analysis, however, is partially invalid in the case of the Nagarattars, since the particular space where a woman stays, i.e. both the room in a house during menstruation and the wedding pavilion, seem to have the significance of protecting the woman from the evil effects which come from the outer area. Since women are supposed to be particularly susceptible to evil during both menstruation and before the *muhuurtam*, they are to be protected.

---

is not used in the Shiva temple. Neither *kunkum* nor sacred ash is given to the devotee in any Vaishnava temple, but only a sandal paste.

[17] Among the Nagarattars, the wedding pavilion is called the *kottahai* as *'pandal'* is used to signify the pavilion installed at the time of a funeral.

As far as the Nagarattars are concerned, the factor of protecting the ritual purity of the other house members from the menstrual pollution of a girl is less likely, since she is expected to remain at home even during the menstrual period. There is no separate hut arranged for a menstruating woman. During the wedding, the temporary seclusion in the *kaliyaana viidu* also intensifies the theme of protection.

At the climax of the ritual, the importance of the *ul viidu (kaliyaana viidu)* is highlighted. After the preparatory ritual officiated over by the Brahman priest, she goes back to the *kaliyaana viidu* and awaits for the auspicious time *(muhuurtam)*, surrounded by her female relatives. She is also expected to change her *saree* there with the help of her female relatives, as it is usual for a bride to wear red with gold embroidery when she comes out to receive the *taali* at the climax. Since the *kaliyaana viidu* in which she stays belongs to her father, this stage demonstrates that she is still under her father's jurisdiction and he protects her from evil until the most auspicious time comes. In some areas, the *taali* is tied in this room itself, as an extra precaution.

5.3.9 Muhuurtam: *Auspicious Moment*

Before the bride comes out from the *kaliyaana viidu* dressed in a red *saree,* the Brahman *puroohita* and his Brahman assistants leave the spot temporarily until the *taali* is tied around the neck of the bride.[18] The Brahman priests leave as their presence at the most auspicious moment is undesirable (i.e. inauspicious), because of their association with funeral rituals. This makes a striking contrast with other non-Brahman wedding rituals in which the presence of the Brahman priest is essential at the *muhuurtam*, as Good reports in the case of household weddings among the non-Brahmans (1991: 114–15) as well as temple weddings (ibid.: 117).

On the other hand, the Nagarattars only require Brahman priests when formal rituals are necessary for praying to the gods, thus explaining their presence at the wedding. In any case, a Brahman

[18] Since Brahman priests are not supposed to eat in any non-Brahman house, the Nagarattars arrange for a Brahman house in the village to provide light meals. During the various rituals at weddings and *saandi*, I noticed that the Brahman priests took drinks such as coffee, milk, juice, etc. in the Nagarattar houses although there were strict Brahmans who would drink nothing but milk.

priest is required at the wedding. The couple pray to the gods for protection before tying the *taali*, and it is with this that the Brahman priest assists the couple and he also guides them in Sanskritic rituals. The Brahman priest again assists the married couple to pray to the gods for protection at *saandi*. Brahmans are particularly required for the purification of the ritual setting. When they celebrate puberty and/or *tiruvaadirai*, the Brahman priest is unnecessary.

After the bride changes her *saree* in the *kaliyaana viidu*, she comes out, and stands on the platform while the groom stands below.[19] As the higher position of the bride signifies, she is accorded honour and respect as a representative for the affinal side of the groom, thus implying that the groom's side accept the bride as a 'gift of a virgin' *(kanya daan)* with respect, honouring the giver. After two knots of the *kaluttiru* are tied by the groom, the final knotting is done by the groom's mother and/or his sister.[20] According to Kolenda (1984), the help of the groom's sister or mother in tying the *taali* in a South Indian wedding makes a striking contrast to that of the North Indian wedding. In the South, the groom's sister helps marry off her brother's wife, thus signifying the cooperation between the groom and his female kin in getting the bride to become part of their family, while in the North (e.g. among the Rajputs), it is the bride's brother's wives who help marry off their husband's sister by massaging her, by grinding rice, and by rubbing *dhal* (gruel made of ground chickpeas), rites which end her virginity (Kolenda 1984: 110).

Among the Nagarattars, during the whole process of tying the *kaluttiru*, the auspiciousness embodied in the *kaluttiru* is stressed. After the *kaluttiru*, the *taali* is put around the neck of the bride by the groom. Nowadays, quite a few brides from the lower middle class cannot afford *kaluttiru*, yet the customary ritual of tying the

[19] In the southern region, the couple enter the *kaliyaana viidu*, and tie the thread of the *kaluttiru* inside the room, surrounded by the closest relatives of both parties, expressing the exclusive character of this auspicious but critical moment.

[20] According to an elderly Nagarattar, tying the knots of the *taalis* was done by the elders until the early twentieth century. In one letter he mentioned as a record, the groom was expressing his satisfaction at having acquired the right to tie the *taali*, as this was done by the groom in other communities. The custom of asking the elders of the relatives to tie the *taali* also appears to imply that the tying of *taali* was considered to be a crucial moment which needed to be protected by the kin and the affines.

kaluttiru before putting on the *taali* still takes place. The bride's family hire the *kaluttiru* from one of their relatives, and return it after the wedding is over. As this clearly shows, the ornament is supposed to have such strong powers of regenerating auspiciousness that it is imperative that they have the *kaluttiru* at least for the ritual to ward off evil before they tie the *taali*. The auspiciousness of the *kaluttiru* reflects the status of the *sumangali*. Even if the woman is eighty, if she is still a *sumangali* she will not give it to anybody, even her daughter. She may lend it to a relative if it is needed, however. Therefore, the *kaluttiru's* association with the *sumangali* is strong, and it should not be melted down while she remains a *sumangali*. If the woman dies as a *sumangali*, the *kaluttiru* should be handed down to her daughter or granddaughter, but if she loses her husband, the *kaluttiru* is melted down or disassembled, and what is left is given to her daughter. If a daughter receives the *kaluttiru* from her mother or grandmother, it should be worn as it is. The receiver may add some more gold pieces, but because of the 'auspiciousness' of the *kaluttiru* handed down from the mother/grandmother, the receiver is not supposed to have it melted down or disassembled.

After the *taali* is tied, the couple exchange garlands three times to reconfirm their unity and they then approach the audience to receive blessings. They are also guided by their maternal uncles and their wives to the entrance hand-in-hand, and also to the back of the house so that all the ancestors can bless the couple and all those who are in the house can see the married couple and give them their blessings *(kumbitta kattikiladu)*. The unusual aspect of the Nagarattars' wedding is that they do not request their parents to be present at the crucial moment, i.e. at the *muhuurtam* while it is their maternal uncles whose presence is requested. As I will explain later, this is quite unusual even compared to other non-Brahman castes, although this very fact emphasizes the maternal uncle's link with the marriage ritual as the auspicious agent.

According to a middle-aged *aacchi*, showing the couple to all the people in the house has a dual significance. In the past, widows did not attend weddings nor did they enter the *walavu waasal* to observe the ritual. They stayed in the kitchen and the couple had to go there to receive blessings from them. The couple also seek blessings from their 'ancestors' who are represented by the old photographs hung in several parts of the house.

Among some non-Brahman castes, a procession seems to be practised after the *taali* tying, consisting of the couple and a few close relatives (Good 1991: 116–17).

5.3.10 Signing the Isai Padimaanam

After this is done, the *isai padimaanam* is signed by the fathers of both parties. As I have explained, this is a document stating the marriage contract arranged between the two families. The importance of the *kaliyaana viidu* is represented here as well, as this is where the two parties should sign the contract. After this is done, the couple worship the deities and the ancestors attached to the *kaliyaana viidu* and then come out of the room.

5.3.11 Manaavalai Sadangu: *Ritual Performed at the Platform*

The groom sits with his relatives while the bride remains at the platform waiting for another ritual to be performed. The bride's mother comes with a plate on which a yellow triangular mound of turmeric is placed as a symbol of Pillaiyar (Vinayaga). There are also seven cups containing salt,[21] rice (uncooked), tamarind, cotton, turmeric, sacred ash, betel leaves, and areca nuts.

The groom's mother applies each item under the chin of the bride three times and she also applies it to her own neck. The groom's sisters, if there are any, do the same to the bride both in the house of the bride as well as in the house of the groom in the evening. After these applications, the groom's mother pours water on the mango leaf held by the bride. The bride receives it, worships it, and pours it on the ground three times. The same thing is repeated by her sister-in-law.

The significance of this sequence of the ritual was explained to me by several Nagarattars, both male and female, as that which establishes the relationship between the bride and her mother-in-law. According to them, the ritual symbolizes a 'promise' that the bride makes that she will follow the instructions of her mother-in-law thereafter, while her mother-in-law accepts her as her daughter.

[21] Kolenda, reporting the wedding ritual of North Indian Rajputs, maintains that the symbolic significance of salt and rice used in the wedding ritual, put in a pot and heated up, is that of semen and egg, a representation of sexual union (1984: 109).

The application of materials by the bride's mother-in-law can also be interpreted as the assistance of a female affine to help her daughter-in-law assimilate into the groom's family symbolically, since at the wedding a woman becomes a wife, who shares food with her husband and his family, and as Parry (1985) says, food intake is the crucial part of the ritual.

Assimilation of the bride into the groom's family is also encouraged by the groom's sister; thus she, too, should repeat the ritual done by the bride's mother-in-law. In case the groom has no sister, a classificatory sister of the bride, i.e. the groom's female parallel-cousin would take part. In the case I observed, the groom's paternal uncle's daughter took on this role both at the bride's house and at the groom's house. At this point, both the bride and her mother-in-law (and the sister-in-law) stand on the same level even if the sister-in-law is younger than the bride. Thus, the ritual does not consider the importance of hierarchy between the two, based on seniority of age but appears to stress co-operation between the bride and the groom's female family members, i.e. the mother, grandmother, and the sister of the groom. The grandmother's role, however, is not as central as that of the mother and the sister: she welcomes the couple at the entrance of the ancestral house in the evening, greeting them with the ritual of *aarati,* although any senior female relative of the house may assume this role. She also blesses the *taali* before it is tied around the neck of the bride, but again it is usual for this to be done by other senior relatives and friends as well.

The wedding ritual contains the process of the transformation of the bride from a girl *(kanni)* to a mature, marriageable woman. As I have already discussed, the role of the maternal uncle in the wedding is crucial as he is a mediator between the bride's lineage and that of her husband's. When the bride is transferred to her husband's lineage, the process of transformation is symbolized in the application of food (rice, salt) and other items such as sacred ash and cotton which are also daily household materials which are taken from the house of the groom. By applying these both to herself and to her daughter-in-law, the mother-in-law expresses that the bride has now become her 'daughter', i.e. a family member who will share the same substances that make up the body and the same items which are necessary for daily worship (sacred ash and cotton which is used for the wick of the lamp). Eating together in the same house implies that the participants are of the same family. If a man and woman eat together there are sexual connotations (i.e. husband and wife, see section 5.3.14). By applying both the sacred ash and the cotton used as the wick of the lamp, the bride has become part of the groom's family and, as such, will worship the same ancestors and deities.

5.3.12 *The Transfer of Auspicious Materials*

After the mother-in-law's ritual, three ritual items are brought in to express the newly-established relationship between the groom's mother and the bride. First, there is a silver container with paddy and aubergine on top. The mother-in-law touches the aubergine and repeats the same action to her daughter-in-law as above (touching the bride's neck and her own after touching the ritual object). Next, a plate with a tiny silver doll *(kolavi)* wrapped in a red cloth is handed to the mother-in-law, and she repeats the same action. Both the aubergine and the silver doll represent the future offspring of the bride, and thus the bride's mother-in-law is expressing her wish for grandchildren and blessing the bride in this ritual.

The ritual plates used by the mother-in-law are carried into the *kaliyaana viidu* by the female relatives of the bride who stand beside her. Third, a *sleit vilakku* (a large silver lamp stand with a candle inside) is carried in by the paternal aunt *(attai)* of the bride to the place where the *koolam* is drawn. Without being touched by either party, it is transferred to the bride's mother-in-law's side by the bride's paternal aunt. The Brahmans are not supposed to enter the setting until this ritual is over.

There is thus a sequential transfer of goods — first, the aubergine and paddy implies the prosperity of the household, as both are essential food items and symbols of fertility (they are also used in the puberty ceremony). Secondly, the transfer of the symbol of a child, i.e. *kolavi,* wrapped in red silk, symbolizes hope for progeny. This ritual is repeated when the bride takes leave of her father's ancestral house, and also when she enters that of her husband.

5.3.13 Agni Puujai: *The Ritual Offered to the Fire God Agni*

The *puroohita* returns to help the couple conduct a ritual for Agni, the fire god. The fire is lit, *ghee* is offered to the god, and the couple walk round the fireplace holding hands, taking seven steps. After this, the couple enter the *kaliyaana viidu* for a prayer to the gods, jumping over a straw bag *(kottan)* of paddy.

Binding the couple's hands with a red silk towel and walking around the sacrificial fire is a typical Sanskritic ritual called 'seven steps' which is common among the Brahmans also (Good 1991: 173). According to Good, this ritual is more important to the Tamil Brahmans than the tying of *taali* (ibid.).

A Tamil Smartha Brahman woman told me,

Even if the *taali* is tied around the neck of the bride, anybody who is against the wedding can stop the wedding and nullify the unity while the *saptapadi* (seven steps) is performed. The most important and essential ritual in our wedding is the *saptapadi* as this is when we take a vow in front of the fire god.[22]

5.3.14   Feeding the Groom

As soon as the couple returns to the platform, the bride feeds the groom for the first time *(manaavarai saappaadu)*. A silver plate with ghee, rice, *dhal,* and vegetable curry is placed before them. They sit on the platform, and the bride feeds the groom twice with her right hand and then she washes her hand.[23]

A woman is only allowed to feed a man with her own hand if he is her husband, and so this ritual signifies that the bride and the groom have become husband and wife. After this ceremony, the couple approach the elders for their blessings and the relatives of both parties sign the notebook as a record of their attendance *(moi panam eludal).* [24]

---

[22] Kolenda writes that circling of the fire has now become a regular part of non-Brahman wedding ceremonies, although this does not seem to have been so until recently (1984: 106–7).

[23] Unlike some other Hindu castes, the Nagarattar bride does not eat the leftovers.

[24] As Good reports, the *moy* collection among the non-Brahman castes in Terku Vandanam, which consists of contributions of small amounts of money by those attending the wedding constitutes a substantial amount for non-Brahman castes in general (1991: 121). However, *moy* collection among the Nagarattars takes place only at weddings and it is regarded as token money accompanied by the attendance signatures of close relatives.

5.3.15 Manjar Niir: *Taking Oil and Turmeric Baths*

At the end of the ceremony, the couple take a ritual 'bath' in order to 'cool down' their body and return to their normal condition. According to senior Nagarattars, it was a custom to take a real bath by pouring water from the pot onto the bodies of the couple. This is no longer practised as the Nagarattars have stopped 'infant marriages' in which the participants were children. Nowadays, the couple simply wet their heads, and soak part of the end of the *saree* and the *veetti* in the yellow water. They are given a handful of oil to put onto their heads and then a small quantity of *shikakaai* (shampoo). The relatives of both sides then splash the couple with turmeric water which causes much enjoyment. Ritual bathing with turmeric water is supposed to cool the body and make it ritually pure. Thus after the climax of *taali* tying which symbolizes sexual union (i.e. the heat), the couple is cooled down by this ritual to regain normality.

Taking an oil bath is an essential purifying ritual before attending any auspicious ceremonies or visiting the temples on auspicious occasions. A turmeric bath is believed to be auspicious. Applying turmeric to the skin is believed to beautify women and the Hindus in southern India consider its yellow colour to be auspicious. Taking an oil bath and/or applying turmeric over the face and body is auspicious; it is believed to 'cool the body', and makes the person ritually pure.

The ritual climax of the wedding is represented by 'heat' and should be cooled down, in a similar way to the rituals for a goddess in a village festival. The goddess, when accepting the blood sacrifice, is at the peak of expressing her *shakti*. After she is satisfied with the offering, she is cooled down and appeased by the purification ritual (Shulman 1980: 91; Fuller and Logan 1985: 91). Similarly, the climax of the wedding ritual representing the 'heat', i.e. sexual union, should be cooled down, so that the couple can resume a normal life. The purifying bath symbolizes this process.

5.3.16 Kudi Alaippu: *Bidding Farewell to the Mother's House*

In the evening, the bride goes to the *walavu waasal* of her father's ancestral house and prostrates herself before her close kin, i.e. her grandfather, grandmother, father, and mother. Because of her newly acquired status as a *sumangali,* her younger cousin sisters and her junior brothers and cousins formally prostrate themselves in front of her and bid her farewell while she is standing and she receives their greeting. This kind of formal prostration is done towards senior people but is not performed until the receiver gets married and acquires a formal social status. This formal expression of respect confirms that the bride is already a *sumangali.*

Her paternal grandfather, representing her natal family, gives her a plate of gifts and the cash dowry, and a few coins are tied to the end of her *saree* as charms to maintain her financial security. The bride is then taken by car to a house near the groom's ancestral house until it is time for the *pen alaippu.* Traditionally, the bride's party prepares a snack for both the bride's and the groom's parties. In the past when people travelled to the groom's village on a bullock cart, they had to spend a lot of time on the journey and so a light packed-meal was necessary. Even though now a car is used and it is only a few minutes ride, they still follow the tradition: both parties stop beside the temple tank of the groom's village and they eat the meal even if they are not hungry. It is customary to eat by the temple tank as people used to search for water so that the bullocks could drink. The coins tied to the end of the *saree* are considered to be auspicious agents, essential to the ceremony. When money is used on auspicious occasions, it is usually accompanied by a ceremonial gift of betel leaves and areca nuts, and it is expected to be reciprocal, i.e., those who are given money and ceremonial gifts should give something in exchange either immediately or at some point in the future. However, if the ritual is inauspicious, e.g. a funeral, the relatives refuse to accept any money gifts. Only the service castes, i.e. Brahman *puroohita,* barbers, and Parayas (undertakers), receive money. As I explain in a later part of this chapter, gifts given at funerals symbolize the expiation of sin and pollution, and so any money in this context is strictly regarded as a 'payment' *(sambalam)* for professional services (cf. Good 1991: 124).

5.3.17 Pen Alaippu: *Inviting the Bride to the Groom's House*

The bride arrives at the groom's house with her relatives at an auspicious time in the evening, and is welcomed with *aarati* by an elderly woman of the family. Even widows are allowed to do the *aarati* ritual, especially because the ritual is now in the final stage.

Three large pots *(padayal)* of water are put in front of the *kaliyaana viidu*, and the couple are supposed to search for the silver idol of a small child once again *(kulam waarum pillai)*. As soon as this is over, the bride enters the *kaliyaana viidu*, with the groom and the relatives, and prays to the ancestors in front of an offering of food on banana leaves, comes out and repeats the ritual *(manaa-varai sadangu)* that she had performed with her mother-in-law, in her father's ancestral house.

The bride then participates in basket-carrying rituals with the relatives of both sides (see the next section), and after the *undiyal* (final money calculation) is over, the guests start to leave, bidding farewell to the members of the house. Finally, the bride's relatives and parents take their leave after they have talked and said good-bye. The bride is then introduced to every member of the groom's family.

5.4   *Veevu:* Gift-Giving

During the wedding ceremony, there are three gift-giving rituals which are symbolized in the act of carrying *'veevu'* (it is also spelt as *velvu*), or the wedding gift. The first one is called the *ammaan veevu* and is the gift sent by the maternal uncle of the groom to the bride's house. The second is the *kaliyaana veevu* (wedding gift), and the third is the *mudar warsham veevu* (first year gift), which comes from the bride's family as part of the *siir* (gift from the bride's mother's house) written in the marriage contract.

The gifts which are carried in the *veevu* are an essential part of the *siir*, i.e. gifts from the bride's mother's house. In addition, *maamaa veevu (ammaan veevu)* comes from the groom's and the bride's maternal uncles, symbolizing the financial help of the 'mother's people' from both sides. If the bride and the groom are cross-cousins, the chances are that the bride's father-in-law is also her maternal uncle or the groom's father-in-law is his maternal uncle, who give the present. *Veevu* symbolizes the financial assistance from both the bride and the groom's family and the exchange relationship between the two houses.

As Dumont also reports, gifts from the bride's house *(siir)* are carried in a number of baskets (1983: 81), and giving gifts in a

Fig. 5.4. *Veevu*-carrying ritual

basket seems to be quite widespread all over Tamil Nadu as part of the *siir*.[25]

5.4.1 Ammaan Veevu *(or* Maamaa Veevu*)*

Ammaan veevu is the traditional gift from the maternal uncle at the wedding of his sister's first child. It is given to the first child only when it gets married, whether it is male or female. It consists of sweets, biscuits, fruits, pumpkin *(palangi kaai)*,[26] banana leaves,

[25] However, I could not verify whether gift-giving in a basket is combined in the wedding ritual among other castes as well. I did not come across ethnographic reports that *'veevu irakka'* exists as the wedding ritual among other castes.

[26] Pumpkin is believed to be a 'hot' vegetable which heats the body (Beck 1969). It is also believed to increase sexual desire, and so Brahmans avoid eating pumpkin when they have to conduct special rituals.

sugar, and traditionally a live goat with red silk tied around its neck which was cooked for the celebration meal after the wedding, but nobody gives a live goat these days. In addition to this, two measures of paddy are carried in a *kottan* (a straw bag).

The most unusual aspect of the *veevu* is its carriers. The *maamaa veevu*, after being carried into the *walavu waasal* by the servants from the house of the maternal uncle, are picked up and carried by the bride and the relatives of the bride and the groom, to the *kaliyaana viidu*. Each *veevu* is carried by two people, one from the bride's family and the other from the groom's family. The bride has to carry the *veevu* several times as the significance of the ritual is to demonstrate her status as the housewife of the new *pulli* she has established. The groom sits on the floor observing the ritual, and does not participate, because the domestic economy of the *pulli* is controlled by the wife with the help of her relatives and her husband's relatives.

The transfer of *veevu* also signifies the mutual respect shown by both parties. When the *veevu* is carried into the house, the maternal uncle places it on the *koolam* which is drawn on the floor of the entrance of the *walavu waasal* on which there is also an auspicious lamp carried from the bride's side. The groom's paternal grand-father or paternal uncle then hands it to the bride's party who place it back on the *koolam*. When the groom's paternal grandfather or paternal uncle lifts it, he places it on top of his head to show respect to the other party.

The Nagarattars told me that these acts are symbolic of the way the *veevu* were carried to the house of the bride in the past. According to one elderly Nagarattar, the gift of provisions is the legacy left from the days when the wedding lasted for three, five, or even eleven days.

In those days, we used to have only one ritual per day. We carried all the provisions in *kottans* from the groom's village to the bride's house on foot. The bride's side received them with great respect, which they showed by receiving them on their heads before placing them on the floor.

5.4.2 Kaliyaana Veevu

This is the gift from the parents to the couple. A number of *veevu* are carried from the entrance to the *walavu waasal* by servants, and placed in the *kaliyaana viidu* by the bride and the male relatives.

The significance of both *veevus* is that the manager of the household economy is now the newly-married wife, and the male relatives of both sides show their willingness to cooperate with her. The non-participation of the groom in this ritual is important because it shows that he is ready to endow his wife with the responsibility of household management, while his wife, by carrying the *veevu* with the relatives of both sides, expresses her readiness to cooperate with the relatives.

5.4.3 Mudar Warusham Veevu: *Gift for the First Year*

This is the gift which was traditionally given at the couple's first celebration of Pongal and Deepavali. The gifts used to be sent by the bride's family on each occasion as the fulfilment of a promise written in the *isai padimaanam,* but this custom has changed so that the bride's family send them all on the day of the wedding itself. The transaction takes place in the same way as the *maamaa veevu* and the *kaliyaana veevu.* The gifts consist mostly of food provisions and pots for cooking *pongal* (rice gruel), in addition to the auspicious gifts of betel leaves and areca nuts. Banana leaves and brown sugar are also given as they are essential for preparing ceremonial meals.

In the ritual which I observed, five stainless-steel *kottans* of fruits and coconuts and a lamp were carried in to the house by the bride's grandfather and uncles. They were placed on the *koolam* on the floor of the entrance to the *walavu*. Each male relative of the groom's side tied a towel around his head before lifting the *kottan* with the bride, as if he had carried it a long way, and then the stainless-steel *kottans* were carried into the *kaliyaana viidu*.

5.5 Undiyal: **Settling the Account**

After these rituals are over, the bride's and groom's parties sit in a corner, face to face, and settle their accounts. Traditionally, this is the occasion on which the bride's party hands over the cash dowry to the groom's party on a plate with betel leaves and areca nuts.

On one occasion I witnessed, the groom's father, after receiving the dowry on the plate from the bride's father, handed it to the couple with an application form to open a joint bank account which was filled in by both parties at that time so that the money

Fig. 5.5. Workers cleaning the cooking
vessels after the wedding ceremony

would go immediately into the couple's account. The money for
the groom's mother *(maamiyaar siir danam)* had already been
handed over before the wedding took place.

Concerning the *undiyal,* one senior Nagarattar explains that they
want to clarify money matters referring to the *muraichittai* and *moy
panam eludal* in front of both the parties. If they have forgotten to
give any of their relatives money that was due to them, they have
to rectify the situation there and then.

5.6 Departure of the Bride's Party

After the bride's closest relatives are given money and gifts, they
are ready to leave. The bride's father, mother, grandfather, grandmother, brothers and sisters, and even the bride herself are all
given an auspicious amount of money such as Rs 21, 101, 51,
etc., with some gifts by the groom's parents. They take their time

Fig. 5.6. An *aacchi* hands the gift to each servant and checks the account books as her domiciliary stewards surround her

in bidding farewell to the groom's party, and at this point the other guests bid farewell and leave without any gifts. Around two hundred gifts, consisting of stainless steel vessels with betel leaves, areca nuts, *kunkum* powder, turmeric, and a packet of sweet biscuits are given to the close kin of both parties. A token amount of ritual money is also given to the closest kin of the bride before they take their leave.

5.7   Gift-Exchange and 'Mother's House'

As the whole process of wedding-gift transactions shows, the exchange between the bride's party and the groom's is mutual and ceremonial. Dumont, reporting cases among non-Brahman castes like Piramalai Kallars, Nangudi Vellalars, and Ambalak-karars, stresses the mutual gift-giving involving the bride's and the groom's houses (1983: 82–3). However, there are a few significant differences between such cases and the Nagarattars. First, there is no gift-exchange between the two families at funerals.

There are further differences between Dumont's non-Brahman castes and the Nagarattars. According to Dumont, marriage gifts are categorized into several 'prestations' and 'counter prestations' (ibid.: 80–6). He names *parisam,* a sum of money which is paid to the bride's side from the groom's family as a gift. This amount becomes part of the expense on jewellery which the bride's side spends (although the bride's side should spend at least twice as much on the bride's jewels, according to Dumont).

Secondly, among the non-Brahman castes like the Piramalai Kallars, each ceremonial visit of the groom's side to the bride's house is accompanied by a number of baskets *(siir),* containing foodstuffs and other articles for consumption, and this is increased and handed back from the bride's side. These cyclical prestations

Fig. 5.7. Three brothers present the gift of diamond *taali* to their sister when her husband celebrates the *saandi*

and counter-prestations between the bride's house and the groom's house are both called 'siir' by Dumont, and are defined as external prestations. On the other hand, the money collected among both families on marriage, called *moy,* which helps the relatives contribute to the expenses of the marrying families, he calls internal prestation (he maintains it is often called *surul* by local people).

A number of differences distinguish the case of the Nagarattars from what Dumont reports. First of all, *parisam* given to the bride's side by the groom's side is only token money, such as Rs 11 or so, although this money is always accompanied with the gift of gold of a few sovereigns, as an auspicious accompaniment. The gold given by the groom's side is more important, and it is combined in the *taali* or *kaluttiru* by the bride's side later. Therefore, Dumont's contention of gift-exchange (prestations and counter-prestations) is applicable at this level. The groom's side also sends the gift of wedding *sarees* and a few toilet items for the bride, accompanying the gold pieces.

Secondly, among the Nagarattars, *siir* means only the gift sent from the married woman's mother's house to the married (or marrying) daughter at the wedding and after the wedding. The counter-prestations which are returned as a gift from the groom's side to the bride's side such as the case of fruit, baskets, sweets, etc. are not called *siir.* However, as Dumont mentions 'masculine *siir*', there seem to be some castes which call the prestations from the groom to the bride *siir* as well (ibid.: 82). Thirdly, *moy,* as I have already mentioned, is not a substantial contribution, since the amount is less than Rs 1 (mostly between 25 to 50 paisa). Moreover, the distinction between the internal prestations *(moy)* and external prestations *(siir)* does not appear to be of much use in the case of the Nagaratttars, since the sole importance of the gift centres around the gift from the 'mother's house' to the married woman, and this alone is called *siir.* Even if the gift included her husband's clothes or children's clothes, the receiver of the *siir* is the married woman.

Among the Nagarattars, the successive gift-giving from the mother's people starts on the day of the wedding, and continues throughout her life, and the relationship between her and her brother is inherited by her children. The day after the wedding, after the newly-married couple have been to the temple to worship the deities, they go to the bride's natal family's house for lunch or supper. The bride's family give Rs 21, or 101 to the couple in addition to fruits and betel leaves and areca nuts as a ceremonial gift. The couple again visit the bride's mother's house the following day, for another meal *(rendaam wali)*, and then visit the maternal uncles' houses of both sides, and have either lunch or tea there. Such visits made by the newly-married couple are rewarded with the money gift given by the bride's natal family and maternal uncles. According to the Nagarattars, it is only after these three visits are made to the close kin of the bride's side that the couple may go to the houses of others, and this is when the couple becomes 'ordinary'. This custom may be practised to ease the psychological isolation of the bride from her natal family as the relationship between her newly-established house and her mother's house is firmly established by these visits. However, the establishment of such relationships between the couple and the wife's people are also made by the gifts given to them on their visits, particularly just after they get married. The rule that the newly-married couple cannot begin an ordinary routine life until they visit the wife's people is consistent with the latter being the most important gift-givers.

Because of this 'established relationship', the importance of the bride's mother's house to neutralize abnormal situations can be observed even after a man has taken a trip abroad. The Nagarattars believe that long ocean journeys are dangerous and so after a man has crossed the ocean and has returned to his natal village, he must visit his wife's 'mother's house' and have at least one cup of coffee or tea. Then after he has resumed 'normality' he goes back to his own house to his wife and family. A woman who has been abroad also observes this custom. She goes to her 'mother's house' to have a cup of coffee before going home to see her children.

The area in which the Nagarattars can readjust to normal life, and the safe zone for both the husband and wife, is the wife's 'mother's house' where they eat some food, which nourishes and helps the couple to return to normality before going home.

In the following, I shall contrast the Nagararattar wedding with other weddings starting with that of the Brahman's, since the latter is in sharp contrast to the Nagarattars in terms of the expressions of hierarchy of gender and that of the wife-giver and wife-taker. The conspicuous difference between the Brahmans and the non-Brahmans can be observed in terms of the ritual role of the affines; among the Nagarattars, the role of the parents of the bride and groom are not essential while the role of the Brahman's maternal uncle *(ammaan)* and paternal aunt *(attai),* and especially that of the maternal uncle, is crucial. Another difference exists in the concept of *kanya daan,* or the gift of a virgin. While it is clearly expressed in the Brahmanic wedding ritual, it is completely absent among the Nagarattars. I shall now discuss the hierarchical relationships between the wife-giver and wife-taker which is clearly expressed in the Brahmanic wedding, especially in the ideology of *kanya daan.*

5.8   The Ritual of *Kanya Daan* in the Brahmanic Wedding Ritual

The Brahmanic wedding can be summarized in ten significant rituals: (1) *nalangu* (ointment); (2) *kaasiyattra,* i.e. the groom leaves for Benares, the sacred city, in order to become a world renouncer; (3) *unjal* (when the couple sit on a swing and are worshipped as divine figures by the five *sumangalis* or the auspicious married women whose husbands are alive); (4) *homam* (offering of *puja* to the fire god); (5) foot-washing of the groom by the bride's parents; (6) *kanya daan* (the bride sits on the lap of her father as the gift of a virgin); (7) *mangala sutra or taali kattu* (the tying of the *taali* or the wedding pendant around the neck of the bride by the groom); (8) seven steps *(sapta padi);* the lifting of the left toe of the bride with the right finger of the groom; (9) *ammin mudikkiradu,* (the groom places the bride's right foot on the *ammin,* the grinding stone ; (10) *kumbitta kattikkiladu* (receiving the blessing from the attendants.) Several rituals are of particular interest when considering the Brahmanical gender hierarchy. The *nalangu* is a blessing in which elders and *sumangalis* place some oil on the head of the bride and groom. By repeating this ritual several times until the wedding ritual starts, the couple's status is supposed to be elevated to divine status. Thus this ritual itself does not convey any gender hierarchy. However, as Bennet (1984) maintains in her discussion of a Nepalese vedic wedding, the status of the bride (but not of her husband) is deliberately lowered after elevating the status of the couple to a semi-divine status.

The male 'dilemma' is ritually expressed in *kaasiyattra* in order to signify the ritual superiority of the husband over his wife. As a Brahman who belongs to the caste who seeks the highest religious value, the groom leaves the wedding hall to take up the life of *sanniyaasi*, the world-renouncer. According to Brahmanic values, ultimate freedom from *samsaara* (life of repeated rebirths) is possible only after observing religious discipline as a world-renouncer. However, the bride's father comes and reminds him of the life of *grhasta* (householder), offers his own daughter and asks the groom to marry her. Therefore, by repeating this ritual, Brahman males are reminded that their religious ideal is *sanniyasinhood* the attainment of the life of *sanniyasin*. However, they are going to be married, and so are expected to live a contradiction, since marriage leads to a worldly life as a householder and thus the 'renunciation' of the pursuit of the ideal religious goal. The bride, living a worldly life without the right to pursue the highest religious goal, has indirectly forced the groom to lead a worldly life too by marrying her. This is the justification for their subsequent hierarchical relationship in married life.

Among the Brahmans, ritual status is endowed patrilineally. However, only male members are endowed with the full-fledged status of ritual officiates. Brahmans also maintain that world renunciation is the highest possible religious achievement of the true Brahman (Dumont 1970*b*: 43; Heesterman 1985: 155). The idealized 'reluctance' to get married and start a life as a householder implies a dilemma between the ideal of world renunciation and the worldly life as a householder. In addition, it may also express the reluctance to accept the bride as the *kanya daan*. Parry (1989*b*), in his discussion of 'the gift' in India, argues that a hierarchical relationship between the giver and receiver exists when 'the gift' embodies a strong religious connotation as the expiation of pollution or 'sin'. Quoting Raheja (1986), Parry demonstrates that the gift of a virgin *(kanya daan)*, which is said to expiate the sin of the father, also fits into the same category of religious gift as a poisonous one. Parry maintains that the Brahmanic dilemma exists because of the gap; only the meritorious Brahmans who are detached from normal worldly life can receive the *daan* without harming themselves. Therefore, the Brahmanic priests who receive the *daan* for their living feel that undigested sin is accumulating within them and that in the hypergamous Brahmanic culture, wife-takers are considered to be ritually superior as they are the receivers of the *kanya daan*, the most meritorious gift by the bride's father (1989*b*: 67). By receiving a bride as the *kanya daan* from the person whose ritual status is lower than the receiver's, the groom's side symbolically endangers their ritual status. This situation, according to Parry, is consistent with the fact that the the bride herself is stereotypically represented as the source of division and conflict within the joint family into which she has married (ibid.: 73). In other words, she pollutes and causes danger to the family she is marrying into. As Heesterman argues, the ideal Brahman, by virtue of vedic knowledge, is not overcome by evil by receiving gifts: an ideal Brahman is self-contained and independent, and in order to maintain his independence, he does not engage himself in the world, but renounces it (1985: 44). Thus a Brahman is constantly facing the dilemma of choosing between renunciation and the householder's world. Taking a bride as a gift is necessary to have offspring and continue the line, yet accepting it itself means being tied to this world. This dilemma is well expressed in the *kaasiyattra* as well as the Brahmanic concept on women's menstrual pollution. Other rituals such as foot-washing, *kanya daan, ammin mudikkiradu,* and *arundati,* all appear to emphasize the gender hierarchy between the bride and groom which is created at the moment of *kaasiyattra.*

5.9 The South Indian Brahman Wedding

The modern Brahmanic wedding is much simpler and shorter than it used to be, especially if it is conducted in a wedding hall.[27] In the wedding I attended in 1994 in Karaikkudi, the whole process took two days in a far simpler form than in the past. On the first night, *nalangu* was held, as was the betrothal ceremony *(nicchaital)*[28] in which presents (such as *sarees* for the bride and suits for the groom) were exchanged. On the following day, the major rituals were held.

The groom undergoes the ritual of status transformation, i.e. from birth (when he is given a name) to adulthood. As a Brahman he wears a *puunul,* a sacred thread to signify his Brahmanic status. Offerings are made to the patrilineal ancestors of the bride's father and a series of Brahman priests (in this case, eight Brahmans) sit on the floor below the platform where they receive *daanam* (gift to the Brahman priests for religious merit) from the bride's family as representatives of the bride's father's patrilineal ancestors. As

27 Until the 1940s, the wedding would last for three days.
28 (Thurston and Rangachari 1909: ii. 278).

these two rituals show, the groom's status is confirmed as the successor to the patriline. Male sexuality, i.e. male maturity, is also strongly marked as expressed in the above status transformation. Male ritual superiority is also stressed as they alone are endowed with the right to chant the *mantra* in this kind of public ritual.

After the ancestors are worshipped by the bride's family members and close relatives, the *kaappu* (a yellow thread which signifies protection) is tied around the couple's wrists: the groom's is tied by the priest, but the bride's is tied by the groom, again reinforcing the gender hierarchy. In the third stage, the ritual *kaasiyattra* is conducted. The groom's loin cloth is tucked up as an expression of departure, and he carries a stick and a rice bundle, while a close relative holds an umbrella for him as he starts to depart for Kasi (Benares) for religious study. His father-in-law comes out from the wedding hall, and offering two coconuts smeared with turmeric, he declares to his son-in-law that he has a daughter to offer him as a bride (following the guidance of the Brahman priest, this sentence is announced in Tamil). The bride, accompanied by her female relatives, comes out to the entrance of the hall and is officially introduced to the groom by her father.

Then the bride and groom are lifted onto the shoulders of their respective maternal uncles, as a legacy of traditional child marriage, and exchange their garlands. This is the only ritual in which the maternal uncles play a major role in the wedding rituals. After this, the couple enters the wedding hall hand-in-hand, where a swing is already set up. The ritual called *unjal* (the swing) starts. The couple, sitting on the swing, receive the worship of five *sumangalis* who are mostly classificatory aunts from both sides. This ritual is said to lift the status of the couple to divinity, i.e., Vishnu and his consort Lakshmi, before the highlight of the wedding ritual. The *sumangalis* wash the feet of the couple and wave the red and yellow rice balls. According to the Brahmans, these balls are to feed and pacify the *peey* (evil spirits). Each *sumangali*, singing songs, faces the couple on the swing, waves the tray three times clockwise and three times anti-clockwise, and then throws a ball north, south, east and west to ward off evil spirits.

After this, the couple proceeds to the main platform, towards the ritual hearth. In preparation, the bride's father washes the feet of the groom, assisted by his wife. Foot-washing is a typical vedic ritual which expresses respect with a strong religious connotation:

the person whose feet are washed is ritually higher than the washer, and thus signifies the hierarchical relationship between the *guru* and disciple or husband and wife. In this context, the ritual rank of the father of the bride is deliberately lowered in relation to his son-in-law. As the receiver of the sacred gift, i.e., the gift of a virgin, the groom's ritual status is higher than the bride's father's.

Next, *kanya daan,* i.e. the gift of the virgin, is carried out. The father of the bride sits on the chair and the bride sits on his lap while the groom stands in front of them. The Brahman priest of both sides announces the *gootra* (the patrilineage to which they belong) of the bride and groom in order to express the legitimacy of the marriage. Before the *taali* (a gold pendant to signify the married status of the bride) is tied around the neck of the bride, her Brahman priest takes the *taali* and ties it around a piece of wood which symbolically represents the bar which pulls the bullock. This ritual is called *nuhattadi* (it literally means a yoke). The two *taalis* are touched by the Brahman priest and then by the groom who places the wood on the head of the bride. She vows to be under the guidance of her husband, as symbolized by the bullock controlled by the wooden bar. According to the Brahmans, this ritual signifies the teaching that the bride should not forget that she must keep pace with her husband but must not go ahead of him. According to a Brahman wife in her late forties, the wooden piece was much more like a real yoke when she married more than twenty years ago and that it felt very heavy when placed upon her. After this, the *taali kattu* (tying the *taali)* takes place with the bride again sitting on her father's lap. The first knot of the *taali* is tied by the groom.

Next comes the worship of the fire god, Agni, by offering oblation and then the ritual of seven steps *(sapta padi)* takes place. The groom, bending towards the bride, holds the middle toe of the bride's right foot with his left hand, and gradually leads her towards a stone grinder *(ammin).* Counting seven steps altogether, the groom places her right foot on the stone grinder. After putting the bride's foot on the stone grinder, he points to the sky, showing his bride the star Arundati, a symbol of the loyal and faithful wife.

This is said to be the most crucial part of the Brahman wedding (Thurston and Rangachari 1909: ii. 286), but confusion arises between this ritual and the rituals of walking around the fire, also referred to as *sapta padi* (Good 1991: 173). During the wedding I attended, the placing of the bride's foot on the grinding stone was called *sapta padi* and the bride and the groom walked round the hearth three, not seven times. Each time they sat down in front of the hearth, offering *ghee* and puffed rice, given to them by the bride's brother (see Bennet 1984: 84, for the similar ritual role of the bride's brother in the high-caste Hindu weddings in Nepal). After this, the couple received blessings from the elders, while an odd number of Brahman *puroohitas* (five *puroohitas* in this case) continued to chant *mantras* on the platform. Although there are slight differences between the Aiyars (Smartha Brahmans) and the Aiyangars (Vaishnava Brahmans), the above features described seem to be common to most Tamil Brahman weddings nowadays; particularly since they started to use wedding halls and to engage priests who are not from their own area, which contributes to the standardization of the rituals.

The Brahmans insist that it is not the *taalikattu* which is the most crucial part of the wedding, but the *sapta padi,* i.e. when the groom touches the right middle toe of the bride and puts her foot on the grinding stone. The ritual does not take place among the Nagarattars but some other non-Brahman castes seem to have taken it up with certain modifications.[29]

The *sapta padi,* i.e. touching the toe of the wife, combined with *Arundati,* i.e. looking at the star Arundati, are considered by some Brahmans to be more crucial than the ritual of walking around the fire (Thurston and Rangachari 1909: ii. 286), and also seem to be considered as the most important ritual in the North Indian patrilineal high-caste wedding, especially among the Brahmans. For example, in Nepal, among the Brahmans and the Chettri castes reported by Bennet, it is the crucial ritual in establishing the relationship between the husband and wife (1984: 84). Bennet comments that in some pictures of the king's wedding, the groom touched the bride's foot with a handkerchief rather than his bare

[29] I have checked with other non-Brahman communities and the Mudaliyars, an agricultural caste, are the only one in which I have observed the existence of this ritual at their weddings. The Mudaliyars are regarded as one of the higher castes; they are Shaivas, and highly Sanskritized in their manners and customs. For example, they are vegetarians and like the Shaiva Vellalars, also have caste *madams* in several places. At the Mudaliyar wedding I attended in 1986, in the Pudukottai district in Tamil Nadu, Brahmanic themes such as *kanya daan* and *sapta padi* were quite predominant.

hand, since according to an explanation of a priest, men who belong to the younger generation were too proud to touch their wife's foot with their bare hands even during this important rite (ibid.). Yet this priest informant clearly explains to Bennet that 'the purpose of this rite was to ensure that the wife would henceforce be subservient to her husband'. By showing respect for his bride while she still has the semi-divine, high ritual status at the height of the wedding, the groom would touch her foot without debasing his own ritual status. He thus acquires his right to receive respect from her in their subsequent married life (ibid.). Touching the toe of the bride by the groom therefore strengthens the control the husband has over his wife. Similarly, among the South Indian Brahmans, I was told that putting the bride's foot on the grinding stone is to show her that wifely duties involve being faithful to her husband, and being solid and reliable, like the firm grinding stone.

Hierarchy is also expressed between the wife-taker and wife-giver especially in the foot-washing ceremony. In Hindu culture, as I mentioned above, foot-washing is practised as an expression of respect, especially of someone with ritual superiority. Therefore, the disciple washes the feet of his *guru* and the priest washes the feet of the divine image. Among the high-caste Hindus in Nepal, the wife washes the feet of her husband before every meal and the father washes his virgin daughter's feet in the ancestral worship ritual, since, in the hypergamous setting, she is already expected to marry into a family which is ritually higher than that of her father (ibid.). During the high-caste Nepalese wedding ceremony described by Bennet, the bride's father also washes her feet and drinks the water three times, gives her some money, and worships her by touching his forehead to her feet. Then he washes the groom's feet in the same way and the whole sequence is repeated by the bride's mother, her mother's co-wives, her father's brothers and their wives, etc. signifying their acknowledgement of their lower status in relation to the bride's husband (ibid.: 81) The wife's inferior status in relation to her husband is combined with her high status in her natal family. Although South Indian Brahmans do not require the brides to wash feet and drink the water in which their husband's feet are washed, the relationship between the bride and the groom is still hierarchical. Compared to such Brahmanic practice, non-Brahman weddings especially those of the Nagarattars in South India, form a striking contrast.

5.10   Komutti Chettiyar Wedding

Komutti Chettiyars (or Goomti, Koomati Chetti) are a trading caste of Telugu origin and are especially renowned as jewellers and grocery merchants. They also call themselves *Vaishya* (the third category in the vedic hierarchy signifying merchants), and traditionally follow a Brahman *guru* (Thurston and Rangachari 1909: ii. 306–48). However, unlike the Nagarattars, they do not specialize in long-distance trade, although their families do live jointly. Their joint houses are patrilineally organized, but tend to have a male head who is the most senior man in the family. They tend to merge all the members' property so that the dowry carried by the bride is handed over to her mother-in-law. I have seen many of this kind of joint houses shared by three to four generations, even in the big cities, although unlike the Nagarattars, the conjugal facilities are not economically autonomous. Nonetheless, the relationship between the wife-giver and wife-taker is quite equal which can be seen from their strong preference for bilateral cross-cousin marriage. The role of the maternal uncle as the bride's guardian is also less strong among the Komutti Chettiyars than among the Nagarattars.

I noted these features while observing their wedding rituals. In contrast to the Nagarattars however, the Komuttis consider the Brahman priest to be their *guru* while the Nagarattars see the Brahman priest to be an inauspicious agent at an auspicious occasion. Yet, in spite of this, the Komuttis strictly adhere to Brahmanic ways, for example, the *kaasiyattra* ritual. Instead of the groom pretending to be a 'world-renouncer', he wears a silk turban, jewellery, silk clothes, and behaves like a 'king', who is stopped not by his father-in-law, but by his brother-in-law, in a casual, friendly manner. Although the equality between the wife-giver and wife-taker is stressed by the Komuttis, the hierarchical relationship between parents and children is expressed by the latter washing the former's feet. In addition, the mother-in-law/daughter-in-law relationship is shown to be more hierarchical than that of the husband and wife, since the bride is expected to wash her mother-in-law's feet and not those of her groom. The first foot-washing ceremony takes place soon after *kaasiyattra* when the bride's parents wash their daughter's feet. This might be considered as a replacement of *nalangu*, when the status of the bride is elevated to divinity. The groom's feet are also initially washed by his parents. The second foot-washing is done later both by the bride and groom to their own parents. This order therefore, would signify the elevation of their parents' status, since the bride and groom, after receiving the foot-washing, become semi-divine figures. The third one is performed by the bride who washes her mother-in-law's feet, signifying that the relationship with her female in-laws is more important to the bride. However, this does not lower the status of the bride's natal family. Instead, the Komutti wedding ritual deliberately equates the ritual status of both sides at the beginning of the wedding. The bride, groom, and their parents sit on benches facing each other. The fathers then apply sandal paste to each others' arms, symbolizing their equality. In order to stress this, the two parties even switch benches for a second application of the sandal paste. In addition, each father ties the *kaappu* around his own child's wrist. As this sequence of ritual shows, the father's role is more important than the maternal uncle's, in comparison to the Nagarattar wedding.

Several Brahmanic motifs are also taken up by the Komuttis, such as *sapta padi*. However, it is expressed quite differently: in *sapta padi*, the bride's toe is lifted by the groom and then touched to seven betel nuts which are placed on a large plantain leaf on the floor. Moreover, after the *taali* is tied, a unique ritual takes place which involves the Brahman priest. In this ritual, the Brahman priest is a jovial and comical figure, who teaches the wisdom of life using the sweetness and sourness of food. Having the Brahman priest play the part of a talkative figure is somewhat unusual although it does fit with his role as their caste *guru*, even if it differs greatly from the role of the priest among the Brahman caste, as well as that of the Nagarattars. In this ritual, the priest, pointing to the salt (symbol of difficulty in life) and the *dhal* (chickpeas, symbol of sweet things) on the floor, asks the bride and then the groom to choose either of them. When each has chosen, the priest explains the connotations of salt and *dhal.* Finally, he explains to the couple that the real sweetness of life exists in the combination of both, i.e., hard and smooth, and that the couple should be united to accept both. Secondly, the priest explains the difficulty of family life using a doll, stressing that the co-operation and discussion between the husband and wife are crucial to sustain a family life, especially after their child is born.

As this humorous part of the ritual shows, the relationship

between bride and groom is one of equality at least in important decision-making processes, and the role of the Brahman priest as teacher, rather than ritual specialist who maintains ritual purity and pollution, is clearly demonstrated.

5.11 Arcot Mudaliyar Wedding

The wedding of the Arcot Mudaliyars, from Madras, commences with *nalangu,* which takes place between two and seven days prior to the wedding. *Maappillai alaippu* (inviting the groom to the bride's house) takes place on the morning of the wedding, as does further oil bathing and *nalangu,* in order to elevate the status of the bride and groom to divinity. The *arasaani kaal* (auspicious pole) is installed by five *sumangalis* with the help of the priest. The groom washes the feet of his parents and in exchange, his parents bless him by throwing yellow rice, signifying the hierarchical relationship between child and parents.

Kaasiyattra is also performed, but like the Komuttis, it is the groom's brother-in-law who comes and fetches the groom who is dressed up like a king. In this case however, the brother-in-law does the foot-washing of the groom and gives him a new pair of shoes as an expression of affection. According to an Arcot Mudaliyar, this signifies the blessing of the brother-in-law who offers him a gift to express his goodwill.

Kanya daan takes place between the bride's parents and the groom's parents, although it is quite different from the Brahmanic version. The bride holds the coconut on a plate, while her mother pours water and her father touches the coconut as well. The plate is then passed on to the groom and his parents. It can be seen that the emphasis is on the transaction between the bride's parents and the groom's, just like the expression of equality between the wife-giver and wife-taker among the Komuttis. After the *taali* is tied, the bride places her feet on the grinding stone *(ammin)* and the groom puts the toe ring on her left toe, and they take seven steps round the fire *(sapta padi)* There is no lifting and touching of the bride's toe by the groom.

Another conspicuous feature is that there is no specific ritual role for the maternal uncle in their wedding. However, this seems to be due to the fact that in this community, it is always the maternal uncle who is given the first preference to marry the girl.

If the mother's brother is often the groom, it is difficult to assign him any conspicuous role as the girl's maternal uncle.

5.12   Kamma Naidu Wedding

The Kamma Naidus are a caste of Telugu origin (i.e. from Andhra Pradesh), who were traditionally successful landlords. Nowadays they are mainly agriculturalist-cum-landlords, traders, and entrepreneurs who are extremely successful in the Coimbatore area of Tamil Nadu. Thurston and Rangachari tell us that in Tamil Nadu, Kamma women are more active participants in production than those who live in Andhra Pradesh (1909: iii. 94). Unlike women of other high-castes, the Kamma women maintain that they have enjoyed relative gender equality both at home and within their caste due to their economic activities because they used to work with men in the fields as supervisors. According to these women, there is no profession which is prohibited to them: they can take any jobs they want or participate in either their father's or their husband's business. Even when they are married and have children, there is no stigma attached to being a working mother. However, unlike the Nagarattar women, their dowry is minimal. They are given gold jewellery which is far less valuable than that of the Nagarattars', and they cannot claim any share of their father's business as their dowry. Instead, they are expected to earn their economic autonomy. They may work either in the family business or be white-collar professionals, and in both cases, they receive encouragement and financial support both from their fathers and brothers, and even from their husbands. The men, as corporate 'investors', benefit from allowing their women to participate in production outside the domestic sphere. As a matter of fact, Kamma women are renowned for being 'forward' in Tamil Nadu as many of them are white-collar professionals as well as businesswomen.

The wedding I saw in February 1995, took place in Coimbatore in Tamil Nadu. In spite of the fact that they claim to be *kshatriyas,* following the vedic tradition, and engage Brahman priests for ceremonies, their wedding ritual shows less evidence of a gender hierarchy between the bride and the groom than Brahmans or other high castes such as the Komuttis or Arcot Naidus.

Unlike Brahmans, the rituals are officiated over by both the bride and groom, although there exists a gender division of rituals.

The preparatory ritual of the previous night is performed by the bride, while the groom does the major rituals on the day of the wedding. The first foot-washing ceremony in the wedding hall is carried out by the bride's parents who wash their daughter's feet while the groom's feet are washed by his parents, as both the bride and groom are considered to have been elevated to the status of semi-divine figures. The second foot-washing ceremony takes place before the *taali*-tying ritual in which the bride and groom wash the feet of their own parents. The crucial part before tying the *taali* is the pouring of water over the hands of the bride and groom which takes place after the bride and groom are separated by a silk screen on the platform. The bride's mother, assisted by the father, pours water over the hands of the bride and the groom who, together, are holding a coconut below the silk screen. After this ritual, a *taali* is tied around the neck of the bride.

The egalitarianism between the bride and groom is expressed in the foot-washing ceremonies as seen above, in whicn neither the bride nor her father washes the feet of the groom. There is no *kaasiyattra,* but the meticulous preparatory rite focuses on the elevation of the bride and groom to semi-divine status as expressed in *nalangu* and the pouring of yellow rice and the sprinkling of flowers, yet there is no ritual to lower the status of the bride while retaining the high status of the groom.

A hierarchical relationship between wife and husband is sym-bolized by the control of the wife's sexuality as is the case with the Brahmans, while the reverse tendency may imply a sharing of decision-making power between husband and wife, as is the case with the Nagarattars and Kammas. Hierarchy that exists between a wife-giver and a wife-taker expresses a hypergamous tendency, as seen in the *kanya daan* ritual. The rituals of the Komutti Chettis demonstrate a deliberate negation of this, which underlines their isogamy. A hierarchy between parents and children is strongly expressed among the Komuttis, on the other hand, and less strongly by the Arcot Mudaliyars and Kammas, which would imply a continuous bond with the bride's and groom's natal families as well as their assurance of caste membership endowed by their parents. In the case of the Brahmans, this is much weaker, although the daughter's relationship with her father is expressed when the former acts as the religious 'gift' for the latter to expiate sin. Lack of parent/child relationship is conspicuously less important for the

Nagarattars, where the *pangaalis* and maternal uncles act as primary ritual performers.

5.13   Gender Hierarchy and Hypergamy

As these comparisons clearly show, two major points are noticeable in hierarchical expressions in the wedding rituals: (1) the gender hierarchy between husband and wife; (2) the hierarchy between the wife-giver and wife-taker. In discussing these two points, I have demonstrated that the strength of the hierarchy can be studied by comparing several rituals performed during the wedding ceremony, especially if the Brahmanic-vedic wedding ritual is used as the yardstick of comparison. However, through the study of the weddings of various castes, it has also become clear that the role of the maternal uncle is not always conspicuous, although the absence of a clear role for the maternal uncle does not necessarily mean that the wedding ritual as a whole conforms to the Brahmanic mode.

The Brahmanic ideology as expressed during the wedding rituals, stresses control over women, over their reproductive capacity and sexuality. Although control of female reproductive capacity and sexuality is universally observable among other castes and certainly among the Nagarattars, among the latter this theme is not as dominantly expressed as that among the Brahmans. The Nagarattar theme of sexual control is closely associated with the bilateral cross-cousin marriage, and not the hierarchical relationship between the groom and his father-in-law.

In this sense, I agree with Beerman who argues that the so-called Sanskritization (i.e. the imitation of the manners and customs of the upper castes, especially the Brahmans', by the lower castes) suppresses females. He maintains that females have the least autonomy and equality with men in the Sanskritized segments of Hindu society (1993: 370), and that the lower castes which are striving for upward mobility in the traditional manner suppress women by the imposition of the Sanskritic norm (ibid.: 370). This position is backed up by the comparisons I have made between the various wedding rituals in Tamil Nadu which have been considered in the wider context of kinship and alliance. Throughout such a comparison, it has become clear that the emphasis on gender hierarchy differs considerably between that of the Brahmans and of the Nagarattars and other castes such as the Komuttis and the Kammas. Endowing women with religious status could also be one of the strategic ways in which they can maintain the ritual prestige of the caste. While the men were engaged in long-distance trade, the women would look after the household and domestic activities, participating in religious activities in their own right. Egalitarianism between husband and wife might thus well be based on their rational calculation as merchants, which is based on the principle of exchange on a reciprocal basis, in a way that is similar to the Kammas whose egalitarianism is strongly based on regarding their women as a workforce who can share in the men's business as equal partners.

For Brahmans, whose assets are based on knowledge, there can be no loss of assets as long as their patriline is secure, which may partially explain why they do not practise bilineal property transfer. Among Brahmans the statuses of men and women are based on a completely different principle from that of the Nagarattars. Traditionally, Brahman men were landlords and priests, and so had more time to spend at home while wives were busy performing household chores. Under these circumstances, ritual initiation, especially the privilege of chanting *mantras* is reserved only for sons and not for daughters. This is a drastic difference between the Brahmans and the Nagarattars, since as I mentioned, the Nagarattar women are endowed with equal ritual status with the men which is clearly demonstrated in the egalitarianism between the bride and the groom in the wedding ritual. Relative egalitarian gender hierarchy has also been expressed among the Kammas followed by the Mudaliyars and the Komuttis although the latter two show stronger inclinations to take up Brahmanic influences.

However, this does not nullify the fact that even under such a relative egalitarianism, the Nagarattar male can still exercise control over his wife's reproductive power and her sexual activities, as is also the case of other castes mentioned. For higher caste women, control over their sexuality is given to a particular man who is entitled to exercise it even after death. As it is clearly observable in the worship of *sumangali* (married auspicious woman), control over women's sexuality among the higher castes does not allow them to divorce or to get remarried after they become widows. By forbidding widow remarriage, their caste as a whole keeps on controlling their sexuality. On the other hand, women of lower caste appear to enjoy more freedom: they do remarry after divorce or becoming widows. Unlike higher caste women, sexual control over them from their male relatives appears to be far less. Yet their extramarital sexual relationships are often the result of the exploitation of higher caste men rather than the result of their sexual freedom. The bitterness about men's sexual exploitations is often expressed by the *aacchis* themselves.

Servants marry off their daughters to bad men. Although they spend a lot simply to get their daughters married, the men just enjoy sex for a while and discard them when they are pregnant. Their men are mostly drunkards and beat their wives.

Aacchis are also aware of the sexual exploitation of the Nagarattar males towards poor women. Talking about one of her young servants, an *aacchi* says,

Her father is a Nagarattar but her mother isn't. After enjoying life living with her for several years, he returned to Coimbatore where his family was waiting, leaving his daughter with his illegitimate wife. Her mother got some money while he was with her, but was left penniless. Now she is working as a labourer in Karaikkudi.

Although Hindu family law allows children of illegitimate birth to inherit a share of their father's property, most women lack the means to claim it in the court.

How can you prove that she is really that Chettiyar's child? The man may claim that woman had several illicit relationships so she can never claim her daughter is his.

Aachis are aware of the fact that gender hierarchy between men and women can easily make them pawns and even if they are lucky enough to get married, the privileged status of married woman may suddenly be taken away if her husband dies. For this calamity, they have no remedy.

5.14 Auspiciousness and *Sumangali*

Sumangali is the highest and most desirable status to women in Hindu society. In Sanskrit, *su* means *subam*, or auspiciousness, as does *mangala*. In India married women whose husbands are alive are auspicious and good, as it implies the well-being of the family. Reynolds claims that *sumangali* means a married woman and mother (1980: 38), but in fact, *sumangalis* are not necessarily mothers, at least for the Nagarattars.

In India in general a woman is not considered to have obtained a proper status until she has produced a son. Yet at least among the Nagarattars, a married woman whose husband is alive is of the utmost importance: even if she does not have a child, she can adopt a son, and infertility of a woman is not grounds for divorce. Strict monogamy which is supported by the well-defined marriage contract (see Chapter 4) also helps maintain the status of a *sumangali*. For a woman, a husband is an essential prerequisite for the assurance of her status as an *aacchi* although losing her husband in her later stage of life may not be so uncommon especially because women in general enjoy longer life than men. If her husband dies, she immediately loses this auspicious status; she can never remarry and remains a widow for the rest of her life.

Widows are ritually inauspicious and are unwelcome in the formal sphere on ceremonial occasions. For example, when the bride's people go to meet the groom who is waiting at the temple, both men and women form the procession, but widows will not participate for fear of bringing any inauspicious elements to the ceremony. If the widows are young, their lives are made miserable, as people say that it would be due to her previous bad *karma* that her husband died. In the village, numerous stories circulate about how young widows are tortured and suspected by their husband's relatives as being the cause of their husband's deaths.[30] A widow in olden days, used to be excluded from social gatherings and was expected to live a life of religious austerity. It is inauspicious to see either a widow or a lone Brahman[31] first thing in the morning, it is said, as neither have any symbolic alliance of reproduction.

On the other hand, seeing a *sumangali* first thing in the morning is 'good' (*nalladu*), i.e. auspicious. A red spot on the forehead, coloured *saree*, and the *taali* around her neck are symbols of her

[30] In one village, for example, I heard about an incident which took place in the 1950s. A nineteen year-old Nagarattar widow who lost her husband just a year after marriage, committed suicide because people gossiped that she had killed her husband through her bad *karma*, and that she was having affairs with other men after the death of her husband.

[31] A lone Brahman in this context symbolizes a world renouncer, i.e. *sanniyaasin*, who is not a householder.

status. If her children and husband have important engagements on a particular day (e.g. examination, business contract, journey, etc.) they would ask her to arrange it so that they saw her first as soon as they left the house.

The auspiciousness of the *sumangali* is well represented in the ritual of *sumangali praatanai* which is quite popular among the Brahmans. In it, five *sumangalis* are invited, and asked to take an oil bath in the house of the ritual officiant. Turmeric, *sikakaai*, coconut oil, and other items are all provided by the householder and his wife, and a new *saree* is given to at least one of the invited *sumangalis*. All *sumangalis* are given a plate of gifts on which areca nuts and betel leaves, money, *kunkum*, fruits, turmeric, sweets, etc. are presented. Good food is given to them as a treat, and as the embodiment of Lakshmi, the *sumangalis* are sent off with the utmost respect. The *sumangalis* who are invited are relatives and thus this worship is to celebrate the procreative power of the *sumangalis* who belong to the kin and the affine of the officiate and to pray for their prosperity.

Auspiciousness, as Marglin (1985) correctly claims, is strongly connected to fertility, birth, and growth. A man is never welcome without his wife at any auspicious function. If any marriage alliance negotiations are organized, a man is always asked to come with his wife. A man is not considered to be a complete figure until he is married. If he dies before marriage, he is not mourned as a full-fledged adult, so that there is no proper funeral, and only the closest relatives participate. 'Do not go to the temple alone. Prayers will not be heard without a wife' is a saying which indicates that all auspicious activities should be carried out as a couple.

Among the Nagarattar caste, the acquisition of *aacchi* status starts with marriage, thus *sumangalihood*. Although not all *aacchis* are *sumangalis* and especially powerful *aacchis* are often old widows, they start to acquire social status as adult women when married, i.e. as *sumangalis*. As guardians of their husbands, they play a crucial role as the active participants in maintaining the alliance between their husbands' and their own natal family. They receive a liberal amount of economic support from their natal families, especially when their parents are alive, and even after they are dead, the relationship between these two families continues, as the basic funds of their parents are held by their brothers in order to be able to continue sending gifts on ceremonial occasions.

The fragility of the status itself makes them aspire for it and makes them celebrate it, especially when their husband turns sixty. In the following chapter, I shall discuss the ritual of *saandi* as the celebration of *sumangali*.

Chapter 6

The Ritual of *Saandi*

6.1 *Saandi*

I F a man reaches sixty and his wife is still alive, it is Nagarattar custom for him to celebrate his continued health with his wife. Although *saandi* appears to be a celebration for the man, it is in fact a celebration for the *sumangali*, since, to have a husband who has reached sixty is itself an auspicious thing for the *sumangali*. She has every reason to pray for his longevity, as the status of *sumangali* depends on her husband's well-being.

Saandi was originally called '*shasti abda puurti*', i.e. the completion of the sixtieth year (*shasti* means sixty in Sanskrit). According to Kane (1973), the term *saandi (shanti)* denotes the propitiatory rites for averting a deity's wrath, a calamity, or unlucky event (ibid.: ii/1.719) The celebration called *saandi* however, in this context, is exclusively held when her husband has completed his sixtieth year, that is, when he actually becomes sixty-one. He celebrates it in the month he was born, and on the day when his birth star *(nakshatra)* is current. For example, if someone was born on *Anusham* star day in *Margali* (one of the Tamil months), he would have his celebration when the same star was current in *Margali*. Since this star is current every twenty-seven days, it may be so twice in one month, in which case the latter occurrence is taken as the day of celebration (Fuller 1992: 263–4). According to one elderly Nagarattar, *shasti abda puurti* has three purposes. First, it celebrates the completion of the sixtieth year; secondly, it is the occasion of the *saandi* (*saandi* means 'ritual' in Sanskrit) or *parihaaram*, (i.e. praying for longevity by chanting *mantras* to ward off evil, as the sixty-first year is thought to be critical for a man); and third, it celebrates *kaliyaanam* (the second round of wedding celebrations with his wife). *Shasti abda puurti* is the Brahmanic name for the ritual, but I shall use the term *saandi* as this is how it is most referred to by the Nagarattars. In

Fig. 6.1. Inspecting the *siir: sumangalis* go to the
wife's brother's *walavu viidu* where *siir* is displayed

addition, *saandi* in the Nagarattars' sense is quite different from
shasti abda puurti.

Brahmans conceive of life as divided into four stages: *brahmachari*
(unmarried student), *grhasta* (householder), *vana prastha* (dweller
in the jungle), and *sanniyaasin* (world renouncer) (Dubois 1906:
160). In the third stage, the wife is allowed to accompany her
husband and live in seclusion with him but in the last stage the man
should renounce even his wife and live in complete solitude. The
ritual of *shasti abda puurti*, therefore, is to mark the third stage of
a man's life and prepare him for the last stage (world renunciation),
and also to pray for his peaceful death. Although such is the Brahmanic ideology, most Brahmans nowadays do not follow this pattern and the ritual of *saandi* is held mostly to pray for longevity.

For the Nagarattars, *saandi* is the second biggest occasion for
gift-exchange after weddings. For the Brahmans, *shasti abda puurti*
is a ritual. They insist on the meticulous details of each ritual while

the Nagarattars take very little notice of the ritual side, instead devoting themselves to lavish gift-exchanges.

A middle-aged Brahman woman said that she would not spend more than three thousand rupees on her husband's *shasti abda puurti,* as the number of essential items is limited to the *homams* (fire ritual), and meals for a small number of her kin, i.e. her parents, her husband, her children, and herself. She was very critical of the 'money-mindedness' of the Nagarattars who, she said, pamper themselves and engage in meticulous gift-giving. 'The Nagarattars do not think of the real meaning of *saandi!*'

On the other hand, the Nagarattars consider gift-giving as the essential part of the ritual. The minimum budget for a lower-middle class Nagarattar *saandi* is said to be around Rs 20,000.[1] People in the middle range spend around Rs 30,000 to 50,000, and the upper class record was set in 1991 by one of the richest Nagarattars, M.A.M. Ramasamy, who was said by local people and relatives to have spent more than Rs 20,000,000 ($1 million).

Although Ramasamy's case is not typical, gift-giving during *saandi* is always costly for the Nagarattars. There are three major gift-exchanges: first, *siir* (the gift from the 'mother's house' which is given to the wife by her brother); secondly, the gifts given to the relatives by the officiant of the *saandi;* and thirdly, the feast from the officiant for all those attending the *saandi.* Although gifts are given to the officiant from his children, they are smaller than those offered by the officiant couple.

According to local people, celebration of *saandi* has become more and more popular since the 1960s, and even urbanized non-Brahmans like the Kallars, Maravars, and Vellalars have started to celebrate *saandi* as an auspicious ceremony in function halls in the cities.

However, for non-Nagarattars, the role of the wife's brother as the gift-giver is not crucial. For the Nagarattars, on the other hand, the most important aspect of *saandi* is the reconfirmation of the relationship between the couple and the wife's natal family, especially the wife's brother.

Saandi renews the tie between the man and his wife's brother. At the wedding, the bride's parents and her mother's brother are the gift-givers. At the *saandi,* this role is taken up by the wife's

[1] At that time, one pound was approximately equivalent to Rs 22–25. Devaluation of the Indian rupee took place in June and one pound became Rs 45.

brother who reconfirms his support of his sister by sending gifts. A man's wife's brother is regarded as a dependable ally, while a wife regards her brother as a protector, so the gift he gives her is an expression of his everlasting support.

As Beck (1974: 5) suggests, in Tamil society uni-sex relationships (those between two males or two females), are concerned with the transmission of rights and duties, while cross-sex relationships (male to female) are conceived somewhat differently. While the uni-sex relationships are concerned with authority and practicality, cross-sex relationships are characterized by the good and beneficial aspect of life. Procreation, prosperity, general well-being and the magical force of blessings or curses are involved in the cross-sexual relationships. Along with mother–son and husband–wife relationships, the brother–sister relationship is thought of as one of the strongest bonds (ibid.: 5).

Thus, the Nagarattar celebration of *saandi* expresses a strong bond between husband and wife, and also strengthens the existing bond between brother and sister. It is considered to be a renewal of marriage, but, unlike the first marriage ceremony which is held in the bride's house, rituals only take place in the husband's ancestral house. The wife is already included in her husband's kin as a member, and another *taali* which is brought in to the husband's father's ancestral house, is given to honour the sister who has already become the centre of the house into which she married. In most cases, by the time a man celebrates his *saandi,* his wife's parents are dead (or at least well past their prime). While her parents are alive, or at least while the woman's mother is alive, the wife can expect monthly provisions from her natal family to help her own nuclear family budget.

If her parents are dead, her brother takes over the responsibility, sending gifts at least twice a year on Deepavali (the annual celebration of the festival of lights held in the autumn) and Pongal (the celebration of the newly-harvested crops held in January). These gifts are considered to be part of the *murai* (contract, or promise, which is written at the time of betrothal as part of the payment from the wife's natal family to the conjugal family). If it is difficult for the brother to carry out his gift-giving regularly, he may, if he is conscientious, open a bank account for her so that she would automatically receive a fixed amount on Deepavali wherever her brother may be. To neglect this duty may well breed feelings of resentment in the sister, as her brother would not be fulfilling his moral duty to her.

Murai is part of the traditional responsibility assigned to the 'mother's house' as an obligation to the married daughter. Although *murai* literally means 'promise', the sending of gifts to a married woman from her natal family is considered to be an expression of affection rather than a 'duty'. If her brother dies, her nephew takes over this responsibility, but it is regarded as an expression of sincere affection for his aunt. Thus, the celebration of *saandi* is the reconfirmation of unity between brother and sister in their remaining years.

6.2 Gift-Giving at a *Saandi*

6.2.1 Gifts Given to the Family Members and Affines

The officiants of the *saandi,* i.e. a male Nagarattar and his wife, regard the occasion as an opportunity to show their affection for

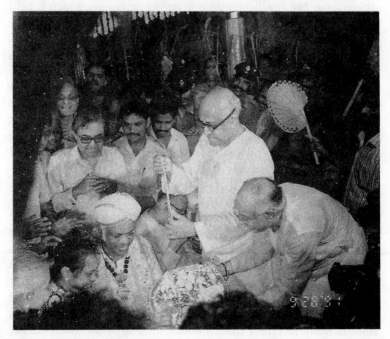

Fig. 6.2. The plate of the diamond *taali* is carried by two males

their kin and affines. The officiating couple's children and grand-children are most favoured in the gift-giving of the *saandi*. Next comes the man's wife's side, i.e. the man's brother-in-law (the wife's brother), and the man's brother-in-law's wife and children. The wife's parents, if they are alive, her sisters and their husbands, along with their children and grandchildren, are also important. *Pangaalis,* i.e. the husband's brothers and their wives, his married sisters and their husbands, etc. are of secondary importance compared to the wife's side. A middle-aged *aacchi* said, 'In the *saandi*, you must be especially good to *dayaadi* (the mother's people).'

The *aacchi* was saying that her husband should give gifts to his children and grandchildren, and then to his mother's brother and his family (wife, his children and grandchildren). A boy (or a girl) is connected to his (or her) maternal uncle through his (or her) mother, as the gifts sent from his (or her) maternal uncle are directed to his (or her) mother. A man, after marriage, receives gifts from his father-in-law through his wife. Later, this role is taken over by his brother-in-law, yet the official receiver of the gift is still his wife.

6.2.2 Feeding Relatives and Friends

Everyone at the ceremony who is not amongst the above-mentioned close kin, belongs to the second category of gift-receivers. If the couple is well off, they may give gifts to the *pangaalis* of the man. However, more importance is given to the feast. The couple entertains a number of guests, as they would at a wedding. If the family is rich and they want to give a feast at their ancestral house, the co-operation of their relatives is necessary as feeding hundreds or thousands of guests requires a great deal of preparation. In addition to the cooks and servants who work in the kitchen, additional people are needed to guide the guests into the dining hall and look after them. 'Unless they are escorted, guests won't go and eat. While they are eating, the ushers should always remind the servers to add second or even third helpings.'

It is usually the custom that a relative of the couple accompanies each guest and stays for ten to twenty minutes until the guest finishes eating. The eldest male of the husband's *pangaali* stands at the front veranda of the joint house, and asks guests whether they have eaten. If any of the guests have not, they are immediately taken to the service quarter.

Not giving a guest anything to eat is bad. If someone is in a hurry and does not have time to eat, we would at least pack something up for the guest to eat at home.

In South Indian culture, eating food in someone else's house is an expression of respect: it shows that the guest has accepted equality of status, at least ritually. It is for this reason that people are keen to entertain and feed outsiders in their own house. If the guest accepts food in the house of a host, it demonstrates that the status of the host is either equivalent to or even higher than that of the guest. No man or woman can accept food from people of lower status.

6.2.3 Daanam *to the Brahmans*

Since conducting *saandi* in their ancestral houses is getting more expensive, there are some Nagarattars who use halls attached to the Shiva temples. According to the *puroohita* who works in the *devastaanam* (temple administration) office in Pillaiyarpatti,[2] a convenient package *saandi* can be arranged. As part of this package, the *devastaanam* office lends the *taali* for the ceremony, which is not for the wife, but for the old Brahman couple who would receive *daanam*. A small *taali* is supposed to be presented by the Nagarattar couple to a poor Brahman couple who are invited to receive it as the *daanam*. Instead of giving it to them, the *devastaanam* office lends it for the ritual, and the old Brahman couple is given Rs 51 instead. I was told: 'The Brahmans are to imagine that a real *taali* is presented as *daanam*.'

6.2.4 *The Budget of a Modest* Saandi

A modest ceremony costs approximately Rs 4,500: Rs 1,500 for *puuja, hoomam,* and rental fee of the halls and Rs 3,000 for food served to around two hundred people. (When I attended a budget-conscious *saandi* even the number of pots was reduced to less than half the ideal. There were less than thirty there, because the hiring charge of pots varies with the number hired.)

---

[2] Pillaiyarpatti is one of the nine lineage temples of the Nagarattars. Their *devastaanam* office runs several halls that are to be engaged for such purposes and they are used mostly by lower-middle class to middle class families.

The gift-giving budget, which is the largest, is not included in this amount. The Nagarattars cannot omit the gift-giving, since it is an essential step in their praying for longevity. In return for their gift-giving, the Nagarattars expect good wishes, although the Brahman priests insist that the couple's longevity is assured because of their powerful *mantras* and rituals. When the gift-giving starts in the middle of the ritual, the Brahman *puroohitas* leave the spot to take light meals because it is tedious for them, and their presence is unnecessary.

The most expensive items are the *sarees*, i.e. the *'pattu saree'* (silk *saree*, see Chapter 4 for more discussion). Then come the men's clothes such as the *veetti* (loin cloth worn by men) and a towel, and the children's clothes such as shirts and trousers. I was told that the most expensive gifts should be given to the 'mother's people', i.e. both the wife's and the husband's maternal relatives.

6.2.5 *Gift Given by the Wife's Brother*

The *taali* which is worn by the wife on the occasion of *saandi* is made of gold and diamonds. The number and size of the diamonds depends on the wealth of the brother. It is not at all necessary to have a diamond on the *taali* if the brother cannot afford it. It is presented by the wife's brother or her maternal uncle, with additional gifts and cash. The gift which is carried from the wife's 'mother's house' is called *'siir'*, and as I describe in the following section, the *siir* is displayed and inspected by the *aacchis* of the wife's and the husband's relatives before it is carried to the ancestral house of the husband. Since their parents are quite likely to have died by the time the couple celebrate the *saandi*, it is essential for the wife's brother or the maternal uncle to assume this duty.

6.2.6 *The* Saandi *of a Middle-Class Family: Case Study*

Meena Aacchi celebrated her husband's *saandi* in 1989, on which she spent Rs 1.5 lakh (Rs 150,000). This came out of her own money, which she had saved and kept in the bank in her own name, and had originally been part of her dowry. Since her husband had not been able to make the family rich, Meena Aacchi had to organize and bring up her children using her own money. Her friends and relatives praised her for being able to conduct a *saandi* without the means of her husband.

She presented *sarees* (about Rs 1,200–2,500 each) to twenty-one women who were close relatives, and she also gave *veetti* (Rs 250) to fifty-one close male relatives (total estimated cost: Rs 75,250). For *puja* (rituals), around Rs 5,000 was spent. A *veetti* and a towel (Rs 50) were given to twenty-one priests who chanted *mantra* (est: Rs 1,050).

Four meals were served to the guests: breakfast, lunch, tiffin, snack and supper (Rs 25,000). Fifteen cooks served and five hundred people were invited. They spent Rs 6,000 on decorations, photographs, a video, and music. For the diamond *taali* and a ring, Rs 25,000, plus Rs 6,000 for a ring for the husband, were spent. Meena Aachi had to arrange to purchase the diamond *taali* by herself, since her brother was unable to buy one for her.

Two hundred relatives were given stainless-steel trays, Rs 10 in cash, betel leaves, areca nuts, and one coconut each (total: Rs 6,000). Meena Aacchi gave each of her adult children a 1 kg silver basket (Rs 30,000). She gave an old Brahman couple a small *taali* (Rs 1,000) and donated a *saree* and sandal paste to the temple (Rs 1,000).

She hired a car (transport expenses including petrol: Rs 2,000), paid Rs 61 to each of the guests, and gave one plastic bag to hundred guests (Rs 8 per bag = total Rs 800). A religious book *(Ramayana)* was also given to a hundred guests (Rs 3 x 100 = 300). An electric generator and gas light were necessary for illumination (Rs 500). After the function, Meena Aacchi and her husband went to Rameshwaram for two days with their children and grandchildren. Altogether, twelve members went (Rs 1,000). Meena Aacchi calculated the total cost to be Rs 156,150.

Meena Aacchi received Rs 50,000 from her elder brother as a gift, but even though this amount was more than the cost of the diamond *taali,* she still complained that it was not sufficient. She more or less paid for the whole function out of her own pocket. According to her friends, Meena Aacchi's husband was a modest bank employee whose salary was not enough to marry off their children. It was therefore Meena Aacchi's dowry and savings which enabled their children to marry.

She was not happy that her elder brother seemed to show little affection for her. 'My brother is a rich man, and since I am his only sister, he should have given me more.' However, she also understands the difficulty of his financial condition: he has five daughters and only one of them is married so far. With four more daughters to be married, it would have been difficult for him to send her more. In fact, it would generally be thought that Meena Aacchi's brother had fulfilled his moral obligation, since in spite of having four unmarried daughters he had still managed to show his 'affection' for his sister to a certain extent.

6.3 *Siir* and the Brother–Sister Relationship

The *siir* is a collection of the most important gifts given to the wife from her natal family either at the wedding or during the *saandi* of her husband. *Siir* is decorated and displayed in the ancestral house of the wife's father, which would probably have been inherited by her brother, before it is sent to the ancestral house of the husband, where the *saandi* ritual is held.

Fig. 6.3. M.A.M. Ramasamy and his wife surrounded by married and unmarried women who are their close kin

Meena Aacchi also complained that her mother's house should have arranged the diamond *taali* for her along with other gifts such as a ring, one or two *sarees* and a *veetti* and shirt for her husband. She should also have received a gift of money accompanied by fruit, nuts and sweets, coconuts etc. Although the money was given beforehand, all such arrangements were made by her, and she had to send the diamond *taali,* which she bought herself, to her brother's ancestral house so that everything could be sent at once after having been displayed there.

Before the gifts are carried to the ancestral house of the husband, a few *aacchis* related to the wife come to the wife's brother's ancestral house to inspect the *siir* displayed in the waiting room adjacent to the open courtyard. The wife's sister-in-law (the wife's brother's wife), should entertain the visitors with coffee and snacks. This is exclusively a women's inspection and no males accompany them.

On the morning of the *saandi* of Ramasamy, I accompanied the group of women who went to inspect the *siir* that was to be sent to Sigappi Aacchi, the wife of Ramasamy. Ramasamy and Sigappi Aacchi are cross-cousins and belong to the VS line, which I discussed in Chapter 3. According to the local newspaper, Ramasamy celebrated the grandest *saandi* in 1991, attracting 120,000 people to Chettinadu.

Although the scale of the *saandi* was unusually large, it still presented Ramasamy with an opportunity to express the two 'cross-sexual relationships of the kin nucleus' (Beck 1974), i.e. the husband/wife, and brother/sister relationships. Moreover, since Sigappi Aacchi's brother was an adopted son, this case shows that the role of the brother can be taken over by either one of her parallel-cousins or an adopted brother. The gift, in this context, is also the expression of the alliance between her husband and her adopted brother who are united through her. Although her parents are dead, she is protected by the fact that her husband is her cross-cousin, so that the family into which she married was already known to her, and her relatives were also those of her husband. Although she has no children, and she and her husband are thinking of adopting a son, infertility does not weaken her position because of the closely interwoven relationships of kin and affines created by cross-cousin marriage.

6.4 The Inspection of *Siir*

About a dozen *sumangalis* who are related to the couple accompanied Sigappi Aacchi to inspect the *siir* in the ancestral house of her brother. No men were to be present at this informal ceremony as it is customary for the *siir,* i.e. the auspicious gift, to be appreciated first by *sumangalis.* On arrival, the women inspected the items, touching them and admiring the display in the women's area, where they normally sleep (Fig. 1.1 in Chapter 1). A square platform had been set up, on which dozens of gifts were arranged with colourful decorations on an auspicious red carpet. The gifts consisted of fruit, sweets, coconuts on silver plates, and for her husband, a *veetti,* shirt, and a gold ring. For Sigappi Aacchi there was a *pattu saree,* a gold chain, and a diamond *taali* with a bundle of money along with a container of *kunkum* and sandal paste which are essential for auspicious rituals. *Siir* also functions as a public demonstration of respect paid by a brother to his sister. The more

Fig. 6.4. Posters which advertise the *saandi* ceremony of M.A.M. family

important his sister's husband is to the brother, the more he should care about the content of the *siir* sent on this day.

Women, on the other hand, appear to take a rather informal role when they inspect the *siir*. They touch the items, assess them, and discuss them over coffee. Although the atmosphere is quite informal, it is nevertheless a ritual. By touching them, and talking about ancestors in the photograph, the *sumangalis* add auspiciousness to the gifts which are sent to the sister from her brother. Goods and money turn into auspicious objects after this ritual. In order to get the blessings and turn the materials into auspicious things, *sumangalis* are asked to come to touch and inspect them. In fact, even ancestors are expected to participate in this kind of gathering to add some auspiciousness. In the corridor surrounding the *walavu*, there were a number of old photographs including those of Sigappi Aacchi as a child with some of her relatives, sitting with their elders. I was told to go around the corridor to see these photographs and ask the women gathered there, about them.

Seeing the old photographs and remembering the ancestors is said to be good, especially at such an auspicious occasion, and thus this procedure is also part of the custom associated with auspicious moments. Photographs are especially useful for remembering ancestors, since for the Nagarattars, ancestor worship does not extend to generations whose stories are not remembered and talked about by succeeding members. The rest are combined as the ancestors in general and worshipped at the beginning of the *padaippu*.

This informal inspection is important to reassure the sister of the economic support of her brother who must not lose face by presenting poor items. Furthermore, the visit emphasizes the importance of the auspiciousness associated with *sumangalis* and ancestors as the protective auspicious power to be attached to the *siir* before it is sent to the ancestral house of Sigappi Aacchi's husband.

6.5 The Ritual of *Saandi*

The ritual of *saandi*, according to a Brahman *puroohita*, follows two themes: one is the second-time marriage and the other is the prayer for the couple's longevity. The first part is represented in the repetition of the marriage ritual which would have taken place decades ago. For example, the marriage is announced by the installation of the *muhuurta kaal* (auspicious pole) seven days before the ceremony starts. A specialist called the *muhuurta kaaran* (he is a Pandaaram, i.e. a caste who work for village temples as priests) comes and installs a pole at a corner (north-east) of the *walavu waasal.* This announces their wedding and is a repetition of the wedding ritual.

The preparation of the ritual is started on the previous day by a few *puroohitas,* and sixty-five pots are prepared in the courtyard. The wife wears a *kaluttiru* (hand-shaped gold ornament which is given at her wedding) and the *taali* which she normally wears. Her husband wears *rudraksha,* a necklace which is a symbol of spiritual discipline.

The beads of *rudraksha* are made from special fruit from a tree grown in the Himalayas, and normally there is no decoration. *Rudraksha* is used for rituals, to count the number of chanted *mantras.* However, the *rudrakshas* worn by the Nagarattars are joined with gold, and have a large gold ornament in the centre. Moreover, the *rudraksha* worn by the officiant is usually handed down by the *pangaali* of the officiant. In other words, the same *rudraksha* is worn by the officiant's father, (probably by his grandfather), his elder brothers, and will be worn by his younger brothers. Thus, sharing *rudraksha* symbolizes the idea of joint property shared among the *pangaalis,* which is represented in their ancestral house. Even though the Nagarattars wear *rudraksha* on *saandi,* this is not the symbol of a step forward to world renunciation but a symbol of worldliness: wealth and kinship ties are reinforced by the ceremony of *saandi.*

His wife puts on *kaluttiru* to represent her auspiciousness for the evening ritual which takes place on the eve of *saandi abisheekam* (water pouring ritual, a highlight of *saandi*). As I discussed in Chapter 4, the *kaluttiru* is an auspicious symbol and is also considered to be an important economic asset for married women.

Brahmanic *saandi* also shares the same themes, i.e. longevity and reconfirmation of marriage, yet according to the Brahman *puroohita,* their focus is on the power of *mantra* and rituals in order to live a peaceful life as a couple and to prepare for painless deaths with the help of spiritual powers. The Nagarattars also depend on the power of *mantras* and rituals as they, too, feel *mantras* are essential in the process of ritual to attain longevity. Yet this desire for longevity is particularly stressed through their dependence on *sumangalis* as ritual specialists.

The first installation of the brick platform in the courtyard is done exclusively by the *sumangalis* who are related to the couple. In the ritual I observed, the *sumangalis,* in order of seniority, placed a lotus petal on each brick before cementing it. Lotus petals are a symbol of auspiciousness, wealth, and purity, as the goddess of wealth, Lakshmi, is depicted sitting on a lotus flower.

The platform where the couple sit is also decorated by the *sumangalis.* When the couple pray to their ancestors at the *ul viidu,* they are also exclusively assisted by their relatives, again, especially by the *sumangalis.* As is the case at weddings, the Brahmans do not have any part in the ritual, nor are they allowed to enter the *ul viidu.*

When the ancestral worship starts, the Brahman priests take a break. The gift-giving starts, in the continued absence of the Brahmans. In the ceremony I observed, the gift-giving continued for nearly one and a half hours, yet it was not an exceptionally long one by Nagarattar standards.[3]

After the gift-giving is over, the couple are accompanied by relatives to the nearby temples, usually the Vinayaga temple and the local village goddess's temple, such as the Mariyamman temple. On their return, they sit on the platform and the *puuja* starts with the Vinayaga *puuja* in order to pray to Vinayaga, the elephant god for a good beginning. During *saandi* the priests are supposed to chant *mantras* many times, in auspicious numbers such as 108 or 1,008 times as a whole. When the prescribed number of chants is completed, those attending the function pour holy water onto the couple. Since finishing the chants takes quite a long time, priests start chanting on the eve of the *abisheekam* ritual so that they can reach the required number by noon on the day of *saandi.* The *puroohitas* start chanting *mantras* from early in the morning.

As soon as the ritual is started on the eve of the *saandi abisheekam,* people come one after another and prostrate themselves in front of the couple to receive gifts, and on the day of *saandi abisheekam,* the couple receive gifts from the visitors. In the meantime, breakfast is prepared and people go and eat. Traditional music is played whenever there is an important ritual, as it is supposed to drive away any evil in the atmosphere. Several close relatives come with gifts for the couple. Garlands, a ring and a chain, *sarees* and a *veetti* are put on

---

[3] Sometimes, gift-giving is done separately from the ritual, especially if those who are given gifts are numerous, as was the case in Ramasamy's *saandi.*

plates as gifts from the couple's children. These gifts are blessed by the children and then presented to the couple.

Three hearths are temporarily set up for the *saandi*, in which special wood with a herbal mixture is burnt to add religious power to the *mantra*-chanting. According to the priest, the wooden sticks are believed to create smoke with beneficial medical effects when inhaled. The priests contrive to chant *mantras* until the *muhuurtam* (auspicious moment), during which a new diamond *taali* is put around the neck of the wife. As with the wedding ceremony, the *taali* is placed on a plate, carried by either the son and daughter or by the wife's brother and his wife, and is blessed by close relatives by being touched. The *taali* is then kept in the *ul viidu* until the next most auspicious moment comes.

Before the couple takes *abisheekam* (the water pouring ceremony as an expression of ritual blessing and purification) the priest brings sesame oil in a black iron bowl. *Abisheekam* is a purification ritual which blesses the receiver. It is also part of temple rituals in which the priest pours water onto the sacred idol to 'cool' the deity and to keep the divine in good humour. While kin and affine can perform this ritual, servants are not supposed to do so. The water contains lime juice, milk, turmeric, etc., which are traditionally supposed to 'cool down' the body and thus make the person ritually pure and auspicious (See Chapter 5 for a detailed discussion). Since the *mantra* has been chanted for two consecutive nights and the water is believed to have absorbed both the effect of *mantra* and the herbal effect which has been created from the smoke of the hearth, it is the ritual of pouring water itself which is believed to increase the longevity of the couple.

The black iron bowl is believed to ward off evil and the sesame oil is the essential material for an oil bath, the most auspicious ritual bath. The couple do not smear oil over their bodies but merely dip their fingers in it and put a few drops over their head, merely to signify the oil bath.

When the priests complete the required number of *mantras*, the chief priest starts to pour the water from the pot onto the couple, and the guests come in front of them, and pour water. Most of the guests come as a couple and the water pouring ceremony continues for nearly one hour until the last few pots of water are poured by the couple's sons and their wives.

The role of the son is crucial, since he is the last one to finish pouring, as heir of the house of the officiant. If there is no son, the paternal nephew assumes this position. (In the case of Ramasamy, since there was no child, the water was poured by the adopted son of Ramasamy's deceased brother's widow.) After this is over, the couple go to the changing room, change into a new *saree* and a new *veetti* which are given to them by their children, and then return to sit on the platform and prepare to give *daanam* to a Brahman couple in order to ward off evil before their own ritual of *taali*-tying.

At the *saandi*, it is usual for a poor and elderly Brahman couple to be invited onto the seat on the platform. They are given a garland and one small gold *taali* by the recipient of the ritual. The *taali* given to the Brahman is a *daanam* to make the *taali*, making the ritual of the Nagarattars auspicious: it is usually approximately one gold sovereign, which is a symbol of the blessing the Brahman couple gives to the Nagarattar officiant in exchange for receiving a gift. The Nagarattar officiant and his wife, after giving a *taali* to the old Brahman couple, accompany them to the entrance of the house to show respect for the elderly couple.

The couple then come back to the platform and the *puroohita* starts the ritual to conduct the marriage of the couple again. The husband blesses the diamond *taali* and the gold chain on the plate, putting *kunkum* on them for auspiciousness, and the husband's *pangaali* touches the *taali* and hands it to the husband. The *sumangali* from both the husband's *pangaali* and the wife's side help in this ritual. After the *taali* is put around the neck of the wife, the *kunkum* is smeared on the forehead of the wife and the *taali* itself, by the husband, and then the couple exchange garlands three times, just like in their original wedding.

At the 'real wedding', the Brahman priest is asked to leave the house just before the *taali* is tied as the Nagarattars believe him to be highly inauspicious. At this ritual of *taali*-tying at the *saandi* the priest stays. This is partly because more than two Brahman priests are not as inauspicious as one Brahman. (According to local people, seeing more than two Brahman priests at a time first thing in the morning is ritually neutral, i.e. neither auspicious or inauspicious.)

There are a number of Brahman priests who are chanting the *mantra* and moreover, the priest is needed as soon as the *taali* is tied. However, the *taali* is never to be touched by the Brahman and is handled only by the close relatives who surround the couple. After the *taali* is tied, the couple's relatives come one after another to receive yellow rice as a blessing. Those who are older than the couple sprinkle the yellow rice on the head of the couple to bless them for longevity. Yellow rice is supposed to be highly auspicious.

When this is over, the couple come out of the house, where a cow is waiting for them. The cow faces away from the entrance, and the recipient's wife conducts the *aarati* (a lamp waving ceremony) on the back of the cow and decorates its head with a garland.[4] When the whole ceremony is over, the couple and their relatives settle their accounts as they return to the house.[5]

6.6 The 'Palace of Chettinadu' *Saandi*

On the afternoon of Ramasamy's *saandi,* well before the *siir* was carried in to 'The Palace of Chettinadu', the crowd had increased to an uncontrollable size. Even well before seven o'clock in the morning, the entrance of the Palace was blocked by the police as a huge crowd had already flooded into the palace from all over Chettinadu. The *walavu waasal* where the whole ritual was held became as hot and humid as a steam bath, since the opening of the *waasal* was completely sealed with the decorative roof and the space was crowded with more than a thousand people. When the turmeric water was poured onto the couple, the *waasal* was full of thousands of people, pushing and bumping into each other and the police started to worry about accidents. Even on the day before the *saandi* there had been a huge crowd at seven o'clock in the morning, which had blocked the approach to the entrance of the Palace. On the second day, the crowd had already begun to build up at six o'clock, and the courtyard where the ritual was held was again very hot because of the crowd and the closed ceiling.

The weather was hot outside and there was no breeze. In the huge crowded space, all the guests were drenched with sweat, and neither the officiating couple nor their close relatives could come out from the *waasal* to rest. Those who were not known to the couple were the most liberal in their consumption of food and snacks; in addition

[4] According to elderly Nagarattars, seeing the back of a cow first thing in the morning is always auspicious, therefore, the procedure of the ritual is arranged so that the couple can see the back of the cow as soon as they come out from the house.

[5] Relatives are paid for performing rituals for the couple. The amount and the gift given depends on the financial condition of the couple.

to the villagers there were hundreds of gypsies and beggars who were camping around the area in an attempt to reach the food in the service area. This was tolerated, as it is a taboo to refuse meals to anybody and it would be a bad omen for the auspicious ceremony. A lot of the close relatives left the palace without eating, as the food halls were fully packed and nearly impossible to enter.

People who were known to the couple even came from abroad to show their goodwill. For example, Sigappi Aacchi's brother's children, some of whom are now settled in the United States, all came with their babies to attend. Even those who rarely left their houses came, as not coming at all signified the cessation of the relationship. At the main hall of the palace in the two days before *saandi*, Ramasamy was constantly receiving male guests, while Sigappi Aacchi was surrounded by her male home stewards and women guests in the women's quarter, busily giving gifts.

As the celebration of *saandi* approached, the whole Chettinadu area and Madras city were full of posters of Ramasamy's *saandi*. Along with posters of Ramasamy's *saandi* those of others who were close political allies were displayed. There was the minister and MP who was a close relative of Ramasamy, and there was the president of the political party which Ramasamy was supporting. All the local newspapers and television covered the *saandi* and a video film was taken to focus on important guests.

As this shows, *saandi* serves not only to renew the tie with relatives but also to demonstrate the wealth of the officiant. The element of competition in holding a grand function permeates the weddings and *saandi* of the Nagarattars more than other castes, since the scale of the function becomes a strong indicator of wealth and prosperity. If they succeed in impressing their relatives and business partners by holding a grand function, they are given augmented social status in return (i.e. increased business credibility). Ample gift-giving is also an expression of the generosity and prosperity of the giver, which is also a factor in the formation of their social status.

For nine days, between 20 and 28 September 1991, the Palace in Chettinadu received a constant flow of guests. During this period, meals were served four times a day: breakfast with coffee or tea, lunch, a light meal in the evening with sweets, and supper consisting of *idli, doosai,* or *idiappam,* with some sweets and coffee and tea. The menu was purely vegetarian and chosen several days ahead by Sigappi Aacchi. Except for 26, 27 and 28 September, the meals were served in the two dining halls of the Palace. However, because they expected the number of the guests to increase from 26 September, food halls were arranged in six places in adjacent houses, which were Ramasamy's *pangaali*'s houses. These houses were entirely open for use during the *saandi* function, since additional cooking facilities and resting quarters for relatives were needed.

Invitation cards were sent to 30,000 people, yet the actual number of people who visited the Palace from 10 to 26 September alone reached 20,000. On 27 September, the number of visitors reached 40,000, and by the 28th, it was 60,000. Therefore, the total number that attended the *saandi* was 120,000, according to the servants who supplied plantain leaves on which to serve food to the guests. Not only the meals but also small snacks and cold drinks were given whenever groups of villagers or guests arrived. Over two days (27th and 28th alone), approximately 15,000 bottled cold drinks provided by the Palace were consumed.

The meals consisted of at least eleven items (on the day of *saandi*, it was twenty-two items), and for supper alone, they served five to six items. All the guests, and the host couple, ate the same meal in one of the service quarters.

Their food service even extended to Brahman *swamiji*, a leader of one Brahman *madam* in Bangalore. Although Brahmans never eat in non-Brahman houses, one *achariya*, a *madam* head, visited them with a group of a dozen Brahman disciples, and they all had lunch with Ramasamy and Sigappi Aacchi. The cost of each meal was also extraordinary. According to one of the stewards who organized the food section, one meal cost Rs 90 per person which was an extremely generous amount as usually middle class Nagarattars would spend around Rs 7 to 8 or less per meal.

Several days before the ceremonies were conducted, villagers from nearby areas came in a group with a large garland to pay their respects to Ramasamy on the veranda of the entrance where he sat with his male relatives and friends. The villagers were then led to the internal area where the *walavu* was situated. Sigappi Aacchi was seated there with her sister-in-law and several female friends. She sat beside two store-rooms with a notebook listing categories of gifts to be given.

Two store-rooms were filled with the stock of gifts arranged in categories, and according to the closeness of the relationship, those who came were given gifts. For example, on the day of the *saandi,* three kinds of *pattu sarees* specially arranged by Sigappi Aacchi were to be given to each of the closest female relations so that they all wore the same 'uniform' three times during the *saandi.*[6]

Villagers who came with garlands were given some soft drinks and a packet of biscuits with betel leaves and betel nuts in a small stainless-steel container, all put in an inexpensive cloth bag. Those who helped the family for three days were given a slightly better gift: a packet of biscuits in a vinyl bag with areca nuts and betel leaves with *kunkum* and turmeric in a small stainless-steel container. Villagers who had been in the service of the family were given a *veetti* or cotton *sarees.* However, refusing to take the one offered and claiming more expensive goods seems to have been a regular occurrence, according to the house stewards: 'Some villagers demanded a *saree* or *veetti* even though they hadn't worked for the Palace at all!'

The work of gift-giving was left entirely to Sigappi Aacchi. After Ramasamy received his guests and exchanged a few words, he told most of them to receive gifts from his *aacchi.* The selection and purchasing of gifts is all in the hands of the *aacchi,* as well as organizing the 'poor feeding' (meal service to the poor which is held in temples). Those who visited the Palace would first see Ramasamy if it was a man or a couple. Ramasamy would then tell them to go and see his *aacchi* and receive gifts. If it was a woman, she would directly go to Sigappi Aacchi. Sigappi Aacchi sat beside a small desk, checking the items with a small notebook and her steward then brought out the gift, and handed it to her. She then handed it to the receivers who prostrated themselves in front of her, and with a word of gratitude, left.

6.7 Gift-Giving in the *Saandi*

After observing an apparently endless series of gift-giving for several days, I wondered about the motives and what it was meant to achieve. The Nagarattars I questioned instantly replied that the gift-giving was not just useful but absolutely essential.

[6] There is a photo of all the *sumangalis* surrounding Ramasamy and Sigappi Aacchi. It is interesting to see that the couple is surrounded only by the auspicious women from the relatives, as if the attendance of their husbands is implied by the presence of the *sumangalis.*

First of all, Ramasamy is supposed to be the richest Nagarattar, and he is the heir of the aristocratic family. It is therefore necessary to have a grand ceremony to match his status and wealth. It is also a good demonstration and advertisement for their business. In addition, the couple is childless (although they are going to adopt a son), and so they haven't conducted any marriages after their own and to compensate for their lack of opportunities for grand ceremonies they are having a particularly grand *saandi.*

The Nagarattars would consider a man most worthy if he were trustworthy and socially credible, as well as having a degree of religiosity which would lead him to make donations to charity. In order to meet these requirements, the Nagarattar men engage in business wholeheartedly and are never wasteful. Excessive consumption at ceremonies is not considered to be a waste, but a part of the expression of generosity, since by feeding hundreds and thousands, a man can increase his religious merit.

Therefore, their purpose in spending large amounts of money on ceremonies is similar to their expenditure on charities and patronizing temples. According to Bayly, Indian merchants consider 'name' or 'credit' as an essential element of their effectiveness (Bayly 1983). Their constant capital investment in temples and pilgrimage centres is combined with their interest in broad business activities as traders and merchants in an attempt to acquire credibility in the places where they cannot depend on local kinship support.

Although the daily life of the Nagarattars is said to be frugal, the heavy expenditure on ceremonial occasions such as weddings and *saandi* does not contradict this ethic. The capital investment is made in order to attract publicity and also to renew the ties not only with kin and affines but also with friends and business partners. Employing the mass media to demonstrate a family's wealth is similar to the traditional Nagarattar strategy of investing in temples to acquire prestige and merit.

6.8 The *Aacchi* as *Sumangali* and Manager/Protector of the House

Among the Nagarattars, the arrangement of a big function is mostly done by the *aacchi,* and for this, co-operation and help from other *aacchis* is essential. What Beck calls the uni-sexual relationship is highlighted in this co-operative network. Her mother-in-law, and some elderly wives of the *pangaali* as well as her mother, sisters and cousins help. If the house is large, she has servants and home stewards who are engaged for both business and domestic activities. For example, during the whole ceremonial procedure, Sigappi Aacchi was surrounded by her managers who came from the offices of their companies. In South Indian society, having male servants at home is quite exceptional in an ordinary house, although for mercantile houses it is more common.

Therefore, the bigger the house is, the more work at home is assigned to the *aacchi*. Her field of work is neither completely public nor private nor is her power completely informal. In other words, both men and women of the Nagarattar caste acknowledge the importance of kinship related alliances as their sense of identity largely depends on this, and an *aacchi's* field of activities plays an important part for her husband's identity and well-being.

On the night of the *saandi* ritual, Sigappi Aacchi had to work late at night after all the other family members and guests had gone to sleep. She took a late supper with her dozens of home stewards who were sitting on the floor beside the dining-table. While eating, they chatted and gossiped about the people who were known to both parties. A sense of co-operation and unity existed between the male servants and the *aacchi*, which confirmed her position as the manager of the house. Chatting and gossiping with servants about various matters also gives her valuable information in which she should be well-versed, since male servants travel and come from various regions carrying news from other places. In mercantile communities, keeping clerks and domiciliary managers at home is important, and if the business is on a small-scale, women sometimes engage in moneylending, turning their house into an office. If this is the case, the help of male servants is essential, as the *aacchi* can then maintain a distance from the male customers, and they can manage their business by sending male servants as messengers and even money collectors.

Yet the *aacchi's* role is not only that of a manager but also a ritual specialist: her role as *sumangali* starts from the moment when the installation of the auspicious pole *(muhuurta kaal)* is over. The installation of a pole in one corner of the *walavu waasal* is an announcement of an auspicious ceremony, just as it is at a wedding. Three days before the ceremony, *sumangalis* start to build the platform in the centre of the *waasal* where the pots are supposed to be placed and where they carry out the lotus petal ritual as mentioned earlier. After the first brick was placed by Sigappi Aacchi, the *sumangalis* from her side and her husband's relatives installed each brick while praying for the longevity of Ramasamy. A conch shell was then blown by one of the women to announce the ceremony.

These *sumangalis* then decorated the platform with auspicious signs *(koolam)* as well as the front door and the plank on which the couple sat. They lit auspicious lamps both in the *ul viidu* and at the entrance of *walavu*. All the *sumangalis* wore the *sarees* given by Sigappi Aacchi, and they all accompanied the couple to the temple where they prayed for a good beginning to the ritual, a simulation of *sumangali praatanai*, which I discussed at the beginning of this chapter. When the photograph was taken, Ramasamy was surrounded by the *sumangalis* from among his relatives who were dressed in the same *pattu sarees,* as if he were protected by the auspiciousness of these women.

Even after the *saandi* was over, and the whole group including Ramasamy had gone to bed and the ground floor of the Palace was deserted, the work of Sigappi Aacchi was not yet over. At 8:30 p.m., she was still sitting with her stewards in the corner of the *walavu* facing a mound of garlands and the leftover gifts, sorting them out to be carried into the store-room. In another room, there was also a huge mound of unused gifts. After this had been arranged, she still had to go round the *walavu waasal* paying her respects to all the ancestors in the photographs, touching them and receiving blessings from them. She also visited the room where an enormous photograph of Ramasamy's mother overwhelmed other photographs of Ramasamy's grandfather, grandmother, his father and his dead elder brother. She applied *kunkum* to each one of the photographs, and did the same to her forehead and to her two *taalis* which hung around her neck in order to obtain blessings from the ancestors.

This aspect of a *sumangali's* daily life shows that she is the protector of the house. She needs her husband to maintain her auspicious status, and, for this, she prays to the ancestors for protection. Both the wife's and the husband's ancestors' interest are combined in protecting the husband. The prosperity of the house and the life of the husband are essential to the *aacchi,* and in this respect, co-operation of all the *sumangalis* of kin and affines is requested, especially at auspicious ceremonies: being *sumangalis* of his kin and affines, they have every reason to protect the life of Ramasamy by giving blessings.

The auspicious status of a *sumangali* is not affected even if she does not have a child. Although Sigappi Aacchi is childless, she could adopt a son from her husband's clan temple division, and after arranging his marriage, she would be called *'periyaacchi'* (big *aacchi*) and exercise leadership in her own house. This shows, that at least among the Nagarattars, the *sumangalihood* is more highly regarded than motherhood itself.

When I commented that it was rather hard for Sigappi Aacchi to deal with all the tedious work long after all the other family members had gone to bed, one of her relatives, a middle-aged *aacchi* objected: 'Of course, she has to do it. However tired she may be, it is after all, her *saandi.*' As this comment clearly shows, the *saandi* is in fact a celebration of the *sumangali* who has prayed for her husband's longevity so that her status may be preserved.

Discussing the position of a woman in Tamil society, Beck (1974: 7) writes about the presence of a 'kin nucleus', i.e. that the woman is surrounded by males: her husband, her brother, her son, and her father. In Tamil society, rights and duties stem primarily from men's relationships with other men (i.e. father-son-grandson, or brother-in-law/son-in-law and father-in-law), while women, at the centre surrounded by men, are the source of power. A goddess, in a myth, provides the energy potential from which all else, including her husband, was later formed.

However, a mythical woman or a goddess is a highly ambivalent figure, as she may bring not only prosperity and rain, but also famine and disease. In folklore, if a female was not treated properly, she could cause a calamity to befall a male, or 'burn' those who behaved wrongly. Therefore, in order to maximize the constructive application of their power, women must at all times be connected to and contained by their male relatives, and in compensation such men stand to benefit from the blessings and good luck that flow from a woman who is chaste and whose power is controlled and well managed. A virgin sister's blessing can win battles for her fathers and brothers, while a chaste wife can increase a husband's prosperity and fighting power. But if a man should mistreat a woman who is under his protection, or ignore her just demands, he opens himself to her curse (ibid.). Four male relatives, i.e. her father, brother, husband, and son, protect the woman in order to direct her energies towards constructive ends, which in the case of the Nagarattars, as well as of most Tamil castes, is the prosperity of two families through co-operation.

According to Beck, therefore, the relationship between males and females in Tamil kinship is of a different order than that between persons of the same sex, such that cross-sex links have to do with the general themes of prosperity and power while uni-sex relationships have to do with descent, authority, and rights and obligations of a more formal and everyday sort. It is from this that the difference between cross and parallel relationships stems. Cross-relatives are people with whom one should be friendly and familiar, and exchange gifts, while parallel-relatives are people with whom more formal and more restrained interaction is expected. In the South, the woman's husband and her brother are classificatory cross-cousins in terms of kinship terminology, and her behavioral patterns express co-operation and friendship.

The Nagarattars also fit Beck's argument well, and the role of the *aacchi* in the context of Tamil culture is defined in the way Beck claims. Sigappi Aacchi who is married to a cross-cousin, is protected by the kinship nucleus, as discussed by Beck, even though she does not yet have a son. A child, in her case, can be adopted. The woman in the centre, even if she cannot have a child, is protected, and serves to 'cement' the relationships of four males, while men are the 'girders or beams of the structure' (ibid.: 20).

6.9 Auspiciousness in the Web of Kinship

Pure and impure, as Dumont (1970a) maintains, is an essential value system in Indian society and structures social hierarchy in India. Between men and women, there is also a hierarchical difference based on this value system: women suffer from menstrual pollution while men do not. Therefore, men are fit to officiate over rituals without much difficulty while women are not. However, as the Dumontian argument also stresses the complement of the pure and the impure, both need the other to make a complementary opposition; husband and wife are complementary and indispensable to each other. Husband and wife make a pair, which is considered to be a basic unit in Tamil society.

For a married woman, especially of higher caste, her essential virtues are associated with purity *(suttam)* in the form of chastity and cleanliness, since it protects her family and brings prosperity. There is a Tamil saying: 'Cleanliness can feed you for life.' As the guardian of home life, a woman is expected to be neat and clean. In this sense, cleanliness, purity and auspiciousness are interrelated, as they are all closely associated with reproductive activities and home life.

Although women are classified as socially inferior to men, and their reproductive capacity is under the control of men, women are essential to give men a social identity. Only after marriage can a man or a woman achieve an acceptable proper social status. A woman as a wife is strongly associated with auspiciousness (*mangalam,* or *subam*).

As soon as a *sumangali* becomes a widow, she has to remove her *taali* as it is an object which is only to be associated with auspiciousness. It is melted down or disassembled, and given to her daughter or granddaughter. However, if a woman dies as a *sumangali,* neither her *taali* nor her *kaluttiru* are melted down because they have remained with a *sumangali,* and are still auspicious objects, and so they are handed down to her daughter as such. Because of the history of the object, i.e. *kaluttiru* and *taali* which are associated with the life of a woman who died as a *sumangali,* they become auspicious agents.

Auspicious events, states, or auspicious objects are pure as they are symbolically associated with reproduction and prosperity which is sometimes stressed as the feminine power, i.e. *shakti.*

Generally, the physical transformations that women pass through entail simultaneous transformations of their religious status. A girl *(kanni)* as a virgin is pure and auspicious and is fit to participate in religious rituals. Sometimes, these girls are requested to become the vehicle of the divine spirit at village festivals. She loses this ritual purity when she begins to menstruate, although she is still auspicious. However, she is still pure in another sense, since her reproductive potentiality is under protection as a virgin. This potentiality can be utilized through the right channel (i.e. correct marriage) in the near future, and because of this potentiality, she is still said to be 'pure'. When she becomes a *sumangali,* she is no longer a virgin, yet her status as a 'pure virgin' is replaced by another stage as a married woman whose sexuality is properly channelled to her husband's family. Therefore, she becomes the most appropriate person to deal with auspicious household rituals, but she loses this status the moment she becomes a widow. Losing her husband, she loses the proper channel of reproduction, and since there is no replacement (remarriage), unless her reproductive power is channelled into a religious path (ideally), she becomes a threat to her affine. Choosing to be a religious widow is the only way for her potential reproductive power to benefit her family and the affine.

On the other hand, a man's significance in relation to ritual purity and auspiciousness does not really fluctuate. Except for a few occasions when he is affected by external circumstances, his ritual purity is less affected by his physiological process. However, a man suffers from the gravest pollution, i.e. the death pollution, when he becomes the chief mourner at a funeral both for his unmarried children and his parents. Although his wife and daughter also suffer from death pollution at this time, their degree is not as grave as his since, being women, they can never become chief mourners or attend the cremation. At the funeral, women send off the corpse which is accompanied by men who are close kin to the dead. As soon as they are gone, women start to clean the house to ward off death pollution.

Men accept death pollution from their parents partly because they receive most of the property left behind, and partly because they are not reproductive agents. Women, on the other hand, suffer from pollution, when they give birth to a child. Yet because of this reproductive capacity, they should not be polluted by death. In this respect, there is a sexual division of ritual pollution: women suffer from birth and menstrual pollution while men suffer from death pollution. In addition, sexual division of auspiciousness and inauspiciousness is attached to these two kinds of pollution: the former is auspicious but the latter is inauspicious. When his wife gives birth to a child, a man does not go to the temple for a few days, since he is supposed to share a certain degree of birth pollution, in the same way as his wife shares death pollution from his parents to a certain degree. His wife undergoes a longer period of ritual pollution after giving birth, just as he undergoes the gravest ritual pollution of death as a chief mourner. However, birth pollution is highly desirable while death pollution is not.

Madan (1987), along with Marglin (1985), claims that auspiciousness is a progressive movement directed towards growth, life, and the future, while inauspiciousness is a regressive movement directed towards destruction, death, and the past. Similarly, Good, in his life-cycle ritual analysis, formulates a scheme composed of four elements: the wedding as auspicious and pure, the ritual for the ending of mourning as inauspicious but pure, birth and puberty ceremonies as impure but auspicious, and lastly, the funeral as both impure and inauspicious (1991: 209).

Good's argument however is focused more on the dichotomous structure of the two levels, i.e. the auspiciousness/ inauspiciousness on one level, and pure/impure on the other (ibid.: 210). However, in the analysis of the ritual symbolism of the Nagarattars, I shall emphasize the clear sexual division of rituals between these two levels, and also stress the exclusive nature of auspiciousness *(subam)* which is rather neglected in the central part of the arguments of the authors mentioned above. *Tiruvaadirai,* the puberty ritual, and *padaippu* (ancestral worship) represent this exclusiveness in their rejection of the professional priest (i.e. Brahman *puroohita*). Although the Brahman *puroohita* is needed as funeral priest for purification, once purified, and the deceased has become an ancestor, there is no need for further purification. Therefore, as the desirable and pure agents, the ancestors are worshipped by the members of the lineage (mostly the members of the joint family) and for this ritual, the chief ritual officiant is the eldest male while women are only the assistants. Although the situation is auspicious, the ancestors are not really directly associated with procreation: being kin, they alone cannot become the symbol of reproduction. Exclusiveness of auspiciousness at the wedding is directly connected to procreation, on the other hand. At *muhuurtam,* when the bride receives the *taali,* the Brahman priest is requested to leave the house, as his presence is believed to be inauspicious. The *taali* and the *kaluttiru* are to be handled only by the close relatives, especially *sumangalis* or maternal uncles and their wives, since by being affines of the bride and the groom's families, they are auspicious and generate procreative symbols. Even in the rituals of *saandi,* although the Brahman priests do not disappear from the spot, the couple is surrounded by their close relatives, and the diamond *taali* is handled only by such people. In other words, the interactions of kin and affines as demonstrated in the wedding is strongly auspicious and pure as the representation of procreation.

The auspiciousness is expressed as the web of kinship in which professional specialists are avoided as unwanted elements: although

a washerman, *Muhuurta Kaaran,* and a Brahman priest are employed in the preliminary stage, they are unwelcome at the crucial
moment, since they are not kin or affine. Auspiciousness is generated only from the close interaction between the kin and affine:
since the kin cannot reproduce without affine, the presence of
cross-relatives, i.e. the maternal uncle and cross-cousins, is essential
in auspicious rituals.

In order to generate auspiciousness in the purest atmosphere,
both kin and affines are needed to symbolize procreation, while at
the funeral, the deceased should be looked after only by the family
and the *pangaali,* i.e. the kin. The auspiciousness of a *sumangali* is
guarded and generated by the web of kin and affines and she
functions as the mediator and adhesive between her kin (i.e. her
father and her brother) and her husband and son.

Chapter 7

Nagarattar Widowhood

7.1 Widowhood

ALTHOUGH widows in South Indian society are contrasted with the *sumangali* as the representation of inauspiciousness and economic insecurity, widowhood needs to be reassessed as an unavoidable stage of life which a lot of Indian women undergo. Most women live longer than their husbands and widowhood carries both trauma and liberation. While widows are no longer auspicious, they can enjoy the status of being considered the heirs to their husbands' property. It is especially so among the Nagarattars since unlike other caste women, Nagarattar widows are relatively well protected in terms of their economic autonomy. While socially, they cease to be sexually active beings irrespective of their biological age, they no longer need to be under the control of the male partner. They may stay in their husband's ancestral house alone, or live in their own house until their death, may travel with other widows or on their own.

While traditional Hindu laws do not allow a married daughter to inherit the property of her parents, a widow can. This was the case until the enforcement of the Hindu Succession Act in 1956. This allows the female heirs (both married and unmarried) to inherit the ancestral property (i.e. joint family property) in equal shares with their brothers (Rao 1995: 314). The problem of this act however, is that it is not retrospective except for the three southern states (Kerala, Andhra, and Tamil Nadu) which have special state amendments to make it retrospective. In other words, these three states allow married women to claim an equal share with their brothers of their parents' ancestral property (ibid.: 324–8).

Along with her children, a widow may inherit her deceased husband's property left by his father and enjoy it until her death. Although the property she inherits from her deceased husband passes not to her heir (such as her married daughter or her own brother's son) but to the next heir of the male from whom she inherited it, she can still use it till her death. Thus if she has no male child, her deceased husband's brother or his male descendant inherits it after her death.

Sad cases are often cited to me by other castes that as soon as the father dies, the son takes over the house his parents lived in as well as the property. His mother, as a widow, although she is entitled to enjoy these till her death, has to live without a house or any income since she lacks the means to appeal to the court. Indeed, one of the biggest tragedies of Indian women is that unless they have special means of earning a living or savings of their own, as widows, they are forced to live in poverty since they have to depend on the mercy of their sons. Therefore, the traditional arrangement of the Nagarattars to allow widows to stay in their husbands' ancestral house conforms to the orthodox Hindu law and if the minimum requirement of their living is provided, i.e. food and lodging, widowhood, especially after the widows are sixty, is not so bad, according to most Nagarattar women.

Older Nagarattar women get used to the way of fulfilling their lives in their old age as widows. Some senior aged widows do volunteer work in 'community service' and try to make marriage alliances as free mediators and negotiators; thus, well-informed widows are extremely popular in the community. They are invited to the ceremonial functions, keep in touch with people regularly so that they know the latest information: who is going to get married, details about unmarried young men and women, who failed in business, who went abroad, what kind of assets there are, and so on. Their associations are not limited to rich and powerful houses. Informative *aacchis* are quite accessible and acquire their popularity through constant socializing. They keep on being informed through conversations with other women. Their news is often more quickly circulated than men's. Unless they are out of town, they can go to any house if they are invited to the functions. Thus, widowhood cannot always be taken negatively.

Women in this stage may move more freely than in earlier stages; as they grow older, they develop their associations not only through women but also through their husbands and fathers, as well as sons and their friends. The kinship network and well-planned economic security play important roles in securing their social status before they undergo the last stage. I shall next discuss a Nagarattars funeral since this represents two fundamental characteristics of Nagarattar kinship: (1) the relative weakness of their concept of death pollution, since due to complete caste endogamy, they regard each other as being ritually equal; and (2) the clear ritual division of the affines playing a key role at weddings and kin playing a key role at funerals.

7.2 Funeral Procedures

Good (1991: 132) puts the death ritual in three stages in order to give an analytical description: (1) the disposal of the corpse; (2) the rites in the cemetery one or three days later; and (3) the subsequent purificatory rites at which prestations are exchanged, which normally take place sixteen days after the first stage. Following this, I shall sketch the death rituals of the Nagarattars. However, among the Nagarattars, the rites in the cemetery take place on the day after the cremation, and the mourning period lasts no longer than six days. Therefore, the interval between (1) and (3) is fairly short.

7.2.1 The Day of Death

When a death occurs in a Nagarattar house, the body is cleaned with rose-water and ash (and *kunkum* for a *sumangali*), covered with a white cloth (or a red cloth, if it is a *sumangali*), and kept in the ancestral house. It is first kept in an intermediary area, and then moved to the *walavu waasal* while the *pangaalis* of the deceased officiate over the rituals.

A white *veetti* with a tuft of grass tied in each corner with mango leaves placed on it is held aloft by four poles. Unlike the case of the Asaris reported by Good (ibid.: 133), in the Nagarattar funerals, there are no professionals like the musicians and the barber in the ritual held in the ancestral house. Just like the Brahman funeral, there is no music. The conch shell is blown by one of the *pangaalis* as well.

The body, wrapped in white cloth, is covered with a bamboo mat, and taken to the *walavu waasal* where a *pandal* is put up. If the deceased is a man, his male *pangaalis* go round the body in a clockwise direction and then their wives and children do the same. Even if it is a married woman (or widow), her husband's *pangaalis* perform the same rituals. Setting up the *pandals* and preparing for the funeral is the job of the *pangaalis,* and there is no role for the *dayaadi* (mother's people). In other words, the funeral ritual emphasizes the patriline of the deceased while the wedding emphasizes the marrying person's matriline. Even when a married woman dies, she receives proper homage from her husband's kin and all the expenses are met by her husband.

An *aacchi* told me: 'The mother's people would come and grieve with the people in the house, but this is of course, not a formality.' Contrary to the wedding and other auspicious occasions, there is no payment given to the ritual participants except for the professionals such as the priest. Giving money to relatives in auspicious circumstances is good, but money is not to be given to relatives and not to be received from others at funerals, especially not to or from the *pangaalis.* Only service castes get payments for duties performed at funerals.

A male *pangaali* blows the conch shell, which is also different from an auspicious ceremony, when the conch shell is blown by a married woman who is related to the family. After the conch shell is blown, the body is taken out and put into a cart and only the male *pangaalis* accompany the cart to the cremation ground. There is no musical band accompanying the group, and both the barber priest and the Parayas are awaiting for them in the cremation ground.

As soon as the body is gone, the women clean the house with water. However, although the corpse is regarded as a pollutant, the Nagarattars maintain that they still express more respect for the corpse than the Brahmans.

We always wrap the body with a new mat since we do not like to keep the body on the bare floor, like the Brahmans, as it looks very crude. We use the new mat to pay homage to the deceased and after the body is gone, we wash it and reuse it for some other purpose. On the other hand, the Brahmans keep the body wrapped in a white robe without covering it with a mat. Because they feel that only the spirit is important, they do not place much importance on the body. They treat the body as if it is rubbish and do not show it any affection.

A tall lamp with five angles is lit in a corner of the *walavu* throughout the mourning period. The same lamp is used on the auspicious occasions with five wicks, but for funerals, they use only one wick to signify that it is an inauspicious period.

7.2.2 Cremation

In the villages of Chettinadu, the Nagarattars usually have their own cremation ground which is separate from those of other castes. A few Parayas who have been hereditarily attached to the Nagarattar cremation ground wait for the funeral procession to come and assist in the cremation. The chief mourner is tonsured by a barber at the side of the compound and he takes a bath at the other side where there is a well. He changes his *veetti* there and comes to the platform where the body is to be cremated.

The Parayas cover the body with cow dung, straw, and clay and then, after the body is covered completely, an opening is made around the face into which each participant pours rice[1] soaked in water, some coins, and a few extra drops of water.

According to Good (1991: 135), this is called mouth money (*vaaykkaasu*), and is the prerequisite of the Vettiyan. According to Dubois (1906: 485), this is meant to stop the hunger and thirst of the deceased. This opening is then sealed and the body is covered with mud. The chief mourner goes clockwise round the body three times, carrying on his left shoulder a clay pot filled with water, accompanied by a barber. Each time the chief mourner circles the corpse, the barber makes a hole in the pot with a sickle so that the water pours out of it onto the ground (Good 1991: 135). In the meantime, the mourner kindles a fire with a wooden stick which he holds in his right hand. After three rounds, the mourner throws the pot over his shoulder. When the fire has been lit, the mourner and his accompanying party leave the spot and they are not supposed to look back. The Parayas pour kerosene onto the fire and tend it throughout the night.

The chief mourner, accompanied by the *pangaalis,* goes to the Shiva temple. He does not enter but waits for a Brahman *puroohita* at the side of the temple tank. The *puroohita* comes to the tank and sits at the steps of the tank and is given gifts by the chief mourner.

Daanam or religious gifts are only given to the Brahmans. The purpose behind this is to create merit for the deceased. Today, the

---

[1] According to the Nagarattars, this raw rice should be removed freshly from the husk in a wooden pounder, and this should be done by the daughter of the deceased. If there is no daughter, either the brother's daughter or the wife's sister's daughter *(mahal)* can replace her.

simplest way of giving *daanam* is to give Rs 50 to the Brahman, but traditionally, items such as pots filled with water (a symbol of fertility and thus auspiciousness), a new *veetti*, vegetables, and a torch, are given.

A more conspicuous gift is that of a cow or a calf *(goo-daana)* which, as Parry (1985: 619) and Dubois (1906: 483) maintain, is indispensable at least among the Brahman castes, if one wishes the deceased to arrive in heaven. This custom is popular among the Nagarattars. Purchasing a cow, according to a Nagarattar, is not as expensive as may be imagined. 'A cheap one can be available at around Rs 500 to 800. It does not matter whether it is lean or old. A cow is a cow.' Early in the morning the following day, the *pangaalis* take the bones from five parts of the deceased's body, which are put in a small box.

7.2.3 *Fifth Day: The End of the Mourning Period*

Traditionally, mourning ended on the sixteenth day, but nowadays, it ends on the fifth day.[2] In the morning, the Brahman priests begin preparing for the rituals in the women's quarter. The men and women are relieved that the mourning is at an end and are happy to chat with each other in their own quarters, so they pay little attention to the Brahman and his work. Seventy *donnai* cups (small cups made of leaves) are laid out with different things inside each. According to a *puroohita*, the seventy *donnai* cups are divided into five groups in the following manner. Three-fifths are given to the ancestors: this role is played by the *puroohita* in the ritual, and the *puroohita* receives them as *daanam*. One-fifth is given to lord Vishnu: this role is played by a Vaishnava Brahman or a Brahman connected with a Vishnu temple. One-fifth is to be given to lord Shiva: this role is played by a Brahman Shiva temple priest (Gurukkal).

The *donnai* cups should contain a minimum of ten items such as black grams, chickpeas, salt, raw sugar, turmeric, raw rice, auber-

---

[2] According to one *puroohita*, Brahmans observe mourning for twelve days, which is less than non-Brahmans. This is because they observe stricter disciplines than other castes and are thus 'purer'. Non-Brahmans now have the longest mourning period, since they have not changed their custom. Other castes have a much shorter mourning period. Among the Maravars in Chettinadu area, for example, the mourning period lasts for only two and a half days.

gine, bittergourd, tamarind, turmeric, etc. A *puroohita* sits in front
of a pot decorated with white thread placed on a mound of yellow
rice. The pots, according to the *puroohita*, symbolize the deities
and the deceased. The *puroohita* starts the Vinayaga *puuja* with
turmeric made into a small pyramid shape (this is to symbolize
Vinayaga). The mourner comes to the *puroohita* and is given the
thread *(puunal)* around his shoulder. This is a sacred thread which
symbolizes the status of the twice-born, who is entitled to receive
the service of the Brahman *puroohitas*. The *puroohita* sprinkles
yellow rice and then water with a mango leaf onto the Vinayaga,
i.e. the yellow pyramidal mound of the turmeric. He chants the
names of gods to invoke and request their presence and then he
chants the deceased person's name, *gootra*, birth star, etc. He then
sprinkles rice and flowers onto the pot and the chief mourner.

Next, at the corner of the setting, the priest worships the goddess
Lakshmi with a special lamp chanting her eight names. He puts
kus grass on the coconut placed on the pot. (*Kus* grass keeps evil
away.) Five Brahmans and the *puroohita* start chanting *mantras*
together, and the *puroohita* sprinkles water from the pot onto the
chief mourner as part of the purificatory ritual. The chief mourner
and his wife sip a few drops of *panchakaaram* (a mixture of five
ingredients, i.e. milk, curd, cow's urine, rice, and *ghee*) that has
been given by the *puroohita* for purification. The female relatives
receive the *panchakaaram*, after prostrating themselves, and then
the males follow suit. The mourner goes with the *puroohita* to the
corner where Lakshmi is worshipped, sits beside him, and copies
his chanting of the names of gods. The chief mourner stands and
places the *kus* grass in front of each of the six Brahmans sitting in
a row facing North. After some water is sprinkled, a big banana
leaf is placed in front of each of them on which water is sprinkled.
Raw rice and vegetables are then placed on each of the leaves.[3]

Five rupees, betel leaves, areca nuts, long vegetables, and pumpkin pieces are added to each *donnai*. Then two Brahmans put a
white *veetti* up as a curtain and the *puroohita* sits behind the curtain
facing the chief mourner who is sitting on the other side of the
curtain. The chief mourner passes money and other gifts to the

---

[3] This is only a pseudo-feast, and all the food put on the leaf is 'raw', because
Brahman priests refuse to dine with non-Brahmans in order to preserve their
ritual purity. At the funeral of a Brahman, real cooked food would be given to
the Brahman priests, since they are ritually equal.

puroohita through the space between the curtain and the floor. He then takes a bath and wears a new thread given to him by the *puroohita*. A fire is lit for the *homam* (offering of *ghee* to the fire god). The change of the sacred thread symbolizes the termination of pollution, and the new start in the mourning house.

The *puroohita* makes balls of uncooked rice, *milahu*, honey, and yellow rice coloured with turmeric. One ball is for the paternal grandfather, one is for the father, and another is for the deceased. These three balls are mixed together so that they make one big ball and later, the ball is thrown into a pond, tank, or river.[4]

One box which contains a few bones of the deceased is buried in one corner of the house, and after a few days, this is taken out and carried to a sacred river (e.g. Ganges, Yamuna) for immersion. At the ritual I attended, the box was taken to Rameshwaram, a famous pilgrimage centre by the sea in the south of Tamil Nadu. Some Hindus take the bones as far as Benares, which is the most desirable final destination. The Nagarattars have rest houses for caste members in almost all famous pilgrimage centres in India, so that they can stay there at a reasonable rate (Rs 10 to 15 per day, for a family) for as long as they want.

7.3 Caste Endogamy and Pollution

Comparing the Nagarattar funeral with other funerals, I have noticed three major differences. First, there is no gift-giving from the wife's natal families nor is there any ritual role assigned to the people from the *dayaadi*. While the ritual role of the affines (i.e. *dayaadi*) especially that of the maternal uncle's role in auspicious occasions is stressed, the Nagarattar funeral does not assign any role to the affines. When a married woman dies, all the expenses are to be met by her husband or her son. Except for the minimum gift of *saree* and a few bottles of rose water to cleanse the body, her natal family has no obligation to meet the funeral expenses or to give gifts. All the funeral procedures are conducted by the *pangaalis*, the husband's patrilineage. Although some castes do practice gift-giving to the chief mourner and the role of his affines as the givers

---

[4] According to Parry (1985: 628), the Funeral Priest (Mahabrahmans in Benares, i.e. Kasi) is supposed to take up the place of the deceased (ghost) and eat the meal there, in order to absorb the sin of the deceased and send him or her to heaven.

is still stressed (cf. Dumont 1983), among the Nagarattars the mourner does not receive any substantial gift from his affines at the funeral. This might also express the Nagarattars' emphasis on the *pulli* (conjugal family) as an economically autonomous unit, since a Nagarattar man maintains,

You must always keep the money aside for funerals for your family members. If the money is not enough to hold the funeral, you might borrow some from your father or brother. However, you have to return it as quickly as possible.

Secondly, unlike most other castes who deliberately refrain from eating in the mourning house excepting the closest kin, the Nagarattars do serve meals to all the visitors in the mourning house. Moreover, it is an obligation for those who attend the funeral to eat there, since it is considered an expression of condolence. This custom is extremely rare and so far, I have not heard of any other caste who would cook a meal in the mourning house to serve the visitors, since eating there is considered to be ritually polluting. Thirdly, while other castes in general do not send the women to the cremation ground at all, the Nagarattars send them the following morning. After the cremation takes place, the women visit to pay homage to the deceased. This is also quite unusual and would go some way to explain part of their gender relationships in the ritual context of funerals. Focusing on these three points, I shall explain the gender relationship as it appears in a funeral.

7.4 Absence of Gift-Giving from the 'Mother's House'

Several castes make the close kin and affines participate in both funerals and weddings as crucial ritual specialists. For example, Srinivas (1952) describes how the kin, i.e. the patrilineally inherited joint ancestral house members among the Coorgs, perform essential functions on both auspicious and inauspicious occasions, in the major life-cycle rituals. On both types of occasion, members of the friendly *okkà*, i.e. those who are called *aruvas*, who are also classificatory affines, come and help the members (ibid.: 124). The *aruvas* have frequent marriage alliances with another *okka*, so that the relationship between these *okkas* is closely tied with mutual help and gift exchange relationships. Similarly, the matrilineal Nayars who have mutual co-operative relationships with the friendly *tara-vads* called *enangans* who are also the classificatory affines, come and assist at both the funerals and weddings.

However, as far as the Nagarattars are concerned, there is a clear distinction between kin and affines at weddings and funerals, although both take place in their ancestral house *(walavu viidu)*. While weddings and auspicious rituals are attended by the affine, i.e. ' mother's people', they are not involved with funerals. Funerals are taken care of by the *pangaalis:* they are the people who would come and assist the chief mourner and his family. Yet they refuse to accept gifts for that service.

The close *pangaalis* often help the family when there is a sudden death at the house and when there is no chief mourner to accept the death pollution. For example, at the funeral I attended, the son (who had been adopted) was away from home and did not manage to reach the house before his father's cremation. A festival for a village goddess in a shrine situated very close to the house was about to be held, so the family was forced to perform the cremation immediately so that the auspicious festival was not polluted. Because the son could not get there in time, a nephew took the role of the chief mourner. In this way, some other *pangaali* can replace the chief mourner if they have to conduct a funeral without the son. The person who takes the position would accept the pollution, have his hair tonsured and cremate the body of the deceased as the chief mourner. This kind of ritual division of labour exists between the *pangaalis* and the affine.

Affines are related to auspicious ceremonies and reproduction, while the *pangaalis* look after death. This explains how the funeral pollution is associated with the right to the ancestral property, since it used to be shared by the close kin male member group who are patrilineally related. However, the fact that even the death of a married woman is looked after by her husband's *pangaalis* implies that her membership is already completely transferred to and is secured in her married house. Among the Nagarattars the expense of the funeral and the labour to conduct the funeral are met by her husband's family. Yet this is not very common among other castes even among the Chettiyars. For example, a Velan Chettiyar maintains that in his community, the funeral expenses for a married woman should be met by her natal family. Similarly, among the Kallars, Maravars, and Ahamudiyars, gifts of money and commodities come from the woman's mother's house as is discussed by Dumont (1983).

No gift is given by the *dayaadi* and no role is assigned to any of the *dayaadi* at the funerals. Also, women, once married, do not need to undergo the ritual pollution of their natal family, since they have already become part of the affines with respect to their brothers. Although a woman who has lost her parents mourns and grieves, and does not wear brightly coloured *sarees* for a few days, she does not receive death pollution. When she dies, death pollution is shared by her husband, her children, and some close *pangaalis* of her husband, but not by her natal family members. If they wish, they may go to the temples and visit other people's houses, although they may be too grief-stricken to do so. In this sense, Nagarattar women once married, appear to be severed from their natal families, as they do not undergo the official mourning period of their families like other patrilineal castes (cf. Good 1991). However, unlike the case of the Tanjore Brahmans (Gough 1956) or Nambudiri Brahmans, such a transfer of membership to a husband's lineage does not imply the wife's isolation from her natal family but rather implies her right to share her husband's property. If she dies before her husband, she is enshrined as the guardian of her husband's lineage as *periyaacchi* (big *aacchi*). If she becomes a widow, she is entitled to enjoy her husband's property including the space given at *walavu viidu*. Until her death, she can enjoy the space there and often the house that the husband built in addition to a share of the management of her husband's business. Such a systematic arrangement for widows shows that her right of managing her husband's property is compatible with that of her sons. A Brahman woman in her late fifties lamented,

In our community, a widow has no right to her husband's property. Everything goes to her son as soon as her husband is dead. Therefore, if the son wants he can even kick her out from the house without giving her any money. And this often happens.

7.5 Guest-Feeding at the Funeral

Feeding the guests in the mourning house is quite unusual in India yet the Nagarattar mourner feeds the participants, throughout the mourning period. He even gives a small gift to the participants on the last day of mourning.[5] Feeding the guests would have taken almost two weeks in olden days, since a lot of them would be working abroad and it would have taken them some time to get there. Although feeding nowadays takes only three days, it still requires a great deal of money, since they have to feed at least two hundred to five hundred people who might be at the mourning house. In addition to the expenses which involve funeral specialists such as the *puroohita,* a senior Nagarattar maintains that the Nagarattar family should always keep such money aside for the funeral of any family member. 'Only when you are well prepared for such an occasion, can you be a full-fledged man', he maintained,[6] if you are a married man. It is a shame if a man has not prepared anything for a funeral.' To a Nagarattar, the family of a man with social standing should be able to arrange a funeral for him and for his wife and for his unmarried children.[7]

Feeding the guests also carries significant meaning when compared with other castes. People normally avoid feeding guests since people taking food in the mourning house fosters pollution. Cooking itself is prohibited among the Brahmans and the Nayars; thus, it is an essential task of the close relatives who live nearby to cook food and deliver it to the mourning family. However, in the case of the Nagarattars, eating in the mourning house is an obligation of the visitor, since sharing the food symbolizes sharing of sorrow with the mourners. It is quite important to note the fact that most mourners who come are Nagarattars: the Brahmans who work for them would come but would not be requested to take food there although all the Nagarattar visitors would stay and eat, or if one is in a hurry, coffee is at least to be consumed before one leaves the house.

[5] On the final day of mourning, the participants are given small gifts, things like stainless-steel cups with *poriyal* (popped rice) in addition to betel leaves and areca nuts. Stainless-steel cups, as I explained in the previous chapter, symbolize auspiciousness, because of their scratchless, unbreakable quality. *Poriyal* also signifies auspiciousness by its colour (whiteness) and puffy quality (good harvest).

[6] However, in reality, there are some families who have to borrow money from the relatives if there is a sudden death.

[7] If someone dies before getting married, he or she is not given a proper funeral, i.e. the guests are limited to the close kin, and no Brahman priest is required, or no grand meals are served to the guests. If it is a child, the funeral is far more simple. According to Good (1991: 144), the corpse of a child is not to be cremated and should be buried, and only adults are supposed to be cremated.

Sharing the death pollution strongly demonstrates an egalitarianism based on caste endogamy. Therefore, as all Nagarattars are equal in terms of ritual status, it is possible to make alliances with good families if any of the family members achieve economic success.

7.6 Gender Division in the Funeral Ritual

Women do not accompany the body to the cremation ground, but 'purify' the house while the men are away. Thus, there is a clear gender division at the funeral: the women, who are associated with reproduction, are not supposed to undergo death pollution as the chief mourner. On the other hand, at the birth of a child, a woman undergoes a polluted period for one month. She cannot go to a temple until this period is over, although a lot of women maintain that this period of taboo is reserved for women after birth to rest in a secluded separate place.

In the case of the Nagarattars however, the concept of 'pollution' is relatively weak. During my research, my informants from the Kamma Naidus and Gownders also expressed a relatively mild concept of pollution as compared to Brahmans, Komutti Chettiyars, or Shaiva Vellalar Pillais. The latter group strictly maintain that they should not take any food (even a cup of coffee) in the mourning house, while both the Kammas and Gownders maintained that they can offer food as long as it is not cooked in the mourning house, although the visitors do not need to take it. However, only the Nagarattars maintain a specific custom of assigning women to visit the cremation ground the following morning after the cremation. A senior Nagarattar male explains,

We ask women to go and check if there is any emotional entanglement the deceased person has left in this world. If there is, it would show in the bones. Women just go and check it.

However, this role is never given to the young unmarried women. It is taken over only by old senior widows and married women of the kin. In other words, married Nagarattar women, along with men, are assigned roles to send off the deceased, and this also expresses their status as the 'female' *pangaali* of the deceased person.

7.7 Widows and Their Autonomy

Widows are said to be ritually inauspicious, but they are not considered ritually impure. By living a religious and austere life, they are actually purer than married women from a ritualistic perspective. Indeed elderly widows who lost their husbands in their old age are not particularly inauspicious and are treated with considerable respect. They can bless their grandchildren at *Tiruvaadirai*, and welcome the newly married couple at the entrance of the house with *aarati* ceremony. The only prohibition among the Nagarattars seems to be that they tend to avoid participating in the women's group to fetch the bridegroom *(maapillai alaippu)* nor would they stand near the ritual platform when the *taali* is tied around the neck of the bride (see the ritual part of wedding). Among the Nagarattars, widows can even achieve a ritually elevated status by getting initiated into the second stage of Shaiva initiation after which they are entitled to conduct a *puuja* to the lingam (Shiva) in their own houses.

Nonetheless, a widow, especially a young one, still suffers from the loss of social status as a *sumangali*. When her husband dies, all the jewellery is taken away from her and she no longer wears a *taali*, a symbol of auspiciousness and the capacity of reproduction, since to avoid risking blemishing the caste code, there is no chance of remarriage for a high caste Hindu woman. She is left the option of a religious life so that she can aspire to the *moksha* (the final liberation) through religious discipline. In this sense, her life and status resemble those of the *sanniyaasins* (world renouncers). They are not polluted but considered inauspicious and so are kept away at the moment of tying the *taali*. A temple priest told me that in the past *sanniyaasins* had not been welcome inside the temple because they were inauspicious and were believed to take away the temple's *shakti* (cosmic power) which also symbolizes reproduction. Although most *sanniyaasins* nowadays visit the temple, the stigma of inauspiciousness attached to widowhood still remains in South Indian culture.

To die as a *sumangali* is a desirable fate for women because of the hardships they potentially have to suffer as widows. If a woman dies as a *sumangali*, she is worshipped as the guardian to her husband's lineage. Her corpse is wrapped in a colourful *saree* and a red spot *(pottu)* is put on her forehead for auspicious decoration.

She is cremated in a grand manner by her husband and his relatives, but nothing positive is attached to the funeral of a widow.

The following is an excerpt from a funeral song *(oppaali)*, sung by the Nagarattar widows in the area of Chettinadu. Funeral songs describe the misery of widows in olden days and the *oppaalis* of the Nagarattar women are famous for the richness of their poetry and the full and vivid descriptions of their lives. I quote from a book written by Somalay (1953 : 441) because I could not collect *oppaali* directly from the women, as singing them on a normal occasion is inauspicious.[8]

> The goldsmith who made the *taali* should have known.
> The man who wove the *saree* should have known.
> The man who fixed up the day of the marriage should have known.
> One of them could have given us the warning . . .
> I bought a *saree*.
> Before I use it, my husband is dead.
>
> I was cleaning the floor.
> Suddenly people fixed my marriage.
> Now I am a widow.
> People take away my jewels.
> What are you going to do with them?
> You give me a piece of cloth.
> What is this?
> This is the inauspicious thing.
> Saints use this to wipe their hands.
> Such a cloth is given to me to hide my heart.

No woman feels positive about widowhood. On becoming a widow, she has to remove all her jewellery, including her *taali*, and is not supposed to wear coloured *sarees*, but only white ones. She has to hide herself away and keep social contacts to the minimum. She is simply inauspicious, although she is also considered clean and pure.

However, in real life, they still have to continue their lives and are expected to shoulder far more responsibility to manage the family. Since they are already married, they are no longer

[8] When I attended a funeral, I heard an old woman sing an *oppaali* with a particular tune, expressing her despair and heartbreak in the way she sang. The songs are mostly learnt by heart while attending funerals. According to Somalay, *oppaalis* are widespread in Chettinadu, and a famous Nagarattar movie producer and poet, Kannadasan, has taken most of his themes and tunes from lullabies and *oppaalis* sung by his mother and his female relatives.

under the control of their parents. In order to survive, they are even encouraged to take jobs or manage their husbands' property skillfully. If they have small children, their position as the bread-winner is further justified so that both close kin and affines extend help and coach them until they can handle everything by themselves. After getting their children married, old senior widows seem to be able to enjoy more freedom than they would have had in their married life. In terms of travelling more freely and doing things as they wish, they are far more liberated than young married women in some respects. Indeed, although people tend to stress the dark side of widowhood, there is a positive side as well.

Of course, I felt sad when I lost my husband since we used to be together. However, after several months, I recovered from such sorrow and started to work much harder. I sold my husband's land and purchased a flat in Madras in order to let it out. I also managed a farm with the help of my husband's aunt. She gave me a lot of advice and we've been very close. I could marry off my three children. I often go back to Chettinadu. Sometimes, I visit my friends' houses, go on pilgrimage with them.

A Nagarattar woman in her middle thirties maintains that her maternal grandmother used to tell her that she had been far more liberated after having become a widow.

I do not think marriage can be everything for women. If they have children and have the power to earn their own living, they would be able to enjoy life far more as widows. Marital relationships are full of stress and hardships. However, once you become a widow, no one will pressure you to get married any longer. You are much freer as a widow.

Even some of the women of the Kamma Naidus and the Gownders admit that widowhood can be a relief after a conjugal relationship.

My maternal grandmother as a widow had a more relaxed life than she had as a wife. By looking after the land left for her, she saved well, brought up her children and enjoyed a freedom she could not have had with her husband.

The relative freedom of widows has been stressed by scholars studying other societies (cf. Rogers 1975; Skinner 1993). Of course, this view is not shared by everyone, especially if there is no way for a widow to earn her own living.

In India widows in general are said to be one of the poorest sections of society, since most of them, without any means to earn their own living, have to depend on the mercy of their kin. Earning power is associated more with men and Hindu custom does not prohibit widowers from remarrying. Such asymmetry shows how uneven rights and privileges between men and women are, although in real life, not all widowers are assured of remarriage. If the man is economically weak, it can be difficult, and a wealthy widower might also not remarry if he is in his fifties, since it may create problems between the children of his first and second wives.

Men are mostly caught between their new wife's and their deceased wife's children. Therefore, remarriage might not necessarily be an advantage for them. Grown-up children would object to their father's remarriage, since it would create problems of property transfer. Therefore, in order to avoid such problems, most senior men would not remarry but would prefer to hire a cook who caters their food and does daily laundry.

Thus, some Nagarattars mention that extra-marital sexual activity sometimes took place between female servants and widowed Nagarattar men, while rich men would sometimes keep concubines (see Chapter 2).

In short, the problems of widowers are less to do with economics and more to do with the availability of day-to-day services including sex and their children's nursing. On the other hand, a larger number of widows lose their basic means of survival. They become liabilities either to their natal family or to their husbands', and tend to be treated as a burden (see Meenakshi's case in Chapter 2). To have a young widow in the house is a burden to the family, since they have to be responsible for keeping her chaste to the deceased husband in order not to soil the family name. Widows used as domestic labour are still common while among the poor, there are some who cannot even find a place of shelter. Even among the high castes, women do complain that they lose a place to stay in as soon as their husband dies. 'If the husband dies, the son takes over the entire property and he won't give anything to his mother.' Troubles can occur between the mother-in-law and her daughter-in-law, since the latter's position is much stronger if her husband takes over the property.

In the case of the Nagarattars however, due to their tradition of economic autonomy preserved in *pulli,* widows tend to maintain relative economic security. Women believe that it is better to keep the kitchen separate even if they live under the same roof. A middle-aged *aacchi* says,

Quarrels always start from the kitchen. Therefore, it is better if you do not interfere with your daughter-in-law, especially in her kitchen. If I become a widow, I would prefer to live in my own house rather than to live with my son, just like my mother. You can also go back to Chettinadu and stay in the *walavu viidu* of your husband. You have a right to stay there as a widow. It would be much more comfortable if you could manage on your own.

Indeed, the Nagarattars' arrangement of preserving the joint household works to the advantage of the poor, since being a joint house, they have the right to live in it even if they are financially down-trodden. In this sense, the widow's right to live in her husband's *walavu viidu* is a welfare provided by the community. I have come across a number of widows living in the old *walavu viidus* of Chettinadu on their own. Even when some of them share the space with another widow or with some families who are their husbands' *pangaalis,* they strictly keep the principle of keeping a separate kitchen, and they do keep separate accounts and maintain that that is the way to live in peace. Indeed, I have noticed that Nagarattar widows prefer to live on their own rather than with their sons, even though it is not economical to live alone. Among other castes, whether the family is rich or poor, it is common for a son to live with his mother after his father dies while among the Nagarattars, it is more common for old widows to stay in their husbands' house on their own, with a minimum number of servants. An *aacchi* explains,

My father left a will stating that she has the right to stay in the present house until her death and manage her own property. Therefore, one of my brothers will take over the house after her death. Leaving a will is quite common among us.

In addition, most women I have come across kept some unaccounted savings called *siruveetu panam* (women's money) for a rainy day. The widows also depend on the strong networking power which they cultivate especially after marriage.[9]

---

[9] Gownders also told me that they have the custom of keeping the *siruveettu panam* out of the money they earned privately, e.g. selling the milk of their cows.

A widow appears to spend a busy life in extra- and inter-household networking. She often visits her kin, affines, and her friends' houses. Pilgrimages and other tourism, as well as the shuttling between Chettinadu and Madras every month are crucial activities without which the Nagarattar network does not function. In other words, her lifestyle exemplifies the Nagarattar women's life in old age: minimum economic security and autonomy but with a fully-integrated life within the community. 'I want to be on my own so that I do not need to beg from anyone even if my husband throws me out.', an *aacchi* in her late forties maintains. Her sense of autonomy is strongly supported both by her economic autonomy and by women's alliances which can be crucial weapons to counteract men's greater economic resources. For example, an *aacchi* said that she had to fight against her own sons in court since they tried to snatch all of her share of her deceased' husband's property. With the support of her daughter and the daughter's husband, she hired a lawyer and won the case against her two sons. In other words, the mother–daughter relationship also attracts her son-in-law as a support she can count on in times of need.

Some childless *aacchis* adopt a son after their husbands' death. Thurston (1909: iv. 263) records a case. A widow, whose wish to adopt a boy was ignored by her brother-in-law, appealed to her husband's clan temple committee and succeeded in adopting a son. This arrangement would, of course, keep her right to manage her deceased husband's property on behalf of her adopted son. Such an appeal would not have been made if she did not have any intra-household networks to consult. As some *aacchis* demonstrate, it is even possible for a widow to maintain a business alliance with her deceased husband's brothers, especially if they are related, e.g. cross cousins. The following story shows such a case.

CASE STUDY.   Visala, forty-six, widow, and a college lecturer.

Visala married at sixteen, and lost her husband at eighteen. She had no child, so she took up higher studies and became a college lecturer. Now she teaches mathematics at a local college for girls at a village in Chettinadu. She says there was a time that she had thought about remarriage. Someone from another caste came forward and proposed to her. She did not accept it, since she did not want to lose all her social connections by this marriage. Moreover, she was economically sound and did not need to remarry for economic reasons. She also did not want to lose her right to her deceased husband's share of the property in Malaysia. It was shared by his two brothers and they were going to sell it to establish a business in India. Although she is a widow, she maintains a fairly busy social life, attending weddings and ceremonies. She built a big house and helps finance her relatives' children for education and job hunting. Her brothers-in-law, who are her cross-cousins, are now her business partners as well. She owns several shops and two auto-rickshaws and is thinking of adopting a grown-up son so that she can become a mother and have grandchildren. However, she will not let her son touch her property until her death.

As seen above, it is possible for a widow to take up the social role of her deceased husband. The process is smoother especially if she has business partners or consultants among the relatives. As already discussed, the membership of a married woman is already transferred to her husband's *pangaali* group so that even at the funeral of her husband or herself, there is nothing her maternal uncle or her natal family members officially do for her. Their moral code therefore maintains that she should try to earn her own living without going back to her natal family. As the legend of the emergence of the Nagarattar caste suggests, the intermarriage of the Chettiyar boys and the Vellalar girls (agricultural caste) makes it possible to imagine that the Nagarattars living closer to the Vellalars might have taken up some customs of the Vellalars. The women especially might have started to save their pocket money by keeping cows or weaving baskets, since their husbands were mostly away on long-distance trade. A similar relationship was suggested to me by the Gownders in Coimbatore District, that Coimbatore Kammas might have copied the former's custom to make women work in the field and become economically autonomous.

Many Nagarattar women still maintain that sons alone can keep the house name and inherit the husband's property. Yet this underestimates the fact that women still exercise their power more effectively through networking. Their power may sometimes underpin men's, especially if it is underwritten by her status as a mother or as a widow. Thus some male Nagarattars state that it is better to leave their joint property to their mother until her death:

My mother handles my father's property very carefully. At the moment, she manages it with my elder brother since other brothers are not in the business. However, she is fair to all of her four sons, so she did not give me money when I built a house. Of course, if we had a sister, the matter would be entirely different. My mother would have assisted her if our sister wanted to buy a house for her family.

Although this man did get considerable financial help from his wife's natal family, this further confirms the economic separation between the mother (widow) and her sons.

Most widows in India are poverty-stricken. Yet even widowhood differs depending on caste tradition and this is why there was no tradition of systematic provisions to support widows. On the other hand, as I discussed in this chapter, several agricultural castes encourage widows to help themselves, e.g. working as day labourers in the fields or looking after their own land. The Nagarattar way of widowhood is also part of such a tradition: although *walavu viidu* in Chettinadu appears to be functioning only as their functional hall, it nonetheless represents a practical idea. As long as there is a common ancestral house, the married women have a place to stay. Living in Chettinadu and visiting each other, widows have a life of economic stability. Their frugality also keeps their food budget to a minimum. They can spend time travelling. Visiting religious centres is their favourite pastime — the Nagarattars have built their rest houses in all the major pilgrim centres in India where members can stay for a small charge.

Although Tamils appreciate *sumangalis* as auspicious symbols, they also accept the fact that widowhood is after all an unavoidable stage for many women. Economic uncertainty is the most crucial worry for the widows who are not able to have the means of remarriage or of earning their own living. In exchange for sexual liberation or the choice of remarriage, the Nagarattars as a community offer an insurance to the widows: by securing them the space to live on their own in their deceased husband's ancestral house and by providing the cheap accomodation in almost all pilgrimage centres, they provide a minimum security and minimum means of leisure for their womenfolk to cope with the last stage of their lives.

Chapter 8

Conclusion: Mercantile Morality and Nagarattar Womanhood

8.1 The Morality of Gift-Giving and Gift-Exchange

When M.A.M. Ramasamy's *saandi* took place on an unprecedented scale, people were especially shocked by the scale of his gift-giving: not only relatives and friends, but all the servants, employees, and guests who went to see him were given gifts of some sort. People talked about such an excessive indulgence in gift-giving as typical of the Nagarattars. Yet on giving gifts, people whispered, the Nagarattars would always consider what they would get in return. Incidentally, Kamala, a non-Nagarattar woman lawyer who married a Nagarattar (see Chapter 2) said to me,

Whenever I attend their functions, they keep on giving me stainless-steel vessels as gifts. I accept them, but tell them that they'd better not to give them if they expect me to return a gift in the future. Because I may forget, I tell them that beforehand. All *aacchis* are so careful and remember whatever they gave or whatever they were given by others and never forget to return another gift on appropriate occasions. Being a non-Nagarattar, I was not brought up in such a culture, and I keep on forgetting things. I appreciate their warmth and enjoy it very much but I only attend ceremonies which are absolutely necessary.

Indeed, the Nagarattars do not expect the same kind of reciprocal relationship from non-Nagarattars: their hospitality towards non-Nagarattars is for self-satisfaction, in other words, gift-giving, without receiving, is an expression of generosity without degrading their status.

As I mentioned in previous chapters, a principle of reciprocity is established in a collective sense in a bilateral, cross-cousin marriage. As I have pointed out, the reverse works at a funeral, as it is

an inauspicious occasion which should not be repeated: the Nagarattars insist on non-reciprocity and the mourner simply gives but
never receives. This non-reciprocal gift as an expression of inauspiciousness is the pair ideology of auspiciousness which is the basis
of reciprocity.

As I have already discussed, Nagarattars regard gift-giving as
reciprocal (which Sahlins might term a 'political' alliance), and the
auspiciousness or *subam* that is intrinsic to the gift-exchange of the
Nagarattars is closely connected to reproduction or fecundity,
which can also lead to a political alliance. Exchanges which take
place on auspicious occasions have marital union as their motivation and objective: kin and affines make gift-exchanges for future
alliances and mutual prosperity at puberty ceremonies, weddings,
and *saandi*. Women, as auspicious agents, are the central figures
in the Nagarattars' scheme of such a gift-exchange. They are producers of future progeny and as such are the most auspicious
valuables exchanged between two lineages. Without marriage, the
lineage can no longer maintain an exchange relationship with the
rest of the Nagarattars. As with the Trobriander's exchange of
valuables, the Nagarattars marital exchanges only take place within
a defined circle, and women, along with other valuables and commodities, are carefully exchanged only within those boundaries.

In contrast to this kind of reciprocal exchange, gift-giving at
funerals is inauspicious and should never be reciprocated. Neither
the maternal relatives nor the affines have any role in funeral rituals
— only the *pangaalis* help the mourner and participate in the
rituals, but they receive nothing in exchange. However, the Nagarattars still express the principle of egalitarianism among themselves
even at the last moment of life: the mourner, on behalf of the
deceased, serves food to all the visitors who come and mourn for
the family. It is the visitors' obligation to have meals in the mourning house as this is an expression of sharing the sorrow with the
family of the deceased and paying respect to the dead. To them,
eating in the mourning house is not a pollution since all caste
members have the same ritual status. Such 'pollution sharing' is
rarely observed among other castes and may confirm the Nagarattars' strong insistence on an egalitarian principle based on perfect
caste endogamy.

For wealthy Nagarattar merchants, the extravagant spending at
the wedding of a daughter is equivalent to reciprocal exchange,

which is necessary to maintain their prestige as well as their personal desire. In one way, that may be similar to modern capitalist expenditure on advertising and commercials. Pompous wedding ceremonies are effective ways of propagating the wealth of a family and increasing the credibility of the merchant, thus his individual desire and capitalistic motivation go hand in hand, since the house can demonstrate its wealth through a large function and generous gift-giving. As Bayly points out in the case of North Indian mercantile families (1983: 376), a large proportion of the family capital is kept for the daughter's wedding, and this is one of the essential ways of advertising to outsiders which eventually benefits the business (Rudner 1994). A wedding connects two houses in a business alliance, thus extending the network and pooling the assets of two families even if neither interferes directly with the other's business concerns.

8.2 Individuality among the Nagarattars

The Nagarattars' well-planned political and economic strategy does not fit in well with Weber's position that Hinduism does not conform to the capitalistic mode of production or ascetic work ethic. Yet as both Rudner (ibid.) and Ito (1966) maintain, the economic power of the Nagarattars is based on a firm kinship structure and not on individualism like Western capitalism. Unlike the western individualist society, people's identity is deeply connected to caste. Particular customs and traditions are deeply embedded in each caste. Thus, a Nagarattar woman maintains,

If I married someone from another caste, I would start worrying as soon as I got up in the morning. I would worry what to cook and how to cook it. I would worry all day about every little thing. Therefore, it would be much easier to marry someone of my own caste.

Collectivism rather than individualism is stressed in such a comment and an individual is well described in the web of her kinship. Caste also appears as the extension of kinship which defines the manners and customs of the individuals. Yet Mines (1994) maintains that it is misleading to argue that Indian society is completely dominated by caste-oriented collectivism as Dumont (1983) remarks. Mines thus demonstrates that the concept of an individual differs between the West and India and that one can not assess an individual only by one valued manifestation — that of Western individualism (1994: 5).

What Indians recognize is not the person separated from the collective identity, according to Mines, but they still recognize personal uniqueness, value achievement, and assess personal motivation and reputation as the features of individuality. Thus Tamils recognize individuals as responsible actors (ibid.: 10). Tamil individuality, according to him, has both exterior and interior dimensions. Therefore, rather than separating the public identity from the private self, the Tamil individuality takes a more holistic attitude (ibid.: 12–13). Therefore, philanthropic activities, or leadership as expressed in local communities as the headman, big-man, or as the head of the *pangaali*, are indicators showing the uniqueness of an individual. In other words, one can aspire to different goals depending upon circumstances and ability, although in many cases, such goals are often achieved through connections that are traced 'at least in part through wives or mothers' (ibid.: 17).

Although Mines criticizes Dumont's confusion about the different concept of an individual, between the Western 'individualism' and Tamil 'individuality', I still doubt whether there is such a concept of the goal as headman or the big-man (*periyavar*) among Tamils, since there is no Nagarattar who mentioned such a concept. A few Nagarattars whom I asked about the notion of *periyavar* maintained that it merely means a man of senior age, and not a man of importance. 'When we want to suggest someone as an important person in our community, we use the term "*mukkiya-maana pulli*" (important conjugal unit)'.

As this statement shows, the Nagarattars' respect for individual autonomy works more to encourage the conjugal unit. Without getting married a man cannot gain social status. Thus, the Nagarattars' ideal is to be autonomous without conflicting with the *pangaalis* and natal family members which is why economic autonomy of the *pulli* is the key. The head of a renowned joint business group, now in his late seventies, maintains he borrowed money from the joint business capital pool in his early twenties to build a house for his family but had to return it with interest as quickly as possible. His group is the only prominent group which has maintained a joint business over three generations and the head now occupies the chairman's position, but his position is more honorary rather than concerned with making decisions in day-to-day business activities.

Unlike the 'real' *pangaali* joint business as seen among the Komutti Chettiyars in which the eldest male as head of the business needs to be consulted in every major decision, the Nagarattars tend to diversify businesses and eventually split into individual units. Therefore, although the eldest male member of the close *pangaali* group is consulted about various things, individuals have much broader business networking to depend on. For example, the wife's brothers are often consulted as they tend to have closer relationships through the wife than their own brothers.

Some are even critical of their own brothers and paternal uncles: '*Pangaalis* fight each other if they have joint property interests.' Conflicting interests between father/son or brother/brother are mitigated by the conjugal couple's economic autonomy supported by the wife's connections with her natal families. While the husband's independence from his natal kin is regarded as crucial if he is to prove his economic capability, his wife's and her natal kin's help are taken for granted. In this sense, both male and female autonomy are achieved in a different manner since the life-cycle of both sexes are different, and the Nagarattars still maintain a more strict sexual division of labour compared with agricultural castes such as the Kammas or the Gownders.

A new approach is thus required to assess the authority and leadership roles in the sphere of both the internal and external household kin relationships. During my research I have noticed that emotional solidarity among female kin is far stronger than between male kin. Women exchange labour far more easily than men: they keep their children in each others' houses, send meals to each other, assist in finding appropriate marriage partners, and lend money to each other without taking interest. On the other hand, men are more reserved and do not talk to or visit each other as often as women do. Indeed, their preference for cross-cousin marriage can be understood as part of that process: the women's network forms such close interactive units that their spouses and children are drawn into this. Therefore, a child, whether a son or a daughter, may feel easier about marrying a member of their mother's family.

The importance Nagarattars attach to social networking within the caste is especially illustrated by the fact that even the city-dwelling and foreign-born Nagarattars repeatdly visit Chettinadu to attend functions of their kin and affines, as well as functions of important friends. The married womens' close associations and networking forms a crucial part of establishing authority, prestige and hence the political-economic relationships of their husbands and children. Without their assistance, Nagarattar males cannot obtain proper caste membership and hence the identity of a proper male Nagarattar (cf. Chapter 2). In addition, the Nagarattars expect married women to achieve their own economic autonomy. When they become widows or when they have to share heavy economic burdens with their husband, they are expected to use the networks which have been cultivated through their female associations. Assistance of their male kin and affines such as brothers, fathers, maternal uncles, or sons-in-law, for example, ensue through these networks.

8.3 Aacchihood; Women's Work, Its Prestige and Female Autonomy

How can I describe the sense of integrity and autonomy in the case of the Nagarattar woman? When I started writing this book, I was trying to answer this question by discussing the 'power' of aacchis: why they seem so distinctly different from women of other castes. The Nagarattar and non-Nagarattar women seem very much the same when they complain about things like the 'dowries' and male egoism etc. Nonetheless, I felt the status of aacchis was more socially accepted and respected by men of their community in general although I still doubt if I can call this their 'power'.

Power can be understood as a network rather than a privilege or physical coercion (Foucault 1977: 26) and mere possession of visible property does not always mean power dominance. Although non-Nagarattars maintain that aacchis carry a lot of dowry and that is why they henpeck their husbands, this is not exactly true. Whatever they carry, the gifts from their parents turn out to be meaningless unless they can claim them to be their own. As I mentioned before, there are some mercantile castes which systematically and completely amalgamate their brides' properties into the patrilineally organized joint family assets. Therefore, the real issue here is the Nagarattar system of pooling the capital within the community, which tactfully conforms with the ideology of pulli-based household economy. In other words, encouraging married women to have their own autonomy was part of their economic strategy as a caste and that is part of the reason why married women have 'power' of their own or to put it the other way around, the community allows married women to retain a certain economic autonomy to be exercised in the family. Although sons inherit business shares and real estate from their fathers, they are not disposable unless they are in real financial trouble. Being sons, they are expected to work hard and thereby increase the inherited property to pass on to their children. Husband and wife are complements in this sense, since while men carry immovables, the wife's crucial assets consist of movables. Even if the parents give her immovable properties such as land, stocks and shares these days, unlike men's assets, they are disposable if cash is desparately needed for some reason. The Hindu morality which supports the traditional Hindu laws also stresses that only after two people get married and become a 'couple', or *pulli*, can a man be regarded as a full-fledged person, which also stresses the woman's first loyalty in the conjugal relationship.

However, unless she has the enormous support and solidarity with women of kin and relatives, she cannot retain her integrity in the conjugal household. As I have already discussed, the kinship structure allows her to retain the support relationships with her natal family and also gives her more occasions through various functions to be in touch with the kin and relatives as broader network.

On the other hand, in North India, a woman's status is often described as being ambivalent: ambivalent, in the sense that as a daughter and as a sister, a woman enjoys high status, while as a wife, her status is low relative to husband and his family members as she lives in a hypergamous context (Ortner 1981; Bennet 1983; Sharma 1984). Jamous, in his recent argument (1992), also claims that even vedic tradition stresses the high ritual status of the daughter in her natal family. As a married sister, her ritual rank is placed high in her brother's family, yet this does not assure her any share in decision-making power with her husband. As a wife, she is expected to follow her husband's decision in the conjugal relationship. Ortner argues that in northern India, compared to the South, there is a strong tendency to lower the status of a wife in relation to her husband, as the bride is completely severed from her natal family and lives isolated among her husband's natal family who are strangers.

This kind of contrast between North and South India in terms of women's status however, is sometimes criticized by the North Indians as too simplistic, not to be applicable to all North Indian castes. There are some castes which do not allow the grooms' side to demand cash from the girls' natal families, as in the case of Modh Banyas and Gujarati Jains which I have already reported. Although North Indian Hindus in general do not allow marriages with close relatives, such castes still do not sever the tie of their daughters with their natal families completely. Their caste traditions sometimes allow married women to receive gifts from their natal families to be kept in their own names, to inherit properties of their parents in their own right. Therefore, the North Indian dislike of marrying close relatives alone cannot necessarily be associated with the low status of married women.

Nevertheless, South Indian states are still said to be more gener- ous in acknowledging women's property rights than the rest of India. As I mentioned before, only three southern states (Andhra Pradesh, Kerala, and Tamil Nadu) acknowledge equal share retro- spectively to the daughters to inherit their parents' ancestral proper- ties. When asked about the reason for this gender egalitarianism, lawyers in Madras told me that in the South, women are better educated than in the North and therefore, state assembly members voted for this amendment hoping to attract women's vote. Yet a female lawyer said to me,

I even argued that the state assembly should give equal rights to their wives to inherit their ancestral properties but the male politicians did not want that. Obviously they are more indulgent to their daughters. They were afraid that if they acknowledge such a right to their wives, the wives would immediately exercise their right and split the house.

Women's higher education may be the consequence of their higher status in their family rather than its cause yet this statement clearly shows the strong emotional ties which are not severed from the natal families even after marriage. 'Affection', which they ex- press to their children is the expectation for future return, which is already moulded in their kinship: preference for cross-cousin marriage assumes that their married daughters do not completely disappear; after several generations, their offspring will come back with property.

In the case of the Nagarattars, this affection for their daughters is more clearly expressed and moulded in their bilateral cross-cousin marriage as their basis of egalitarianism. By allowing a married woman's property to be kept in her name and to be transferred to her daughter, the Nagarattars maintain a strong bond between the married daughter and her mother, since even after marriage, the daughter retains the right to inherit her mother's property when she has died. Unlike men's inherited property, women's property is not tied to the joint family property and so is treated as self-acquired property, which is disposable by the owner as he or she wishes. Therefore, there was no problem for mothers to leave their property to their daughters while from the father's self-acquired property, the daughter can also get part of her property as a 'gift', which, they claim, has been given out of 'affection'.

In the West, women often face a dilemma regarding their conjugal relationships and female solidarity as Stivens (1981: 181) maintains. In my opinion, South Indian women do not seem to face such situations as frequently as women in the West do. However, I agree with Stivens that female solidarity could also work to maintain women's subordination to men (ibid.). As I have discussed, Nagarattar women are the sustainers of the kinship oriented ideology, and yet they are forced to act contradictorily: while they propagate the ideal of monogamy, they are expected to tolerate concubinage as part of the necessary evil of the system, in exchange for securing their status as the sole legitimate wife, *aacchi*, the married Nagarattar woman. As long as they stick to kinship as their supporting system, they have to bear with other factors as well: no divorce, no widow remarriage and no intercaste marriage. Breaching these rules and stepping out from their kinship-oriented caste means a real 'freedom' from the web of tightly woven kinship. Some dared to commit it and disappeared from the community yet for most of the Nagarattar women, it is too risky a gamble however poor they may be. Bitter feelings about money-mindedness cannot overcome the risk of losing their social identity or losing the chance to give authentic caste membership to their children. Kinship morality, supported by women, thus also works to bind women.

Kinship ties women heavily to the household as unpaid labourers: reproduction, welfare of the family members, and socializing are the major tasks assigned to them, among which socializing is hardly ever recognized positively by male members as part of productive activities. The big difference of the Nagarattars from most other communities, in my opinion, exists here: their domestic orientation does not stop them from engaging in socializing activities. In the eyes of other castes, *aacchis* are too outwardly socializing, not only with kin and relatives but through them, they tend to have more extended networks outside their own community. The Nagarattars' excessive indulgence in ceremonial functions shows how the community as a whole considers the socializing essential to the survival of the caste. Thus, the whole family should often stop their daily routine in order to attend a ceremony. Women's attendance at the ceremonies outstrips that of men in general, although men are also not supposed to be absent from the ceremonies of their close relatives.

Ceremonies and functions are the centre of their networking activities which highlight the day-to-day socializing activities of women. The network created by women within the community is so valuable that intercaste marriage is a taboo since it breaks down the chain of that network. The lifestyle of the Nagarattars has changed since the 1950s: the men are no longer sent as personnel abroad, nor do most of them live in the *walavu viidu* anymore. However, they don't seem to be willing to change their participation in ceremonies. Even those who are listed as the top entrepreneurs in India, give priority to performing ceremonial duties in their community. The Nagarattars who immigrated to the U.S. or to the U.K. take special leave from their offices and come back to Chettinadu in order to attend ceremonies of their close relatives, sometimes risking their jobs: 'When I went back to my house in San Francisco, I found I was already fired. They said I took leave too often.'

On the other hand, Nagarattar women no longer confine themselves to the house but prefer to have jobs and to earn their own living, especially among the middle-income and lower-income groups, and this trend is increasing. Higher education, for this reason, is getting popular since this is a new opportunity to make a better alliance, to increase prestige and also to acquire a socially acceptable job. This trend seems to be far more prevalent nowadays than at the time when I finished my fieldwork in Chettinadu in November 1991. In those days, upper-middle class people used to have a slight preference for college-educated girls since they said that well-educated girls can teach their children well. On the other hand, less educated girls hardly ever had problems in finding good alliances if their parents were ready to give them a big *siir danam*. Young Nagarattar girls hardly ever expressed an ambition in career-oriented jobs but during the past five years, tremendous changes have taken place. Nowadays, I come across some Nagarattar women lawyers, architects, doctors, and entrepreneurs who rarely have objections from their families to pursue these professions.

Comparing the Nagarattar women's traditional 'work' performed at home and the current trend towards career-oriented jobs, I will focus on the Nagarattars' great concern in assessing women's work in relation to the 'prestige' attached to it. Different evaluation for men and women in the same work often happens in the agricultural labourer class in India and it shows that it is not the quality or quantity of work but prestige which makes up the crucial part of 'work' in society. A woman's status depends partially on the economic rewards her work brings, but also on the prestige attached to that work. How a woman's 'work' (both domestic and non-domestic) is assessed depends on the society in which she finds herself. Some maintain that in the capitalist mode of production, domestic and non-domestic work are polarized thereby alienating women who are confined to the domestic sphere; whereas in the pre-capitalist mode women's domestic labour is not 'privatized' and is on a par with and intermingled with subsistence production. Domestic labour or work can entail productive activity such as cooking, servicing in the domestic area, and the provision of sexual services. It also entails reproduction in an explicitly biological sense, and it involves the socialization of children (Seccombe 1974). However, such a notion of 'labour' is strongly dependent on the Marxist orientation of defining the work by its mode of production and it ignores the factor of 'value' which can be attached to labour. Therefore, I will refer to 'work', rather than 'labour', when it includes the elements of prestige and status which enhance the social standing of the family. In other words, in order to investigate society as a web of relationships, it is more important to discuss labour in terms of value added 'work' — without this, one cannot explain the fact that in some societies the work done by women is not valued while the same work done by men is valued.

In order for women's work to be seen as valuable, both men and women must share the value attached to it: only with this shared value can the work of both men and women receive mutual recognition. There is a cooperation between husband and wife when they share labour and jointly participate in the decision making process. Yet sharing labour in the real sense is only possible when both can realistically evaluate the quality of each other's labour. Without this evaluation, the relationship soon becomes hierarchical and makes sharing a common goal more difficult. In the agricultural labourer class in India a different value is often put on the same work depending on whether it is done by men or women. In spite of the fact that women wage workers do contribute a considerable share to the maintenance of their family, their contribution is undervalued among the unskilled labourer class since their wage work is not considered to be creating 'prestige' for the family.

Kapadia (1995) for example, notes a strong gender hierarchy among the labourer class in South India and maintains that men ignore the fact that women are often the major bread winners. While men's earnings are considered to belong to them alone rather than to their family, women's earnings are seen as family income. In other words, in order to be thought prestigious, income needs to be considered to belong to her, at least as a first step. Otherwise, the earnings of women are regarded purely as necessity, just minimal to sustain the living of the family. Thus keeping women at work is not considered desirable. Among the Scheduled Caste agricultural labourers I studied in 1986, I noticed this process: the senior leader of a local Pallar caste stopped his wife from daily labourer work as soon as he was able to afford it, since keeping women as purely domestic labourers was considered to be more prestigious and an indication of affluence — it showed that the household was not in need of the wage which could have been earned by the woman.

Women's domestic activities can denote affluence in other ways: by engaging a woman solely in domestic work, the family can enjoy an improved living standard, especially when it comes to food. Instead of cooking only once a day in the evening as most agricultural labourer women do, non-working housewives can cook three times a day serving fresh meals to their family. The health and welfare of these family members is thus improved. Among the urban middle class, the enhancement of family status is indicated by housewives exhibiting traditional middle class cultural values such as taking an active role in teaching their own children, socializing with other middle class families, and even copying the latest western cuisine and interior decoration (Caplan, P. 1985). However, Caplan also notes the lack of solidarity among women of the middle class and upper-middle class who belong to the women's organization in Madras city, showing that they lack the shared value attached to the variety of domestic work assigned to them.

On the other hand, where there is not a clear-cut distinction between domestic and non-domestic work, a woman's work is more highly valued, not least because men play a vital role in determining how much prestige certain types of work deserve. For a woman's work to be seen as valuable, men have somehow to be involved in it and share the values attached to it. In this way, the distinction between 'domestic' and 'non-domestic' or 'women's and 'men's' work is blurred, thereby making a woman's contribution more significant.

As for the Nagarattars, the prestige and status of the Nagarattars are deeply rooted in the soil of Chettinadu, a geographical territory which represents 'kinship'. This can be symbolically identified with 'inside' or 'home' in contrast to 'outside' or 'abroad' where men toil hard to earn a living. Even if he has been working abroad for three years, a male Nagarattar can regain or elevate his social status through his wife's participation in prestige creating activities. Compared with other mercantile castes such as the Marwaris and Komutti Chettiyars whom I came across, the big difference exists in the Nagarattar orientation. Since the Nagarattar man worked overseas, women used to look after the household, and one of the *aacchis'* biggest concerns was the temple, the most important prestige-creating institution in olden days. Prestige, an important asset for business at home, is closely tied to the Nagarattars' business credibility. In olden days, it was attached to the temple while these days, the Nagarattars are sensitive enough to understand the prestige their wives and daughters carry for the family if they are well-educated and are engaged in well-qualified jobs.

The quick transformation from house-oriented *aacchis* to career-minded *aacchis* was relatively easy since both were engaged in similar kinds of activities, i.e. prestige-creating work. In this sense, there is no enmity between the career oriented *aacchi* and house-oriented *aacchis*. Indeed, most non-professional *aacchis* still have some kind of work outside their house: charity and running schools are the favourite activities for wealthy *aacchis* while others engage in pawnbroking, moneylending, running a business, etc. Yet none of the Nagarattars look down on the latter. In conclusion, I shall let Uma, one of the foresighted *aacchis*, talk about her ideal *aacchihood.*

Uma's personal goal is to become a prominent *aacchi.*

I want to stand out. However small the field may be, I want others in that field to recognize me as a person of some fame. I want others to respect me for having achieved success in my own field. If you cannot achieve anything in society, what is the use of life?

Uma, who is now in her late forties, married at sixteen and then went to college. She had a daughter before she turned twenty. After having a son in her early twenties, she started work as a part-time teacher at a nursery school. Then after fifteen years experience as a part-time teacher, she recently started a small nursery school on her own.

When I started to work, my father-in-law objected saying that to earn money outside the house is demeaning. My husband explained to him that it is not at all demeaning to earn money as a teacher. Both my parents and my husband persuaded him to give in, saying this is a decent job. Interestingly, my mother-in-law did not object at all. Although she is extremely old-fashioned, she respected my autonomy and ever since I married, she has never interfered with my activities at all.

Uma says she will not interfere with her husband's business, since it is jointly managed by his brother and his father. Similarly, she maintains that they cannot interfere with her business either, although she sometimes consults her husband about financial matters.

The car my family uses is registered in my name, as it was bought out of my income. The refrigerator, which is used at home, is also mine, and was bought out of the profits from my business. But they are all common property. Even though they were bought by me, how can I insist that they are all mine? We share everything among the family members.

On the other hand, she maintains,

Your husband won't throw you out if you are richer than he is. You must be careful and be well prepared for that rainy day so that you can manage on your own. I wouldn't depend on the mercy of my brother or anybody. If my son got married, I would not live with him. If there were no place to live, I would be happy to live in my husband's *walavu viidu*. With a small amount of money to help me survive, I would be quite happy. People respect you only if you can stand on your own feet.

Her married daughter Valli, now twenty-six, is also well trained as a young *aacchi*. She comes to her mother's house almost every day with her baby. As a young *aacchi*, though wealthy, Valli is very careful about spending each rupee. Things given to her and to her babies are carefully counted and most of them kept in cupboards untouched. As for a number of toy animals still in their packaging, she jokes that her daughter will take most of them when she gets married in twenty or twenty-five years' time. Most of her property is still managed by Uma and her husband, because, according to Uma, her daughter is still too young to manage it. 'When she is old enough to manage it by herself, she shall take it on. Until then, she should learn how to manage her own house and how to survive.'

Uma is deft at making decisions and is determined to organize her life according to what she wants. Uma told me that her work at the school was not motivated by money. Her charitable activities such as the cooking and selling of *chutney* are not motivated by money either. 'I do what I can do to help others.'

Like most prominent male Nagarattars, *aacchis* consider charity a crucial way of achieving a successful business and prominence among other *aacchis*. In the same way that a respectable male businessman sometimes tries to achieve prestige and fame by getting involved in charitable activities, prominent *aacchis* also devote themselves to charitable or religious activities. Both Uma and her mother encourage Uma's daughter to run a business if she wants to, but Uma is also careful that her daughter should gain experience before starting, which is why she insists that her daughter is supervised by members of her family until she can manage on her own. 'Nowadays, I feel like helping my son's business as well. When he finishes all his study and starts a business of his own, I shall work with him and help him in whatever he needs.' In this way, she already indicates that her husband and her son are expected to be completely separate in their business activities.

As Uma's case shows, a woman earning money is not frowned upon by the Nagarattars, as this has been a tradition of their caste. However, this economic independence does not mean that Nagarattar women are individualists in the Western sense, since whether they are rich or poor, they live by the morality of their caste. If they have children, they save for them and if they are widows or unmarried, they try to manage by themselves within the means they are given. Almost all Nagarattars I met said that they believe in God and their religiosity is closely interrelated with their mode of economic rationality. A very pragmatic *aacchi* in her early eighties even maintained that she did not believe in *gurus* or even saints, although she believed in God.

Aacchihood exists in the pursuit of autonomy which is achieved by a well planned lifestyle. Marrying properly, bringing up children and marrying them off, are essential for *aacchihood*. In addition, in order to prepare for their life in old age, *aacchis* must save money.

Having associated with so many old widows, I came to feel that it would not be so bad to be like them. Relieved of the burden of managing the conjugal household, and being respected women but with no serious obligations, they can enjoy visiting each other and travelling either on their own or with close female friends. The Nagarattars provide the cheapest lodging facilities in almost all the pilgrimage centres and there are always places reserved exclusively for women travellers.

Aacchihood may well be the ideal state for other South Indian women, although this remains as the ideal state for other Nagarattar women, too. Yet Nagarattar women themselves struggle hard in order to maintain the system: their hard work is the essential core of the economic activities of the community. Just like men in business, they are not supposed to fail in their economic activities. If they do, they may have to disappear without leaving descendants to the community. This is the strict part of Nagarattar *laissez-faire*. Although Nagarattar women are still mostly housewives, their 'work' is as economically productive as the men's work. Without the women's work, the Nagarattar business would not exist. Thus, the women's world is an essential part of the Nagarattar business world.

Glossary

aacchi	elder sister; married Nagarattar woman
aachanai	ritual
aarati	lamp waving ritual
aattal, attai	paternal aunt
aayaa	maternal grandmother
abisheekam	bathing ritual performed during *puuja;* anointment
adai	pancake
aduppu	hearth
aiyaa	grandfather
amangali (vidavai)	widow
ammaa viidu	mother's house
ammaan	mother's brother (= maamaa)
annan	older brother
appaa	father
appattaal	paternal grandmother
arasani kaal	an auspicious wooden plank installed for weddings of the Nagarattars
attaan	older male cross-cousin
bhagavadyaanam	prayer to gods
Chettinadu	land of the Chettiyars
Chettiyar	mercantile caste
chittappa	paternal uncle who is younger than one's father
daanam (or daan)	religious gift given to a Brahman for religious merit
danam	wedding gift (e.g. *siir danam*)
dayaadi	mother's people; affine; maternal relatives
Deepavali	autumnal celebration of new harvest
devadaasi	temple dancer
dhal	gruel made with chickpeas; chickpea sauce

enangan	lineages linked by marriage alliances among the Nayars
Gurukkal	temple priest, usually a Brahman
hundi	1) a treasury box; 2) a bill of exchange
isai padimaanam	mutual agreement, signed by the fathers of the bride and groom on the wedding of the Nagarattars
jaati	subcaste
kaliyaana viidu	marriage house (=*ul viidu*)
kaliyaanam	marriage
kaluttiru	a gold wedding pendant unique to Nagarattar women
Karaikkudi	a town in Chettinadu
karanavan	a male Nayar head of a *taravad*
koolam	auspicious floor decoration drawn with rice powder
koovil maalai	a garland sent by the clan temple on the Nagarattar wedding
kolambu	soup
Kottahai kaaran	a man who comes to install the lucky pole before wedding ceremony
kottahai	a wedding booth
kula deivam	lineage god
maamiyaar siirdanam	cash paid for mother-in-law from the bride's family before marriage
maappillai	bridegroom; son-in-law
maappillai alaippu	'inviting the groom'; the ritual in which the groom enters the wedding house of his bride's side
madam	Hindu religious institution
manaavalai	wedding platform
mandahappadi	a festival day in which the expense is met by a particular group (caste)
Mariyamman	a village goddess
moy	money-presents given to a newly-married couple
moy panam eludal	the attendance record of a Nagarattar marriage
muhuurtam	auspicious time, especially at a wedding

murai	promise
muraichittai	contract paper which is exchanged at the wedding between the bride and the groom's families
nagaram	town
Nagarattar	a mercantile caste; Natukottai Chettiyar
nahai	jewellery, or the way to count a set of jewellery
nalangu	purificatory ceremony held befor the wedding (among non-Nagarattars)
paahai	a measure equal to the length of outstretched arms
padaippu	ancestral worship ceremony
Pandaaram	a non-Brahman village temple priest
pangaali	patrilineally related relative
pattu saree	silk saree, normally Kancheepuram *saree*
peesi mudittal (nicchaittal)	betrothal
pen	a young woman; a bride
periyaacchi	senior *aacchi (periya* = big)
periyappa	paternal uncle who is older than one's father
petti	small box
Pongal	celebration of a New Year
pulli	a dot, a nuclear household which consists of a husband and wife (plus their unmarried children)
puroohita	family priest, usually a Brahman
puja	worship
puunul	sacred ritual thread worn by male Hindus
puuram kalikkiradu	a purificatory ritual for the bride held in the morning of a Nagarattar wedding
rudraksham	a rosary made of special seeds grown in the Himalayas
saamaan	goods; bridal goods
saami viidu	'deity's room', or an in-house shrine
saandi	celebration of the sixtieth year birthday of a married man
sangu	conch shell
siir	gift to a married woman from her natal family
siir danam (stri dhana)	woman's property given by her natal family on marriage

sleit vilakku	a candle lamp used by Nagarattars for wedding rituals
sondakaaran	relatives
sumangali	a married woman whose husband is alive
taali	a wedding pendant worn by a married woman
tambi	younger brother
taravad	matrilineally organized joint family household among the Nayars
tattaan	goldsmith
tiru mangalyam	marriage pendant worn by the bride
Tiruvaadirai	a celebration for small girls held on *ardra* star day
ul viidu	interior house, a room allotted to a Nagarattar couple
urimai	proprietary right, or a female cross-cousin
uur	village
veetti	loin cloth worn by men
veevu (kottan)	basket, or the wedding gift in a basket
veevu irakka	basket carrying ritual held at Nagarattar weddings
wadi	interest rate, 1 *wadi* equals to 12 per cent
walavu viidu	ancestral house of the Nagarattars
walavu waasal	interior courtyard of an ancestral house
wattahai	territorial division
wattal kulambu	vegetable soup made of dried vegetables

References

ABU-LUGHOD (1986), *Veiled Sentiments*. University of California Press.

ANONYMOUS (1987), *Tulaavuur aatina varalaaru* (Tamil). Thulavur: Thulavur Shaiva Aadinam.

APPADURAI, A. (1981), *Worship and Conflict under Colonial Rule: A South Indian Case*. Cambridge: Cambridge University Press.

AYYAR, A. (1938), *Manual of Pudukottai*. Pudukottai: Pudukottai Dharbar Office.

BARNARD, A. and A. GOOD (1984), *Research Practices in the Study of Kinship: ASA Research Methods in Social Anthropology, 2*. London: Academic Press.

BARNETT, S.A. (1976), 'Coconuts and Gold: Relational Identity in a South Indian Caste', *Contributions to Indian Sociology*. NS 10: 133–56.

BAYLY, C.A. (1983), *Rulers, Townsmen and Bazaars: North Indian Society in the Age of British Expansion, 1700–1870*. Cambridge: Cambridge University Press.

—— (1986), 'The Origins of *Swadesh:* Cloth and Indian Society, 1700–1930', in A. Appadurai (ed.), *The Social Life of Things*. Cambridge: Cambridge University Press, 285–321.

BECK, B.E.F. (1969), 'Colour and Heat in South Indian Ritual', *Man*. NS 4: 553–72.

—— (1972), *Peasant Society in Konku: A Study of Right and Left Subcastes in South India*. Vancouver: University of British Columbia Press.

—— (1974), 'The Kin Nucleus in Tamil Folk-lore', in T.R. Trautmann (ed.), *Kinship and History in South Asia, Michigan Papers on South and South-East Asia*. Ann Arbor, Michigan: University of Michigan Press, 1–28.

BEERMAN, G. (1993), 'Sanskritization as Female Oppression in India', in B. Miller (ed.), *Sex and Gender Hierarchies*. Cambridge: Cambridge University Press, 366–92.

BENNET, L. (1983), *Dangerous Wives and Sacred Sisters: Social and Symbolic Roles of High-caste Women in Nepal*. New York: Columbia University Press.

BOURDIEU, P. (1990), *The Logic of Practice*. Stanford University Press.

CAPLAN, L. (1984), 'Bridegroom Price in Urban India: Class, Caste and Dowry Evil among Christians in Madras', *Man.* NS 19: 216–33.

CAPLAN, P. (1985), *Class and Gender in India: Women and Their Organization in a South Indian City*. London: Tavistock Publications.

CHANDRASEKHAR, S. (1980), *The Nagarattars of South India: An Essay and a Bibliography on the Nagarattars in India and South East Asia*. Madras: Macmillan Company of India.

DANIEL, E.V. (1984), *Fluid Signs: Being a Person the Tamil Way*. Berkeley and Los Angeles: University of California Press.

DAS, V. (1977), *Structure and Cognition: Aspects of Hindu Caste and Ritual*. Delhi: Oxford University Press.

DAVENPORT, W. (1986), 'Two Kinds of Value in the Eastern Solomon Islands', in A. Appadurai (ed.), *Social Life of Things*. Cambridge: Cambridge University Press, 95–109.

DAVID, K. (1973), 'Until Marriage Do Us Part: A Cultural Account of Jaffna Tamil Categories or Kinsman', *Man.* NS 8: 521–35.

DIRKS, N. (1987), *The Hollow Crown: Ethnohistory of an Indian Kingdom*. Cambridge: Cambridge University Press.

DOUGLAS, M. (1966), *Purity and Danger*. London: Routledge.

DUBOIS, A. (1906), *Hindu Manners and Customs*. Madras: Higginbotham.

DUMONT, L. (1970a), *Homo Hierarchicus: The Caste System and Its Implications*. Chicago: University of Chicago Press.

—— (1970b), *Religion/Politics and History in India*. Paris and the Hague: Mouton.

—— (1983), *Affinity as a Value: Marriage Alliance in South India with Comparative Essays on Australia*. Chicago: University of Chicago Press.

—— (1986), *A South Indian Subcaste*. Delhi: Oxford University Press.

EPSTEIN, T.S. (1962), *Economic Development and Social Change in South India*. Manchester: Manchester University Press.

FABRICIUS, J.P. (1972), *Tamil and English Dictionary*. Tranqubar: Evangelican Lutheran Mission Publishing House.

FOUCAULT, M. (1977), *Discipline and Punish: The Birth of the Prison*, trans. by A. Sheridan. New York: Penguin Books.

FULLER, C.J. (1976), *The Nayars Today*. Cambridge: Cambridge University Press.

—— (1984), *Servants of the Goddess: The Priests of a South Indian Temple*. Cambridge: Cambridge University Press.

—— (1989), 'Misconceiving the Grain Heap: A Critique of the Concept of the Indian Jajmani System', in J.P. Parry and M. Bloch (eds.), *Money and the Morality of Exchange*. Cambridge: Cambridge University Press, 33–63.

FULLER, C.J. (1992), *The Camphor Flame: Popular Hinduism in India.*
New Jersey: Princeton University Press.

FULLER, C.J. and P. LOGAN (1985), 'The Navaratri Festival in Madurai',
Bulletin of the School of Oriental and African Studies, vol. XLVIII, part
1: 79–105.

GANDHI, G. (1983), *Tamil Nadu District Gazetteers: Pudukottai.* Madras:
Government of Tamil Nadu Press.

GOOD, A. (1991), *Female Bridegroom.* Oxford: Clarendon Press.

GOOD, A. and A. BARNARD (1984), *Research Practices in the Study of
Kinship: ASA Research Methods in Social Anthropology, 2.* London:
Academic Press.

GOUGH, K. (1956), 'Brahmin Kinship in a Tamil Village', *American
Anthropologist.* 58: 826–53.

—— (1959), 'The Nayars and the Definition of Marriage', *Journal of
the Royal Anthropological Institute.* 89, 23–34.

—— (1961), 'Nayar: Central Kerala', in D.M. Schneide and E.K. Gough
(eds.), *Matrilineal Kinship.* Berkeley and Los Angeles: University of
California Press, 298–384.

GREGORY, A. (1980), 'Gifts to Men and Gifts to God: Gift Exchange
and Capital Accumulation in Contemporary Papua', *Man.* NS 15:
626–52.

GREGORY, J. (1982), *Gifts and Commodities.* London: Academic Press.

HEESTERMAN, J.C. (1985), *The Inner Conflict of Tradition: Essays in
Indian Ritual, Kingship, Society.* Chicago: University of Chicago
Press.

HIRSCHON, R. (1984), 'Introduction: Property, Power and Gender
Relations', in Hirschon (ed.), *Women and Property — Women as
Property.* New York: St Martin's Press, 1–22.

IFEKA, C. (1989), 'Hierarchical Woman: The "Dowry" System and its
Implications among Chirstians in Goa, India', *Contributions to Indian Sociology.* NS 23: (2): 261–84.

ITO, S. (1966), 'A Note on Business Community in India, with Special
Reference to the Nattukottai Chettiars', *The Developing Economies,*
vol. A. Tokyo: 367–80.

JAMOUS, R. (1992), 'The Brother-Married-Sister Relationship and Marriage Ceremonies as Sacrificial Rites: A Case Study from Northern
India', in Coppet (ed.), *Understanding Rituals.* London: Routledge,
52–73.

KANE, P. (1973), (1968–77) *History of Dharmashastra,* 5 vols. Poona:
Bhandarkar Oriental Research Institute.

KAPADIA, K. (1995), *Siva and Her Sisters.* Boulder, Colorado: Westview
Press.

KOLENDA, P. (1984), 'Woman as Tribute, Woman as Flower: Images of "Woman" in North and South India', *American Ethnologist*, 11, 98–117.

LEACH, E.R. (1960), 'Introduction', in Leach (ed.), *Aspects of Caste in South India, Ceylon and North-West Pakistan.* Cambridge: Cambridge University Press, 1–16.

—— (1961), *Rethinking Anthropology.* Cambridge: Cambridge University Press.

—— (1976), *Culture and Communication: The Logic by which Symbols are Connected.* Cambridge: Cambridge University Press.

LEWIS, G. (1981), *Day of Shining Red: An Essay on Understanding Ritual.* Cambridge: Cambridge University Press.

MADAN, T.N. (1987), *Non-Renunciation: Themes and Interpretations of Hindu Culture.* Delhi: Oxford University Press.

MAHADEVAN, R. (1978), 'Immigrant Entrepreneurs in Colonial Burma — An Exploratory Study of the Role of the Nattukotai Chettiars of Tamil Nadu,1880–1930', *Indian Economic and Social History Review,* XV (3): 329–58.

MAHER, V. (1984), 'Work, Consumption and Authority within the Household: A Moroccan Case', in Wolkowitz and McCullagh (eds.), *Of Marriage and the Market: Women's Subordination Internationally and its Lessons.* Routledge, 178–92.

MARGLIN, F. (1985), *Wives of the God-King: The Rituals of the Devadasis of Puri.* Delhi:Oxford University Press.

MAUSS, M. (1990), *The Gift: The Form and Reason for Exchange in Archaic Societies,* trans. W. Halls. London: Routledge.

MENCHER, J. and H. GOLDBERG (1967), 'Kinship and Marriage Regulations among the Namboodiri Brahmans of Kerala', *Man.* NS 2: 87–106.

MINES, M. (1984), *The Warrior Merchants: Textiles, Trade, and Territory in South India.* Cambridge: Cambridge University Press.

—— (1994), *Public Faces, Private Voices: Community and Individuality in South India.* Berkeley and Los Angeles: University of California Press.

MOORE, M. (1985), 'New Look at the Nayar Taravad', *Man.* NS 20: 523–41.

NAGARAJAN, K. (1983), *Rajah Sir Annamalai Chettiyar.* Chidambaram: Annamalai University Press.

NISHIMURA, Y. (1987), *A Study on Mariyamman Worship in South India.* ILCAA, Tokyo University of Foreign Studies.

—— (1993), *Kinship, Marriage and Womanhood among the Nagarattars in South India.* Ph.D. dissertation, University of London.

NISHIMURA, Y. (1994), 'Marriage Payments among the Nagarattars in South India', *Contributions to Indian Sociology*. NS 28 (2): 243–72.

—— (1996), 'South Indian Wedding Rituals: A Comparison of Gender Hierarchy', *Anthropos*. 91: 411–23.

ORTNER, S. (1981), 'Gender and Sexuality in Hierarchical Societies: The Case of Polynesia and Some Comparative Implications', in S. Ortner and H. Whitehead (eds.), *Sexual Meanings: The Cultural Construction of Gender and Sexuality*. Cambridge: Cambridege University Press, 359–409.

PANT, P.C. (1995), *The Law of Marriage, Divorce and Other Matrimonial Disputes*. Delhi: Orient Publishing Company.

PARKIN, D. (1992), 'Ritual as Spatial Direction and Bodily Division', in D. Coppet (ed.), *Understanding Rituals*. London: Routledge, 11–25.

PARRY, J.P. (1979), *Caste and Kinship in Kangra*. London: Routledge.

—— (1980), 'Ghosts, Greed and Sin: The Occupational Identity of the Benares Funeral Priests', *Man*. NS 15: 88–111.

—— (1985), 'Death and Digestion: The Symbolism of Food and Eating in North Indian Mortuary Rites', *Man*. NS 20: 612–30.

—— (1989), 'The Gift, the Indian Gift, and the "Indian Gift" ', *Man*. NS 21: 453–73.

—— (1989), 'On the Moral Perils of Exchange', in J. Parry and M. Bloch (eds.), *Money and the Morality of Exchange*. Cambridge: Cambridge University Press.

PRICE, P. (1979), 'Resource and Rule in Zamindari South India, 1802–1903', Ph.D. dissertation, University of Wisconsin.

RABINOW, P. (1977), *Reflections on Fieldwork in Morocco*. Berkeley and Los Angeles: University of California Press.

RAHEJA, G. (1989), 'Centrality, Mutuality and Hierarchy: Shifting Aspects of Inter-Caste Relationships in North India', *Contributions to Indian Sociology*. NS 23: 79.

—— (1988), *The Poison in the Gift: Ritual Prestation, and the Dominant Caste in a North Indian Village*. Chicago: University of Chicago Press.

RAM, K. (1991), *Mukkuvar Women*. London: Zed Books.

RAO, G.C.V. (1995), *Family Law in India*. Hyderabad: S. Gogia & Company.

REYNOLDS, H. (1980), 'The Auspicious Married Woman', in Wadley (ed.), *The Powers of Tamil Women*. Syracuse, New York: Maxwell School of Citizenship & Public Affairs, 35–60,

ROGERS, S.C. (1975), 'Female Forms of Power and the Theory of Resources in Cultural Dominance: A Model of Female/Male Interaction in Peasant Society', *American Ethnologist*. 2: 727–57.

RUDNER, D. (1985), 'Caste and Commerce in Indian Society: A Case

Study of Nattukottai Chettiars, 1600–1930', Ph.D. dissertation, University of Pennsylvania.

RUDNER, D. (1994), *Caste and Capitalism in Colonial India: The Nattukottai Chettiars.* Berkeley and Los Angeles: University of California Press.

SAHLINS, M. (1972), *Stone Age Economics.* London: Tavistock Publications.

SECCOMBE, W. (1974), 'The Housewife and her Labour under Capitalism', *New Left Review.* No. 83: 3–24.

SHARMA, U. (1984), 'Dowry in North India: Its Consequences for Women', in Hirschon (ed.), *Women and Property — Women as Property.* New York: St Martin's Press, 62–74.

SHULMAN, D. (1980), *Tamil Temple Myths: Sacrifice and Divine Marriage in the South Indian Saiva Tradition.* New Jersey: Princeton University Press.

SIEGLEMAN, P. (1962), 'Colonial Development and Chettiar', Ph.D. dissertation, University of Minnesota.

SINGER, M. (1968), 'The Indian Joint Family in Modern Industry', in Singer and Cohn (eds.), *Structure and Change in Indian Society.* Chicago: Aldine Publishing Company, 423–52.

SKINNER, G. (1993), 'Conjugal Power in Tokugawa Japanese Families: A Matter of Life or Death', in B.D. Miller (ed.), *Sex and Gender Hierarchies.* Cambridge: Cambridge University Press, 236–70.

SOMALAY (1953), *Chettinadum Tamilum* (Tamil). Madras: Waanadi Padippakam.

SPOONER, B. (1986), 'Weavers and Dealers: The Authenticity of an Oriental Carpet', in A. Appadurai (ed.), *The Social Life of Things.* Cambridge: Cambridge University Press, 195–235.

SRINIVAS, M.N. (1952), *Religion and Society among the Coorgs of South India.* Oxford: Clarendon Press.

—— (1984), *Some Reflections on Dowry.* Delhi: Centre for Women's Development Studies.

—— (1987), *The Dominant Caste and Other Essays.* Delhi: Oxford University Press.

STIVENS, M. (1981), 'Women, Kinship and Capitalist Development', in K. Young, C. Wolkowitz and R. McCullagh (eds.), *Of Marriage and the Market: Women's Subordination Internationally and its Lessons.* Routledge: London, 178–92.

STRATHERN, A. (1971), *The Pope of Moka: Big Men and Ceremonial Exchange in Mount Hagen.* Cambridge: Cambridge University Press.

STRATHERN, M. (1984), 'Subject or Object? Women and the Circulation of Valuables in Highlands New Guinea', in Hirschon (ed.), *Women and Property — Women as Property*. New York: St Martin's Press, 158–74.

TAMBIAH, S.J. (1973*a*), 'Dowry and Bridewealth, and the Property Rights of Women in South Asia', in J. Goody and Tambiah, *Bridewealth and Dowry*. Cambridge: Cambridge University Press, 59–169.

—— (1973*b*), 'From Varna to Caste through Mixed Unions', in J. Goody (ed.) *The Character of Kinship*. Cambridge: Cambridge University Press, 191–229.

THURSTON, E. and K. RANGACHARI (1909), *Castes and Tribes of Southern India*, 7 vols. Madras: Government Press.

TRAUTMANN, T.R. (1981), *Dravidian Kinship*. Cambridge: Cambridge University Press.

TRAWICK, M. (1990), *Notes on Love in a Tamil Family*. Berkeley and Los Angeles: University of California Press.

WEBER, M. (1963), *The Sociology of Religion*. Chicago: Beacon Press.

—— (1985), *The Protestant Ethic and the Spirit of Capitalism*. London: Unwin Paperbacks.

WEINER, A. (1976), *Women of Value, Men of Renown: New Perspectives in Trobriand Exchange*. Austin: University of Texas Press.

—— (1985), 'Inalienable Wealth', *American Ethnologist*. 12: 210–27.

YALMAN, N. (1971), *Under the Bo Tree: Studies in Caste, Kinship and Marriage in the Interior of Ceylon*. Berkeley and Los Angeles: University of California Press.

Index